Weimar on the Pacific

WEIMAR AND NOW: GERMAN CULTURAL CRITICISM

Edward Dimendberg, Martin Jay, and Anton Kaes, General Editors

Weimar on the Pacific

*German Exile Culture in Los Angeles
and the Crisis of Modernism*

Ehrhard Bahr

UNIVERSITY OF CALIFORNIA PRESS
Berkeley   •   Los Angeles   •   London

University of California Press, one of the most distinguished university presses in the United States, enriches
lives around the world by advancing scholarship in the
humanities, social sciences, and natural sciences. Its activities are supported by the UC Press Foundation and
by philanthropic contributions from individuals and institutions. For more information, visit
www.ucpress.edu.

University of California Press
Berkeley and Los Angeles, California

University of California Press, Ltd.
London, England

First paperback printing 2008

Library of Congress Cataloging-in-Publication Data

Bahr, Ehrhard.
    Weimar on the Pacific : German exile culture in Los
Angeles and the crisis of modernism / Ehrhard Bahr.
        p. cm.—(Weimar and now : 41)
    Includes bibliographical references and index.
    ISBN 978-0-520-25795-5 (pbk : alk. paper)
    1. Modern (Aesthetics)—California—Los Angeles.
2. German—California—Los Angeles—Intellectual life.
3. Jews. German—California—Los Angeles—Intellectual life.   4. Los Angeles (Calif.)—Intellectual life—
20th century.   I. Title.
BH301.M54B34 2007
700.89'31079494—dc22   200700207

Manufactured in the United States of America

16   15   14   13   12   11   10   09   08
10 9 8 7 6 5 4 3 2 1

The paper used in this publication meets the minimum
requirements of ANSI/NISO Z39.48-1992 (R 1997)
(Permanence of Paper).

Contents

Illustrations

Abbreviations

AT   Adorno, Theodor W. *Aesthetic Theory*. Ed. Gretel
Adorno and Rolf Tiedemann, newly trans. and with a
translator's intro by Robert Hullot-Kentor. Minneapolis:
University of Minnesota Press, 1997.

Berman Berman, Russell A. *The Rise of the Modern German
Novel: Crisis and Charisma*. Cambridge, MA: Harvard
University Press, 1986.

DE   Horkheimer, Max, and Theodor W. Adorno. *Dialectic of
Enlightenment: Philosophical Fragments*. Ed. Gunzelin
Schmid Noerr, trans. Edmund Jephcott. Stanford, CA:
Stanford University Press, 2002.

DF   Mann, Thomas. *Doctor Faustus: The Life of the German
Composer Adrian Leverkühn As Told by a Friend*. Trans.
John E. Woods. New York: Alfred A. Knopf, 1997.

GBA   Brecht, Bertolt. *Werke: Große kommentierte Berliner und
Frankfurter Ausgabe*. Ed. Werner Hecht et al. 30 vols.
Frankfurt/Main: Suhrkamp, 1988–2000.

GW   Mann, Thomas. *Gesammelte Werke in dreizehn Bänden*.
13 vols. 2nd, rev. ed. Frankfurt/Main: Fischer, 1974.

Leppert Adorno, Theodor W. *Essays on Music*. Trans. Susan H.
Gillespie, with introduction, commentary, and notes by
Richard Leppert. Berkeley: University of California Press,
2002.

MM   Adorno, Theodor W. *Minima Moralia: Reflections from Damaged Life*. Trans. E. F. N. Jephcott. London: Verso, 1978.

PMM   Adorno, Theodor W. *Philosophy of Modern Music*. Trans. Anne G. Mitchell and Wesley W. Blomster. New York: Seabury Press, 1973.

Poems   *Bertolt Brecht Poems 1913–1956*. Ed. John Willett and Ralph Manheim with the cooperation of Erich Fried. New York: Methuen, 1976.

Emigration is the best school of dialectics. Refugees
are the sharpest dialectic thinkers.

Bertolt Brecht, Refugee Conversations, 1940

Preface

After completing my graduate work at the University of California, Berkeley, in 1966, I accepted a teaching position at the University of California, Los Angeles. I loaded my graduate-student library onto the backseat of my Volkswagen bug and drove to Southern California. When I turned into a gas station in Westwood, the Los Angeles suburb where the university is located, the gas station attendant commented on one of the books in the car, a collection of Thomas Mann's short stories with a lavender book jacket. I vividly recall the gas station attendant involving me in a lengthy discussion of Mann's *Magic Mountain*. I took it as a good omen. What better welcome to Los Angeles could there be for a teacher of German literature?

I was aware that Thomas Mann had lived in Los Angeles and had left the city only fourteen years earlier. Until June 1952 he had often visited his beloved Westwood to have his hair cut—visits that were regularly recorded in his diary: "Gone to Westwood for a hair cut" *(Nach West-wood zum Haarschneiden)*. But in 1966, when I arrived, his diaries had not yet been published, although I had heard from his son, Michael, who taught German at U.C. Berkeley, that they were ready for transcription and the first volume was scheduled for publication in 1975. I was unaware, however, that in the 1940s Thomas Mann had planned to retire in Los Angeles; it was here he wanted to see his grandchildren grow up. In 1952 McCarthyism inspired him to change his plans. Personal attacks on him, including in Congress, had made him apprehensive, and he feared that the history of the Weimar Republic would repeat itself in the United States. He returned to Europe in June 1952 and settled in Switzerland, where he died three years later. I still recall listening to his Schiller address on the radio in West Germany in 1955.

Although I was trained in the history of German literature, I was not aware in 1966 that so many canonical authors of modern German literature had lived in exile in Southern California and produced their major works here. My experience at the gas station in Westwood, however, had alerted me, and for the next thirty years I researched this phenomenon that was so important not only to German literature, but also to German modernism more generally, including architecture, film, music, and philosophy. I eagerly met Marta Feuchtwanger, one of the last representatives of the German exile group of the 1940s, and I became acquainted with the second- and third-generation exiles, including the children of Arnold Schoenberg, Nuria, Ronald, and Lawrence; Schoenberg's daughter-in-law, Barbara, who was the daughter of the exile composer Erik Zeisl; and Lawrence Weschler, the grandson of the exile composer Ernst Toch. I also made the acquaintance of Walter Wicclair, director of the *Freie Bühne,* the only German-language theater in Los Angeles, who kept alive the memory of many of the exile writers in his public readings in the 1960s and 1970s, and Marta Mierendorff, who was the most dedicated chronicler of the German-speaking exiles in Los Angeles.

At first this research was simply the subject of personal interest rather than my main scholarly pursuit, as my primary field of research at the time was German literature of the eighteenth century. My first book was about irony in the late works of Goethe, although my work was influenced by Thomas Mann's view of Goethe as an ironic writer. I changed my research focus when John M. Spalek of the University of Southern California established exile research as a legitimate field in the study of German literature in the United States. I was only too happy to join his group and contribute an article to his *Deutsche Exilliteratur seit 1933: Kalifornien,* the authoritative work on German exile literature in Los Angeles. My article dealt with the participation of Thomas Mann and Lion Feuchtwanger in a writers' conference at UCLA in 1943, a conference that was devoted to the recruitment of literature, film, and music in the war against the Axis powers. In the 1980s, my interests expanded to include exile culture in general, and I added architecture, film, music, and philosophy to my fields of research. This shift was influenced by the trends in German studies in the United States that I helped to initiate as a member of the American Eighteenth-Century Studies Society and the

German Studies Association. In the 1990s, I had the good luck to participate as a consultant to two major exhibitions at the Los Angeles County Museum of Art dealing with modernism in Germany and the exile of modernism from Central Europe during the 1930s. I consider this book the summary of my research spanning more than thirty years, since my arrival in Los Angeles in 1966.

I am grateful to the students at UCLA who gave me the opportunity in the 1990s to test my ideas and interpretations in classes and seminars on German exile culture. They helped me to define my topic and broaden my field of study. I particularly want to thank all the students of the graduate seminar "German Exile Culture in Los Angeles," which I taught in the fall quarter of 2001. Their insights and criticism helped to enrich the contents of this book.

Many colleagues and friends offered invaluable suggestions, especially Frank Baron, Stephanie Barron, Franz H. Bäuml, Russell A. Berman, Donald G. Daviau, Erich A. Frey, Ruth Goldschmidt-Kunzer, Harold von Hofe, Peter Uwe Hohendahl, Thomas S. Hines, Ruth Klüger, Lutz P. Koepnick, Wulf Koepke, Jill Anne Kowalik, Herbert Lehnert, Peter Loewenberg, James K. Lyon, Peter H. Reill, Walter H. Sokel, John M. Spalek, Guy Stern, and Hans R. Vaget. Chapter 6 is dedicated to Thomas S. Hines, chapter 9 to Herbert Lehnert, and chapter 10 to Hans R. Vaget, in gratitude for their support and counsel.

The University of California, Los Angeles, through its Academic Senate Committee on Research, supported the preparation of the manuscript through a number of grants. I thank Andrew Hewitt and Hans Wagener, chairs of the Department of Germanic Languages, for providing me with an office on campus that made my research much easier. For archival materials, I relied on the helpful staffs at the Charles E. Young Research Library and its Special Collections at UCLA, the Akademie der Künste Archiv in Berlin, the Architecture and Design Collection at the University of California, Santa Barbara, the Deutsches Literaturarchiv in Marbach am Neckar, the Feuchtwanger Memorial Library at the University of Southern California, the Getty Research Institute in Los Angeles, the Harvard University Archives, the Horkheimer Archives at the University of Frankfurt, the Keystone Archive in Zurich, the Theodor W. Adorno Archives in Frankfurt, the Arnold Schönberg Center in Vienna, and the USC Cinema-Television Library. I offer my sincere thanks to these institutions. I extend my heartfelt appreciation to Juergen Nogai, of Santa Monica, who took the photos of the exiles' residences in Los Angeles without institutional support.

I thank Martin Jay, Anton Kaes, and Edward Dimendberg, the editors of the Weimar Series, for accepting this title for publication in the series "Weimar and Now: German Cultural Criticism." The manuscript benefited from three anonymous readers who evaluated it for the University of California Press.

Portions of this book are based on the following works, which have been reconceptualized and rewritten. They are used by permission: "The Anti-Semitism Studies of the Frankfurt School: The Failure of Critical Theory," *German Studies Review* 1 (1978): 125–38, reprinted in *Foundations of the Frankfurt School of Social Research,* ed. Judith Marcus and Zoltan Tar, 311–21 (New Brunswick: Transaction Books, 1984); "Neu-Weimar am Pazifik: Los Angeles als Hauptstadt der deutschen Exilliteratur," in *Weimar am Pazifik: Literarische Wege zwischen den Kontinenten: Festschrift für Werner Vordtriede zum 70. Geburtstag,* ed. Dieter Borchmeyer and Tilman Heimeran, 126–36 (Tübingen: Niemeyer, 1985); "Paul Tillich and the Problem of a German Exile Government in the United States," *Yearbook of German-American Studies* 21 (1986): 1–12; "Literary Weimar in Exile: German Literature in Los Angeles, 1940–1958," in E. Bahr and Carolyn See, *Literary Exiles and Refugees in Los Angeles,* 1–17 (Los Angeles: William Andrews Clark Memorial Library, 1988); "Die Kontroverse um das 'Andere Deutschland,' " in *Deutschsprachige Exilliteratur seit 1933: 2. New York,* ed. John M. Spalek and Joseph Strelka, 1493–1513 (Bern: Francke, 1990); "Art Desires Non-Art: Thomas Mann's Dialectic of Art and Theodor Adorno's Aesthetic Theory," in *Thomas Mann's Doctor Faustus: A Novel at the Margin of Modernism,* ed. Herbert Lehnert and Peter C. Pfeiffer, 145–60 (Columbia, SC: Camden House, 1991); "Dialektik des Nihilismus: Thomas Manns Benjamin-Lektüre und der Faust-Roman," in *Crisis and Culture in Post-Enlightenment Germany: Essays in Honour of Peter Heller,* ed. Hans Schulte and David Richards 415–31 (Lanham, MD: University Press of America, 1993); "Los Angeles als Zentrum der Exilkultur und die Krise des Modernismus," *Exilforschung: Ein Internationales Jahrbuch* 20 (2002): 199–212; "Goethe in Hollywood: Thomas Mann in Exile in Los Angeles," in *Goethe im Exil: Deutsch-Amerikanische Perspektiven,* ed. Gert Sautermeister and Frank Baron, 125–39 (Bielefeld: Aisthesis, 2002); "Exiltheater in Los Angeles: Max Reinhardt, Leopold Jessner, Bertolt Brecht und Walter Wicclair," *Exilforschung: Ein Internationales Jahrbuch* 21 (2003): 95–111; "Thomas Manns Vortrag 'Deutschland und die Deutschen': Vergangenheitsbewältigung und deutsche Einheit," in *man erzählt Geschichten, formt die*

Wahrheit: Thomas Mann—Deutscher, Europäer, Weltbürger, ed. Michael Braun and Birgit Lermen, 65–80 (Frankfurt/Main: Lang, 2003); "Modernism and Anti-Modernism in Franz Werfel's Work in Exile," *Die Alchemie des Exils: Exil als schöpferischer Impuls,* ed. Helga Schreckenberger, 179–89 (Vienna: Verlag Edition Praesens, 2005).

I was fortunate to have as my editor at the University of California Press Niels Hooper, who shepherded the manuscript through the process of evaluation and production. Copyeditor Sharron Wood worked miracles to turn the manuscript into a readable book—a major achievement when dealing with an author like Theodor W. Adorno, whose difficult style is an integral part of his philosophy. Special thanks go to project editor Mary Severance, who kept the undertaking on track and answered my frantic e-mails within the hour.

I am dedicating this book to the memory of the exiles and refugees and to my wife and family, who were convinced that this story needed to be told. My wife, Diana, shared with me her research on the World War II internment camps for Japanese Americans and their political activism to seek redress. German-speaking exiles in Los Angeles were affected by the same evacuation orders, although these orders were not, in the end, carried out for them as a group. On the basis of my wife's research I was able to trace the impact of the threat of forced relocation on Bertolt Brecht's California poetry of 1942.

I wrote this book in English not only to express my gratitude for a rewarding life of teaching and research in Los Angeles, but also to introduce this story to an audience that may not be fully aware of this chapter in the history of Los Angeles. This chapter in history has an impact far beyond Southern California and is of global significance for the production of cultural artifacts during a time of persecution and genocide.

Introduction

For almost a century, Los Angeles has occupied a space in the American imagination between innocence and corruption, unspoiled nature and ruthless real-estate development, naïveté and hucksterism, enthusiasm and shameless exploitation. In his book *Landscapes of Desire*, William A. McClung has shown that "two competing mythologies of place and space—one of an acquired Arcadia—a found natural paradise—and the other of an invented utopia—an empty space inviting development—" have shaped the image of Los Angeles (dust jacket; 4–5). There have been numerous attempts to counter this impression and to portray the city as one with intellectual substance and authentic artistic character, but they have gone largely unnoticed in the popular imagination of this global city, which has not only been the entertainment capital of the world since the 1920s, but has also become a center of international commerce, news management, and immigration in the last four decades.

Some of these attempts to revise Los Angeles's image were made by German-speaking exiles from Nazi-occupied Europe, who settled in great numbers in the area during the 1940s and early 1950s. Their presence in Los Angeles conferred upon the city the moniker "Weimar on the Pacific," a title that incorporated the name of the charming little town in Thuringia that served as a center of German classical culture and as the birthplace of German democracy. Weimar was the residence of Goethe and Schiller during the golden age of German literature at the end of the eighteenth century, and it was the site of the National Convention where

FIGURE 1. Goethe-Schiller Monument by Ernst Rietschel (1857) in front of
the National Theater in Weimar during the 1920s. Photograph courtesy of
Foto Marburg / Art Resource, NY.

the constitution of the new German Republic was adopted after World
War I in 1919. But it was neither the town of Weimar nor the German
capital of Berlin that most influenced the Weimar on the Pacific, but
rather the two periods of cultural production associated with Weimar:
German classicism of the eighteenth and early nineteenth centuries and
the culture of the Weimar Republic. The American West Coast afforded
the refugees from Nazi-occupied Europe a haven from persecution and
a place to live and work until the end of World War II.

Although these refugees did not succeed in changing the image of Los Angeles, their presence and creative efforts during the war years and the 1950s are often cited as examples of the city's intellectual and artistic potential. Any book on Los Angeles published today—for example, the publications by Mike Davis, David Fine, Kevin Starr, and William A. McClung—will cite one or two of the illustrious German refugees of the 1940s, and some make an argument for or against the vitality of the city based on their presence. David L. Ulin, as well, included some of the exile writers in his literary anthology *Writing Los Angeles* of 2002.

Los Angeles has not played a great role in the German popular imagination, though Hollywood usually figures as a metonym of the film industry and is conceived as a modern Sodom and Gomorrah. The glamour of the movie industry is acknowledged, but it is also resented. Even hard-boiled intellectuals like Bertolt Brecht, who felt at home in the sin city of Berlin of the 1920s, became provincial and puritanical when they delivered their verdict on Hollywood. In his diary of July 17, 1942, Brecht referred to the movie industry as the "center of global drug-trafficking" (GBA 27: 116). In the German imagination, Santa Monica, or, for that matter, Los Angeles in its entirety, was considered a suburb of Hollywood, as many of the German biographies of Brecht demonstrate (see, for example, Klaus Völker's *Brecht-Chronik* of 1971, or Franz-Josef Payrhuber's *Bertolt Brecht* of 1995).

It is difficult to reconstruct the German-speaking exile community in Los Angeles of the 1930s and 1940s. There is a wealth of anecdotal material, but the social history of this community remains to be written. Michael A. Meyer's 2002 article on the creative elite of the refugees from Hitler's Germany and their middle-class audience in Los Angeles in the 1930s and 1940s and Ruth E. Wolman's oral history *Crossing Over* of 1996 constitute a promising step in that direction. About 10,000 to 15,000 refugees came to Southern California between 1933 and 1941 to escape political and racial persecution in Hitler's Europe. According to Gerald D. Nash, a noted historian of the American West, the refugees

made a profound cultural contribution to the West and the nation. Some worked in the movie industry; others were active in science, literature, the theater, music, art, psychiatry, and other fields. Constituting the cream of the European intelligentsia, they brought an intellectual maturity and sophistication to cultural life in the West that it had previously lacked. (Nash 179)

As this quotation shows, the German exile community was defined and continues to be defined in terms of the cultural products of its elite rather than in terms of the entire community's search for a social, political, and religious identity and its adaptation to the new environment. The problems of accommodation and achievement may have been similar for the group as they were for the elite, but with the exception of a short history of the Jewish Club of 1933 in Hollywood (Roden 482–94), *Die Westküste,* the biweekly West Coast edition of *Aufbau/Reconstruction* (the newspaper of German Jewish immigrants in New York), and the oral history interviews of eighteen refugees recorded by Wolman in *Crossing Over,* there are no reliable data except for the letters, diaries, and memoirs of the cultural elite. The editorial policy of *Aufbau* conveyed three principles to their readership: loyalty as citizens of the United States, attachment to their Jewish faith and tradition, and cultivation of their German cultural heritage (Steinitz 13). About 70 percent of the German immigrants were Jewish, and the majority were interested in swift assimilation. This interest did not prevent their identification with the German cultural tradition, as the programs of the Jewish Club of 1933 indicated. The club members welcomed those of the Weimar cultural elite in Los Angeles for lectures and readings, and they supported German theater, cabaret, and other musical events. They continued to speak German with each other, though they interacted with Americans at their places of employment. There is, however, not much beyond the anecdotal known about the everyday lives of German-speaking exiles— whether they mingled with nonexiles, which features of Los Angeles most captivated or appalled them, or how institutions such as the University of California, Los Angeles, figured in their exile experience—although historians can answer these questions in detail for Bertolt Brecht, Thomas Mann, or Arnold Schoenberg.

Institutions such as the University of California, Los Angeles (UCLA) and the University of Southern California served exiles as resource centers and functioned as places of employment for Schoenberg, Hans Reichenbach, Ludwig Marcuse, and a few others, but they never played an active role in the exile experience, as did Columbia University and the "University in Exile" at the New School for Social Research, both in New York. Columbia granted affiliated status to the Frankfurt School, and the New School for Social Research hired the largest number of refugee scholars of any American university, offering them a place where they could continue the German tradition in the social sciences (Krohn, *Intellectuals in Exile,* 59).

The history of German-speaking exile in Southern California would be incomplete without reference to the conservative German-language press, the activities of the German Consulate in Los Angeles between 1933 and 1941, and the various rallies of the American Nazi party in Los Angeles County. The conservative German-language press, the *California Staatszeitung*, the *Sued-California Deutsche Zeitung*, and the *California Demokrat*, tended to support the "new" Germany under Hitler. There was even an outspoken Nazi paper, the *California Weckruf*, published from 1935 to 1938 by the German-American Volksbund, the central Nazi organization on the West Coast (see Bander 195–213). The German Consulate protested events that they considered anti-German and arranged visits of Nazi VIPs such as Leni Riefenstahl, who traveled to the United States with her film of the Berlin Olympics and visited Los Angeles in November–December 1938. Due to protests by the Hollywood Anti-Nazi League her film was never screened, but Riefenstahl met with Walt Disney, while other studio heads refused to see her. The German-American Bund movement was well organized in Southern California and staged Nazi rallies at the former Hindenburg Park in La Crescenta in the 1930s and early 1940s, celebrating events such as the Anschluss of Austria in March 1938 and the "liberation" of Sudetenland in October 1938. The largest rally took place on April 30, 1939, when a brigade of 2,000 German American Bund members came to hear West Coast Bund leader Herman Max Schwinn and "American Fuehrer" Fritz Kuhn, who spoke from a stage draped in swastika banners (Los Angeles Times, May 14, 2006, B2).

The gaps in our knowledge about Weimar on the Pacific are similar to those in our knowledge about New York, or Paris on the Hudson: the historical record of the émigrés who fled France in 1940 is mostly limited to an account of the French intellectuals and artists living in wartime Manhattan (Mehlman, *Émigré New York*). The life of the group is preserved only in terms of the achievements of its elite, such as Maurice Maeterlinck, Denis de Rougemont, André Breton, Marcel Duchamp, Simone Weil, Louis Rougier, Antoine de Saint-Exupéry, Saint-John Perse, and Claude Lévi-Strauss. Although the German exiles were not, like the French, divided by politics (some French émigrés supported de Gaulle and the Free French government, while others backed Pétain and the Vichy government), otherwise the groups exhibited many similarities. Like Thomas Mann, Saint-John Perse was employed as a consultant to the Library of Congress, for example, and the Ecole Libre served a function similar to that of the Frankfurt School.

As Weimar on the Pacific, Los Angeles could have served as an icon of intellectual and artistic resistance to the Nazi regime. It was, after all, no small matter that so many artists and intellectuals left the country when the Nazis came to power. The fact that the cultural elite left Germany in droves, found refuge in Los Angeles in the 1940s, and were most productive during that decade could have served East and West Germany as inspiration for the reconstruction of their country after 1945, but this did not happen. Although the German Democratic Republic made an effort to persuade Heinrich Mann to return as president of the newly founded Academy of Arts in East Berlin in 1949, its cultural policies were focused on the exiles that were living in Moscow. The Federal Republic of Germany did not publicly invite any exiles to return. Those who returned did so on their own or were invited by individual cities or private parties. At the time Los Angeles was not thought of a center for German exiles, and even today only a few Germans are aware that Bertolt Brecht, Thomas Mann, Alfred Döblin, and many others wrote their greatest works in an American city on the Pacific Ocean.

The reason for this is not a dearth of publications. The German-speaking architects, actors, artists, composers, movie directors, philosophers, and writers who lived in Los Angeles have been featured in individual monographs—sometimes major figures such as Thomas Mann, Bertolt Brecht, Theodor W. Adorno, and Fritz Lang have been the subject of three to five of them—but these figures have never been studied as a group and with a focus on the crisis of modernism. The only study that comes close is John M. Spalek's collection of articles on the exile writers in Los Angeles—*Deutsche Exilliteratur seit 1933: 1. Kalifornien,* published in 1976—but even this work does not present an overall assessment. Moreover, it is not accessible to the English reader. Cornelius Schnauber's *Hollywood Haven* of 1997 is a useful tourists' guidebook, listing "the homes and haunts" of the Los Angeles exiles, but it is hardly an analysis. The same applies to Holger Gumprecht's *"New Weimar" unter Palmen* of 1998, a popular introduction to the subject. The only monograph on Nazi refugees in an American city is Helmut Pfanner's *Exile in New York* of 1983, which focuses on German and Austrian writers after 1933. New York may have had a larger community of refugees, but it could not boast of a group of artists and intellectuals as prominent as those in Southern California. In the realm of politics, a chapter on Los Angeles in an East German history of exile in the United States—*Exil in den USA* of 1980—presents the city as a center of antifascist engagement and artistic activity.

In addition, there are, of course, some Hollywood monographs, such as John Russell Taylor's *Strangers in Paradise* (1983), devoted to exiles in the movie industry, and Otto Friedrich's *City of Nets* (1986), a social and cultural history of Hollywood between 1939 and 1950. In his *Fluchtpunkt Hollywood* (1986), Jan-Christopher Horak assembles the filmographies of more than eight hundred anti-Nazi refugees who came to Southern California between 1933 and 1945. Saverio Giovacchini provides an assessment of film and politics during the New Deal in his *Hollywood Modernism* (2001), calling attention to the contributions of European film directors who arrived in Hollywood from Nazi Germany. He argues that "the convergence in Hollywood of radical American artists, and of refugees from European fascist dictatorships, provided Southern California with a new generation of filmmakers, inclined to attune the Hollywood screen to the political reality of the day" (2). Giovacchini's description of "Hollywood democratic modernism," which tried to popularize and "to politicize modernism while broadening the size of its audience," demonstrates some parallels with exile modernism.

Anthony Heilbut's study *Exiled in Paradise* (1983) is a social and cultural history of the German-speaking émigrés that covers their presence in the United States from the 1930s to the present, and Jarrel C. Jackman's and Carla M. Borden's essay collection *The Muses Flee Hitler* (1983) concentrates on cultural transfer and adaptation between 1933 and 1945. Los Angeles is mentioned extensively in these studies, but it is not the focus. The same applies to the studies by Alexander Stephan and Hans-Albert Walter, the handbook of German emigration edited by Claus-Dieter Krohn and others, and the biographical dictionary of Central European émigrés edited by Werner Röder and Herbert A. Strauss.

Martin Jay provides another interpretation of the historiography of the forced migration from Germany for the catalogue of the exhibition "Exiles and Emigrés" at the Los Angeles County Museum of Art in 1997, arguing that its scholarship has been politically charged in America as well as in the two Germanies. Whereas for the two postwar states of 1949 exile research served as political legitimation, in the United States it tended to allegorize migration "into a moment of brief and tenuous resistance to the dominant ideologies, political and scholarly, of American life" (334). Jay, however, records a growing disinterest in exile research since the end of the Cold War that has also been echoed in Germany. German scholar Claudia Albert raises the question whether exile studies have come to an end. Martin Jay states that, for the United States, "with the passage of time and the gradual disappearance of the exiles themselves from [American] cultural life, other intellectual currents have emerged to supplant those they transplanted to American soil" (334). He lists these new currents as French theory, the French and English versions of Freud, poststructuralism, postmodernism, and gender studies. These strains of thought are global concerns, and they touch upon the future of exile studies in general, but they do not directly address Weimar on the Pacific, which is still awaiting its final assessment, as current histories of Los Angeles—Mike Davis's *City of Quartz* (1990) and Kevin Starr's *The Dream Endures: California Enters the 1940s* (1997), for example—show.

One of the first scholars to introduce a "poetics of exile" was Bettina Englmann, who in her *Poetik des Exils* (2001) reviewed a number of canonical (Brecht, Döblin, Mann, Werfel) and noncanonical works in the framework of modernity. The consensus in German literary history is that there was no continuation of Weimar modernism in exile. Fredric Jameson shares this point of view in his book *A Singular Modernity* (2002) when he says that modernism in Germany was "abruptly cut short . . . in the early 1930s" (167), obviously ignoring its continuation in exile. Englmann shows that exile literature did not revert to antimodernism, as had been claimed by the majority of German literary historians, but continued to develop new forms of modernism that show especially in the works' fractured relationship to reality *(dekonstruktive Mimesis)* and self-reflective narration *(Autoreflexivität)*. Although Englmann does not use the term "modernism," which was relatively new to German critics—they prefer *Moderne* (modern period) and *Modernität* (modernity); see Gerhart von Graevenitz as well as Silvio Vietta and Dirk Kemper—she opened a new discussion on literary modernism in exile. Two years later, Angelika Abel in her *Musikästhetik der klassischen Moderne* (2003) applied the term "modernism" explicitly to the works of Thomas Mann, Theodor W. Adorno, and Arnold Schoenberg in exile. My study argues that there existed a specific German exile modernism in Los Angeles. In Fredric Jameson's terminology this modernism would figure as "transitional modernism" between the "classical modernism" or "high modernism" of the 1920s, on the one hand, and the "late modernism" after World War II, on the other (150–51, 165–68). There was no late modernism in German literature after World War II, according to Jameson (182), but a good case could be made for writers of the 1950s and 1960s, such as Günter Grass, Uwe Johnson, Paul Celan, and Peter Weiss. Most important for this discussion is the conclusion that modernism is not monolithic, but rather there are a multitude of modernisms.

My survey of exile studies is by no means complete. Instead, it is a sketch of the state of exile studies as they affect the history of Los Angeles. This book is not intended to be another publication on German exile literature, but rather a study of a significant chapter in the cultural history of Los Angeles. Literature is only part of this culture, which also includes architecture, film, music, philosophy, and theater. This study is by no means meant to be comprehensive, but selective in its material and subject matter. And it intends to make the crisis of modernism its focus because it was an international crisis that found a specific German answer in Los Angeles.

As defined by Raymond Williams in his seminal lecture of 1987, modernism is the response to "the greatest changes ever seen in the media of cultural production" at the end of the nineteenth century ("When Was Modernism" 33). As he observes, "photography, cinema, radio, television, reproduction and recording all [made] their decisive advances" during that period. Williams considers the 1890s as the "earliest moment" of the movements that developed into schools of determined self-advertising and self-promotion, such as Futurism, Imagism, Surrealism, Cubism, Vorticism, Formalism, and Constructivism. He concludes that the movements were "the products, at the first historical level, of changes in the public media" (ibid. 33). The new metropolises were centers of innovation, offering themselves as "transnational capitals of an art without frontiers" (ibid. 34). In this context he mentions Paris, Vienna, Berlin, London, and New York, naming them collectively "the eponymous City of Strangers." This type of locale he defines as most appropriate for "art made by the restlessly mobile emigré or exile, the internationally anti-bourgeois artist" (ibid. 34). He describes how writers such as Apollinaire, Joyce, Beckett, and Ionesco were moving to Paris, Vienna, and Berlin in order to meet exiles from the Russian Revolution, who were arriving from the East and bringing with them postrevolutionary manifestos:

> Such endless border-crossing at a time when the frontiers were starting to become much more strictly policed and when, with the First World War, the passport was instituted, worked to naturalize the thesis of the non-natural status of language. The experience of visual and linguistic strangeness, the broken narrative of the journey and its inevitable accompaniment of transient encounters with characters whose self-presentation was baf-

fling unfamiliar, raised to the level of universal myth this intense, singular narrative of unsettlement, homelessness, solitude and impoverished independence. (ibid. 34)

Raymond Williams's identification of the mythical exile as the producer of modernist art or literature makes his definition especially attractive to my study, even if I must challenge his final conclusion that the concept of modernism is "crucially interpreted and ratified by the City of Emigrés and Exiles itself, New York" (ibid. 34). It is my thesis that for German modernism during the 1940s, Los Angeles became the City of Emigrés and Exiles that was most appropriate for that decade's modernist art and literature, and that the exiles had to adopt a dialectical stance toward the image of Los Angeles as a natural paradise in order to perceive it as the cityscape of modernism. I have therefore adopted as the motto for this book Brecht's assertion from his *Refugee Conversations* (1940): "emigration is the best school of dialectics" (GBA 18: 264).

This is a most daring assertion because Los Angeles was still an idyllic garden city in the early 1940s. There was a downtown area with department stores and high-rises, but none of the buildings was higher than city hall, with its twenty-six stories (a law prohibiting buildings taller than city hall was in effect until 1956). The rest of the city consisted of urban sprawl, with low-income housing in the northeast (Chavez Ravine) and east (Boyle Heights and East Los Angeles, or the so-called barrio), as well as in the south-central part of town (Watts). The middle class and affluent lived in apartment buildings and houses on the so-called "Westside" (Beverly Hills, Westwood, Santa Monica, Brentwood, and Pacific Palisades). Hollywood was the only western suburb that housed both the rich and the poor within its borders. Even if a strong case can be made that during World War II Los Angeles became a major center of the defense industry and an important port of embarkation for the war in the Pacific, and that it thus soon turned into a modernist metropolis in spite of its idyllic setting (see Gerald D. Nash and Arthur C. Verge), it was not the grim, gray city of alienation that Raymond Williams had in mind when he named New York the city of modernism. His image of a modernist writer was that of a lonely author "gazing down on the unknowable city from his shabby apartment" (34). But in Los Angeles, the German exile writers were living in bungalows or flats, surrounded by lush gardens that some of them resented with a vengeance. Both Brecht and Alfred Döblin made negative comments about the gardens surrounding them. Full of contempt, Brecht, when looking at his garden on 25th Street in Santa Monica, exclaimed, "They [the Americans] have nature here" (GBA 27:12). And Döblin dwelled on the fact that he had to spend a lot of time "in the greenness" of flourishing vegetation, complaining that he was not a cow (Kesten 238). These statements illustrate the unease they felt when confronted with the garden city of Los Angeles, and their need to reconstruct the image of the cityscape in their minds. To be sure, the exiles from Central Europe were attracted to Los Angeles because of the tropical climate, the prospect of employment by the movie industry, and the lower cost of living compared to New York. But perhaps it was this startling contrast between the city's paradisiacal setting and the awareness that the most brutal warfare ever had been unleashed that made Los Angeles the most appropriate locale for art that dealt with both the reality of fascism and World War II and the hope for a better future. The idyllic landscape functioned like a Hollywood movie set that produced alienation because of its apparent perfection.

The history of modernism before 1933 shows that its representatives tried to project in their works a transformation of society, even though they were keenly aware of their political impotence and disposed to the critique of naïve utopias. This tendency explains the anticapitalism of modernism and its alignment with socialism, but also its susceptibility to radical solutions that resulted in fascist modernism. Modernism had always been divided, although this division did not become apparent until 1933. Prior to that year most modernists had associated their movement and its goals with a general progressiveness, but the political events of 1933 made clear that a progressive modernism had failed and a totalitarian modernism had triumphed. Vladimir Mayakovsky, Pablo Picasso, Ignazio Silone, and Brecht had supported communism, while Gabriele d'Annunzio, Filippo Tommaso Marinetti, Wyndham Lewis, Ezra Pound, Ernst Jünger, and Gottfried Benn had moved towards fascism, which was beginning to extend its rule over Europe and the rest of the world.

I would argue that Los Angeles became the battlefield for the wars of German exile modernism in the 1940s, with Brecht, Lion Feuchtwanger, and Heinrich Mann on the left, Alfred Döblin and Franz Werfel on the right, and Thomas Mann and Arnold Schoenberg in the middle. Admittedly, this arrangement of armies oversimplifies the complex group dynamics and alignments within German exile modernism, but it serves as a blueprint for the discussion in this book. I adopted this blueprint from Russell A. Berman's monograph *The Rise of the Modern German Novel* (1986), in which he treats three competing versions of modernist prose

writing: "fascist modernism, leftist modernism, and a modernism of social individuality" (vii). Berman considers these categories ideal types
that were to be "understood as forms of address designed to generate the
new communities of readers. The rise of the modern German novel and
the associated aesthetic innovation are inseparable from the various programs for social and political transformation inscribed in the texts"
(vii–viii).

In case of fascist modernism, this "new community" was a charis-
matically inspired readership (205); in the case of leftist modernism, it
was an appeal to "the collective" to obtain a voice of its own (234); and,
finally, in the case of the modernism of social individuality, it was a "rational" readership, "oriented toward the possibility of a new social individuality" (262–63). Berman was most concerned about the cultural
rupture around 1900 and the creation of communities of readers that the
competing strategies of modern writing tried to establish (vi). I fully
agree with Berman's charge that the Frankfurt School never resolved the
critical question of this cultural rupture, but I am focused on the ruptures
within modernism around 1933, or rather the final split of modernism
into three competing strategies. I consider this split the crisis of modernism. Although this split had been a long time coming, it became an
undeniable fact when the Nazi party had accomplished its political
takeover in Germany and driven a great number of modernist artists,
writers, and composers into exile. I do not use the term "fascist modernists" for the conservative exile writers, because their writing strategies
cannot be associated with writers such as Ernst Jünger and Hans Grimm.
Neither do I address the strategies for creating communities of readers,
but the topic of the appropriate audience for esoteric art and literature
is discussed, as it is thematized in the works.

The term "German-speaking exiles" (or "German exiles") as it is employed throughout this book includes Austrians, Czechs, Poles, and
Hungarians, all participants in a Central European culture and who
spoke German as a common language. The term refers to their linguistic and cultural heritage rather than their nationality. Many of the actors,
directors, writers, and composers of Weimar culture were born in Austria, Czechoslovakia, Hungary, and Poland. They came to Los Angeles
via the Berlin of the Weimar Republic: Schoenberg, Fritz Lang, and Max
Reinhardt came from Vienna, Franz Werfel from Prague, actor Peter
Lorre and film director Michael Curtiz from Hungary, and actor
Alexander Granach, actress and screenwriter Salka Viertel, and Billy
Wilder from Poland.

The Nazi measures that caused their exile were totally different from previous methods of political expatriation. The Nazis established categories with the intent to deprive certain groups of their means of subsistence, their property, their rights as citizens, and—in the so-called "Final Solution" *(Endlösung)*—their lives. Among these categories were the so-called non-Aryans, the Marxists (or those labeled as such), and the intellectuals and artists who had resisted the rise of the Nazi party. Literature and the arts had become special targets of political propaganda, as it was the declared goal of the new regime to erase fourteen years of "cultural bolshevism." All writers, actors, artists, composers, and musicians were required to become members of the Reich Chamber of Culture *(Reichskulturkammer)* in order to practice their profession. The Reich Chamber of Culture was a branch of the Ministry of Propaganda and dealt with all sectors of cultural activity. One of its primary purposes was to achieve a uniform national culture under the leadership and control of the Nazi government and to purge from German cultural life all Jews and persons considered politically unreliable.

In February 1933, two members of the Prussian Academy of Arts who were critical of the Nazi party were forced to resign: the artist Käthe Kollwitz and the writer Heinrich Mann. Thirteen other members resigned in protest, including Ricarda Huch, Thomas Mann, and Alfred Döblin. In early April, Hitler issued the Law for the Restoration of the Civil Service, which required the dismissal of Jews and politically unreliable persons from the civil service. This law retroactively validated the dismissal of composer Arnold Schoenberg by the Prussian Academy of Arts, and of the artists Max Beckmann, Otto Dix, Paul Klee, and Oskar Schlemmer by the art academies in Berlin, Dresden, Düsseldorf, and Frankfurt/Main. On May 10, 1933, books were burned at public ceremonies in most university cities in Germany. Minister of Propaganda Joseph Goebbels presided over the ceremony in front of the University of Berlin. He began his speech by proclaiming the end of "the age of overblown Jewish intellectualism" and specifically targeted the works of the Jewish "city-slicker literati" *(Asphaltliteraten).* During the same month lending libraries and bookstores received their first blacklists, which included more than 150 "unacceptable authors." In July 1933, the Bauhaus school of architecture in Berlin was closed. In October 1933, Hitler laid the cornerstone of the House of German Art in Munich, the museum that was inaugurated in 1937 as a counterpart to the exhibition "Degenerate Art." The exhibition "Degenerate Music" was to follow in 1938, staged in Düsseldorf in conjunction with the national musical festival, the Reichsmusiktage, and prepared by the Reich Chamber of Music, a branch of the Reich Chamber of Culture, under the supervision of Goebbels.

The number of writers designated by name and singled out for personal persecution was relatively small in May 1933. There were not more than fifteen names on the list for the book burning in Berlin, and these included an author no longer alive, Karl Marx. The number of authors who chose exile, however, exceeded fifteen by far. These writers were joined by artists, actors, directors, composers, musicians, scientists, and scholars, and all became part of a mass emigration of German and Austrian Jews, members of the Communist and Social Democratic parties, trade unionists, and individuals from various professions and political parties. Accurate statistics are available only for the number of Jewish refugees, which had reached 283,000 by May 1937. The annexation of Austria in 1938 added another 95,000, the takeover of Czechoslovakia a year later another 23,000. The mass emigration included more than 1,500 authors, including journalists and university scholars; of these 1,500, approximately 200 were novelists, playwrights, and poets. There are no statistics available for artists in other fields, but it is safe to call this one of the largest emigrations of writers and artists recorded in history, comparable to the exodus of intellectuals from Constantinople, the center of Byzantine culture, after its capture by the Ottoman Turks in 1453.

The most remarkable aspect of this exodus of 1933 was that almost all the prominent writers of the Weimar Republic chose exile over compromise with the Nazi regime. The figures are not as impressive for the artists, actors, directors, conductors, and composers. If they were not Jewish, they could continue to eke out a living in Germany, as some of them did (Anton Webern as a composer and Otto Dix as painter, for example), but the stories of those who stayed behind, such as Ernst Barlach and Emil Nolde, show how demoralizing the daily surveillance by the Nazi authorities could be. Of the writers, only Gerhart Hauptmann—the "King of the Weimar Republic," as Thomas Mann had called him in his famous speech "The German Republic" (Von deutscher Republik) in 1922—stayed behind. The playwright, who had been in the avant-garde at the turn of the century and had been responsible for important innovations in German naturalist drama, had moved too far to the right of the political spectrum to recognize and fight fascism. The list of authors who went into exile includes Bertolt Brecht, Hermann Broch, Alfred Döblin, Lion Feuchtwanger, Heinrich and Thomas Mann, Robert Musil,

Anna Seghers, Franz Werfel, and Stefan Zweig. Six of these writers made
Los Angeles their home during at least part of the period from 1940 to
1958: three of them (Heinrich Mann, Feuchtwanger, and Werfel) died
here, while three others (Brecht, Döblin, and Thomas Mann) returned to
Europe after the war.

Although some of the exiles were Austrians, Czechs, or Hungarians,
I subsume them here under the label of Weimar because most of them
had been corresponding members of the Prussian Academy of Arts in
Berlin, the Bauhaus, Berlin theater companies, or the German movie industry. The exiles represented the best of Weimar culture, and they carried their culture into exile.

After the collapse of the Weimar Republic in 1933, there was a tendency among its survivors to idealize its cultural achievements. Peter
Gay, a historian of the Weimar period, refers to the "legend of Weimar,"
which began with the "Golden Twenties," and points out the danger of
mythologizing the era as a golden age. To construct a flawless ideal of
Weimar, he said, is

> to trivialize the achievements of the Weimar Renaissance, and to slight the
> price it had to pay for them. The excitement that characterized Weimar
> culture stemmed in part from the exuberant creativity and experimenta-
> tion; but much of it was anxiety, fear, a rising sense of doom. With some
> justice, Karl Mannheim, one of its survivors, boasted not long before its
> demise that future years would look back on Weimar as a new Periclean
> age. But it was a precarious glory, a dance on the edge of a volcano.
> Weimar culture was the creation of outsiders, propelled by history into the
> inside, for a short, dizzying, fragile moment. (*Weimar Culture* xiv)

Yet the Weimar Republic also produced a chauvinist pan-German and
racist literature that glorified the war experience and German "soil and
blood." This literature was in full bloom in the late 1920s, when war
novels and peasant novels flooded the literary market. A system of
defamation, repression, and persecution of progressive intellectuals was
already in practice before 1933. The historiography of the Weimar Republic shows that the depiction of the period from 1926 to 1930 as a
golden age is one-sided (see Karl Dietrich Bracher, Walter Laqueur, Hans
Mommsen, Detlev Peukert, and Heinrich August Winkler). Reactionary
civil servants and judges controlled key positions in the government and
in the courts. They were supported by a right-wing press that attacked
all forms of modernism in literature, music, and the arts. In effect, German fascism had grown out of the resistance of the German middle class
to the threat of rapid modernization in all areas of life, including indus-

trialization, urbanization, rationalism, internationalism, and socialism. In short, German fascism was to a certain degree a counterrevolution against modernism, and since the manifestations of modernism were most conspicuous in the realms of literature, music, and the arts, these became important battlegrounds for the conflicting ideologies and their proponents. The rapid and pervasive changes achieved by modernism in Germany between 1919 and 1933 created a tremendous backlash. In this respect, Hitler and the Nazi movement must be regarded as products of the Weimar Republic as well.

Peter Gay characterizes the Weimar Republic as "an idea seeking to become a reality" (*Weimar Culture* 1). The constituent assembly for the new republic of 1919 was held in Weimar primarily for reasons of security, but soon the city of Goethe and Schiller came to symbolize the hope for a humanist, pacifist, and cosmopolitan Germany. The constitution of the German Republic reflected these values, promising in its preamble to "renew and strengthen the [German] Reich in liberty and justice, to preserve peace at home and abroad, and to foster social progress" (*Weimar Republic Sourcebook* 46). Friedrich Ebert, the first president of the Weimar Republic, referred explicitly to "the spirit of Weimar" in his inaugural speech at the Weimar National Theater on February 11, 1919, when he declared that "the spirit of the great philosophers and poets must again guide us in our life. We must deal with the great societal problems of our time in the same spirit, as Goethe understood them in the second part of *Faust* and in [his novel] *Wilhelm Meisters Wanderjahre:* not to wander off into the metaphysical realm or to lose ourselves to theory, but to address the practical problems of our life with clear eyes and a firm hand" (*Goethe im Urteil* 488).

Ebert's invocation of the spirit of Weimar was designed to counter the spirit of Potsdam, the former residence of the Prussian kings. The Weimar Republic, however, could never overcome the aggressively militaristic, authoritarian, and antimodernist tradition that was associated with Potsdam. It was no accident that Hitler staged a symbolic meeting of the German parliament in the Garrison Church of Potsdam on March 21, 1933 (after the burning of the Reichstag building in Berlin on February 27). This date celebrated the anniversary of the opening of the first Reichstag under Bismarck. The Garrison Church was built by the first Prussian king, Frederick William I, and under its altar was the crypt of the Hohenzollern dynasty. This celebration prepared the new members of parliament for the vote on the "Enabling Law" on March 23, 1933, which gave Hitler the absolute power to pass any law without parliamentary approval. Only the Social Democratic Party was opposed. The "Day of Potsdam" symbolically marked the end of the Weimar Republic.

The history of the Weimar Republic is the history of two German traditions—Weimar and Potsdam—in conflict with each other, and it was this dichotomy, as Peter Gay notes, that contributed to the republic's defeat. Because many of the exiles reflected that dichotomy themselves, it would be an oversimplification to claim that one Germany stayed behind in 1933 while the other went into exile. Bertolt Brecht once declared that everything bad in him had a German origin. He nevertheless continued to write for a German-speaking audience.

From 1933 to 1940 most of the European countries provided a haven for German and Austrian refugees, though some did so reluctantly. London, Paris, Prague, Moscow, and Zurich became centers of German exile culture, with German-language newspapers, periodicals, publishing houses, and theaters. But after the defeat of France in 1940, one of the few escape routes remaining was across the Atlantic—to South America, Mexico, the United States, or Canada. The U.S. Immigration Act of 1924 permitted European immigration according to a system of quotas, which limited the number of immigrants annually to 3 percent of the number of each nationality already present in the United States. Between 1933 and 1941 more than 130,000 German and Austrian immigrants entered the United States. Because of many special restrictions on immigration, however, the German quota remained unfilled during all but one of those years.

In 1940 the United States government, under President Roosevelt, established a number of official and semiofficial agencies, such as the National Refugee Service and the Emergency Rescue Committee, to ease immigration restrictions and to save German, Austrian, and other European expatriates from deportation to German concentration camps. These agencies were assisted by the American Friends Service Committee in a large-scale rescue operation of German, Austrian, and other European exiles trapped in "unoccupied" France after the Vichy government agreed to return all former German citizens to Nazi jurisdiction. Lion Feuchtwanger, Heinrich Mann, and Franz Werfel were saved by an American rescue mission that brought them illegally across the Pyrenees to Lisbon, a point from which they were able to travel by ship to New York. By early 1941 more than six hundred antifascist intellectuals and artists, not only from Germany and Austria, but also from France and Italy, were saved this way, among them Marc Chagall, Jacques Lipschitz, and Marcel Duchamp.

Most of the German-speaking refugees who came to the United States between 1933 and 1941 settled in New York City, but a great many went on to Los Angeles, which became the most important center of German exile culture during the 1940s. Although New York may have reminded the exiles of the Berlin of the Weimar Republic, Los Angeles provided them with an environment that allowed not only for the import of Weimar culture, but also for its creative continuation and further development. To be sure, some were attracted by the mild climate, the low cost of living, and the opportunities afforded by the motion-picture industry. Hollywood had attracted European intellectuals since the end of World War I. German directors and actors such as Ernst Lubitsch, Friedrich W. Murnau, Erich Pommer, Conrad Veidt, and Emil Jannings had been involved in the production of silent movies for the European market. As well, writers like Erika and Klaus Mann (*Ein heiteres Reisebuch* [A Happy Travelogue], 1929) and Arnold Höllriegel, who wrote under the pseudonym Richard A. Bermann (*Hollywood-Bilderbuch* [Hollywood Picture-Book], 1927; *Lichter der Großstadt* [Lights of the Metropolis], 1931) had written about the charm of life on the West Coast.

Furthermore, Los Angeles had not been as severely affected by the Depression of 1929 as elsewhere in the United States, or at least it had recovered better than other cities. Anton Wagner's geographical and economic study of Los Angeles, published in German in the mid-1930s, provided solid evidence of a boom and promising development (*Los Angeles: Werden, Leben und Gestalt der Zweimillionenstadt in Südkalifornien* 131–42). Tourism, the film industry, the local garment industry, oil exploration, aircraft manufacture, and California's agriculture provided a solid base for economic recovery. In the early 1940s, investment capital moved to California because of the development of new high-tech industries. As soon as the defense industry was mobilized to supply the U.S. and Allied forces with arms, minorities and women became employed in addition to the traditional workforce.

Among the exiles, Hollywood also had the reputation of being politically progressive and an active supporter of the struggle against fascism in Europe. The Hollywood Anti-Nazi League (HANL), formed in 1936, conducted mass meetings at the Shrine Auditorium. Between 1937 and 1939, the HANL sponsored a number of rallies in support of the Spanish Republic in its war against Franco. The stimuli for the HANL had been a banquet by the film industry to raise funds for the American Guild for German Cultural Freedom (which had been a great success), and a benefit concert by the Los Angeles Philharmonic Orchestra under the direction of Otto Klemperer, with works by Arnold Schoenberg and Ernst Toch on the program. In 1937, the German playwright Ernst Toller spoke in support of the Spanish Republic at the invitation of the HANL, and in 1938 Thomas Mann gave the public address "The Coming Victory of Democracy" at the Shrine Auditorium. That the HANL was later investigated by the House Un-American Activities Committee (HUAC) and branded as a Communist front was an indication of the change in the U.S. political climate after World War II (Ceplair and Englund 83–128; 254–98). The HUAC hearings in 1947 revealed in retrospect Hollywood's internationalism and its support of the Popular Front during the 1930s.

But perhaps even more important for the exiles was the fact that there was a large German-speaking community in Southern California, a critical mass that enabled Weimar culture to continue and even thrive in exile. No other city can compete with Los Angeles for the title of capital of literary Weimar in exile between 1940 and 1958. In other fields of culture, such as architecture, film, and music, a higher degree of acculturation was required to succeed. German exile literature in Los Angeles was completely deterritorialized; it was written exclusively in German and translated into English only for the purpose of publication. Gilles Deleuze's and Félix Guattari's criteria for a "minor literature"—deterritorialization, politicization, and collectivization (16–27)— can certainly be applied to German literature in Southern California. As Deleuze and Guattari explain, "Everything in [minor literatures] is political. . . . everything takes on a collective value. . . . there are no possibilities for an individuated enunciation that would belong to this or that "master" and that could be separated from a collective enunciation. . . . what each author says individually already constitutes a common action, and what he or she says or does is necessarily political, even if others aren't in agreement" (Deleuze and Guattari 17).

Cultural historians have criticized Los Angeles of the 1940s for not being as mature as New York as a center of American culture, or even for being a symbol of anticulture, but they have failed to take into consideration the fact that Los Angeles's lack of a cultural infrastructure provided an opportunity for Weimar culture not only to reestablish its identity in exile, but also to fulfill its promise. In an environment with an established cultural infrastructure, where the influences of competing cultures could have proved overwhelming, this second flourishing of Weimar culture might not have been possible.

This concept of a second flourishing of Weimar culture is, however, misleading. It belies not only the negative experience of the collapse of the Weimar Republic and the subsequent exile of its intellectual and artistic elite, but also the failure of its culture and the impending crisis of modernism. Even if some writers and artists continued working on projects that they had started before they went into exile, there was no simple continuity. The exiles had to question their individual arts and to reflect on their future missions. Their creative works had obviously failed them. No one had expected literature and the arts to prevent the rise of the Nazis to power in Germany and military rule over Europe, but the exiles—with few exceptions—had not anticipated the collapse of the Weimar Republic. Some of them were even guilty of undermining or attacking the new democracy. None was surprised by the terrorism unleashed, but all of them were stunned by the popular success of the regime that had deprived them of their citizenship and driven them into exile. Now the question was not only how to fight this regime politically, but also how to preserve the utopian potential of modernist literature and art. Was modernism no longer a viable option, or could changes be implemented to prevent modernism from becoming reactionary? For some exiles conservatism, a return to established values and techniques, was thought necessary. Others tried to reconstitute modernism and give it a new meaning and function.

This crisis of modernism, which, with respect to exile literature and art, has not been studied with sufficient theoretical awareness, is at the center of this study. Rather than presenting another interpretation of canonical works, I focus on these works as examples of the crisis of modernism and the creative solutions offered by a loosely assembled group of exiles that settled in Los Angeles during the 1940s. My thesis is that they reconstituted modernism in such a way that they were able, on the one hand, to maintain its experimental structure and to present a vision of modern life with universal reach, and, on the other hand, to add new aspects to modernism that reflected political and historical change.

Foremost among these new aspects was the insistence on the dialectic as a structural element and intellectual argument in art and literature. The exile experience and legitimation of modernism in exile is grounded in what Fredric Jameson called in reference to Adorno "the persistence of the dialectic" (the subtitle of *Late Marxism*). In their California exile Brecht, Thomas Mann, and Schoenberg practiced dialectic to an increasing degree. Aesthetic self-reflexiveness, as well as juxtaposition and montage, were subsumed under the dialectics of representation.

The reconstituted modernism also reflected a new responsiveness to the audience. Artists and writers realized that the time of elitist isolation was over. They became aware that they needed to engage a wider audience to gain support for their analyses of past failures and their development of a new and authentic response to the mass destruction and genocide facing them. This responsiveness required an increased awareness of history and current events; it necessitated a critical review of nationalism and the failure of democracy in Central Europe, as well as an understanding of the emergence of German fascism and the events of World War II. The "German Question" is a frequent topic of exile modernism, and works of art were often produced with the intent to record events and provide analyses and solutions.

In works of exile modernism, human suffering—especially the Holocaust, or Shoa—was often a focus. A continuing discussion of the horrifying consequences of anti-Semitism was necessary since more than half of the exiles were Jews, and Christians and Jews alike felt they needed to come to understand the catastrophe so that their escape and survival did not become meaningless (see Starr, *The Dream Endures*, 367).

In this context every statement, even the unpolitical or private, becomes political, as Gilles Deleuze and Félix Guattari observed (17). Conversions and religious vows have political repercussions, as the examples of Alfred Döblin and Franz Werfel showed. Their personal expressions took on a collective quality, and both writers had to face a critical reception of their actions and works.

Among the formal features of exile modernism, the most obvious is the avoidance of closure. Exile modernism privileges open-ended narrative construction. Paradox, ambiguity, and uncertainty—common features of modernism generally, but now exacerbated by the experience of forced migration—became the litmus test of exile modernism (see also Lunn 34–37).

Many of the exiles saw themselves as continuing the tradition of Weimar as it was represented by Goethe and later by Friedrich Ebert. As Ludwig Marcuse, who taught German literature at the University of Southern California, recalls, he found himself sitting in Los Angeles

> in the middle of the Weimar Republic: with [Max] Reinhardt and [Leopold] Jessner and [Fritz] Kortner and [Ernst] Deutsch; with Thomas Mann, Berthold Viertel and Bruno Frank . . . and every year more literature arrived, so that we were soon as complete as we had been in Sanary, [the French resort on the Mediterranean where many of the Weimar exiles

had settled before 1940], shortly before. You don't feel such a foreigner
when you're surrounded by friends who are also foreigners. And even if
some of them weren't your friends, at least they weren't enemies. I hardly
realized there were any Americans here. And I felt that a poor person isn't
quite as poor in Los Angeles as in New York. (*Mein Zwanzigstes Jahrhundert* 266)

Thomas Mann, who modeled his life as a writer after Goethe in terms of
"identification and unio mystica" (GW 13: 169), cultivated the Weimar
image, especially when he wrote his version of the Faust legend. Thomas
Mann's identification with the "Goethe myth," as he called it, represented his identification with German culture. His use of the term
"myth" reveals that he was aware that this identification was an artificial construct, but he nevertheless pursued this construct with great
determination because he believed in its beneficial effects on his own
writings and his politics. Mann's imitation of Goethe became his imper-
sonation of Goethe, and Los Angeles became his Weimar on the Pacific.
When asked about the progress of his *Doctor Faustus* by a colleague in
a letter of October 1944, Thomas Mann responded that this question
sounded as if it were directed at the sage of Weimar. He was amused by
the question, yet he felt "mythically attracted," because some of the better German qualities were associated with Goethe's *Faust* (letter to Erich
von Kahler, October 20, 1944, *Briefe 1937–1947*, 397). Even Bertolt
Brecht, who adamantly opposed German classicism, as well as the
Weimar Republic, could not escape the Weimar model. When he fled
from the advancing German armies to Vladivostok to catch a ship to the
United States, he read the famous account of Schiller's escape from his
tyrannical prince in Wurttemberg in 1782. After his arrival in Los Angeles, Brecht took stock of his own plays in July 1943 and found that his
dramatic production over the last ten years did not compare badly with
that of Weimar classicism (GBA 27: 159). In "Garden in Progress," his
most important exile poem written while he was in Los Angeles, he identified with Schiller's opinion that "beauty must die" (see chapter 3).

American observers also considered the German exiles in Los Angeles as representatives of Weimar, be it Goethe's Weimar, the Weimar Republic, or both. When the *New Yorker* published a piece on Thomas
Mann in Los Angeles in December 1941, the editor could not resist printing Janet Flanner's article under the title "Goethe in Hollywood," suggesting that German culture, symbolized by Goethe, had been exiled to
the United States, and that Southern California was its new domicile.
Later, at a conference of the Hollywood Writers' Mobilization at UCLA

in 1943, the speaker who introduced Thomas Mann and Lion Feuchtwanger compared the West Los Angeles telephone directory to an issue
of *Kürschners Almanach,* a who's who of the arts, literature, and music
of the Weimar Republic. The idea that Los Angeles was the "new
Weimar" was established during these years, and many of the exiles cultivated it to promote their cause.

This book is not intended as a comprehensive history of this group or
of their works created in exile, but rather as a collection of case studies
that have relevance for German modernism in exile. Even the description
of the exiles as a "group" must be qualified, because they were frag-
mented in their associations and politics. Only their migration from Central Europe provided a common denominator.

Film is not as fully represented in this book as the number of refugees
attracted by Hollywood would suggest. The Los Angeles film industry
employed more than eight hundred professionals who had fled Germany
and Austria, but the studio regulations and working conditions demanded such strict adaptation to American ways that the development
of exile modernism in Hollywood films was nearly impossible, as, the career of Billy Wilder showed, for example. As John Russel Taylor comments, Wilder "remained foreign enough to be colourful . . . , but at the
same time . . . he had observed closely enough to know just how far he
could go without becoming unacceptable to American tastes. He had, in
other words, become an American filmmaker, though with continental
trimmings" (201).

Although Saverio Giovacchini gives much credit to exile film directors
and their contributions to "Hollywood democratic modernism" (27–35,
64–71), it was still Hollywood modernism. Exile modernism in film had
a better chance in independent productions outside the studios, as Charlie Chaplin's *The Great Dictator* (1940) and Fritz Lang's *Hangmen Also
Die* (1943) show.

Musicians, including composers, conductors, performing artists, and
other music professionals, constituted another large group of exiles.
Among the composers there were, in addition to Arnold Schoenberg,
Hanns Eisler, Friedrich Hollaender, Erich Wolfgang Korngold, Ernst
Toch, Erik Zeisl, and, later, Ernst Krenek in Palm Springs. Among the
conductors were Bruno Walter and Otto Klemperer, and among the performing artists Eduard Steuermann (pianist) and Lotte Lehmann (opera
singer), who resided in Santa Barbara (see Merrill-Mirsky). While
Korngold, who was discovered as a child prodigy by Gustav Mahler,
dedicated his musical talents while in exile exclusively to the movies,

both Eisler and Toch showed that it was possible to both compose for the movie industry and continue writing their own compositions. Hollaender continued his career that began with writing songs for *Der Blaue Engel* (The Blue Angel) in Berlin in 1930, composing music for more than 120 films in Hollywood.

Literature may be overemphasized in studies of exile modernism because of its narrative content that is readily subject to interpretation, but writers also constituted the third largest group of exiles in the arts, as Los Angeles was home to more than thirty writers who were well known in Central Europe. This study concentrates on selected works by Brecht, Döblin, Werfel, and Thomas Mann that cover the spectrum of exile modernism. In addition to these often-mentioned authors, the following are discussed in detail in the Los Angeles volume of *Deutsche Exilliteratur*, edited by John M. Spalek and Joseph Strelka in 1976: Günther Anders, Raoul Auernheimer, Vicki Baum, Emil Bernhard, Paul Elbogen, Lion Feuchtwanger, Bruno Frank, Leonhard Frank, Curt Goetz, Hans Habe, Oskar Jellinek, Hans Kafka, Stephan Lackner, Heinrich Mann, Ludwig Marcuse, Alfred Neumann, Alfred Neumeyer, Alfred Polgar, Erich Maria Remarque, Wilhelm Speyer, Friedrich Torberg, and Joseph Wechsberg. This list does not include any of the screenwriters, such as George Froeschel, Felix Jackson, Gina Kaus, Fredrick Kohner, Jan Lustig, Walter Reisch, Francis Spencer, and Salka Viertel.

The absence of visual art in this study is historically justified since few of the painters and sculptors of the Weimar Republic came to Los Angeles. Oskar Fischinger (1900–1967), abstract film animator and painter, Anna Mahler (1904–88), sculptor, and Gertrud (1908–71) and Otto Natzler (b. 1908), ceramicists, were exceptions. Anna Mahler had spent the war years in London and came to join her mother, Alma Mahler-Werfel, in Los Angeles in 1945. During the 1950s she taught in the art department at UCLA. Galka Scheyer (1889–1945), best known for her association with the Blue Four artists, Vasily Kandinsky, Paul Klee, Lyonel Feininger, and Alexei Jawlensky, brought concepts of European modernism to Los Angeles, where she settled permanently in 1933. She had come to the United States as an art dealer in 1923, but was never able to attract any of the painters who were persecuted by the Nazis to Southern California. Although she had no gallery of her own, she exercised considerable influence on art collecting in the Los Angeles area. Galka Scheyer's Blue Four collection is now housed at the Norton Simon Museum in Pasadena.

Architecture is given special attention because it provides the most visible examples of modernism in Los Angeles. Although its most prominent representatives, Richard Neutra and Rudolph M. Schindler, had already arrived in the 1920s, they nevertheless contributed to the reputation of the exiles due to a common misconception that modernist architects had to be exiles from Germany or Austria. Indeed, some of them were, as, for example, Victor Gruen (1903–80), founder of Gruen Associates, which produced a number of impressive commercial designs in Los Angeles. Neutra and Schindler, however, were immigrants and combined internationalism and regionalism for a modernism of their own that can be compared and contrasted with exile modernism.

The philosophy of the Frankfurt School, or the Institute for Social Research, is given a prominent position in this study because it reflects the alienation of the exiles and provides a theory to deal creatively with this alienation. The Frankfurt School, one of the think tanks of the Weimar Republic, affiliated with the University of Frankfurt, had moved into exile, first to Switzerland, then to Paris, and finally to New York, where it was affiliated with Columbia University. In 1941 the Frankfurt School moved to Los Angeles, and its director, Max Horkheimer, and his close friend and collaborator, Theodor W. Adorno, had close contacts with the various circles of exiles in Los Angeles, from Schoenberg and Werfel to Fritz Lang, Thomas Mann, and Brecht. Horkheimer and his wife were official witnesses at the Manns' naturalization as U.S. citizens in 1944, while Adorno set two poems by Brecht to music for voice and piano in 1943: "In Sturmes Nacht" (During a Stormy Night [GBA 15: 76]) and "Das Lied von der Stange" (The Song of the Flagpole [GBA 15: 20]).

Adorno's observations on exile as "damaged life" articulated a commonly shared experience. As he says in his *Minima Moralia*, written between 1944 and 1947, in regard to immigrant writers and artists living in the shadow of Hollywood, "Every intellectual in emigration is, without exception, mutilated, and does well to acknowledge it to himself, if he wishes to avoid being cruelly apprised of it behind the tightly-closed doors of his self-esteem. . . . Between the reproduction of his own existence under the monopoly of mass culture, and impartial, responsible work, yawns an irreconcilable breach" (MM 33).

Adorno draws attention especially to the expropriation of language and the weakening of the "historical dimension" that informed the exiles' knowledge (MM 33). Referring to the writer who made himself feel at home in his writings, he declares, "For a man who no longer has a homeland, writing becomes a place to live." But Adorno had to admit that "in the end, the [exile] writer is not even allowed to live in his writing" (MM 87). Such observations made him an expert on exile culture. Edward Said based his "Reflections on Exile" of 1984 on *Minima Moralia,* quoting Adorno (184–85) and confirming that exile is "terrible to experience" (173; see also "Movement and Migrations," 332–33). Said adds a historical dimension, conceding that the twentieth century was "indeed the age of the refugee, the displaced person, mass immigration," but he warns against transforming exile into a metaphor of modern culture: to think of exile informing literature "as beneficially humanistic [was] to banalize its mutilations" (174). In the postmodern era "exile" has assumed a totally different connotation, as Hamid Naficy has shown in his study of Iranian television in Los Angeles of 1993, when he declared that "exile must also be defined by its utopian and euphoric possibilities" (6). This idea was absolutely alien to Adorno and Said.

It is generally agreed that Theodor W. Adorno's essays on music greatly influenced the conception of Thomas Mann's novel *Doctor Faustus* and that the novelist clearly benefited from reading Horkheimer and Adorno's "Philosophical Fragments," which were published in 1947 under the title *Dialektik der Aufklärung* (Dialectic of Enlightenment). This type of influence is not as clear with other authors or composers, but we can detect parallels and convergence in spite of many conflicts. Although Bertolt Brecht's participation in the seminars of the Institute for Social Research in Los Angeles is a matter of record, he considered them useless and made some very malicious comments about Horkheimer and Friedrich Pollock in his diary, calling them "twin clowns" (August 1941). Nor did Arnold Schoenberg find much to praise in Adorno's essays on his works, although they were highly complimentary of Schoenberg's compositions and characterized them as "incomparably superior" to those of Igor Stravinsky, associating Schoenberg with progress and charging Stravinsky with "permanent regression" (PMM 212). Nevertheless, *Dialectic of Enlightenment,* the central text of the Frankfurt School in exile, provides an excellent hermeneutical tool for my approach.

Chapter 1 is devoted to the explication of *Dialectic of Enlightenment,* as it provided a trajectory for exile modernism to follow, while chapter 2 focuses on the concept of the "culture industry," as defined in *Dialectic of Enlightenment,* and on Adorno's *Philosophy of Modern Music (Philosophie der neuen Musik)* of 1949 and his late *Aesthetic Theory (Ästhetische Theorie)* of 1970. The process of enlightenment had proved both progressive and regressive and culminated in a crisis around 1933 that needed not only political action to decide its outcome, but also philosophical reflection to chart the future course of enlightenment. Chapter 2 shows how Adorno in his book on Schoenberg and Stravinsky integrated the development of modern music into the historical process and identified resistance to society as the function of art. Later in his aesthetics Adorno added the concept of art as historical record and the permanent language of human suffering.

Chapters 3 and 4 deal with Brecht's lyric poetry and his drama *Galileo* as paradigms of dialectics in exile modernism. Brecht had to reinvent Los Angeles as a city of exiles in order to be productive as a poet. Therefore, his California poetry is not mimetic, as it has previously been interpreted. Brecht's *Galileo* is shown to be an extension of the discussion of modern science in *Dialectic of Enlightenment*. It takes the debate to a new level, involving the audience in making a decision about the role of science in the atomic age.

Chapter 5 is a discussion of Brecht's concept of "dialectic theater" and the principles of film noir as they were employed by Fritz Lang in his anti-Nazi film *Hangmen Also Die*. Brecht had developed the story together with Lang and believed that the film would be constructed in the manner of "epic theater," but he did not realize that film noir, although dialectical in its story line and manipulation of reality, was based on suspense and surprise, which were anathema to dialectic theater.

Chapter 6 contrasts immigrant modernism with exile modernism. When Austrian-born architects Richard Neutra and Rudolph M. Schindler arrived in Los Angeles shortly after World War I, their goal was to combine the best features of Austrian and American modernism in their architecture. This combination resulted in a style that was called California modern. Because the style was designed to address regional needs and conditions, it did not reflect the goals of exile modernism. The only exceptions, perhaps, were Neutra's designs for public housing during the 1940s and 1950s (influenced by concepts of public housing during the Weimar Republic and the First Republic of Austria), which were denounced as evidence of "creeping socialism" during the Korean War. On the other hand, the California modern style does not show the break of 1933 that is the defining characteristic of exile modernism.

Chapters 7 and 8 deal with Franz Werfel and Alfred Döblin, as authors of avant-garde literature who turned to antimodernism in exile. Werfel abandoned Expressionism and turned to writing popular novels, while Döblin continued the form of the modernist novel in his *November 1918*, but advanced a history of salvation that was in conflict with modernism. The absence of dialectics in their works underscores their alignment with antimodernism and their "regress to mythology" (Horkheimer and Adorno). Although Werfel and Döblin were both Jewish, they showed an affinity for Catholicism that influenced their works. Both turned to Catholicism during their escape from France—Döblin in Mende and Werfel in Lourdes—and Döblin even converted later in Los Angeles. On the other hand, Werfel—in spite of his strong affinity for Catholicism since childhood—never abandoned Judaism and returned to modernism in his last novel, *Star of the Unborn*.

Chapter 9 discusses the political factions among the exiles with respect to the rise of fascism in Germany, the war against the Axis powers, and the reconstruction of postwar Europe. Although the majority maintained that there was a clear distinction to be made between Germans and Nazis and advocated the theory of two Germanies, Thomas Mann introduced a dialectical concept of *one* Germany, both good and evil. This concept was close to that of Robert Gilbert Lord Vansittart (1881–1957), whose opinion dominated the Anglo-American debate about the future of Germany during the 1940s. According to the former British diplomat, there was no difference between Germans and Nazis and the German nation must be disarmed and reeducated. The dialectical conception of Thomas Mann's formula provided, however, a more productive approach for dealing with Germany's past and future than that of Vansittart.

Chapter 10 explains the role of dialectics as a structural element in Thomas Mann's novel *Doctor Faustus*. The author's collaboration with Theodor W. Adorno reinforced this element not only as the essence of Faust's career as a German composer, but also as the basis for the allegory of Germany and its history. In addition, Adorno's concept of the "identity of the non-identical" enabled Mann to show that the life and works of Adrian Leverkühn not only reflected German history, but also contradicted it. The "identity of the non-identical" also became a structural element for Leverkühn's last composition, which marked his "breakthrough" as an authentic work of modernist art. It functions both as "historiography of its epoch" (Adorno) as well as an expression of human suffering.

Chapter 11 reevaluates the controversy between Thomas Mann and Arnold Schoenberg regarding the employment of twelve-tone composition in *Doctor Faustus*. It draws on the conflict to show that the novelist had the highest respect for the composer and his achievements. His personal dedication to Schoenberg in a copy of *Doctor Faustus* indicates that Thomas Mann was aware that the composer represented the true modernist—a recognition that his Faust figure never deserved until perhaps his last composition. Schoenberg's choral and instrumental music, composed in Los Angeles, is presented as the most important achievement of exile modernism in its refusal to make compromises with mass culture and its attempts to find content and forms that speak to contemporary audiences. Finally, the corpus of Schoenberg's exile compositions is compared to the works of his fellow exiles, Brecht, Döblin, Mann, and Werfel.

The conclusion deals with Weimar culture in Los Angeles as a hidden legacy that is not difficult to trace. Not only are artifacts of German exile culture, such as films, novels, plays, and poetry as well as homes, theater venues, and award-winning architecture, still extant, but the memory of that culture endures within institutions such as the Los Angeles Philharmonic, the Los Angeles County Museum of Art, the Norton Simon Museum, the residential theaters at the Mark Taper Forum and the Odyssey Theatre Ensemble, and, last but not least, the library and film archives at the University of California, Los Angeles, and the University of Southern California. This kind of memory is not limited to high culture, but is also extended to the Weimar salons in Los Angeles, among them the most famous by Salka Viertel that was attend by the various factions of the exile community during the 1940s.

CHAPTER I

The Dialectic of Modernism

When Theodor W. Adorno (1903–69) and Max Horkheimer (1895–1973) began to write their *Dialectic of Enlightenment (Dialektik der Aufklärung)* in 1941, they unintentionally provided a theory for the experience of exile in Southern California and for a modernism that had become questionable to its practitioners who felt out of place in the vicinity of Hollywood. Developed in discussions between Horkheimer and Adorno and recorded by the latter's wife, Gretel Adorno, *Dialectic of Enlightenment* was completed in mimeographed form under the title *Philosophical Fragments (Philosophische Fragmente)* in 1944 and first published under its current title by the publishing house Querido of Amsterdam in 1947. It was most fitting that Querido published this book because it had been the most important publisher of the exiles since 1933. Later, pirated editions were circulated during the student revolution in West Germany around 1968, and the book was republished by Fischer in Frankfurt in 1969.

Read in terms of the Weimar iconography of Los Angeles, this book is also a theory of modernism; its pessimism reflects the crisis of modernism after 1933. What is most remarkable about Horkheimer and Adorno's theory is that it covers such a wide field of creative endeavors and affected even those who had never heard of it or disagreed with it. Bertolt Brecht's sarcastic remarks about the Tuis (his nickname for the intellectuals of the Institute for Social Research, derived from the anagram "Tellect-Ual-In") are well known, and he even planned to write a novel on the Tuis. Yet Adorno raised issues about the authentic recep-

FIGURE 2. Max Horkheimer during the 1940s. Photograph courtesy of Universitätsbibliothek Frankfurt am Main, Archivzentrum, Max Horkheimer-Archiv.

tion of art in his chapter on the culture industry that were similar to those the playwright addressed in his *Short Organon for the Theater (Kleines Organon für das Theater)*, a new theory of the theater that was conceived in Los Angeles at the same time as *Dialectic of Enlightenment* and later printed in East Berlin in 1949.

Horkheimer had come to Los Angeles from New York in April 1941 for health reasons. His doctor had advised him to move to a more temperate climate because of a heart condition. Adorno followed him in November 1941. After his arrival, Adorno sent an enthusiastic letter to his parents on November 30:

> The beauty of the landscape is without comparison, so that even a hard-boiled European like me is overwhelmed. The proportions of mountains and ocean remind me of the French Riviera, near San Remo or Mentone, but it is not as sub-divided and *privé*, but on a much larger scale and more open. The silhouette of the mountains reminds me of Tuscany. The view from our new house lets me think of Fiesole. . . . But the most gorgeous are the intensive colors that you cannot describe. A drive along the ocean during the sunset is one of the most extraordinary impressions that my rather nonchalant eyes have ever had. . . . The southern architecture and the limited advertising have created a kind of *Kulturlandschaft* [cultured landscape]: one has the impression that the world here is populated by some human-like creatures and not only by gasoline stations and hot dogs. (*Briefe an die Eltern*: 107–8)

Both Adorno and Horkheimer settled on the Westside, Horkheimer in a bungalow at 13524 D'este Drive in Pacific Palisades and Adorno in a duplex at 316 South Kenter Avenue in Brentwood. For financial reasons Adorno preferred a rented apartment that was large enough for his library and a grand piano, while Horkheimer had the funds to build a new house that also had room for his friend Friedrich Pollock, a member of the Institute for Social Research who lived in Los Angeles until 1942 and to whom the mimeographed version of *Dialectic of Enlightenment* was dedicated in 1944 (Wiggershaus 312). Horkheimer described his daily routine during that time in a letter of August 12, 1942, to theologian Paul Tillich, a colleague from the Johann Wolfgang Goethe-University in Frankfurt, who had also been exiled to New York in 1933:

> My life runs quite a regular course. In the morning, I take a short walk with Pollock, after which I write notes and drafts for a fairly methodical study; in the afternoons I usually see Teddie [Adorno] to decide on the final text with him. . . . The evenings belong to Pollock. . . . In between, there are seminars and business to do with practical questions involving the Institute. For nearly two months now I have been able to say that we are working on the real text. . . . There is already an imposing series of preliminary notes, but the final formulation of them will take years. This is due partly to the objective difficulties of the task of producing a formulation of dialectic philosophy which will take account of the experience of recent decades, and partly to our lack of routine, the cumbersomeness of thinking, and the lack of clarity on important points which we are still laboring under. (*Gesammelte Schriften* 17: 313)

Other members of the institute who came to Los Angeles included Leo Löwenthal, who was credited in the introduction of *Dialectic of Enlightenment* for his contributions to the chapter on anti-Semitism; Herbert Marcuse, who was likewise credited for parts of the book; and Friedrich Pollock, but all three left for Washington, D.C., when they were offered employment by government agencies that were involved in the war effort, such as the Office of War Information (OWI) and the Office of Strategic Services (OSS) in the case of Löwenthal and Marcuse and the Department of Justice in Pollock's case. According to Horkheimer's plan, Marcuse was supposed to set up an office of the institute in Santa Monica and to participate in the book on dialectics, but these plans were abandoned when Marcuse accepted the job offer from the OWI in 1942. Although Horkheimer benefited from the theoretical work of the other members of the Institute for Social Research, he was also somewhat relieved when they accepted jobs with the U.S. government, because the institute's funds were running low and some of the members' salaries had to be cut.

Horkheimer was the director of the Institute for Social Research, which was founded in 1923 in Frankfurt/Main and ten years later moved into exile, first to Geneva, then to Paris, and finally, in 1936, to New York, where it was affiliated with Columbia University. With Horkheimer's move to California the institute's activity shifted to the West Coast, although the Los Angeles office was considered only a branch office until the New York office closed in 1944. In Paris and then later in New York, the institute issued the *Zeitschrift für Sozialforschung,* continued in English as *Studies in Philosophy and Social Science,* which published seminal articles by members of the institute between 1933 and 1941. Martin Jay and Rolf Wiggershaus have written comprehensive histories of the institute.

It is important to note that Horkheimer tried to imitate the New York office and affiliate the Los Angeles office with a local university. It was his plan to establish a branch *(Zweigstelle)* at the University of California, Los Angeles, in 1940, but the proposal was turned down by Robert G. Sproul, the president of the University of California, because the institute was not prepared to submit its appointments and promotions to peer review, as was required for faculty members of the University of California. The institute had planned to appoint Horkheimer as director of research and Herbert Marcuse as his assistant. They were prepared to lecture and conduct seminars on eighteenth-century philosophy, German and other European philosophy from the middle of the nineteenth century to the present, the history of sociology since August Comte, and the history of ideas during the sixteenth and seventeenth centuries. The institute was willing to contribute $8,000 annually in support of this venture, but the university was not persuaded by the financial offer ("Memorandum"). In 1949, both Adorno and Horkheimer returned to West Germany, convinced that they "would be able to achieve more there than elsewhere" (DE xii). They reestablished at the Johann Wolfgang Goethe-University in Frankfurt/Main the Institute for Social Research, which played a decisive role in the intellectual and political culture of the Federal Republic of Germany, even after Adorno and Horkheimer had died. The term "Frankfurt School" was first used to refer to members of the institute by outsiders in the 1960s, but the group's founders and spokesmen adopted the label without hesitation. In Germany it is customary to speak of a first and second generation of the Frankfurt School (Wiggershaus 1). Jürgen Habermas, Adorno's most distinguished student in West Germany, belonged to the second generation and continued the tradition of the Frankfurt School long after Adorno had died, and even when Habermas was no longer associated with the Goethe University. In the United States, the most common way of referring to the Frankfurt

FIGURE 3. Institute of Social Research in Frankfurt/Main during the early
1930s. Photograph courtesy of Universitätsbibliothek Frankfurt am Main,
Archivzentrum, Max Horkheimer-Archiv.

School was to use the term "critical theory," because much of the
group's work was done in exile and not in Frankfurt (Kellner 1).

It is my argument that *Dialectic of Enlightenment* provides a comprehensive assessment and analysis of modernism and its crisis during
the 1940s. Since it is not limited to the discussion of aesthetics or art—
although they form an important part of the modernist project—it has
universal appeal and relevance, as indicated by the chapter "Elements of
Anti-Semitism." It has been argued that Adorno and Horkheimer were
not really familiar with American culture and treated most subjects with
an obvious European bias, but this element of alienation served to explain the specific exile situation in Los Angeles to a degree that they
themselves may not have been aware of. As foreigners they suffered from
displacement, and their alienation, also inherent in modernism, required
a new and philosophical response. It was not simply that they rejected
modern America, but that they needed to reject it in order to identify and
analyze the crisis of high culture. As Peter Uwe Hohendahl has persua-
sively argued, Adorno was aware of the problematic position of modernism before he came to the United States and "was therefore critical of

a position that would identify 'bad' mass culture with America and 'good' high culture with Europe." The difference between Europe and America was the greater extent of "the systematic transformation of literature and the arts under the impact of monopoly capitalism" in the United States, but it was a difference only by degrees (Hohendahl 22). As Adorno says in his autobiographical essay about his experiences as a European scholar in America, he resisted adjustment and socialization not out of arrogance, as was sometimes suspected, but as a methodology of research. He did not want to perceive American phenomena as obvious, as Americans typically did, but rather wanted to "alienate" these phenomena so that they might reveal elements essential to them that were hidden to the American observers. Adorno admitted that he was indebted to Brecht for his use of the term "alienation" ("Scientific Experiences" 217). He also could have referred to Brecht's "Refugee Conversations" of 1940, in which the playwright says that "emigration is the best school of dialectics. Refugees are the sharpest dialectic thinkers. They are refugees as a result of changes and their sole object of study is change" (GBA 18: 264). This describes exactly the position that Adorno and Horkheimer took when writing *Dialectic of Enlightenment*. Adorno says that in the United States he was "liberated from a naïve belief in culture, [and] acquired the ability to see culture from outside." There was not the "reverential silence [that] reigned before everything intellectual as it [did] in Central and Western Europe far beyond the so-called cultivated classes." The absence of this respect induced in Adorno "the spirit to critical self-reflection." A few pages later he alluded to Hegel as the master dialectician who had emphasized that "speculative thinking is not distinct from so-called healthy common sense *[gesunder Menschenverstand]* but rather essentially consisted in its critical self-reflection and self-scrutiny" ("Scientific Experiences" 239–42).

It is important to emphasize that Adorno and Horkheimer did not believe that German high culture was destroyed by the Nazis in 1933, but rather that its destruction was a long process that had begun already during the 1920s. Therefore, they did not expect German culture simply to be restored after World War II, but instead expected it to be reconfigured in terms of American mass culture (Hohendahl 33). Modernism was not immune to German fascism. On the contrary, fascism had developed its own modernism, and left-wing modernism had adopted some of the stylistic features and topoi of fascist modernism, as Adorno and Horkheimer did not hesitate to show in regard to Alfred Döblin, a fellow exile in Los Angeles. The protagonist of Döblin's famous novel

Berlin Alexanderplatz was compared to desperate characters in mediocre films (DE 123). The year 1933 marked only the date of the final split between right-wing, left-wing, and central modernism that was effected by the external force applied by German fascism, and even that split was not clean, as the examples of Brecht and Werfel showed.

When Adorno and Horkheimer announced their project—namely, the presentation of their momentous discovery that "humanity, instead of entering a truly human state, is sinking into a new kind of barbarism," in the preface of their *Dialectic of Enlightenment* (xiv)— in 1944, they were looking back at a learning process of more than ten years. This insight, which had the ring of a similar declaration by Friedrich Schiller in his *Letters on the Aesthetic Education of Man* of 1795, dated back to the 1930s. Although it was the French Revolution that served as a sobering influence on Schiller, it was the experience of the collapse of the Weimar Republic and the rise to power of the Nazi party that shaped Adorno and Horkheimer's assessment of modern culture and its development. Realizing that the conditions of Nazism were already present in the Weimar Republic of the 1920s, Adorno and Horkheimer came to the conclusion that enlightenment always contained the seeds of its own destruction or reversion to mythology, or irrationality, unless it reflected on this "regressive moment" (DE xvi).

Although they acknowledged the presence of the individual self and were convinced that "freedom in society is inseparable from enlightenment thinking," Adorno and Horkheimer nevertheless believed that this very notion, "no less than the concrete historical forms, the institutions of society with which it is intertwined," already contained "the germ of regression" (DE xvi). They saw this regression as universally apparent not only in the 1920s and 1930s, but also in the 1940s, and not only in Central Europe, but also in the United States. Since their argument was not strictly historical, but instead based on structures, patterns, and process, they could claim that the threat of fascism existed also in the United States (Hohendahl 34). Although in fact the United States was involved in a war against fascism as of December 1941, Adorno and Horkheimer were eager to point out similarities in the forms of mass control and mass entertainment used in Nazi Germany and the United States. In this context, fascist Germany appeared as "the alternative version of modernity" (Hohendahl 34). As Hohendahl explains, "For Adorno and Horkheimer, an analysis of the American society included, explicitly and implicitly, an analysis of modern Germany, since they saw both the political system of the National Socialists and the organization of culture in North America as aspects of the same historical dialectical of reason" (34). While Adorno and Horkheimer admitted that the increase in economic productivity had furnished "the conditions for a more just world," they saw the individual "entirely nullified in face of the economic powers." Even if the economic apparatus provided better for individuals than ever before, they vanished "before the apparatus they serve[d]" (DE xvii).

Adorno and Horkheimer considered the "disenchantment of the world" the legacy of the Enlightenment. They employed Max Weber's famous formulation to explain the Enlightenment in terms of the dissolution of myths and the overthrow of "fantasy with knowledge" (DE 1). They saw this phenomenon initiated by Francis Bacon (1561–1626), the father of modern science. Although Bacon was credited with the inspiration behind the Royal Society, established in 1660, and figured as founder of the inductive method in modern science, he emerges as a less favorable figure in *Dialectic of Enlightenment*. Here he appears as a promoter of preindustrial capitalism that used scientific knowledge and method in order to reduce nature to a resource for economic production. Using Bacon as their prime example, Adorno and Horkheimer explain the Weberian "disenchantment of the world" as a result of the scientific dominion over nature. While for Max Weber the "disenchantment of the world" is a general tendency toward rationalization in all areas of human endeavor, Adorno and Horkheimer reduce it to the impact of science on society. Adorno and Horkheimer show Bacon to have introduced science as a tool for the economic exploitation of nature in his "Praise of Human Knowledge." Quoting from his works, they expose his program, pointing out that Bacon had singled out the printing press, artillery, and the compass as the three things that changed the world: the first in the domain of learning, the second in the domain of war, the third in the domain of treasure, commodities, and navigation. Bacon believed that knowledge made man "the master of nature" and that kings could not buy knowledge "with their treasure, nor with their force command" (DE 1). This proud pronouncement was met with total disagreement by Adorno and Horkheimer, who had the benefit of historical hindsight in concluding that, for the modern period, "knowledge, which is power, knows no limits, either in its enslavement of creation or in its deference to worldly masters. Just as it serves all the purposes of the bourgeois economy both in factories and on the battlefield, it is at the disposal of entrepreneurs regardless of their origins" (DE 2).

The mechanical methods that evolved during the seventeenth century

turned into the technology of the twentieth century, which was branded
in the *Dialectic of Enlightenment* as "the essence of [modern] knowledge." Adorno and Horkheimer perceived modern technology as disre-
garding original thinking and producing only "method, the exploitation
of the labor of others, [and] capital" instead (DE 2). It was not difficult
for them to see "the radio as a sublimated printing press, the dive bomber
as a more effective form of artillery, remote control as a more reliable
compass." They perceived as the goal of science that human beings "seek
to learn from nature . . . how to use it to dominate wholly both it and
human beings" (DE 2).

The next step of their argument was that "human beings have dis-
carded meaning" in the process of rationalization: "on their way toward
modern science, . . . the concept is replaced by the formula, the cause by
rules and probability" (DE 3). By limiting the process of rationalization
to the progress of modern science, Adorno and Horkheimer assigned all
other categories, such as substance and quality, activity and suffering,
and being and existence, to philosophy and claimed that "science could
manage without such categories" (DE 3). It was science that subjected
everything to "the standard rule of calculability and utility" (DE 3). By
identifying the Enlightenment with modern science and its application in
the form of technology, Adorno and Horkheimer concluded that the Enlightenment recognized as "an existent *[Sein]* or an event *[Geschehen]*
only what can be encompassed by unity *[Einheit]*," and declared that "its
ideal is the system from which everything and anything follows" (DE 4).
With this conclusion they placed Gottfried Wilhelm Leibniz, for example, exclusively in the realm of science and pronounced "the multiplicity
of forms . . . reduced to position and arrangement, history [diminished]
to fact, things [changed] to matter" (DE 4). In their attacks formal logic
was singled out as "the high school of unification" that "offered Enlightenment thinkers a schema for making the world calculable" (DE 4).
Declaring that "number became enlightenment's canon," they resorted
to Marxist arguments when they included in this discussion an argument
that bourgeois society was "ruled by equivalence." According to Adorno
and Horkheimer, equivalence "makes dissimilar things comparable by
reducing them to abstract quantities. For the Enlightenment, anything
which cannot be resolved into numbers, and ultimately into one, is illusion" (DE 4). It is ironic that this attack was extended to a polemical dig
against analytic philosophy, whose major proponent, Bertrand Russell,
they mentioned by name. It could not have escaped them that Russell
had taught at UCLA during 1939–40 and was denied a teaching position

at the College of the City of New York in 1941 because of his controversial ideas on marriage and family. Russell could have been recruited
as a political ally—John Dewey published a book in his defense *(The
Bertrand Russell Case)*—but Adorno and Horkheimer included him in
their condemnation of analytic philosophy, which—in addition to prag-
matism—dominated American philosophy.

Dealing with myth, the authors of *Dialectic of Enlightenment* again
relied heavily on Max Weber's essays on the sociology of religion, sub-
stituting enlightenment for his principle of rationalization in the process
of disenchantment. Although Weber was ambivalent about rationalization, Adorno and Horkheimer were not. They saw myths as not only
falling victim to the Enlightenment, but also emerging as products of the
Enlightenment. Myths also offered explanations, and that tendency
"was reinforced by the recording and collecting of myths" (DE 5). In
their opinion, the myths that the masters of Greek tragedy employed for
their works were already characterized by the structures of discipline and
power that became characteristic for modern science associated with
Francis Bacon: "The local spirits and demons had been replaced by
heaven and its hierarchy, the incantatory practices of the magicians by
the carefully graduated sacrifice and the labor of enslaved men mediated
by command" (DE 5). The end result was myth being turned into enlightenment, and the mystery of nature that myth was supposed to maintain being turned "into mere objectivity" (DE 6). Men had to pay a price
for this increase of their power, and that price was alienation from nature, over which they exercised their power. The result was that enlightenment stood "in the same relationship to things as the dictator to
human beings. He knows them to the extent that he can manipulate
them. The man of science knows things to the extent that he can make
them" (DE 6).

One of the unique arguments of *Dialectic of Enlightenment* was the
dialectical alignment of myth and enlightenment in a common process in
which myth turned into enlightenment, which, "with ineluctable necessity subjected every theoretical view . . . to the annihilating criticism that
it is only a belief" (DE 7). While "myths already entail enlightenment,
with every step enlightenment entangles itself more deeply in mythology" (DE 8). Or, as they announced in the preface of 1944, "myth is already enlightenment, and enlightenment reverts to mythology" (DE
xviii).

In his book *A Singular Modernity,* Fredric Jameson identifies this
process as the model of modernist innovation: "Each supposed advance

in knowledge and science is grasped as a kind of defamiliarization which relegates the previous moment of rationality to the status of a superstition." He argues that this perspective grounded the "telos of modernist innovation in a far more satisfactory and intelligible process." Each generation feels limited by some artificial conventions, "which it is challenged to replace." What looked like the progressive discovery of new territory "is now seen to be a perpetual process of unnaming and refiguration which has no foreseeable stopping point" (157).

Although Jameson gave this model a positive spin, for Adorno and Horkheimer this process was negative because it was governed by instrumental reason and mythology dominated society as a belief system that, unlike myth, defied explanation. They reinterpreted Hegel's concept of the movement of thought through the ages as a negative process by defining enlightenment as "totalitarian" (DE 4, 18). There was no return to the old forms of myths in harmony of nature, but rather compliance with an enlightenment that highlighted only the negative side of myths.

There was no space reserved for reason to escape this mechanism of domination by either enlightenment or mythology, except for the last sentence of the chapter on anti-Semitism, in which the authors express the hope that "enlightenment could break through the limits of enlightenment" (DE 172). As J. M. Bernstein argues in his analysis, Enlightenment reason turned out to be "disenchanting, rationalizing, and universalizing," and, therefore, negative. He attributed this fact to Adorno and Horkheimer's failure to account for the conditions of reason in *Dialectic of Enlightenment* (*Adorno* 134).

What was different during the time of myth was equalized by enlightenment, but "the identity of everything with everything else [was] paid for" with the loss of individual identity: "Enlightenment dissolves away the injustice of the old inequality of unmediated mastery, but at the same time perpetuates it in universal mediation, by relating every existing thing to every other" (DE 8). In a demonstration of the dialectic of enlightenment, Adorno and Horkheimer show that equality led to social control: "The unity of the manipulated collective consists in the negation of each individual and in the scorn poured on the type of society which could make people into individuals. The horde, a term which doubtless is to be found in the Hitler Youth organization, is not a relapse into the old barbarism but the triumph of repressive *égalité*, the degeneration of the equality of rights into the wrong inflicted by equals" (DE 9). The authors could have pointed to equality as a questionable achievement of the French Revolution, as Horkheimer did in his essay "The Jews and Europe" of 1939, in which he made the French Revolution a forerunner of the Nazi regime, but in *Dialectic of Enlightenment* the authors preferred a more contemporary analogy to make the point that such qualitative changes were typical in the course of European civilization.

Their special distrust focuses on abstraction as "the instrument of enlightenment." They ascribe to abstraction the type of power that fate possessed during mythic time, and they expect abstraction to act like fate by destroying its objects (DE 9). In the modern era the individual is subjected to the domination of abstraction and of industry. They perceive the distance between subject and object as "presupposition of abstraction" as a reflection of the distance that the master keeps from those whom he masters. Domination in the conceptual sphere is based on the foundation of power in reality. Adorno and Horkheimer argue that "the self which learned about order and subordination through the subjugation of the world soon equated truth in general with classifying thought, without whose fixed distinctions it [truth] cannot exist" (DE 10). Horkheimer and Adorno consider even the deductive form of science the reflection of hierarchy and compulsion: "the entire logical order, with its chain of inference and dependence, the superordination and coordination of concepts, [was] founded on the corresponding conditions in social reality, that is, on the division of labor" (DE 16). This socioeconomic approach to abstraction and logic make the individual subject to a kind of power that appears to be universal. Its universality renders power as "the reason which informs reality" (DE 16): "The power of all the members of society, to whom as individuals no other way is open, is constantly summated, through the division of labor imposed on them, in the realization of the whole, whose rationality is thereby multiplied over again" (DE 16).

According to their sociological analysis, the domination of all members by the privileged few always takes "the form of the subduing of individuals by the many." In their opinion, social repression always exhibits "the features of oppression by a collective." They see "this unity of the collectivity and power, and not the immediate social universal, solidarity, which is precipitated in intellectual forms" (DE 16). In light of these conclusions, they could expose the philosophical concepts with which Plato and Aristotle represented the world as merely a reflection of their society and explain that the Greek philosophers only elevated the conditions that substantiated their society to the level of true reality by the claim of universal validity. Quoting Giambattista Vico, who said that the concepts of Greek philosophy originated in the marketplace of

Athens, they elaborate that these concepts reflected "with the same fidelity the laws of physics, the equality of freeborn citizens, and the inferiority of women, children and slaves." Language was seen as complicit with domination:

> Language itself endowed what it expressed, the conditions of domination, with the universality it had acquired as the means of intercourse in civil society. The metaphysical emphasis, the sanction by ideas and norms, was no more than hypostatization of the rigidity and exclusivity which concepts have necessarily taken on wherever language has consolidated the community of the rulers for the enforcement of commands. (DE 16–17)

As a result, ideas became all the more superfluous because they served only as a means of reinforcing the social power of language, and the language of modern science finally put an end to ideas. Adorno and Horkheimer criticize especially the neutrality of the language of science, which serves only to camouflage power relationships. Anything new but powerless is deprived of its appropriate means of expression, while existing power relationships are expressed in a language that pretends to be impartial but actually confirms the power structure in place.

Adorno and Horkheimer attribute the specific untruth of the Enlightenment to the fact that the process was always prejudged from the start. This was a criticism of the mathematical approach in the sciences. They argue that in mathematical procedure, "when the unknown becomes the unknown quantity in an equation," this marks it as something well known "before any value has been assigned" (DE 18). In the tradition of Goethe's scientific aversion toward Newton, they deduce from the procedures of mathematical equations that "Nature . . . is what can be registered mathematically; even what cannot be assimilated, the insoluble and irrational, is fenced in by mathematical theorems. In the preemptive identification of the thoroughly mathematized world with truth, enlightenment believes itself safe from the return of the mythical. It equates thought with mathematics" (DE 18). Adorno and Horkheimer jump to the conclusion that mathematics has been made the ultimate authority in the scientific exploration of nature. Quoting Edmund Husserl, they refer to "Galileo's mathematization of nature" and argue that thinking has been degraded to "an automatic process" that imitates the machine, which thinking produced so that the machine could ultimately replace it. Their conclusion was that "Enlightenment pushed aside the classic demand to 'think thinking,' . . . because it distracted philosophers from the command to control praxis. . . . Mathematical procedure became a kind of ritual of thought. Despite its axiomatic self-limitation, it installed itself as necessary and objective: mathematics turned into a thing—a tool, to use its own term" (DE 19).

Horkheimer employs the negative concept of "instrumental reason" that dominated his later philosophy for the first time in *Dialectic of Enlightenment*—although the German text has *"Werkzeug"* (tool) and not yet *"Instrument"*—as a wholesale attack on analytic philosophy. Instrumental reasoning was characterized as a kind of mimesis that identified universal thought with the world and turned factuality into the unique object of thinking. With a sarcastic reference to positivism as "the court of judgment of enlightened reason," the authors of *Dialectic of Enlightenment* explained that positivism did not deal with atheism because digressions into intelligible worlds were no longer merely forbidden on procedural grounds, but constituted meaningless chatter: "[Positivism] does not need to be atheistic, since objectified thought cannot even pose the question of the existence of God" (DE 19). The business of thought was adjusting actuality, or, in another favorite phrase, mastery of nature. Anything else was declared metaphysical and therefore meaningless, even atheistic.

These arguments also include a criticism of Kant, who had declared in his *Critique of Pure Reason* that there was no form of being that science could not penetrate, but what could be penetrated by reason was not being: "Philosophic judgment . . . aims at the new yet it recognizes nothing new, since it always merely repeats what reason has placed into the objects beforehand" (DE 19–20). Adorno and Horkheimer perceive the defeat of the thinking subject as a backlash against this Kantian philosophy as it constituted itself as "world domination over nature." Nothing was left of the thinking subject but that eternally same *"I think"* that must accompany all his ideas. Adorno and Horkheimer charge that the claim and approach of philosophical cognition was abandoned by Kant. Their goal was to comprehend the given conditions and their underlying causes as such. It was not enough to determine the abstract spatio-temporal relations of the facts in order to grasp them, but, on the contrary, to conceive them as superficial surface phenomena, as mediated conceptual moments that revealed their full meaning only in the development of their social, historical, and human significance. They argue that knowledge does not consist of mere apprehension, classification, and calculation, "but precisely in the determining negation of whatever is directly at hand *[in der bestimmenden Negation des Unmittelbaren]*" (DE 20). In other words, the goal was to negate the surface phenomena as they occurred or presented themselves and to inquire into their causes and conditions. This "determining negation of whatever is directly at hand" constitutes the core of the critical theory developed in *Dialectic of Enlightenment*. The authors charge that mathematical formalism, whose medium is numbers—the most abstract form of the immediate—limits thinking to mere immediacy. They concede that factuality is winning the day, arguing that cognition is restricted to its repetition, and therefore thought has become mere tautology. Their conclusion is that "the more completely the machinery of thought subjugates existence, the more blindly it is satisfied with reproducing it." Their final verdict is that "enlightenment thereby regresses to the mythology it has never been able to escape" (DE 20).

According to Adorno and Horkheimer, mythology confirms the status quo. For philosophy this implies that the world is nothing but "a gigantic analytic judgment" (DE 20). As mythology tends to legitimize factuality—as, for example, the abduction of Persephone in Greek mythology explains the cycle of spring and autumn—it also exercises deception. Likewise, the absorption of factuality into mathematical formalism is a deception since it makes "the new appear as something predetermined which therefore is really the old" (DE 21). Not existence itself but knowledge is without hope for true renewal, since in the mathematical symbol existence is appropriated and perpetuated as a schema. That the production of human existence follows a predetermined schema is the enormous deception perpetrated upon mankind according to *Dialectic of Enlightenment*. This deception was instituted in order to prevent change and innovation, not to speak of revolution.

Adorno and Horkheimer see mythology as permeating the sphere of the profane in the modern world. Reality appears to have assumed the numinous character that the ancient world had attributed to demons. Presented as facts of life, the social injustice from which those facts arise is now sacrosanct, "as the medicine man once was under the protection of his gods" (DE 21). The return to Marxist terminology is camouflaged by the anthropological context when the authors say that not only is domination accepted and "paid for with the estrangement of human beings from the dominated objects," but it also effects "the objectification of mind" and causes "the relationships of human beings, including the relationship of individuals to themselves, [to become] bewitched" (DE 21). The individual is reduced to conventional responses and modes of operation that are expected of him. Industrialism is listed as the cause for the objectification of the souls of men. Here the argument turns exclusively Marxist; the authors say that "with the ending of free exchange, commodities have forfeited all economic qualities except their fetish character, [and] this character has spread like a cataract across the life of society in all its aspects" (DE 21).

With this reference to mass production, the economic argument is turned into a cultural one. The culture of mass production impresses upon the individual a certain number of standardized modes of behavior "as the only natural, decent, and rational ones" (DE 21). Accordingly, individuals define themselves as things, as figures of statistics, "as successes or failures." Their goal is self-preservation, defined as "successful or unsuccessful adaptation to the objectivity of their function and the schemata assigned to it" (DE 21 f.). Everything else, from individual thought to personal crime, is subject to the force of the collective that monitors conduct "from the classroom to the trade union." But even the threatening collective is perceived as only the deceptive surface, under which there are concealed mysterious powers that manipulate the collective as the instrument of power. The brutality that the collective employs to discipline the individual is said to represent "no more the true quality of people than value represents that of commodities" (DE 22). Again, the distorted form that things and men have assumed in the light of so-called unprejudiced cognition is attributed to domination. The fatalism by means of which prehistory sanctioned the incomprehensibility of death is transferred to wholly comprehensible real existence in the modern world. Adorno and Horkheimer do not perceive the modern world as a world without fear due to the rule of reason. On the contrary, they conclude that men are dominated by panic, as they were in prehistory, and that they expect the world "to be set ablaze by a universal power which they themselves [constitute] and over which they are powerless" (DE 22). No doubt, this insight was influenced by the war against Germany and Japan.

Rather than dealing with class struggle, Adorno and Horkheimer concentrate on the division of labor, which results in alienation. In their discussion of the self, they perceive the social work of every individual in bourgeois society as mediated through the principle of self. For one group, labor is supposed to bring an increased return on capital, for another, the energy for extra labor. Their special warning is directed against alienation that they attribute to the bourgeois division of labor: individuals "must mold themselves to the technical apparatus body and soul" (DE 23). Individual thinking is abandoned as being too subjective. Again, analytic philosophy is identified as the culprit and blamed for

having removed the last agency differentiating between individual behavior and the social norm:

> Reason serves as a universal tool for the fabrication of all other tools,
> rigidly purpose-directed and as calamitous as the precisely calculated op-
> erations of material production, the results of which for human beings es-
> cape all calculation. Reason's old ambition to be purely an instrument of
> purposes has finally been fulfilled. (DE 23)

Academic philosophy is blamed for the ills of bourgeois society, as indicated by their statement that "the expulsion of thought from logic rati-
fies in the lecture hall the reification of human beings in factory and office" (DE 23). The process that they analyze is a prime example of the
dialectic they want to elucidate: "Enlightenment [encroaches] on mind,
which it itself is" (DE 23).

This analysis also provides an insight into the dehumanizing effect of
the dialectic of enlightenment. Nature as self-preservation is unleashed
"by the process which promised to extirpate it," manifesting itself "in
the individual as in the collective fate of crisis and war" (DE 23). Adorno
and Horkheimer promote interdisciplinarity, because they consider specialized research an abandonment of reason to instrumental logic. They
express the fear that in a society of theoretical specialists, "praxis must
be handed over to the unfettered operations of world history" (DE 24).
For the sake of self-preservation, the individual defined in terms of civilization resorts to an element of the inhumanity that from the beginning
civilization aspired to evade. Adorno and Horkheimer predict that a time
will come when self-preservation is automated and reason is abandoned
by those who, as administrators of production, profit from its inheri-
tance and now "fear it in the disinherited" (DE 25). Their vision of the
future is painted in dark colors: "The essence of the enlightenment is the
choice between alternatives, and the inescapability of this choice is that
of power. Human beings have always had to choose between their subjugation to nature and its subjugation to the self" (DE 25). Again and
again, they repeat their gloomy predictions that "the curse of irresistible
progress is irresistible regression" (DE 28) and that "enlightenment forfeited its own realization" (DE 33). In the end, they claim "enlightenment is as destructive as its Romantic enemies claim" (DE 33). They do
not preclude the chance that enlightenment might come into its own, but
that will happen only if it surrenders its last remaining agreement with
Romanticism and dares "to abolish the false absolute, the principle of
blind power." They predict that "the spirit of such unyielding theory

would be able to turn back from its goal even the spirit of pitiless progress" (DE 33).

Referring to Francis Bacon as the herald of a new age that introduced modern science as one of the things "that kings with their treasures could not buy nor with their force command," Adorno and Horkheimer identify the modern bourgeoisie as the enlightened heirs of those kings. Not only do they see its power multiplied by the bourgeois economy through the mediation of the market, but they also consider this power extended to such a degree that for its administration it needs the involvement not just of kings, nor the middle class, but of all men. With this democratic turn, an optimistic tone is introduced, a tone that is carried through to the end of the first chapter with the exception of the last sentence. All human beings finally learn "from the power of things . . . to forgo power" (DE 33). There is no reason given for this optimism:

> Enlightenment consummates and abolishes itself when the closest practical objectives reveal themselves to the most distant goal already attained. . . . Today, when Bacon's utopia, in which "we should command nature in action," has been fulfilled on a telluric scale, the essence of the compulsion which he ascribed to unmastered nature is becoming apparent. Knowledge, in which, for Bacon, "the sovereignty of man" unquestionably lay hidden, can now devote itself to dissolving that power. (DE 33–34)

This optimism, however, is dampened by the final sentence, which claims that enlightenment, "in the service of the present, is turning itself into an outright deception of the masses" (DE 34).

Adorno and Horkheimer appended two lengthy expositions of their main points, "Excursus I: Odysseus or Myth and Enlightenment" and "Excursus II: Juliette or Enlightenment and Morality." They had made the case for Odysseus in the introductory chapter, "The Concept of Enlightenment," and needed only to elaborate on their previous interpretation of the Homeric hero as "the prototype of the bourgeois individual" (DE 35). The second chapter on de Sade, however, introduces a new idea that begins with a discussion of Kant's ethics and also relies heavily on Nietzsche's discussions of morality. The chapter begins with a discussion of Kant's classical definition of enlightenment as "the human being's emergence from self-incurred immaturity." They elaborate that Kant's statement that "understanding without the guidance of another person" refers to "understanding guided by reason" (DE 63). But as Kant had failed to derive morality from reason and had to take recourse to treating "moral forces as facts" (DE 67), he identified a dilemma that he had already posed in his *Critique of Pure Reason* and was reconfirmed later by Nietzsche in his *Genealogy of Morals,* namely, that morality cannot be explained in terms of reason. Kant needed the categorical imperative in order to institute his concept of morality. Adorno and Horkheimer argue that fascism and its treatment of people were in a perverse way more in accord with pure reason than the moral teachings of the Enlightenment because the latter were based on claims of reason that could not be substantiated. To illustrate their point, they draw on the shock value of the work of the Marquis de Sade. They declare that his novels were actually a portrayal of Kant's "understanding without the guidance of another person." Sade's protagonist, Juliette in *Histoire de Juliette* of 1797, proceeded rationally and efficiently as she went about her work of perversion: "In the sexual teams of *Juliette* . . . no moment [was] unused, no body orifice neglected, no function left inactive" (DE 69). Adorno and Horkheimer do not hesitate to compare the architectonic structure of the Kantian system to the gymnastic pyramids of Sade's orgies that prefigured "the organization, devoid of any substantial goal, which was to compass the whole of life. What seems to matter in such events, more than pleasure itself, is the busy pursuit of pleasure, its organization" (DE 69). For them, Juliette epitomizes the supreme attack on civilization with its own weapons: "She loves systems and logic. She wields the instrument of rational thought with consummate skill" (DE 74). In regard to self-control, Juliette's directions were related to Kant's as she preached on the self-discipline of the criminal. Juliette believed in science and declared each of the Ten Commandments null and void before the tribunal of formal reason (DE 76, 91). For her, reason displaced all love (DE 91).

Adorno and Horkheimer praise de Sade and Nietzsche for the fact that they did not gloss over or suppress "the impossibility of deriving from reason a fundamental argument against murder" (DE 93). This pessimistic assessment ends, however, on an unexpectedly positive note, changing despair into its dialectic opposite. The fact that de Sade and Nietzsche insisted on reason serves Adorno and Horkheimer as an argument for invoking the secret utopia, contained in the Kantian notion of reason as in every great philosophy: "the utopia of humanity which, itself no longer distorted, no longer needs distortion" (DE 93).

It was not surprising that Adorno and Horkheimer placed the chapter "Elements of Anti-Semitism" last in *Dialectic of Enlightenment,* because Jewish emancipation had been one of the greatest promises of the Enlightenment and was now in gravest jeopardy. However, this chapter, which was supposed to explicate the main points of "a philosophical pre-history of anti-Semitism" (DE xix), is the least convincing. Although the chapter fails to demonstrate that anti-Semitism was central to the dialectic of the Enlightenment project, it points to a problem of modernism and its dealings with anti-Semitism. Neither Brecht nor Döblin made anti-Semitism a central topic of their works during the 1940s, but Lion Feuchtwanger did, as did Thomas Mann, although to a degree his treatment of the subject was quite problematic. Franz Werfel and Arnold Schoenberg made it a central topic of some of their works.

Adorno and Horkheimer offer seven competing theses for their analysis of anti-Semitism in *Dialectic of Enlightenment*. Their presentation of these theses without indicating their preference for one or arranging them according to a hierarchy of validity makes this chapter less than satisfying. For the fascists, according to Adorno and Horkheimer, the Jews were "the antirace, the negative principle as such" (DE 137). This view inevitably led to the extermination of the Jews to secure a fascist world order and world domination. Although this thesis about German fascism was true to the extent that in Germany fascism had branded Jews as absolute evil and intended to annihilate them as such, it did not require an extensive explanation. The issue was different in the case of the liberal point of view that denied the existence of a Jewish national identity. As the authors state, the liberal theory considered the Jews "free of national or racial features," but that they "simply form a group through religious belief and tradition and nothing else" (DE 137). Adorno and Horkheimer were among the first to state that assimilation was the heavy price paid by Jews for the realization of this theory. Yet the practice of this theory had not saved assimilated Jews from persecution. The harmony of society, in which assimilated Jews believed, had turned against them in "the form of the national community *[Volksgemeinschaft]*," from which by definition they were excluded (DE 138).

The second thesis deals with anti-Semitism as a populist movement. Here the authors consider the various elements that in their opinion had contributed to anti-Semitism as a mass movement, and they dismissed political, economic, and social reasons for its development. Anti-Semitism as a populist movement, they conclude, was based on the urge on the part of the masses "to make everyone the same *[Gleichmacherei]*" (DE 139). In other works, it was founded on the pleasure of watching those more privileged being robbed of all their possessions and seeing them lowered below the level of the underprivileged masses. Anti-Semitism was considered devoid of economic benefit for the masses: anti-

Semitism was "a luxury" for the common people (DE 139). Adorno and Horkheimer point to the so-called "Aryanization" of Jewish property in Nazi Germany and to the pogroms in Czarist Russia, both of which rarely brought any economic benefit to the masses but were obviously advantageous to members of the privileged classes. Only as an outlet for the blind anger of the masses did anti-Semitism appear to serve the social function of a ritual of civilization. Men who were robbed of their individuality in modern society were let loose as individuals to find collective approval of their anger. But since the victims were interchangeable according to circumstances—with gypsies, Jews, Protestants, and Catholics serving equally well as scapegoats—there was no genuine anti-Semitism as a populist movement according to Adorno and Horkheimer. Everything alien that appeared privileged became the target of the destructive impulse of the masses that were unable to fully participate in the process of civilization.

Adorno and Horkheimer point to a specific economic purpose of bourgeois anti-Semitism: "to conceal domination in production" (DE 142). The Jews were made the scapegoat for the economic injustice of the capitalist system, whose development is attributed to them. Anti-Semitism, according to Adorno and Horkheimer, is in one sense the self-hatred of the bourgeoisie projected onto the Jews, who in fact were relatively unimportant economically, since they were mostly confined to the sphere of distribution and did not have access to the means of production. Within the distribution sector, however, they became the visible representatives of the whole system, drawing the hatred of others upon themselves. The masses, disappointed in the economic progress that had been promised to them, turned their fury on the Jews in the mistaken belief that what was denied to them was withheld and controlled by Jewish entrepreneurs.

Religious anti-Semitism is dismissed as nonexistent in the context of fascism. According to Adorno and Horkheimer, "Nationalist anti-Semitism seeks to disregard religion. It claims to be concerned with purity of race and nation. Its exponents notice that people have long ceased to trouble themselves about eternal salvation. . . . To accuse the Jews of being obdurate unbelievers is no longer enough to incite the masses" (DE 144). The authors realize, however, that secularized forms of religion were retained by fascism and proved beneficial to the Nazis: "Religion as an institution is partly meshed directly into the system and partly transposed into the pomp of mass culture and parades" (DE 144).

While the authors clearly note that Christianity has become largely neutralized, they nevertheless conclude that Christian rationalizations of anti-Semitism are still of considerable influence. As the religion of the "Son," as they put it, Christianity contains an implicit antagonism against Judaism as the religion of the "Father" and against the Jews as its surviving witnesses. This antagonism was exacerbated by the fact that the Jews, clinging to their own religious culture, rejected the religion of the "Son," and by the circumstance that the New Testament blamed them for the death of Christ.

In the fifth of their theses Adorno and Horkheimer introduce the concepts of idiosyncrasy and mimesis. Anti-Semites were wont to use idiosyncrasy to explain their behavior. Adorno and Horkheimer argue that the emancipation of society from anti-Semitism depends on whether this particular idiosyncrasy is elevated to a rational concept, that is, whether its meaninglessness is recognized. In order to explain their concept of idiosyncrasy, the authors have to turn to some far-fetched theories pertaining to biological prehistory. According to their definition, idiosyncrasy consists of the escape of single human organs from the control of the subject and of reaction to fundamental biological stimuli. Such behavior is based on mimesis, that is, adaptation to nature in a dangerous situation. Uncontrolled mimesis, however, is condemned in modern civilization. Modern man experiences his mimetic heritage only in certain gestures and behavior patterns that he encounters in others and that strike him as embarrassing rudimentary elements that have survived in his rationalized environment. What seems "to repel them as alien is all too familiar" (DE 149). The allegedly typical Jewish gestures of touch, soothing, snuggling up, or coaxing, for example, are enumerated by Adorno and Horkheimer as examples of mimetic behavior developed to survive old forms of domination. Such behavior arouses anger because it reminds modern man of his old fears that must be suppressed in order to survive. The anti-Semite cannot stand the Jew because he reminds him of his old anxieties that he does not dare to admit. He projects his own fears onto the Jew, who, as victim, becomes the false counterpart of the dread mimesis.

The sixth thesis is a continuation of the fifth. Adorno and Horkheimer link the discussion of mimesis (i.e., adaptation to the environment) to false projection (i.e., adaptation to the environment according to individual perception). Anti-Semitism, the authors conclude, is based on a false projection or repressed mimesis, not true mimesis. For mimesis, "the outward becomes the model to which the inward clings, so that the alien becomes the intimately known." False projection, on the other hand, confuses the inner and outer world, defining as hostile the most intimate individual experience: "Impulses which are not acknowledged by the subject and yet are his, are attributed to the object: the prospective victim" (DE 154). In psychological terms, this process is known as transference. According to Adorno and Horkheimer, under fascism this behavior pattern was politicized.

To make projection, as well as the manner in which it was deformed into false projection, understandable, the authors employ a rather naïvely realistic physiological theory of perception. This theory explains the perceptual world as the mirror reflection—controlled by the intellect—of data that the brain receives from actual objects. Adorno and Horkheimer maintain that "anti-Semitism is not projective behavior as such but the exclusion of reflection from that behavior" (DE 156). The individual loses the ability to differentiate, he becomes paranoid, and with his false projection he invests the outer world with the contents of his mind and thus perceives the world as being populated by people who, in his opinion, are bent on destroying him. The Jews appear as a "predestined target" for such projection (DE 164). The authors declare that "the person chosen as foe is already perceived as foe" (DE 154).

Quite astoundingly, in the concluding section of the chapter the authors proclaim with great confidence, yet without any objective proof, that "there are no longer any anti-Semites." Going even beyond this bewildering statement (see Israel 118), they perversely maintain that the German fascists were not anti-Semites, but rather "liberals who wanted to express their antiliberal opinions" (DE 165). Such an aphoristic statement, which contains only a kernel of truth insofar as it points to the decline of liberalism, does not amount to a historical analysis of German anti-Semitism in view of the evidence brought to light by the liberation of the concentration camps—not to speak of the extermination camps—in 1945. It is revealing that the term "concentration camp" is absent from this particular chapter, although it appears in other chapters.

Adorno and Horkheimer become victims of their own theory that fascism is the perversion of enlightenment. Instead of pointing to the policies of the extermination camps or the dangers of the survival of anti-Semitism in postwar Germany, they concentrate their efforts in the last section on detecting potential fascism, including anti-Semitism, in the United States. The seventh and last thesis, added to the chapter in 1947, not only accuses the United States of anti-Semitism, but also places American anti-Semitism on the same level as the Nazi strategy of planned extermination. They consider American anti-Semitism more dangerous for the future than the German variety. In developing their unique thesis, the authors argue that anti-Semitism has always been based on stereotyped thinking. After the defeat of fascism in Europe, stereotyped thinking was all that remained of the anti-Semitism of the period before 1945. Adorno and Horkheimer regard this type of thinking as especially prevalent in the American political party system. They see anti-Semitism surviving in the United States in the "ticket mentality," a political behavior characterized by voting the straight ticket of "belligerent big business" (DE 166). The Allied defeat of Hitler's regime might have eliminated the most obvious forms of anti-Semitism, but the victors had done little to eradicate the causes of anti-Semitism at home. Equating capitalism and fascism in an unhistorical fashion, Adorno and Horkheimer argue that anyone who subscribed to the breaking of the trade unions and the crusade against Bolshevism automatically subscribed also to "the settlement of the Jewish question" (DE 166). As distasteful as reactionary politics may be, such a conclusion was neither historically nor logically true. For Adorno and Horkheimer, anti-Semitism became a coded message in the platform of not only reactionary but also progressive parties, because the progressive parties in America also relied on the "ticket mentality." Without any dialectic mediation the authors maintain that "it is not just the anti-Semitic ticket which is anti-Semitic, but the ticket mentality itself" (DE 172). Adorno and Horkheimer therefore place their hopes for the eradication of anti-Semitism not on the progressive parties, but on the absolute meaninglessness of the fascist program that could be permanently concealed from the undiscerning population "only by their total abstention from thought" (DE 172). Since this abstention will probably not happen, they place their trust in enlightenment, which had "mastered itself and assumed its own power," and "could break through the limits of enlightenment" (DE 172).

Later, when the full extent of the German genocide of the Jews became known, Adorno and Horkheimer realized that their trust in the self-criticism of reason was misplaced. They changed their positions and did not allow any ambiguity in their assessments. In 1951 Adorno issued for the first time his often-cited dictum that "to write poetry after Auschwitz is barbaric" in an essay on cultural criticism and society ("Cultural Criticism and Society," *Prisms*, 34). This essay did not receive much attention until the publication of "Commitment," originally published in 1962, but widely read in Adorno's *Notes to Literature III* in 1965.

It would be naïve to substitute Adorno and Horkheimer's concept of enlightenment with that of modernism because modernism is only a specific phase in the history of the Enlightenment and is related—in the narrow sense—almost exclusively to art, literature, and philosophy, while the Enlightenment also includes science as well as economic and political theory. As they describe it, the Enlightenment expressed "the real movement of bourgeois society as a whole from the perspective of the idea embodied in its personalities and institutions" since the end of the seventeenth century (DE xvi). On the other hand, modernism is the movement in art, literature, and philosophy since the beginning of the nineteenth century, or, as other—more limited—definitions have it, since the turn of the nineteenth to the twentieth century. The underlying principles are, however, similar. As the Enlightenment, in Adorno and Horkheimer's words, "has always aimed at liberating human beings from fear and installing them as masters" (DE 1), so was modernism in its various forms and expressions directed at a utopian society, even if some utopias may not have corresponded to the demands for a more humane society, as it turned out during the crisis of modernism in the early 1930s.

The most obvious parallels between enlightenment and modernism pertain to the future. Although the authors of *Dialectic of Enlightenment* declare that "the wholly enlightened earth is radiant with triumphant calamity" (DE 1), the liberal proponents of modernism had to admit by 1933 that modernism had not kept its promise of more humane conditions. On the contrary, right-wing and leftist strains of modernism were marching in a direction that suggested similar disasters in the near future, as Adorno and Horkheimer had predicted. In this respect, the Enlightenment and modernism had a major concern in common: the "negation of reification" (DE xvii). Borrowed from Karl Marx and Georg Lukács, the term "reification," which stood for the perversion of social relations and alienation in capitalism, is here used to define the negative that was to be overcome by enlightenment. But that promise was not fulfilled. According to Adorno and Horkheimer, authentic thought cannot survive where it is treated as a cultural commodity and distributed to satisfy consumer demands, as it is in capitalist society. Neither can it survive where it is appropriated by nationalist or racist mythologies or subjected to the needs of dictatorships that rule over disenfranchised masses.

While Horkheimer continued to discuss the philosophical implications of enlightenment in his *Eclipse of Reason* of 1947, Adorno began to specialize in the criticism of high art and aesthetic theory. He relied on this bourgeois "confidence in art" when he placed the works of the bourgeois canon at the center of his discussions of modernist literature and music in his later essays, *Philosophy of Modern Music* (1949), which was partially written before *Dialectic of Enlightenment,* and his *Aesthetic Theory,* published posthumously in 1970.

CHAPTER 2

Art and Its Resistance to Society

Theodor W. Adorno's Aesthetic Theory

The geographic proximity of Hollywood confronted Horkheimer and Adorno with the products of the movie studios, which had evolved as a major industry since the early 1930s. The movie industry was hit harder by the Depression than any other. In addition, the technological innovations that enabled the production of sound films and their presentation in movie theaters necessitated new investments in the industry. By the end of the 1930s, however, the movie industry had recovered better than other sectors of the economy, establishing itself as one of the major employers in Los Angeles and promising more work in the years to come. Not only because of films' importance in the local economy, but also in terms of their role in entertaining the masses, the movies had become an important part of American life. Hollywood provided an antidote to the economic realities of everyday life during the Depression, showing viewers a life worth living in the midst of economic misery.

The chapter in *Dialectic of Enlightenment* on the culture industry was Horkheimer and Adorno's most direct response to their exposure to Hollywood. Of course, the film industry of the Weimar Republic during the early 1930s could have provided a similar object lesson. Already before 1933, Joseph Roth had characterized the metropolitan culture of Berlin as an "entertainment industry" *(Vergnügungsindustrie),* but at that time Adorno had been preoccupied with his high-culture music criticism. Only when he came to the United States did he become involved with the modern mass media and their claim to culture. In 1937 he was offered a

FIGURE 4. Theodor W. Adorno at his writing desk, circa 1947. Photograph by Franz Roehn, courtesy of Theodor W. Adorno-Archiv, Frankfurt/Main.

half-time position at the Princeton Office of Radio Research. This work resulted in his essay "On the Fetish Character in Music and the Regression of Hearing," which appeared in 1938 in the *Zeitschrift für Sozialforschung* (Journal for Social Research), the journal of the Institute for Social Research. Adorno's encounter with modern jazz—he tried to categorize it as a commodity of the culture industry—was a disaster because he totally misunderstood it. He could not even pronounce the word "jazz," as is evident from the fact that he associated it with the German word *"Hatz,"* which means "hunting with dogs" and has a decidedly negative connotation. Martin Jay, who reviewed Adorno's articles on jazz in his history of the Frankfurt School, concluded that jazz remained for Adorno "a source of continued horror" (Jay 186) and that he scornfully rejected all claims that jazz was different from the culture industry and deserved special attention. The problem was that Adorno received his introduction to jazz during the Weimar Republic and probably never listened to authentic jazz in the United States (Leppert 330–36; 349–60). The kind of jazz that was available to him during the 1920s was popular dance music that had "very little to do with non-swing American jazz" (Leppert 357). Adorno associated jazz with upper-class entertainment and expressed no regret when it was banished from Nazi radio: "For no matter what one wishes to understand by white or by Negro jazz, here there is nothing to salvage" ("Farewell to Jazz" 496).

Even though Horkheimer and Adorno were deeply involved in the issues of mass culture in the 1920s, it was not in the forefront of their thinking as high culture was. This becomes obvious from Adorno's response to Horkheimer of September 4, 1941, when he raised the question whether they should continue to focus their joint work on art, or whether they should finally start talking about society itself:

> While I was writing the piece on music, I, too, increasingly had the impression that it implied a farewell to art theory, for considerable time at least . . . and I can already tell you that I not only agree with shifting the emphasis onto questions of society as such, but that precisely a knowledge of art makes such a "transition" necessary. (quoted in Wiggershaus 302)

This attitude also accounts for their lack of empirical analysis. It is hard to imagine Horkheimer and Adorno going to the movies in Westwood, as Thomas Mann did, or listening to jazz on Central Avenue, the center of the Los Angeles jazz scene during the 1940s. Adorno was, however, an avid moviegoer in the 1920s. His mentor, Siegfried Kracauer, authored the definitive history of German film of the Weimar period, *From Caligari to Hitler,* in 1947. Adorno mentions a number of invitations to movie studios by directors, such as William Dieterle and Fritz Lang, in letters to his parents, and Adorno and his wife attended parties at the homes of Salka Viertel and Fritz Lang. After he had returned to Germany, Adorno exchanged letters with Fritz Lang, as their correspondence between 1949 and 1967 shows. In *Dialectic of Enlightenment,* however, only a very few film titles, directors, and actors are mentioned. In dialectical fashion, Horkheimer and Adorno discuss modern mass culture in the abstract, in order to position and defend high modernist art in the twentieth century. High culture provided the standard for their

FIGURE 5. Theodor W. Adorno's duplex apartment house, 316 South Kenter Avenue, Brentwood, 2005. Photograph by Juergen Nogai, Santa Monica.

dealing with mass culture. Or, conversely, when they talked about society, they had art on their minds.

Horkheimer and Adorno were trained in aesthetics in the German tradition of Kant and Hegel. Therefore, they spoke again and again of "authentic works of art"— those that avoided "the mere imitation of what already is" (DE 13)—according them a privileged position in the progress of enlightenment. Each work of art that was "closed off from reality by its own circumference" was exempted from the negative effects of enlightenment. This resulted in "the appearance of the whole in the particular" (DE 14). Adorno and Horkheimer claimed for the authentic work of art the "aura" that Walter Benjamin had denied it and had thought was gone in the modernist "age of mechanical reproduction." In Hegelian fashion they considered art "an expression of totality" that "claims the dignity of the absolute." Although they admitted that such occurrences were rare, namely, that art was "an expression of totality" that could claim "the dignity of the absolute," they still thought that at rare moments "the bourgeois world was . . . amenable to such confidence in art" (DE 14). They were keenly aware of the dangers of domination in the realm of art, and even authentic art was not exempt from domination, they realized. Mass culture was subject to similar forms of domination, or it rather constituted a form of domination that was not extraneous to high culture. On the contrary, according to Horkheimer and Adorno, modern mass culture and twentieth-century modernism "owed their existence to the existence of its respective other," as Lutz Koepnick observed in his analysis. Modern mass culture had "emerged out of high art's compromises with public taste and commercial interests" (Koepnick 8).

What recommended Adorno to Horkheimer was Adorno's manuscript "Schoenberg and Progress" of 1940–41, which eventually resulted in his *Philosophy of Modern Music (Philosophie der neuen Musik)*, to which he had added a chapter on Igor Stravinsky in 1949. Horkheimer wrote to Adorno on August 28, 1941, that if he ever felt enthusiasm for anything in his life, it was while reading "Schoenberg and Progress." As a result of his training and his interests, Adorno was predestined to write most of the text on cultural criticism in *Dialectic of Enlightenment*. His development as a major proponent of modernism during the following years was no surprise. Adorno considered his *Philosophy of Modern Music* an "extended appendix," or excursus, to Horkheimer's *Dialectic of Enlightenment*.

J. M. Bernstein characterizes Adorno's stance as an "uncompromising defence of modernist art and [an] uncompromising critique of mass culture as a product of a 'culture industry,' " and he argues that this stance served his opponents, especially the proponents of postmodernism, as a target toward which they could direct their "claims for a democratic transformation of culture." From his opponents' point of view, Adorno was "an elitist defending esoteric artistic modernism against a culture available to all" ("Introduction" 1), but postmodernist criticism was to come about thirty years later.

When Horkheimer and Adorno introduced the topic of "popular mass culture" in *Dialectic of Enlightenment* in 1947, they preferred to use the term "culture industry." This phrase was coined, as Martin Jay has explained, "because of its antipopulist connotation" (216). Both Horkheimer and Adorno dislike mass culture "not because it was democratic, but precisely because it was not. The notion of 'popular' culture, they argued, was ideological: the culture industry administered a non-spontaneous, reified, phony culture rather than the real thing. The old distinction between high and low culture had all but vanished in the 'stylized barbarism' of mass culture" (Jay 216).

With the subtitle to the chapter on the culture industry—"Enlightenment as Mass Deception"—Horkheimer and Adorno pull no punches; it clearly identifies as the target of their attacks the unity, or rather uniformity, of modern mass culture. All mass culture is identical under monopoly capitalism, they argue. Its power is so pervasive that "films and radio no longer need present themselves as art." They clearly understand that films and radio are simply "business," and the authors call their self-identification as "industries" most revealing (DE 95). The culture industry is allied with the most powerful sectors of the economy—steel, oil, electricity, and chemicals—and its audience is identical with the mass of consumers. The products of the culture industry are subject to the same criteria as those of the automobile industry (DE 96–98).

When they were confronted with what they perceived as the drastic impoverishment of aesthetic matter in mass culture Adorno and Horkheimer resorted to Immanuel Kant's aesthetics, clearly revealing their conservative disposition. Kant's formalism, one of the icons of bourgeois aesthetics, "still expected of subjects that they should . . . relate sensuous multiplicity to fundamental concepts" (DE 98). Here Adorno and Horkheimer come closest to the concept of authentic reception as well as the problem of creating a new modernist audience. Authentic reception is free from the control of the culture industry, which not only delivers its products as commodities, but also determines the conditions of their reception.

Adorno and Horkheimer's indictment of the culture industry is that it denies active contribution to the subject. According to Kantian schematism, "a secret mechanism within the psyche preformed immediate data to fit them into the system of pure reason" (DE 98). But since the culture industry provides this service without any individual effort, there is nothing left for consumers to contribute; the producers of the culture industry have already done it for them. Their conclusion is that art for the masses has destroyed the dream but still conforms to the tenets of that dreaming idealism that critical idealism had condemned. To be sure, there is still consciousness *(Bewußtsein)* involved, but in mass art it is the consciousness of the production team that determines details and effects (DE 98). They are designed to ensure order, not coherence: "Lacking

both contrast and relatedness, the whole and the detail look alike."
When Adorno and Horkheimer declare that the prearranged harmony of
the products of the culture industry is "a mockery of the painfully
achieved harmony of the great bourgeois works of art" (DE 99), their
standards are, again, those of a past period.

Film especially came under their scrutiny because of its advanced technology, which enabled it to present the outside world as a continuation
of the film presented on the screen. While the old theater of illusion had
stressed the difference between stage and reality, real life was now becoming "indistinguishable from the sound film" (DE 99). Here Adorno
and Horkheimer come close to Brecht's concept of authentic reception
when they complain that there is no room left for imagination or reflection on the part of the audience, although they address themselves especially to the movies because they think that the movies stunt their consumers' powers of imagination more than any other media. Movies are
constructed so that they debar the spectators from thinking if they are
"not to miss the fleeting facts" (DE 100). The audience reacts automatically because they have been taught what to expect.

Adorno and Horkheimer's common project is based on the standards
of "the great bourgeois art works," and their discussion often turns into
a prescription of modernist art and literature rather than an analysis of
mass culture. This becomes especially obvious in their discussion of style,
in which they concede that the culture industry has achieved unity of
style and harmony of content and form. But for the critical observers this
achievement is just the "aesthetic equivalent of power" (DE 103). For
them, the great artists

> were never those whose works embodied style in its least fractured, most
> perfect form but those who adopted style as a rigor to set against the
> chaotic expression of suffering, as a negative truth. In the style of these
> works expression took on the strength without which existence is dissi-
> pated unheard. Even works which are called classical, like the music of
> Mozart, contain objective tendencies which resist the style they incarnate.
> Up to Schoenberg and Picasso, great artists have been mistrustful of style.
> (DE 103)

Against the background of the products of the culture industry,
Adorno and Horkheimer project their vision of the modernist work of
art, whose essence is to be found in those features in which discrepancy
emerges, "in the necessary failure of the passionate striving for identity"
(DE 103). The style of the great work of art negates itself by risking failure rather than relying on similarity to others and providing only a sur-

rogate of identity (DE 103). These are statements that foreshadowed Adorno's posthumous *Aesthetic Theory* of 1970.

Adorno and Horkheimer identify the culture industry primarily with the democratic culture of the United States, although they do not openly say so. Instead they refer to "the liberal industrial nations" in which movies, radio, jazz, and magazines flourish, and they express a great deal of nostalgia for prefascist Germany, which profited from the time lag of industrial technology. While they speak of the "barbarism" of the American culture industry, which they attribute to technological progress, they wax sentimental about the freedom of culture during the Weimar Republic:

> The German educational system, including the universities, the artistically influential theaters, the great orchestras, and museums were under patronage. The political powers, state and the local authorities who inherited such institutions from absolutism, had left them with a degree of independence from the power of the market as the princes and feudal lords had done up to the nineteenth century. (DE 105)

They belie their own analysis when they declare that the German system of patronage has strengthened "the backbone of art in its late phase against the verdict of supply and demand, heightening its resistance far beyond its actual degree of protection" (DE 105). This is a flat denial of the crisis of modernism that they did not fail to reiterate at other junctures.

Although Adorno and Horkheimer attribute many of the maladies of modern mass society, such as conformity and the myth of success, to the culture industry, they take quite a different approach to amusement. They do not consider "light" art a form of decadence, but point out that "the purity of bourgeois art, hypostasized as a realm of freedom contrasting to material praxis, was bought from the outset with the exclusion of the lower classes. . . . Serious art has denied itself to those for whom the hardship and oppression of life make a mockery of seriousness" (DE 107). Light art they define as the "shadow" of autonomous art, or the "social bad conscience of serious art" (DE 107), because the lower classes have to be satisfied with amusement or distraction. This division between high and low art itself is considered the truth because it expresses the negativity of culture, while the culture industry prefers reconciliation by absorbing light art into serious art. As examples of the latter Adorno and Horkheimer mention the jazz musician Benny Goodman appearing with the Budapest string quartet, or the Budapest musicians playing as uniformly and sweetly as bandleader Guy Lombardo.

Adorno and Horkheimer's second indictment of amusement as dispensed by the culture industry is that it amounts to the prolongation of work. Although it is considered an escape from work, amusement in fact reproduces the mechanization of work to such a degree that the experiences provided are "nothing but after-images of the work process itself" (DE 109). Even cartoons, which were once "exponents of fantasy against rationalism," have degenerated into a reproduction of the cruelty of everyday life: "Donald Duck in the cartoons and the unfortunate victim in real life receive their beatings so that the spectators can accustom themselves to theirs" (DE 110).

Adorno and Horkheimer's prime complaint against the culture industry is that it "endlessly cheats its consumers out of what it endlessly promises," especially in the area of sexual pleasure (DE 111). In comparison to art in which sexual deprivation is presented as negative, the culture industry does not sublimate sexuality, but instead represses it. "Of course, genuine works of art were not sexual exhibitions either. But by representing denial as negative, they reversed, as it were, the debasement of the drive and rescued by mediation what had been denied" (DE 111). Adorno and Horkheimer perceive the secret of aesthetic sublimation as the presentation of "fulfillment in its brokenness" (DE 111). On the other hand, the culture industry only stimulates unsublimated forepleasure, but indicates unmistakably that things will never go too far. To offer something and to deprive the consumer of something are one and the same. In erotic films everything revolves around the coitus because it never takes place (DE 113). The authors declare works of art to be "ascetic and shameless," while the culture industry is "pornographic and prudish" (DE 111). They see in the culture industry a type of deception, epitomized by the daughter's abduction in the cartoon where the father is holding the ladder in the dark. Their interpretation is that the paradise offered by the culture industry is the same old everyday world: "Escape, like elopement, was destined from the first to lead back to its starting point" (DE 113).

Instead of providing amusement as relaxed self-surrender, the culture industry puts entertainment into the service of defending society instead: "To be entertained means to be in agreement" (DE 115). Administered by the culture industry, pleasure is not "escape from bad reality but from the last thought of resisting that reality." Hollywood amusement promises nothing but "liberation . . . from thinking as negation" (DE 116). Even Hollywood's explanations of life are becoming less and less meaningful as they are reduced to advertising slogans. Here Adorno and

Horkheimer's critique of language as an instrument of domination comes into play: "Words which are not means seem meaningless" (DE 118). The culture industry has assumed the power to issue authoritative pronouncements and make itself "the irrefutable prophet of the existing order" (DE 118). As in advertising, words and images are repeated with great monotony. The worship of facts turns the photographic image into a substitute for meaning and right: "Beauty is whatever the camera reproduces" (DE 119). But such a reproduction provides the consumers of culture with nothing but stereotypes that undermine the underlying message. For example, Adorno and Horkheimer compare the ears of corn blowing in the wind at the end of Charlie Chaplin's *The Great Dictator* (1940) with the blond hair wafting in the summer breeze of the German girl whose camp life was photographed by UFA, the well-known Nazi film studio. Chaplin's film deserves acknowledgment as one of the first anti-Nazi films in the United States, and Chaplin was perhaps the most political filmmaker in Hollywood. He produced *The Great Dictator* with his own money in 1939 because the movie industry was afraid of risking a German boycott (Hollywood profitably provided films to the German market until 1941). But, nevertheless, Adorno and Horkheimer subject *The Great Dictator* to their criticism as perhaps a dialectical challenge to their readers. Their conclusion is that the use of the stereotypically idyllic image of the cornfield belies the message of Chaplin's antifascist plea for freedom because Nazi filmmakers produced exactly the same kind of scene to support their ideology (DE 119–20).

In its treatment of the outsider, *Dialectic of Enlightenment* accuses the culture industry of reproducing the prejudices of society. In films the outsider is usually identified as the villain, so that the audience will not get the impression that society would turn against those of good will. There is always room for humanitarian intervention, as long as the beneficiaries of that intervention are willing to become integrated. By emphasizing the "heart of gold," the culture industry does not hesitate to present suffering: life is very hard, "yet therefore so wonderful, so healthy" (DE 122). Here Adorno and Horkheimer perceive the culture industry to be borrowing from art: it offers "to regular movie-goers the veneer of culture they need for purposes of prestige. To all it grants the solace that human fate in its strength and authenticity is possible even now and its unflinching depiction inescapable" (DE 122). Not surprisingly, Adorno and Horkheimer argue that tragedy is reduced to the threat of the destruction of anyone who does not cooperate and that tragic fate has been reduced to just punishment: "The morality of mass culture [has been handed down] from yesterday's children's books" (DE 122). The movies provide the models for acceptable behavior and what one has to do to become accepted by society. This process of integration is repeatedly performed in socially slanted films.

The problem of individuation was never fully resolved during the nineteenth century, as Adorno and Horkheimer concede. Self-preservation in modern class society has kept everybody at the stage of a mere species being *(Gattungswesen)*. Every bourgeois characteristic reveals the harshness of competitive society. But as it progresses, bourgeois society contributes, nevertheless, to the development of the individual. In dialectical fashion, however, "all such progress in individuation [occurs] at the expense of the individuality in whose name it took place" (DE 125). Adorno and Horkheimer jump to the conclusion that "the citizens whose lives are split between business and private life, . . . at odds with themselves and with everyone, are virtually already Nazis" (DE 125). This rash conclusion turns the population of the Western democracies into ready-made fascists. The culture industry profits from this fragility of society by reproducing it. The popularity of movie heroes is based on the effort to imitate rather than achieve individuation. The argument ends with the facetious observation that "for centuries society has been preparing for Victor Mature and Mickey Rooney" (DE 126).

How vapid these film stars appear as individuals is explained in the following terms: "The heroizing of the average forms part of the cult of cheapness" (DE 126). The combination of a film star's status with his or her endorsement of a commercial product ensures "the commodified beauty" (DE 126). Adorno and Horkheimer observe with sarcasm that the culture industry has fulfilled the Socratic notion that the beautiful is the useful. Their anger is directed specifically against the radio, which brings the best orchestras in the world into the living room free of charge. They notice a specific change in the character of the art commodity. While this character is not new, the deliberate admission of the commodity character is. Art has renounced its own autonomy and taken a place among consumer goods. Although Adorno and Horkheimer have to admit that art as a separate sphere in bourgeois society contains an element of untruth, they postulate the autonomy of art, nevertheless, as a condition of its existence in opposition to the market (DE 127). In modern society the use value of art has been replaced by its exchange value. In place of the enjoyment of art there is the prestige of its consumption. Horkheimer and Adorno expose the "unsaleability" of art, promoted by the culture industry in radio concerts, as hypocrisy. The fact that Arturo

Toscanini could be heard free of charge when he conducted the NBC Symphony Orchestra on the radio could not obscure the fact that this was made possible by the profits of the automobile and consumer industries, which kept the radios going with their advertising and the increased sales of radio sets (DE 128).

Since radio was the dominant media of the culture industry of the 1940s in Nazi Germany as well as the United States, Adorno and Horkheimer focused their attention on its dangers. In their eyes, the saving grace of the movie industry was its dependence on ticket sales—a remnant of the liberal era of art consumption, which necessitated some decision making by the consumers. Radio stations, however, did not collect any fees in the United States, and the radio was therefore not subject to any liberal notions of a free market. Its universal availability made the radio "the mouthpiece of the nation" (DE 129). Its illusory form of unbiased authority made it admirably suited to fascism, and, in fact, in Nazi Germany the radio had become "the universal mouthpiece of the Führer" (DE 129). As tempting as it was to perceive the similarity between radio commercials and orders barked by Adolf Hitler in his speeches on the radio, Adorno and Horkheimer had to admit that there was still a difference between the recommendation of a particular brand of detergent and marching orders issued by the Führer (DE 129).

In *Dialectic of Enlightenment* the reduction of culture to advertising is seen as the greatest danger. The more meaningless advertising becomes, the more its omnipotence is enhanced. Advertising that no longer serves to distribute goods to consumers but exists exclusively for its own sake turns into "the pure representation of social power" (DE 132). Adorno and Horkheimer's conclusion is that advertising and the culture industry have merged technically as well as economically. The mechanical repetition of the name of a culture product has become the same as the repetition of the propaganda slogan. The demand for effectiveness has turned technology into a kind of "psychotechnique" that serves to manipulate human beings (DE 133). In conclusion, Adorno and Horkheimer determine that the final effect of the modern media is to induce man to attempt to make himself an efficient "apparatus," conforming to the model presented by the culture industry. Their treasured concept of "personality," which dates back to nineteenth-century Europe, has now become a completely abstract notion scarcely signifying anything more "than dazzling white teeth and freedom from body odor and emotions" (DE 136). As empty as this image of personality in magazine ads and on billboards is, consumers still can, as Horkheimer and

Adorno suggest, see through the products that advertising in the culture industry have compelled them to buy and use, but they never answer the question whether the sweaty Nazi storm trooper with bad teeth could do the same with regard to the propaganda that he was forced to believe.

As a close reading of the chapter "The Culture Industry" shows, Horkheimer and Adorno suggest similarities between Hitler and Hollywood, or between German National Socialism and American mass culture; their dialectical methodology allows them to do so, although they never present this relationship as an equation. The equation took hold among disciples of the Frankfurt School in West Germany and the United States (see Koepnick 6–12). In spite of the totalizing perspective of their assessment of the culture industry, Horkheimer and Adorno's methodology is dialectical enough to avoid such simplistic equations. The last sentence of the chapter states that the consumers who feel compelled to buy and use the products of the culture industry nevertheless "recognize [them] as false" (DE 136). Advertising is valorized as enormously influential but not as absolute as Nazi propaganda.

Adorno's original text, "Schoenberg and Progress," which provided the impetus for *Dialectic of Enlightenment,* centers on the composer and his technique of twelve-tone music, or, as Schoenberg preferred to call it, his "method of composing with twelve tones" (*Style and Idea* 216). In 1948, Adorno added a preface and a new chapter on Stravinsky, who also lived in exile in Los Angeles. Adorno's *Philosophy of Modern Music* (1949) presents Schoenberg and Stravinsky as the "two central figures of musical modernism" (Leppert 551) but neglects their exile experience. In Stravinsky's case, he chose exile in Switzerland in 1910 and then in France in 1920. In 1939 Stravinsky immigrated to the United States, and he died in New York in 1971. Stravinsky lived in Los Angeles from 1941 to 1969, while Schoenberg came to Los Angeles in 1934 and died here in 1951 (see chapter 11). The two composers represented two opposing schools of music in Los Angeles, and their supporters often expressed strong sentiments of belonging to opposing camps and avoided sitting together at concerts. Schoenberg and Stravinsky never met in public or private during those years; although they were present at the same public functions, they chose to remain on opposite sides of the room and, according to eyewitness reports, they never exchanged greetings. Only after Schoenberg's death, in 1951, did Stravinsky become a devotee of his rival's music, studying his scores at the rehearsals and performances of a 1952 Schoenberg retrospective that consisted of four concerts that were part of a private avant-garde chamber music series in Los Angeles

(Crawford 100, 253). In 1953 Stravinsky even wrote a composition in honor of Schoenberg (Crawford 127–28).

For Adorno, Schoenberg and Stravinsky represented extremes that in "meaningful juxtaposition" defined the essence of modern music: Schoenberg stood for progress and Stravinsky for restoration. But it was even more important to Adorno that this juxtaposition permitted "the perception of its truth" (PMM 3). He never discussed to what degree the experience of exile affected this juxtaposition of extremes and made the discussion of its truth a necessity. Nevertheless, he related it to the Enlightenment project, as defined by *Dialectic of Enlightenment,* and saw art as being "able to aid enlightenment . . . by relating the clarity of the world consciously to its own darkness" (PMM 15). According to Adorno, Schoenberg's music was able to do that while Stravinsky's was not, or rather his music avoided addressing that problem.

Adorno's point of departure was history, as reflected by art and specifically by music. He does not, however, classify the history of music in terms of the development of different styles, but rather in terms of its relationship to musical material. This material was traditionally defined "as the sum of all sounds at the disposal of a composer," but Adorno emphasizes that "the actual compositional material is as different from this sum as is language from its total supply of sounds" (PMM 32). Not only is the compositional material reduced and increased in the course of history, but also its specific characteristics are "indications of the historical process" (PMM 32). According to Adorno, the specific characteristics are charged with historical necessity:

> The higher the degree of historical necessity present within these specific characteristics, the less directly legible they become as historical indications. In that very moment when the historical expression of a chord can no longer be aurally perceived, it demands that the sounds that surround it give a conclusive account of its historical implications. (PMM 32)

It is difficult to understand what Adorno means by material. He defines it in Hegelian fashion as "the sediment of spirit *[Geist]*" (PMM 39), that is, as Carl Dahlhaus explains, "nothing less than the objective spirit and the way it is manifested in music" (159). Adorno postulates that the demands made by the material upon the subject are based on the fact that the material is "socially predetermined through the consciousness of man" (PMM 33). The "objective spirit of the material" seems to have its own historical progress. Yet because it is of the same origin as the social process and continually permeated by its traces, even when it is considered as a separate development, it takes the same course, even when "the objective spirit of the material" and society have "become totally unaware of each other and have come into conflict with each other" (PMM 33). From this complex interdependence within the historical process, Adorno concludes that "the altercation of the composer with his material is the same as an altercation with society," precisely to the extent that society is integrated into the work and does not simply face it as a merely external and heteronomous agent, that is as consumer or opponent (PMM 34).

To illustrate his point, Adorno argues that "tonal combinations employed in the past by no means stand indiscriminately at the disposal of the [modern] composer" (PMM 34). He claims that "even the more insensitive ear detects the shabbiness and exhaustion of the diminished seventh chord and certain chromatic modulations in the salon music of the nineteenth century." For the technically trained ear, however, "such vague discomfort is transformed into a prohibitive canon." According to Adorno, "this canon today excludes even the medium of tonality—that is to say, the means of all traditional music. It is not simply that these sounds are antiquated and untimely, but that they are false. They no longer fulfill their function. The most progressive level of technical procedures designs tasks before which traditional sounds reveal themselves as impotent clichés" (PMM 34).

To make his historical argument understood, Adorno refers to the diminished seventh chord that rings false in salon pieces but is "correct and full of every possible expression" at the beginning of Beethoven's Piano Sonata, opus 111. That this chord was not superimposed—it resulted from the structural design of the first movement—but instead reflected "the total niveau of Beethoven's technique" gave the chord "its specific weight" (PMM 35). This chord, however, lost its "specific weight" an in "irreversible" historical process. The chord itself was now "an obsolete form" (PMM 35–36), and as such it represented "in its dissolution a state of technique contradictory as a whole to the state of technique actually in practice" (PMM 36).

The historical tendency of musical material also transformed the status of the composer. He lost the traditional freedom of the artist that idealistic aesthetics had granted him. "He was no longer a creator," as Adorno says (PMM 36). It was neither the century nor the society that imposed external restrictions upon him, but rather "the rigid demand for compositional accuracy . . . that [limited] him" (PMM 36). The composer's efforts were to be directed at executing what the music "objectively [demanded] of him." But in order to comply with such demands, the composer was required to gather all the "disobedience, independence, and spontaneity" that he was able to muster. Such an attitude was required to respond to the "the dialectical nature revealed in the unfolding of the musical material" (PMM 36–37).

Adorno construes Schoenberg's development toward twelve-tone music as an inevitable historical process. Since Adorno perceives this as a dialectical process, it is essential to understand that twelve-tone music was not an endpoint, that musical development would continue indefinitely. Presenting a rough sketch of Schoenberg's development from late Romanticism to Expressionism to twelve-tone music and finally to the "late style" *[Spätstil]*, Adorno expresses distaste for each period except for the last. In its transition from late Romanticism to the atonality of Expressionism, Schoenberg's music appeared to have "elements of barbarism" due to its "purification . . . from all conventions." Protest against conventions had "a regressive tendency." As Adorno reports, "Schoenberg's atonal earliest compositions—particularly the *Piano Pieces [opus 11]*—shocked the audience more through primitivism than through their complexity" (PMM 40–41).

Adorno describes the twelve-tone technique in some detail, explaining the compositional process that began only when the ordering of the twelve tones was established:

> This ordering has made composition not simpler but, rather, more difficult. The twelve-tone technique demands that every composition be derived from such a "fundamental structure" or "row," no matter whether it is a single phrase or a work consisting of several movements. This refers to an arbitrarily designated ordering of the twelve tones available to the composer in the tempered half-tone system, as, for example, c♯–a–b–g–a flat –f♯–b flat–d–e–e flat–c–f in the first of Schoenberg's published twelve-tone compositions. Every tone of the composition is determined by this row: there is no longer a "free" note. This does not mean, however—with the exception of a few very early cases as they appeared in the earliest days of the technique—that this particular row runs its course unaltered throughout the entire composition, revealing only minor alterations of the row and of rhythmic figures. (PMM 61–62)

To this encyclopedic description Adorno adds an account of the variations that Schoenberg applied to the twelve-tone material:

> For the most part he employs the row in four ways: as the basic row; as the inversion thereof, that is to say, by substituting for each interval of the row the same interval in the reverse direction . . . ; as a "crab" in the sense of earlier contrapuntal practice, so that the row begins with the final tone

and ends with the first; and in the inversion of the crab. These four procedures can then, for their own part, be transposed, beginning with each of
the twelve tones of the chromatic scale, so that the row offers itself in forty-
eight different forms for a given composition. (PMM 62–63)

To this straightforward analysis Adorno adds his philosophical commentary.

The total domination of the material, however, turns "against the
subjective autonomy and freedom itself, in the name of which this domination found its fulfillment" (PMM 66). The composer becomes a prisoner of his own system: "The number game of twelve-tone technique and
the force which it exercises" bordered on superstition (PMM 66). This
observation culminates in Adorno's declaration that music that has been
subjected to historical dialectics participates in the dialectic: "Twelve-
tone technique is truly the fate of music. It enchains music by liberating
it. The subject dominates music through the rationality of the system,
only in order to succumb to the rational system itself" (PMM 67–68). By
means of rational organization, liberated music seeks to reconstitute the
lost totality, but it virtually suppresses the subject (PMM 69). As a closed
system that is opaque even to itself, twelve-tone rationality approaches
the realm of myth (PMM 66).

During Schoenberg's last phase, called by Adorno his "late style" in
analogy to a similar phase in Beethoven's career to which Adorno applied the same label, the twentieth-century composer acquired a new
"sovereignty" by liberating himself from his material (PMM 119). The
twelve-tone technique had made the subject "a slave of the 'material,' as
of an empty concept of rules." This degraded the subject "at that moment in which the subject completely [subdued] the material, indentur-
ing it to its mathematical logic." At this point, however, the dialectical
contradiction becomes apparent: "The subject cannot be content with its
subjugation to its abstract identity in the material" (PMM 117). Adorno
considers this renunciation of material "the innermost tendency" of
Schoenberg's late style (PMM 118). "Because the externalized material
no longer expresses anything for him, the composer forces it to mean
what he wishes" (PMM 119). Adorno notices a growing tendency in
Schoenberg toward disassociation from twelve-tone technique and declares that Schoenberg had finally denounced "his fidelity to the sole
domination of material—that very fidelity which he had once designed"
(PMM 123). To prove his point Adorno lists a number of works of the
late phase that were, in his opinion, all "tonal"—the Suite for String Or-

chestra, the *Kol Nidre,* opus 39, and the Second Chamber Symphony, opus 38. In addition, he notices "a more conciliatory attitude towards the public" as their common characteristic, maintaining that Schoenberg recognized "the right to music which, in spite of everything, [was] still valid even in a false society" (PMM 120–21). Although the music of Schoenberg's earlier phases had resulted in isolation from its audience and flight from the public concert hall, the composer began to make use of traditional melodies in his late-style music and to present "what even the enchained consciousness of the consumer still has an ear for" (PMM 122). But Schoenberg's particular manner of conciliation was bound to a special kind of inexorability that continued to present "social truth against society" (PMM 121).

As can be deduced from the polemical subtitle of the second part of *Philosophy of Modern Music,* "Stravinsky and Restoration," Adorno was highly critical of the Russian composer. It is not necessary to present his arguments in detail, because they have no bearing on the crisis of Weimar modernism in exile. Adorno accuses Stravinsky of trying to re-store the essence of music "through stylistic procedures" and limiting himself to ballet music, as, for example, in *Petrouchka,* "arousing only bodily animation instead of offering meaning" (PMM 140). In a com-parison between Schoenberg's *Pierrot Lunaire* with Stravinsky's *Petrouchka* he argues against the latter, claiming that the music tended "to take the part of those who ridicule the maltreated hero, rather than come to his defense":

> Consequently, the immortality of the clown at the end of the work cannot be interpreted as appeasement for the collective, but rather as the threat of evil to it. In Stravinsky's case, subjectivity assumes the character of sacri-fice, but . . . the music does not identify with the victim, but rather with the destructive element. (PMM 143)

Adorno sees the music reduced to the grotesque sounds of the hand organ, which produce "the shock of a modernity . . . degraded to a child-ish level" (PMM 145). Viewing *Le Sacre du printemps*—Stravinsky's most famous and "most progressive" work—in the same light as *Petrouchka,* which he labels in Brechtian terms as "culinary," Adorno concludes that in spite of their differences they "both have a common nu-cleus: the anti-humanistic sacrifice to the collective—sacrifice without tragedy, made not in the name of a renewed image of man, but only in the blind affirmation of a situation recognized by the victim" (PMM 145). In *Le Sacre du printemps* Adorno sees atrocity "presented without

mitigation" (PMM 146). In terms of its technical elements, he characterizes it as "the virtuoso composition of regression" (PMM 148).
Adorno also charges Stravinsky with infantilism and schizophrenia in
Histoire du Soldat and *Renard* (PMM 162, 168). His final denunciation
of Stravinsky's work culminates in the accusation that it was nothing but
"music about music . . . throughout his career" (PMM 182). This verdict
allows Adorno to include the works from Stravinsky's neoclassical period, *Oedipus Rex* and the *Symphony of Psalms*. He condemns Stravinsky's quotations from the music of earlier periods as "universal
necrophilia":

> The idiom, finally developed with such great effort, no longer shocks anyone:
> it is the very essence of everything approved and certified in the two hundred
> years of bourgeois music, treated according to the procedure of rhythmic
> tricks which has meanwhile found approval. . . . The authoritarian charac-
> ter of today is, without exception, conformist; likewise the authoritarian
> claim of Stravinsky's music is extended totally and completely to conformism.
> In the final analysis, this music tends to become the style for everyone, because
> it coincides with the man-in-the-street style in which they have always believed
> and to which this music automatically directs them again. (PMM 204–5)

Adorno's analysis of Stravinsky does not go beyond 1948 and therefore
does not include works such as *The Rake's Progress*, written in the Hollywood Hills between 1948 and 1951, or his twelve-tone compositions,
written after he had abandoned his neoclassical style.

After his return to Germany in 1949, Adorno finally integrated his
divergent ideas on music, literature, and the arts into his comprehensive *Aesthetic Theory*. Although it was published based on his manuscripts only in 1970, after his death in 1969, such an integrated theory
of art was one of his lifelong projects, and he had planned to finish it
during the 1970s. He had formulated and expressed many of the seminal ideas already in the 1940s. For example, the phenomenon of domination, as he exposes in the products of the culture industry in *Dialectic of Enlightenment,* reappears in *Aesthetic Theory*. Adorno
concedes that "autonomous art was not completely free of the culture
industry's authoritarian ignominy" (AT 17). He argues that "the idea
of freedom, akin to aesthetic autonomy, was shaped by domination,
which it universalized," and concludes that this held true as well for
artworks, which reflect and internalize the domination of society. It was
therefore impossible to criticize the culture industry without criticizing
art at the same time.

Adorno held a seminar on aesthetics at the University of Frankfurt during the summer semester of 1950. In the following years he lectured, according to his editors, "four more times on the same topic, the final course extending over the summer and winter terms of 1967–1968, when large parts of the [final version] were already written" (AT 362).

At the center of Adorno's *Aesthetic Theory* is the double character of art as "autonomy and *fait social*" (AT 229). In his explanations Adorno assigns a higher value to autonomy than to the social facts. Bernstein shows that Adorno was indebted to Kant's aesthetics, in this case to his formula characterizing art as "purposeful but without a purpose" *(Zweckmäßigkeit ohne Zweck)*. According to Adorno's adaptation of Kant, art's autonomy is a refusal to submit to the purposiveness of society, but its refusal serves the purpose of instilling the idea of things in the world that are not for exchange (Bernstein 207–9)

Many of Adorno's critics read his *Aesthetic Theory* as an exclusive theory of the autonomy of art (Hohendahl 75–98). However, Adorno attributes the autonomy of art, its independence from society, to the rise of the bourgeois consciousness of freedom. Thus he aligns art with a specific social class during a specific period of time, namely, the bourgeoisie of the nineteenth and twentieth centuries. But Adorno insists that in becoming bourgeois, art made its social aspect more explicit: "Art becomes social by its opposition to society, and it occupies this position only as autonomous art" (AT 225). According to Adorno, art "criticizes society by merely existing. . . . There is nothing pure, nothing structured strictly according to its own immanent law, which does not implicitly criticize the debasement . . . in . . . a total exchange society. . . . Art's asociality is the determinate negation of a determinate society" (AT 226). This analysis led to Adorno's final definition of art as resistance to society. The future of art depended on its power to resist society: "Its contribution to society is not communication with it, but rather something extremely mediated" (AT 226). The means of this mediation is resistance; it reproduces social development in aesthetic terms without imitating it directly.

But this special position of art as autonomous and simultaneously having ties to society is only one aspect of art as defined by Adorno. This aspect must, however, be understood in terms of dialectics. For Adorno art is not constituted by rigid antitheses, but rather by the identity of the non-identical. As he formulates in his *Aesthetic Theory,* art, especially autonomous art, is not "only art, but something foreign and opposed to it. Admixed with art's own concept is the ferment of its own abolition" (AT 4). Art—especially modern art—according to Adorno, is involved in a constant rehearsal of identity: "modern art constantly works at the Münchhausean trick of carrying out the identification of the nonidentical" (AT 23). As the legendary *Lügenbaron* pulled himself out of the swamp by his own hair, modern art derives its identity from the non-identical.

In the relationship between art and society, the problem of the non-identical played a major part, even in terms of technique. As Adorno observes, art had always absorbed objects from outside, but it became one of the distinctive features of modern art that the outside objects were not integrated. Adorno adduces this feature to the pressures social reality exerted on art: "Whereas art opposes society, it is nevertheless unable to take up a position beyond it; it achieves opposition only through identification with that against which it remonstrates" (AT 133).

In his thoughts regarding a theory of the individual artwork, Adorno discusses the question of artistic unity *(künstlerische Einheit)*, that is, the identity of the one and the many in a given work of art. To illustrate his point Adorno chooses an episode from the *Odyssey*, Penelope unraveling a day's weaving at night, and declares it an allegory of art: "What cunning Penelope inflicts on her artifacts, she inflicts on herself. Ever since Homer's verses this episode is not the addition or rudiment for which it is easily mistaken, but a constitutive category of art: Through this story, art takes into itself the impossibility of the identity of the one and the many as an element of its unity" (AT 186–87). Adorno declares that artworks, no less than Hegel's reason, "have their cunning" (AT 187).

With regard to the political function of art, Adorno makes the observation that works of art oppose domination by way of mimesis: "The opposition of artworks to domination is mimesis of domination. They must assimilate themselves to the comportment of domination in order to produce something qualitatively distinct from the world of domination. Even the immanently polemical attitude of artworks against the status quo internalizes the principle that underlies the status quo" (AT 289). Concerning the willful domination within art, in a more narrow sense, a domination to be abolished, Adorno declares, "The proscription of the element of willful domination in art is not aimed at domination but at the expiation of domination, in that the subject places the control of itself and its other in the service of the nonidentical" (AT 289).

Finally, Adorno does not hesitate to declare the notion of formation *[Gestaltung]*, dear to traditional or classical aesthetics, an embarrassing feature, even if it evokes the connotation of structure. In dialectical fashion, Adorno makes the argument that "the category of formation *[Gestaltung]* . . . must be supplemented by the concept of the work's structure. Yet the quality of the work is all the higher, the work all the more formed, the less it is disposed over. Formation means nonformation" (AT 289).

In summary, Adorno understands art in all its aspects not in terms of the opposition or antithesis of some invariable principles, such as life versus art, nature versus mind, or the Nietzschean opposition of the Apollonian versus the Dionysian, but in terms of its "dynamic laws" *(Bewegungsgesetze)*. As Adorno defines it in the introduction to his *Aesthetic Theory,* art "is defined by its relation to what it is not. The specifically artistic in art must be derived concretely from its Other. . . . Art acquires its specificity by separating itself from what it developed out of; its law of movement is its law of form. It exists only in relation to its Other; it is the process that transpires with its Other" (AT 3). In this respect, Adorno's *Aesthetic Theory* can be summarized as a dialectic by which art becomes nonart and yet is totally unable to become nonart. In its difference from nonart, "the artwork necessarily constitutes itself in relation to what it is not, and to what makes it an artwork in the first place" (AT 7–8). Art cannot achieve autonomy without nonart.

Such a summary, however, would be incomplete without reference to the truth content of art and the experience of suffering that Adorno ascribes to art. In the 1940s he may not yet have articulated the concept of art as the *promesse du bonheur,* but he must have promoted the idea of art as the only remaining medium expressing the truth of suffering "in an age of incomprehensible horror" (AT 18), as his remarks on the culture industry, on the one hand, and on Beethoven and Schoenberg, on the other, indicate. The "truth content of artworks" was of greatest concern to Adorno, as it constituted "the objective solution of the enigma posed by each and every one" (AT 127–28). As he formulated it later in typically dialectical fashion, "Art is directed toward truth, it is not itself immediate truth; to this extent truth is its content. By its relationship to truth, art is knowledge; art itself knows truth in that truth emerges through it" (AT 282).

Part of the truth content was the mandate that art represent the suffering of the century. Adorno would rather art "vanish altogether than that it forget the suffering," because he considered suffering to be art's expression and the way in which "form has its substance." This suffering was for him the "humane content" of art (AT 260). Adorno concluded that it was difficult to imagine "what would art be, as the writing of history, if it shook off the memory of accumulated suffering" (AT 261; see also Bernstein 224).

Adorno attributed this property to art throughout its historical development, from its beginnings to the twentieth century. On the other hand, he believed that art in earlier centuries provided solace and consolation *(Trost)*, while modern art was no longer able to offer that. In this context, Adorno referred to Hegel's thesis of art as "consciousness of plight" (AT 18). While the English translation of *Aesthetic Theory* suggests that Adorno's reading of Hegel's phrase *"Kunst als das Bewußtsein von Nöten"*—that is, "consciousness of needs" rather than "plight"—might have been a misinterpretation, this (mis)-reading was essential for his definition of art. Again and again he associated art with suffering for the very reason that suffering had been excluded from art for centuries, when art had a religious function, to inspire redemption. But in view of the atrocities and horrors of the twentieth century, Adorno argued against "art's inescapable affirmative essence," that had "become insufferable" (AT 2). He insisted on art turning against itself, "in opposition to its own concept, and thus becom[ing] uncertain of itself right into its innermost fiber" (AT 2).

CHAPTER 3

Bertolt Brecht's California Poetry

Mimesis or Modernism?

It was Bertolt Brecht who gave Los Angeles a bad name in German literature. Even critics who are not familiar with the original German verse love to cite Brecht's scathing poem comparing Los Angeles to hell. I quote it in full since it sets the stage for my arguments about Los Angeles as the landscape of modernism:

> On thinking about Hell, I gather
> My brother Shelley found it was a place
> Much like the city of London. I
> Who live in Los Angeles and not in London
> Find, on thinking about Hell, that it must be
> Still more like Los Angeles.
>
> In Hell too
> There are, I've no doubt, these luxuriant gardens
> With flowers as big as trees, which of course whither
> Unhesitantly if not nourished with very expensive water. And fruit
>   markets
> With great heaps of fruit, albeit having
> Neither smell nor taste. And endless procession of cars
> Lighter than their own shadows, faster than
> Mad thoughts, gleaming vehicles in which
> Jolly-looking people come from nowhere and are nowhere bound.
> And houses, built for happy people, therefore standing empty
> Even when lived in.
>
> The houses in Hell, too, are not all ugly.
> But the fear of being thrown on the street

Wears down the inhabitants of the villas no less than
The inhabitants of the shanty towns.

(Poems 367; GBA 15: 46)

In the first stanza Brecht refers to Percy Bysshe Shelley's poem entitled
"Hell," which was part of a parody, "Peter Bell the Third," ridiculing a
cycle of poems by William Wordsworth. Brecht had translated the first
ten verses of Shelley's poem in Denmark in 1938, but he needed only the
first stanza for inspiration when he returned to the poem in Los Angeles
in 1941. Shelley's poem begins as follows:

Hell is a city much like London—
A populous and smoky city;
There are all sorts of people undone,
And there is little or no fun done;
Small justice shown, and still less pity.

Los Angeles in the 1940s was surely not a smoky nor even a smoggy city,
but its comparison to hell was an attractive simile for an exile writer who
had to make a living here.

Brecht subjected Hollywood to an even more scathing condemnation
in another poem that denounced it as a place of artistic and intellectual
prostitution:

Every morning, to earn my daily bread
I go to the market where lies are bought.
Hopefully
I take my place among the sellers.

(Poems 382; GBA 12: 122–23)

Honest writers are condemned to earn their living—represented in biblical terms as "daily bread"—by selling screenplays that by their very nature amount to lies. The writers prostitute themselves as the proverbial
whores of the movie industry. This figure of speech is still in use, as shown
by David Mamet's *Speed-the-Plow* of 1985. The protagonists of his play
are screenwriters who call each other "whores" ad nauseam. Despite their
cynical disillusionment, the writers are involved in their own self-
deception. As the same time, however, they cannot escape their self-
indictment as "sellers."

Brecht continues his diatribe against the movie industry in his "Hollywood Elegies" ("Hollywood Elegien"), a cycle of six poems that he
wrote for Hanns Eisler's *Hollywood Songbook (Hollywooder Lieder-*

FIGURE 6. Bertolt Brecht in 1938. Photograph courtesy of Bildabteilung,
Deutsches Literaturarchiv, Marbach/Neckar.

buch), which included other Brecht poems from his exile period in Denmark, in addition to poems by Goethe and Friedrich Hölderlin. Eisler set the poems to music for voice and piano and performed the "Hollywood Elegies" for Brecht and Herbert Marcuse in October 1942. Three of the most negative elegies are variations on the same themes: the utopian site of exile in Hollywood as heaven or hell, and the prostitution of writers and composers by the film industry. Calling Hollywood a "planned village," the first elegy refers to the founding myth of wealthy Midwesterners in the late nineteenth century who sought to create a Christian utopia in Los Angeles. Real estate advertising exploited that myth by promising buyers a utopian life in Southern California. Clever marketing suggested that those who came here would benefit from tremendous savings, even in the realm of religion. According to Brecht's elegy, Hollywood served as both heaven and hell, thereby saving the rich a lot of money. The disparity of wealth in Los Angeles has always been most glaring in Hollywood. The exposure to the glamorous life of the successful serves as both a torment and a punishment for the unsuccessful, as the first elegy argues:

> The village of Hollywood was planned according to the notion
> People in these parts have of heaven. In these parts
> They have come to the conclusion that God
> Requiring a heaven and a hell, didn't need to
> Plan two establishments but
> Just one: heaven. It
> Serves the unprosperous, unsuccessful
> As hell.
>
> (*Poems* 380; GBA 12: 115)

The third elegy introduces the original Spanish name of the city of Los Angeles, El Pueblo de la Reina de los Angeles:

> The city is named after the angels
> And you meet angels on every hand.
> They smell of oil and wear golden pessaries
> And, with blue rings round their eyes
> Feed the writers in their swimming pools every morning.
>
> (*Poems* 380; GBA 12: 116)

The modern angels are the financial backers and starlets of the movie industry. The "smell of oil" alludes to the dependence of Hollywood on the major industries, in this case the energy industry, while the "golden pessaries" and the "blue rings round their eyes" draw attention to their wearers' promiscuity. The last line is a play on words that cannot be reproduced in English. The German word *Schwimmpfühle* is a Brechtian coinage that has three connotations: 1) swimming pool, 2) swamp *(Pfuhl)*, and 3) bed, couch, pillow *(Pfühl)*, implying debauchery. This multiple meaning turns the morning press conference into double prostitution: the financial backers and starlets report on their nightly debaucheries, while the writers are eager to record their sexual escapades for the tabloids (Fuhrmann 60). The fourth elegy includes the composers among the writers who prostitute themselves when they apply for employment by the movie industry. The iconic figure of Protestant church music is forced to produce pornography, while the poet of the *Divine Comedy* walks the streets to sell his diminished sexual charms:

> Beneath the green pepper trees
> The musicians play the whore, two by two
> With the writers. Bach
> Has written a Strumpet Voluntary *[Strichquartett]*. Dante wriggles
> His shriveled bottom.

> *(Poems* 380; GBA 12: 115)

Critics have suggested that the Bach and Dante figures are allegorical portraits of Eisler and Brecht in Hollywood.

Not only orthodox Marxists but also liberal and conservative Brecht scholars have drawn the conclusion from these lines that Brecht's California poetry was anti-American and critical of capitalist society. More thoughtful critics express regret that Brecht did not find any aspect of American culture to his liking. But these critics are missing the point: their arguments are reductive and demonstrate a lack of understanding of modernism. They interpret Brecht's poetry as purely mimetic, but it is not. These poems clearly demonstrate that Brecht needed to translate the utopian images of Los Angeles and Hollywood into an allegory of a modernist city that was ugly and uncharitable. In order to function as a modernist poet he had to assemble a counter-site in which the real site of Los Angeles was "simultaneously represented, contested, and inverted," as Michel Foucault said in a different context (24). To use Foucault's terminology, Los Angeles (and Hollywood) function as a "heterotopia" in Brecht's California poetry.

The distinction that Foucault makes between "utopia" and "heterotopia" is very helpful in identifying the modernism of Brecht's California poetry. Utopias are, according to Foucault, "counter-sites . . . in which the real sites can be found." Utopias function as mirrors: "In the mirror, I see myself there where I am not, in an unreal, virtual space that opens up behind the surface; I am over there, there where I am not, a sort of shadow that gives my own visibility to myself, that enables me to see myself there where I am absent" (Foucault 24). But the material mirror that exists in reality functions as a heterotopia. The heterotopia directs the eyes of the poet toward himself and reconstitutes himself where he is. It makes the place that he occupies "at once absolutely real, . . . and absolutely unreal" (Foucault 24). One could say that the site of one's exile is the heterotopia par excellence.

It is obvious that a more nuanced line of argument is required to do justice to Brecht's California poetry. My first claim is that most dimensions of Brecht's California poetry, except for the anti-American aspect, have simply been disregarded. Critics single out individual poems that seem to confirm their biases, and they neglect to look at the corpus as a whole. My second and more important line of argument is that Brecht's California poetry requires a dialectical assessment in terms of the modernism that shaped his perception of the place that offered him refuge until 1947, when he returned to Europe. Most critics have viewed his poems as mimetic, that is, as realistic representations of the localities and his personal opinions, but they need to be interpreted in terms of their modernist dialectics and their transformation of Brecht's views into objective statements.

As Peter Plagens has argued in his book on art on the West Coast, New York became America's greatest art center because it had "been ugliest the longest" (9). The Westside of Los Angeles, where Brecht and most of the exiles lived, was not as ugly as New York, and it lacked the qualities of poverty and shabbiness that Raymond Williams had considered a prerequisite for modernism. Brecht's poem comparing Los Angeles to hell demonstrates that he needed to establish its ugliness in order to become productive as a poet on the Westside. If he had lived in the slums of East Los Angeles, such a poem would not have been necessary.

Bertolt Brecht (1898–1956) arrived in San Pedro, the harbor of Los Angeles, by ship from Vladivostok on July 1, 1941. He had left Germany for Prague with his wife, actress Helene Weigel, and his son Stefan on the day after the burning of the Reichstag in February 1933. After visits to Paris and southern France, where most of the German exiles had settled, he moved to Denmark, where he stayed until 1939. The threat of a German invasion drove him from Denmark to Sweden and then to Finland in 1940, as he "chang[ed] countries more often than [his] shoes," as he said in his poem "To Those Born Later" ("An die Nachgeborenen") (*Poems* 318–20; GBA 12: 85–87). Finally, in 1941, he received an entry visa to the United States and traveled through the Soviet Union to Vladivostok, where he embarked on a ship that brought him to California. Brecht traveled with not only his wife and two children, but also an entourage of collaborators and lovers, Margarete Steffin and Ruth Berlau. Margarete Steffin was left behind in Moscow because she was seriously ill and died of tuberculosis shortly after Brecht's departure. Ruth Berlau accompanied Brecht and his family to Los Angeles, and later, in 1949, she also followed them to East Berlin. During the first month of his stay in the United States, Brecht and his family lived in a first-floor apartment at 1954 Argyle Avenue in Hollywood and were financially supported by a group of friends that included film director William Dieterle, Fritz Lang, and Ernst Lubitsch. In August 1941, the Brechts found a house on 25th Street in Santa Monica, and later they moved to a larger house on 26th Street that they eventually bought. Brecht and his family applied for American citizenship on the day after the attack on Pearl Harbor.

During his stay, Brecht worked twice for the movie industry, once as a screenwriter for Fritz Lang, and then, in collaboration with Lion Feuchtwanger, as writer of a screen story about a modern Joan of Arc who fought the German occupation of France in 1940. Brecht was very productive during his American exile, writing *Galileo* and *The Caucasian Chalk Circle (Der kaukasische Kreidekreis)*, two of his best-known plays, and creating a corpus of almost three hundred poems; his *Galileo* was performed in English translation in Beverly Hills and New York. Before Brecht left for Europe in October 1947, he testified before the House Un-American Activities Committee (HUAC) in Washington, D.C. The hearings ended with charges against the so-called Hollywood Ten, ten directors and screenwriters who were accused of communist infiltration of the motion-picture industry and sentenced for contempt of Congress in 1948 because they refused to testify. Brecht, who was originally the eleventh member of the Hollywood Ten, reached an understanding with the other ten that he would testify because of his immigrant status (he did not want to risk the loss of his recently obtained exit visa to Switzerland). During the hearings before HUAC, Brecht denied that he had ever applied to join the Communist Party. When asked about *The Measures Taken (Die Maßnahme)*, his didactic Leninist play of 1930, Brecht confused the members of the committee by calling it an adaptation of an old religious Japanese play, a Noh drama. In the end, Brecht went scot-free because he left the United States before any charges could be leveled against him (Ceplair and Eglund 263; Bentley, *Thirty Years of Treason*, 207–20). Brecht's testimony before HUAC was

FIGURE 7. Bertolt Brecht's house, 1063 Twenty-sixth Street, Santa Monica, 2005. Photograph by Juergen Nogai, Santa Monica.

recorded and later made available by Folkways Records, contributing to his rise to the status of an American cult figure.

The urban landscape of Brecht's American poems is Los Angeles, including Hollywood and Santa Monica. It is important to note, however, that the Los Angeles poems do not form the largest group within his corpus, even if one includes the "Hollywood Elegies," which Brecht wrote between 1942 and 1943 for twelve-tone composer Hanns Eisler, and the other California poems he contributed to the *Hollywood Songbook* (*Hollywooder Liederbuch*). The largest number of Brecht's American poems written between 1941 and 1947—almost one hundred—are devoted to the fight against fascism and the war against Nazi Germany. The other poems are either autobiographical, or deal with exile in general, or with death in exile, thematizing the suicide of Walter Benjamin at the Spanish border in 1940, or the death of Margarete Steffin in Moscow in 1941. One group of seven poems, entitled "Theater Poems," expound on the theory of epic theater. Other poems are simply songs that were added to plays or films, such as *The Private Life of the Master Race (Furcht und Elend des Dritten Reiches), Hangmen Also Die,* and *The Visions of Simone Machard (Die Gesichte der Simone Machard).* Then there is the love poetry, addressed to Ruth Berlau, and last but not least there are four long versions of the "Didactic Poem" ("Lehrgedicht"), Brecht's versification of the *Communist Manifesto* in hexameters, in the manner of Lucretius's *De rerum natura.* Because of the prosaic subject matter he never succeeded in this venture, although some friends considered this last work a masterpiece.

Although there is some overlap among these poems, they form self-contained cycles of seven to twenty poems, as, for example, the poems dedicated to Margarete Steffin, or those dealing with the theory of epic theater. One can also talk about a California or Los Angeles cycle of approximately twenty poems, including the "Hollywood Elegies." Brecht also wrote a few poems unrelated to the California poems that were critical of the United States, beginning with "Swastika and Double Cross.1944" ("Hakenkreuz und Doublecross.1944") in 1944 (GBA 15: 115–16) and ending with "The Anachronistic Procession or Freedom and Democracy" ("Freiheit und Democracy") in 1947 (*Poems* 409–14; GBA 15: 183–88). Except for its use of the term "double cross," which functions as metaphor for the treachery of capitalism, the first poem does not expressly refer to the United States, but instead to the alliance of fascism and capitalism. The date in the title suggests that "Double Cross" is to be identified with German state capitalism during the Nazi period and refers to its alliance with fascism in the war against the Soviet Union, symbolized by its emblems of hammer and sickle:

Swastika and Double Cross
Laid waste to the land, it was a shame:
Swastika was afraid of the sickle
And Double Cross feared the hammer.

        (GBA 15: 116)

On the other hand, the slogan "Freedom and Democracy" is an essential part of American political ideology. Brecht's poem is based on a text by Percy Bysshe Shelley, entitled "The Masque of Anarchy, written on the Occasion of the Massacre of Manchester, 1819." Shelley's poem deals with a workers' revolt that took place in Manchester and was bru-

tally suppressed by British government troops. Brecht had translated
twenty-five stanzas of the ballad and referred to it in 1938 to demonstrate that a Romantic poet could write in the realistic style, and that this
did not by any means require "the abandoning of imagination or of genuine artistry" (GBA 22.1: 432). Shelley makes effective use of allegory in
the ballad. At the head of the procession appears Murder, then come
Fraud and Hypocrisy, wearing the masks of members of the government,
and then appear many more "Destructions" disguised as "bishops,
lawyers, peers or spies." Anarchy comes last, "like Death in the Apocalypse." In "Freedom and Democracy," Brecht uses Shelley's ballad to
criticize the introduction of "fake" democracy of the U.S. Occupation
Zone in Germany, where elections took place for local governments in
May 1946 and for state parliaments in 1947. He perceived the elections
as a restoration not only of capitalism, but also of fascism. In spite of the
defeat of the Nazis Brecht was afraid that American imperialists were
ready to accept the return of the Nazis to power in order to extend their
influence over Western Europe. In Brecht's poem, an unnamed com-
mentator observes an "anachronistic procession" on its way to the bal-
lot boxes in Bavaria:

> Spring returned to Germany.
> In the ruins you could see
> Early green birch buds unfold
> Graceful, tentative and bold
>
> As from many a southern valley
> Voters left their houses to rally
> Forming a disjointed column
> Underneath two banners solemn
>
> Whose supports were all worm-eaten
> Their inscriptions weatherbeaten
> Though its gist appeared to be
> Freedom and Democracy.

> (*Poems* 409; GBA 15: 183)

The observer identifies the mouthing of timeworn slogans as a typical
form of popular support for Western democracy by referring to the national anthems of Britain and France, which are intoned together with
the tinkling sound of the U.S. dollar, symbolizing capitalism:

> At the head a featherbrain
> Sang with all his might and main:
> 'Allons, enfants, God save the King,
> And the dollar, Kling, Kling, Kling.'

But rather than indicting U.S. occupation policies, the observer directs his grim satire primarily against the former Nazis returning to power: the trust directors, the teachers, the medical doctors, the scientists, the anti-Semites, the judges, and the artists:

> Poets, painters, and musicians
> Seeking grub and good positions
> Noble souls, who now assure us
> They were no friends of the Führer's.
>
> (*Poems* 411; GBA 15: 186)

The procession moves through the ruins of Munich, the city of the Nazi movement, until it reaches the Brown House, the central office building of the Nazi Party in Germany. Six allegorical figures emerge from the building to join the procession: Oppression, Plague, Fraud, Stupidity, Murder, and Robbery. Finally, even the "great rats" from the ruins follow the procession, "squeaking 'Freedom!' as they flee / 'Freedom and Democracy!' " (*Poems* 414; GBA 15: 188). Although the poem is a denunciation of the perversion of American political values, the tenor of Brecht's ballad is anti-Nazi rather than anti-American. His assessment of U.S. postwar policies regarding West Germany appears to confirm his left-wing commitments, but Thomas Mann expressed similar ideas in his diaries and private letters.

The most pro-American poem of the California cycle is "The Democratic Judge" ("Der demokratische Richter") of 1942—also entitled "The Citizenship Examination" ("Das Bürgerschaftsexamen")—which begins with the lines:

> In Los Angeles, before the judge who examines people
> Trying to become citizens of the United States
> Came an Italian restaurant keeper.
>
> (*Poems* 385; GBA 15: 80)

The narrative could well have been based on a report in the *Los Angeles Times:* the poem tells the story of an Italian restaurant keeper who fails his citizenship examination again and again because his English is not good enough to understand the questions posed to him by a judge in Los Angeles. Asked about the Eighth Amendment of the Bill of Rights, about a successful general of the Civil War, and about the length of term of the president, the Italian gives the stereotypic answer: 1492. After the Italian appears before him three times the judge realizes that the applicant cannot learn the language and asks him how he earns his living. When the judge hears "by hard work," he asks the Italian about the discovery of America at his fourth appearance:

When
Was America discovered? And on the strength of his correct
Answer 1492,
He was granted his citizenship.

(*Poems* 385; GBA 15: 81)

The laconic ending of the poem should have made it into a classic among American high school texts on the United States' Constitution. The didactic example confirms the values of American democracy in simple and convincing terms and without reservation. The judge shows the kind of sympathy with the common people that Brecht considered the essence of American democracy (Lyon, *Brecht in America*, 341–46).

These values were severely tested during World War II by the existence of the so-called "war relocation centers" in California and other western states, the result of the American war hysteria after the Japanese attack on Pearl Harbor in December 1941. It was suspected that Japanese spies had directed the air raids from the ground in Hawaii, and additional acts of espionage and sabotage were expected on the West Coast. Seventy-four days after the Japanese attack on Pearl Harbor, on February 19, 1942, President Franklin D. Roosevelt issued Executive Order No. 9066:

Now, therefore, by virtue of the authority vested in me as President of the United States and Commander-in-Chief of the Army and Navy, I hereby authorize and direct the Secretary of War and the Military Commanders whom he may from time to time designate, whenever he or any designated Commander deems such action necessary or desirable, to prescribe military areas in such places and of such extent as he or the appropriate Military Commander may determine, from which any or all persons may be excluded, and with respect to which, the right of any person to enter, remain in, or leave shall be subject to whatever restrictions the Secretary of War or the appropriate Military Commander may impose in his discretion.

Since the order did not specifically mention any ethnic group, German, Italian, and Japanese aliens all became concerned that they might be affected by these restrictions. In the end, the restrictions were applied only to people of Japanese ancestry residing in the Western Defense Command zones, regardless of whether they were citizens or not. On March 2, 1942, General John L. DeWitt, western defense commander, issued an order that all persons of Japanese ancestry, defined as individuals with a percentage of Japanese blood of one thirty-second or more, be removed from the western portions of Washington, Oregon, California, and southern Arizona. A new civilian agency, the War Relocation Authority (WRA), was created by Executive Order No. 9102 on March 18, 1942, to develop removal plans for the people excluded from the military areas. Some 120,000 Japanese Americans, more than 70 percent of them U.S. citizens, were interned in ten war relocation centers. Only after 1945 did the U.S. government admit that there had not been a single case of Japanese disloyalty or sabotage during the entire war (Hersey 1–66; Pike 22–23).

The internment of the Japanese Americans had a direct bearing on many of the German exiles on the West Coast because they were subject to the same executive order. Legally, the German exiles were considered "enemy aliens" unless they were American citizens or had a passport of a neutral or allied country (Heinrich and Thomas Mann had Czech passports, for example, and Alfred Döblin was a French citizen). Evacuating German Americans and German and Italian resident aliens was considered in 1942, but it was never authorized. In the end, the German and Italian "enemy aliens" were subject only to a curfew, from 8 P.M. to 6 A.M. daily, and their non–work related travel was limited to a five-mile radius of their homes. Austrians were exempt from this regulation because the Allies considered the First Republic the first victim of Nazi aggression. In February 1942, however, this less restrictive treatment of the European "enemy aliens" had not yet been decided, as Brecht recorded with apprehension in his diary on February 26: "We are, because of German descent, enemy aliens, and there is apprehension that we have to leave the coast, unless they make an exception for Hitler's enemies." Brecht was wrong insofar as it was not their German descent that caused them to be considered enemy aliens, but rather their status as immigrants from an enemy country. In the case of the Japanese, however, the War Relocation Authority considered descent and even blood quantum the determining criteria, violating the rights of even those Japanese who were U.S. citizens.

On the same date in February 1942 when he made the diary entry quoted above, Brecht observed the treatment of the Japanese: "The Japanese fishermen and gardeners will be sent into camps. The farmers never liked them and one is afraid of their disloyalty." Thomas Mann, on the other hand, never referred to the evacuation of the Japanese in his diaries except to make a few racist remarks. In his diary and in letters to Agnes Meyer he referred to the Japanese leadership as the "yellow ones" (die Gelben) or, using a kind of Wagnerian terminology, "the yellow archfiends" *(die gelben Tückebolde)* *(Tagebücher 1940–1943* 357; *Briefwechsel* 346, 337). It must be acknowledged that the term "die Gelben" was also once used by Brecht in his poem "Again and Again" ("Immer wieder"), when he referred to the forced exodus of the Japanese Americans from their homes: "At the coast from their homes / The yellow ones move into the barren camps" (GBA 15: 77). Brecht never repeated this racist slip of the tongue, but neither did Thomas Mann continue to refer to the Japanese with racist slurs throughout the rest of the war.

Other restrictions placed on civilians were, however, of great concern to Thomas Mann, at least insofar as they affected his own status. In several letters to Agnes Meyer, the wife of the owner of the *Washington Post,* who had considerable political influence, Mann asked her to intervene to obtain a special travel permit and other exemptions for him (*Briefwechsel* 349, 359, 368). Together with Arturo Toscanini, Albert Einstein, and Bruno Walter, on February 13, 1942, he sent a telegram to President Roosevelt requesting special consideration of antifascist refugees, and he reiterated this request in his testimony before a congressional committee in Los Angeles on March 7, 1942. But the fate of the Japanese American was never Mann's concern. He mentioned that they were treated with "friendliness and patience" during the hearings in Los Angeles, but he never criticized their evacuation and internment (*Briefwechsel* 381).

Brecht reported on the evacuation orders for the Japanese, including American citizens of Japanese ancestry, in his diary of March 25:

> About 100,000 Japanese (including American citizens) are evacuated from the coast for military reasons. It is wonderful how humanism survives in the face of psychosis and hysteria. At the registration bureau, where we also had to register as "enemy aliens," I saw an old Japanese woman who was half-blind. She apologized to the others waiting in line that she needed so much time to complete the registration form. Everybody smiled, the American officials were very polite.

Brecht did not record in his diary his response to the transport of all persons of Japanese ancestry to assembly centers at fairgrounds and racetracks in Los Angeles on May 9, 1942. At that time, posters with evacuation procedures were posted all over the city, explaining that all Japanese were required to report to a Civil Control Station within two days with a limited amount of luggage, which would be carried with them when they departed for the assembly center.

Brecht accepted the official explanation that military troops were used only to protect the Japanese from attacks by Americans. Instead of questioning the explanation, Brecht's main focus was on acts of blue-collar solidarity, such as workers shopping in Japanese stores that they had avoided before. This interest is reflected in his epigram "Fishing Tackle" ("Das Fischgerät"). The Japanese American fishermen on Terminal Island in the Port of Los Angeles were the first to be relocated because they were suspected of giving signals to Japanese submarines that were operating off the California coast. (Although a few Japanese submarines indeed sank some cargo ships off the West Coast and shelled an oil storage facility north of Santa Barbara, it was later learned that their intelligence was not based on shore signals.) Since the Japanese American fishermen were evacuated with only forty-eight hours' notice and were allowed to take only what they could carry in two hands, they had to leave their fishing equipment behind, and their fishing vessels were impounded. Brecht himself owned a treasured fishing tackle that his son had given him as a birthday present. In his epigram he writes that he liked to think that

> this fishing tackle
> Was left to him by those Japanese fishermen
> Whom they have now driven from the West Coast into camps
> As suspect aliens
> To remind [him] of so many
> Unsolved but not insoluble
> Questions of mankind.
>
> (*Poems* 386; GBA 15: 94–95)

What is now considered "a legacy of shame" (Armor and Wright 155) was excused by Brecht in the 1940s as a regrettable but unavoidable action by the authorities. He showed genuine sympathy for the Japanese American workers and did not approve of their removal, but he considered their internment only a reminder of the many "unsolved but not insoluble questions of mankind" that can be postponed for a future solution. The weak conclusion to Brecht's epigram reads almost like an apology for the policies of the U.S. government. If Brecht had been so radically anti-American, Executive Order No. 9066 would have made an easy target for an attack of what he considered American fascism (see also Lyon, *Brecht in America*, 343).

Neither Brecht nor Thomas Mann ever showed any genuine understanding of the fact that the internment of Japanese American citizens was in violation of their constitutional rights. Before the congressional committee that held hearings in Los Angeles on March 7, 1942, Thomas Mann made a point of speaking only on behalf of the German and Italian refugees—"it is not my business to talk about the Japanese problem,"

he said—and pleaded for the exemption of the Europeans from the regulations that were "perhaps necessary in the . . . case of the Japanese"
(Frey 209). For Brecht, the "Japanese problem" was at least a "question
of mankind," although his uncritical use of the phrase "question of
mankind," which has the ring of the abstract humanitarianism of
Weimar classicism, is strangely out of character for his poetry. A newspaper clipping in his diary entitled "Seek to Till Aliens' Land" shows that
Brecht was well aware of the economic advantage to white farmers who
could now acquire Japanese-owned farmland at low prices and cultivate
it without the competition of the Japanese (GBA 27: 62).

In another poem, entitled "Again and Again" ("Immer wieder"), Brecht
focuses on the altruism of man after massacres, reminding his readers:

> Again and again after massacres
> There is a human being, stripping his shirt and using it
> To bind the wounds of his fellow man.

(GBA 15: 77)

The two examples Brecht uses to support this general observation are
from the Soviet Union, where Russian women fed German prisoners of
war who had destroyed their villages, and from the American West
Coast, where the population encouraged the Japanese Americans not to
despair when they were deported to relocation camps:

> From the masses on the sidewalk
> There comes a shout: Don't despair!
> It won't take an eternity!

But the two examples are not congruent, and their juxtaposition is ultimately jarring, especially when the victims at the end of the stanza are
said to feel sorry for their "butchers":

> To the destroyers of their huts,
> Now prisoners in the winter battle,
> The Soviet peasant women give loaves of bread:
> Take the bread, you miserable!

> The butchers are enraged.
> Their victims say of them:
> It's a shame about them.

(GBA 15: 77–78)

Neither the two groups of victims nor the two groups of oppressors have
anything in common. The American bystanders cannot be compared to
the Soviet peasant women, nor can the U.S. government be compared to

the German invaders. The examples must be read as a sequence, as a step from one level to another. The American example is many degrees removed from the Russian situation, which requires much more effort and compassion. The reference to the "butchers," obviously directed against the German leadership, remains strangely oblique.

As in the previous poem, the empathy expressed for the Japanese Americans is stronger than the indictment of the U.S. government. The final line of the second stanza—"It won't take an eternity!"—comes across as a faint apology for an unpopular government action. One would have expected Brecht to protest this obvious injustice, but he portrays it as only a minor calamity that is offset by expressions of kindness by people who have no reason to consider the Japanese Americans their enemies (Lyon, *Brecht in America,* 343), but even this is not clearly expressed.

In order to understand Brecht's California poetry as modernist poetry one has to look at his household poems and at his garden poetry written in imitation of classical Latin poetry that reflects on nature and politics. Ovid is the most obvious model, but he also imitates Horace and Lucretius. The poems devoted to his garden in Santa Monica and the epigrams dedicated to cherished objects in the author's study and household—"Of Sprinkling the Garden" (*Poems* 382; GBA 15: 89), "Reading the Paper While Brewing the Tea" (*Poems* 382; GBA 12: 123), and "The Lovely Fork" (*Poems* 404; GBA 15: 161)—form a special cycle of their own and constitute the nucleus of his modernist exile poetry in Los Angeles. Brecht exploited the antithetical character of the epigram to serve his purposes. In "Summer 1942" ("Sommer 1942"), for example, everyday activities are juxtaposed with events of the war to emphasize the poetic persona's safe life in exile on the one hand, and his awareness of the daily carnage of World War II on the other:

Day after day
I see the fig trees in the garden
The rosy faces of the dealers who buy lies
The chessmen on the corner table
And the newspapers with their reports
Of bloodbaths in the Soviet Union.

(*Poems* 379; GBA 15: 74)

This poem is evidence of a specific poetics of exile that Brecht developed in Southern California. He was fully aware that writing German poetry in Los Angeles amounted to "withdrawing into an ivory tower," as he wrote in a diary entry on April 5, 1942, in which he compared his craft to the art of a goldsmith: "There is something quaint, something oddball, something limited about it." He thus placed the scenes of domestic life in California in the tradition of Theocritus in antithetical opposition to events of World War II, explaining that "the battle for Smolensk is a battle for poetry too" (GBA 27: 79–80).

In another epigram, "The Mask of Evil" ("Die Maske des Bösen"), the poetic persona refers to the image of a Japanese mask in his study:

> On my wall hangs a Japanese carving
> The mask of an evil demon, decorated with golden lacquer.
> Sympathetically I observe
> The swollen veins of the forehead, indicating
> What a strain it is to be evil.
>
> (Poems 383; GBA 12: 124).

Here the realistic observation provides for the humorously dialectical resolution that compassion is so much easier than being evil.

The central poem of this cycle, although not an epigram, is "Garden in Progress" (*Poems* 395–97; GBA 15: 109–10), which is often classified among the Charles Laughton poems, those poems that deal with the translation of *Galileo* by the British actor and with the production of *Galileo* starring Laughton at the Coronet Theatre in Beverly Hills in 1947. This poem should be grouped with Brecht's other garden poems, however, because it is first and foremost a poem about Los Angeles and culture under the threat of extinction.

The garden referred to in the poem was indeed Charles Laughton's garden, which was situated at 14954 Corona Del Mar in Pacific Palisades, close to a steep bluff above the Pacific Ocean. Properties in such a location were subject to landslides, which are a common occurrence in the Los Angeles area, but Laughton was unfamiliar with the phenomenon and was deeply disturbed when his garden suffered a landslide in 1944. As Brecht reported in his diary, Laughton visited him and told him how ashamed he felt bothering Brecht with his misfortune, since he realized that the playwright had not had a roof of his own over his head for more than decade. Later Brecht consoled him with stanzas from this poem, which stress the Schillerian aesthetics of "transitoriness as the essence of beauty" (GBA 27: 202). The indirect allusion to Schiller is remarkable because Brecht had always expressed contempt for the dramatist of Weimar classicism, and a reference to his aesthetics was totally out of character for the modern playwright. But this is precisely the reason this statement requires our critical attention.

The sequence of the stanzas was never established because there is no final manuscript in Brecht's handwriting, only copies with different arrangements of the stanzas in the handwriting of his collaborators. Elisabeth Hauptmann provided a reading for Brecht's collected works of 1976, but this order was never authorized by Brecht (Knopf, *Gelegentlich: Poesie,* 46–53). Reconstructing the sequence, however, is not essential for the interpretation of the poem. There cannot be any doubt that the poem establishes the landslide as a paradigm of exile culture under the threat of destruction. The poem is one of only a few of Brecht's California poems with an English title, and it is highly ironic in its presentation of the garden as a work in progress on the one hand, and as a piece of land progressing downhill on the other. Landslides drag parts of the garden down the cliffs without warning. The narrator sees the completion of the garden in jeopardy; there is no time to be lost:

> Alas, the lovely garden, placed high above the coast
> Is built on crumbling rock. Landslides
> Drag parts of it into the depth without warning. Seemingly
> There is not much time left in which to complete it.
>
> (*Poems* 397; GBA 15: 109)

With the information that the garden is full of plants from all over the world, the poem refers to exile and asylum: the "lord of the garden" took in not "only his own plants and trees, but also the plants and trees of his neighbours" (*Poems* 397; GBA 15: 378). The "exiled" plants thrive more successfully than at home, and some of the bushes, addressed as "immigrants," surprise themselves with the fuller bloom of a daring red, "unmindful of their origin" (*Poems* 396; GBA 15: 109).

The main part of the poem plays on the derivation of the word "culture" from the Latin *colere,* equating the cultivation of the soil with the work of the poet and actor. Laughton's garden serves as a powerful metaphor of culture, precariously placed on the brink of destruction. Both garden and culture are endangered by violence. The pre-Columbian garden sculpture of a granite snake's head serves as a historical reminder of the destruction of old civilizations:

> the Indian
> Granite snake's head . . . lies by the fountain
> As if patiently waiting for
> A number of civilizations to collapse.
>
> (*Poems* 395; GBA 15: 110)

The poem evokes the noise of military tanker trucks rumbling on the Pacific Coast Highway below and the thunder of guns from warships performing exercises in the Santa Monica Bay. The image of a cactus blooming for only a single night to the noise of guns is Brecht's defiant counterexample to death and destruction:

> the Arizona cactus, height of a man, which each year
> Blooms for a single night, this year
> To the thunder of guns from warships exercizing
> With white flowers as big as your fist and as delicate
> As a Chinese actor.

(Poems 397; GBA 15: 109)

The Arizona cactus delivers a moral addressed to both the artist and the writer: they must make use of their brief time to complete their work in spite of looming destruction.

Previously neglected, "Garden in Progress" must be considered one of Brecht's most important exile poems, especially in view of its indirect reference to Friedrich Schiller. Brecht identifies here with an aesthetics that proclaim the short-lived existence of beauty. In his poem "Lament" ("Nänie"), Schiller had argued that the essence of beauty was the fact that it must perish:

> Even beauty has to die; what overcomes men and gods
> Does not move the iron breast of the Zeus of the Styx.
> Only once did love soften the ruler of the shades,
> And even then he sternly called back his gift at the very threshold.
> Aphrodite cannot cure the lovely boy of the wound
> The boar savagely ripped in his delicate flesh.
> When the god-like hero falls at the Scaean gate and
> Falling fulfills his destiny; his immortal mother cannot save him.
> But she rises from the sea with all the daughters of Nereus,
> And laments her glorified son.
> Look, the gods are weeping and all the goddesses too,
> Weeping that beauty must pass, that perfect things must die.

(Penguin Book of German Verse 242)

But "there is splendor" even in this destruction: "to be a lament in the mouths of those we loved" is more desirable than having "no distinction" and going down "to Orcus unsung."

The observation that there are perhaps more positive poems than negative ones in the Los Angeles cycle may help set the record straight and emphasize that an assessment of this corpus would be incomplete and misleading without these positive poems. The three or five poems about Los Angeles as hell—even if they are not representative of the corpus as a whole—are relevant for his poetry if we consider them as modernist.

Brecht's assessment of Los Angeles, including Hollywood, is much more ambivalent than the current criticism of his poetry tends to admit. It matters very little to most critics that Brecht loved to sit "in his little garden in Santa Monica, reading Horace in the pepper tree's shade," as he confessed in his poem "Letters about Things Read" ("Brief über Gelesenes"). The subtitle makes a specific reference to Horace and his *Epistles* II, i. Brecht's poem deals with the function of poetry and poetic excellence:

> I read in Horace of a certain Varius
> Who hymned Augustus (that is, what luck, his generals
> And the Romans' corruption did for him). Only small fragments
> Preserved in another man's work attest
> Great poetic skill. It was not worth to copy more.

> (*Poems* 391; GBA 15: 113)

The poetic persona is delighted to learn that the panegyrics of Lucius Varius Rufus (ca. 70–5 B.C.) were lost in spite of their classical beauty. They were not worth recording because of their utterly abject content (see Hohenwallner 178–85). Brecht was not forced to hymn Hitler, as were his fellow writers who stayed in Germany. Los Angeles offered him refuge from persecution for more than six years. What is important, however, is that he did not let this idyllic refuge temper his attitude concerning the task of poetry. Neither the Los Angeles utopia nor excessive poetic skills were to prevent him from observing the lessons to be learned from the classics:

> With pleasure I read
> How Horace traced the Saturnian art of verse
> Back to the peasant burlesques
> Which did not spare great families, till
> The police forbade lampoons, compelling
> Those with a grudge to develop
> An art more noble and air it
> In lines more subtle. At least that is how
> I construe the passage.

> (*Poems* 391; GBA 15: 114)

The poetic persona interprets great poetry as a response to censorship. Poetic excellence evolves from resistance to oppression. Critical content is the only justification of formal excellence.

Brecht's interpretation of reality as he construed it for his poetic persona also applies to the image of America that we find in his poetry. Although the positive image, associated with the "common people," prevailed, the negative, represented by what he perceived as an alliance of government and big business, appeared more influential. Brecht's initial fascination with America during the 1920s had faded during his first visit in 1935–36 (Lyon, *Brecht in America*, 3–20). The scholarly consensus is that during his American exile Brecht encountered the crassest form of capitalism (Knopf, *Brecht-Handbuch* 2: 142; Knopf in GBA 12: 399; Mennemeier 179), but this applies only to the movie industry, because the defense industry of World War II implemented many of the programs of the New Deal and offered skilled jobs and equal pay to women and minorities. As his poems show, Brecht sided with the "common people" in the United States (Lyon 341–45). This is best demonstrated by one of the photo epigrams that was written for the *War Primer (Kriegsfibel)* but not included in the final edition, which was published in East Germany in 1955. The photo shows an American soldier rescuing a black teenager from an angry mob in downtown Detroit, and the text records the young man's voice and reaction as follows:

> When they had beaten me up and brought me to city hall
> A soldier, who was kind, helped me to escape
> In order to do that he must have been more courageous
> Than in the battles of Kiska and Bataan and El Guettar.
>
> (GBA 12: 273)

Brecht emphasized that common servicemen saved many blacks during the Detroit riots of June 1944, but East German censors did not want any positive statements about American soldiers to appear in the *War Primer*.

Because of his preconceived ideas Brecht sometimes appears to have perceived solidarity among the "common people" that did not exist, as, for example, when he described the reaction of the Los Angeles population to the bombing of Hiroshima and Nagasaki on August 6 and 9, 1945: "When the first newspaper reports reached Los Angeles, people realized that this meant the end of the horrible war and the return of their sons and brothers. But instead the big city rose in mourning. The playwright heard the bus conductors and sales girls in the fruit markets express only fright. Victory had arrived, but it was the disgrace of a defeat" (GBA 25: 65). When one reads of the boisterous victory celebrations on Hollywood Boulevard on VJ Day, one has to remember that they took place more than a week after the bombings, on August 15, 1945, and Brecht was correct in his report of the initial reaction of the "common people" of Los Angeles to the news of the destruction of Hiroshima and Nagasaki in early August.

Brecht's involvement with the movie industry in Hollywood confirmed his anticapitalist bias. The production of *Hangmen Also Die* in 1942, however, cannot serve as a typical example of U.S. capitalism, because Arnold Pressburger was an independent producer and did not represent any of the major studios. Financially Brecht did not fare badly as screenwriter, receiving between $8,000 and $10,000 for the screenplay (Lyon, *Brecht in America*, 64). His conflict with Pressburger and Fritz Lang was about the screen credits that were denied to him, even after a hearing before the Screen Writers Guild and despite the support of Fritz Lang. This hearing shows that Brecht was not naïve in his dealings with the movie industry, and he knew how to defend his claim through the proper channels. It was simply bad luck that he lost.

But there is no denying that Brecht tried again and again to manipulate the system in his favor (Lyon, *Brecht in America*, 58–71), but because he was not a major player he failed to exercise any influence. This did not deter him from submitting new screenplays to the movie industry. When they failed, he sometimes directed his poetic rage against his own willingness to be bought and against the film moguls and bankers who were not willing to pay his price. He was depressed about his failures in playing roulette with film stories, but too proud to admit that he was ready to sell out (Lyon, *Brecht in America*, 72–79). His Hollywood poems served as a sort of evidence that he had not betrayed his political and aesthetic convictions. As he wrote in the poem "The Volunteer Security Guards" ("Die freiwilligen Wächter"), his literary works served as "guards" who were watching him and preventing him from making compromising business deals:

My literary works volunteered
To serve me as some security guards
Who are protecting me in this city of sales.

Expensive houses and houses with exotic furniture
Are out of bounds for me. I am allowed to see certain people
Only if I can prove that it is for business.
I am not allowed to invite them for dinner.
When I talked about buying a beautifully crafted table,

I was met with derisive laughter. If I wanted to buy a pair of trousers,
I would certainly hear: Don't you have one pair already?

They would watch over me in this city
In order to say they know one writer
Who does not sell out.

(GBA 15: 96)

According to the poem Brecht lived a frugal life and was unable to buy any furniture, or even a second pair of pants. It is thus amusing to read Brecht's diary entry in February 1944 in which he records that he bought a new pair of pants when he received the news that Lion Feuchtwanger had sold the film rights to *The Visions of Simone Machard,* for which Brecht received $20,000 for his contribution (GBA 27: 183; Lyon, *Brecht in America,* 78).

But Brecht was too honest to deceive himself that his authentic works would protect him from selling out. He came to realize that in order to write his modernist plays, he needed, as he confessed in a poem of 1942, "Five movies with a happy-end / 10,000 Dollars in hard currency / One or two wars" (GBA 15: 82). This cynicism explains the bitterness expressed in Brecht's Hollywood poems that is rarely encountered in the rest of his California poetry. While his California poems deal with problems of exile, World War II, and the survival of mankind, Brecht's Hollywood poems are directed exclusively against the culture industry. Their bitter tone was derived from the typical exile dichotomy between mundane employment and authentic work that he could not resolve. This dichotomy established a falsely puritanical stance toward Hollywood that fetishized the problem rather than analyzed it. In another poem, entitled "Landscape of Exile" ("Die Landschaft des Exils"), in which the signifiers are clearly identified with the problem, the poem's persona, recording the "gaiety" and "joy" at various stations of exile, is able to admit that "[t]he oil derricks and the thirsty gardens of Los Angeles / And the ravines of California at evening and the fruit market / Did not leave the messenger of misfortune unmoved" (*Poems* 364; GBA 15: 88). But here the position of the observer is clearly identified in contrast to the "gaiety" and beauty of the locale. Nobody would mistake the "messenger of misfortune," as he saw himself, for a happy traveler or adventurous explorer.

The question of mimesis versus modernism is difficult to resolve because of Brecht's concept and practice of realism in exile. Realism is often presented as a predecessor of modernism. As Fredric Jameson suggests, " 'modernist' transformation can be identified as [realism's] cancellation, if not its complete negation" (120). However, Brecht's realism was not mimetic, but critical, and the critical dimension was most important to him. He announced that "the critical element in realism cannot be denied. That is decisive. A mere reflection of reality would not be in our interest, even if it would be possible. Reality must be criticized, when it is formed into a work of art; reality must be criticized in a realistic fashion" (GBA 22.1: 136). A case in point is his poem "California Autumn" ("Kalifornischer Herbst"), which Brecht wrote in 1941, when he lived with his family in a small house on 25th Street in Santa Monica and used to visit William Dieterle, who lived in a country house in the Hollywood Hills.

> In my garden
> Are nothing but evergreens. If I want to see autumn
> I drive to my friend's country house in the hills. There
> I can stand for five minutes and see a tree
> Stripped of its foliage, and foliage stripped of its trunk.
>
> (*Poems* 383; GBA 15: 44)

Brecht employs the conventions of the Latin pastoral elegy to establish the contrast between city and country. He uses the fact that there were no deciduous trees in his garden to criticize life in Los Angeles as unnatural because the plants in his garden do not show the change of seasons. The countryside, on the other hand, is made to appear as natural not only because it shows a tree stripped of its leaves, but also because it is the place where his friend lives and human relationships are cultivated. But Brecht is honest enough to record that there are also deciduous trees in the city that lose their leaves, adding the following lines that suggest the uncertainty of the future: "I saw a big autumn leaf which the wind / Was driving along the road [*Straße*], and I thought: tricky / To reckon that leaf's future" (*Poems* 383; GBA 15: 44). Although the German word "Straße" (street) places the scene in an unmistakably urban context, the English translation introduces an ambiguity with "road" that is not in the original. Brecht's first version of the last three lines, containing instead of "Straße" the word "Rinnstein" (curbstone or gutter) (GBA 15: 340), was even more explicit about the location of the scene and its bleak implications for man's future in the city. For Brecht, the "gutter" was the lowest state of human existence, as the last speech of his Galileo figure shows (GBA 15: 179; see also the next chapter). In the end, he selected "Straße," a less melodramatic term, to present reality, to contest and criticize it, as his poetics demanded.

For Brecht, realism was obviously not a photographic reflection of reality, but instead a creative projection that demonstrated a critical attitude. He developed a model that allowed him to change realist conventions and to present reality, as he transformed it in his poetry. As a realist, Brecht did not want to repeat what was already known. Bettina Englmann provides an acute insight when she says that "Brecht's demand of realist literature was a demand for deconstruction" (104). For this reason, in his poetry Brecht presented Los Angeles as a "heterotopia" that is, "simultaneously represented, contested, and inverted" (Foucault 24). Brecht said that "reality changes; in order to present it, we must change the mode of representation" (GBA 22.1: 410). His California poetry is a prime example of modernist poetics in exile.

CHAPTER 4

The Dialectic of Modern Science

Brecht's Galileo

During his exile in Denmark, Brecht selected Galileo Galilei (1564–1642), an early representative of modern science, as protagonist for a play that he began to write in October 1938. He represents Galileo as a scientist who first resisted the authorities of his time, but, when threatened with torture or death by the Inquisition, complied in order to survive for the sake of science. Brecht presents Galileo's recantation as a cunning device to allow him to continue his experiments in secret and achieve earth-shaking results in his research. Because he recanted Galileo was able to entrust a copy of his manuscript of the *Discorsi* to his student Andrea, who smuggled it out of Italy to Holland, where it was made available to the international scientific community of the seventeenth century. Making an obvious reference to contemporary history, Brecht's Galileo advises his student, "Take care when you travel through Germany with the truth under your coat!" (GBA 5: 106). Although Galileo is depicted as an antihero, his weakness in dealing with the Church is virtually excused in Brecht's work. The preservation of the results of his research outweighs his betrayal of science. As Peter D. Smith has argued, Brecht's Galileo personifies "the archetypal scientist and represents the plight of the intellectual attempting to survive beneath the Nazi regime" (271).

The model for Brecht's Galileo was the Danish physicist Niels Bohr (1885–1962), whose research on the fission of uranium Brecht considered as important as Galileo's studies. There is no parallel in Bohr's life, however, to Galileo's recantation. During the German occupation of

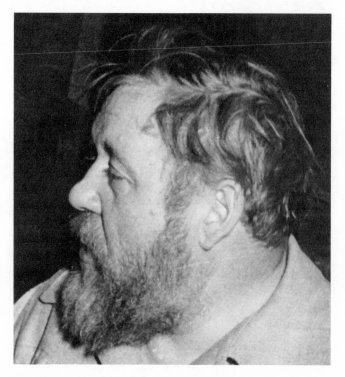

FIGURE 8. Charles Laughton as Galileo in 1947. Photograph
by Ruth Berlau, courtesy of Akademie der Künste Archiv,
Brecht-Weigel-Gedenkstätte, Berlin.

Denmark Bohr escaped to England, but this happened after Brecht's play
was completed. The first version of the play, the so-called Danish version, was finished by December 1938 and premiered in September 1943
in Zurich, Switzerland. Its title was *And Yet It Moves / The Life of
Galilei (Die Erde bewegt sich / Leben des Galilei)*.

Six years after the first version was completed, in December 1944,
Brecht began writing an English version of the play, entitled *Galileo*, in
collaboration with the British movie actor Charles Laughton. The
bombing of Hiroshima and Nagasaki in August 1945 inspired a total
change in the concept of the play and its protagonist. As Brecht says in
the introduction to the second version, the so-called American version,
"the 'Atomic Age' made its debut in Hiroshima in the midst of our
work. Overnight the biography of the founder of modern physics appeared totally different. The infernal effect of the Big Bomb put Galileo's

conflict with the authorities of his time into a new and sharper relief" (GBA 24: 241).

Not only did Brecht and Laughton present Galileo's secret resistance as a myth, but they also made him responsible for the ethical failures of science during the twentieth century. Galileo was now explicitly condemned as a traitor to science and humanity. The model for the new Galileo was Albert Einstein, whom Brecht severely criticized in his diary for his demand "that the atom bomb should not be handed over to other countries, especially Russia." Accusing him of casting the United Nations in the image of Standard Oil, Brecht called Einstein "a brilliant brain in his own field, housed in the head of a bad violinist and eternal schoolboy." Brecht added that it was "dawning on the other scientists who are involved in the production of the atom bomb . . . that freedom of research [might] be considerably restricted if the new source of energy was treated as monopoly of the military" (diary, October 28, 1945).

A third and final version of the play, the so-called German version, entitled *The Life of Galilei (Das Leben des Galilei)*, is basically a translation of the American version into German, although some material was added and the wording in some cases expanded and changed. The German version was first published in 1955 and premiered the same year in Cologne, West Germany. This text was also used for the Berlin production of 1957 that Brecht initiated but was not unable to see performed because he died six months before its premiere. The difference between the American and the German versions is one of emphasis. Influenced by news of weapons of even greater destructive power than the atom bomb, such as the cobalt and hydrogen bomb, Brecht put a more distinctive stress on the ethics of science and the threat of mass destruction in the final German version. The obvious model for this Galileo figure was J. Robert Oppenheimer (1904–67). In his diary on July 8, 1954, Brecht noted that Oppenheimer had "moral objections to the hydrogen bomb," but was now "packed off to the wilderness." He did not accept Oppenheimer's defense, claiming it "reads as if it was by a man who stands accused by a tribe of cannibals of having refused to go for the meat. And then claims by way of excuse that during the manhunt he was only collecting firewood for the cauldron."

Judging from Horkheimer and Adorno's *Dialectic of Enlightenment*, Brecht could not have made a better choice of a figure to represent modern science. In almost every aspect, Brecht's Galileo displays the same scientific attitude for which Adorno and Horkheimer faulted Francis Bacon. Horkheimer and Adorno characterized Bacon as overcoming superstition, on the one hand, but putting a "disenchanted nature" under the control of mankind, on the other. The same applied to Brecht's Galileo. The following quote from *Dialectic of Enlightenment* could apply to both men: "Knowledge, which is power, knows no limits, either in its enslavement of creation or in its deference to worldly masters" (DE 2). The similarities between these figures is not astonishing since both Bacon (1561–1626) and Galileo (1564–1642) were considered founding fathers of modern experimental science and their lives spanned almost the same years. What is perhaps surprising is that both Brecht and Adorno and Horkheimer selected figures from the history of science in order to explain the evils of modernity: the capitalistic exploitation of nature, and that progress had become regression since the beginning of the Enlightenment. While the scholars from the Institute for Social Research saw evil in the development of modern science since the seventeenth century, the playwright expanded upon this concept and connected his Galileo figure to the nuclear scientists of the Manhattan Project of the 1940s. This was a bold conclusion since Galileo delayed progress only by his compliance with the authorities, whereas his peers of the twentieth century developed weapons of mass destruction based on their government-sponsored research.

This is not to suggest that Adorno and Horkheimer influenced Brecht in his choice of Galileo, since Brecht had selected his protagonist in Denmark in 1938, three years before he met the scholars of the Institute for Social Research in Santa Monica. Adorno had reviewed Brecht's *Threepenny Opera* and *Mahagonny* during the late 1920s. Brecht must have met him before 1941, because in his diary he referred to changes in Adorno's physical appearance when he saw him in California. In addition to their social contact in Los Angeles, recorded in Brecht's diary and Adorno's letters, there is also evidence that Brecht attended some of the seminars conducted by Adorno and Horkheimer. The minutes of some of the seminars, available in Horkheimer's collected works, record Brecht's contributions to the discussions. In the long run, however, Brecht kept his distance from the members of the Institute for Social Research and considered their theoretical discussions material for his projected novel about the Tuis, which was to be a satire of the empty talk and lack of political action by intellectuals. Therefore, it is not likely that Brecht would have taken his cue for his new Galileo figure from Adorno and Horkheimer, even though the *Dialectic of Enlightenment* was available in mimeographed form as of 1944.

However, both the Frankfurt School and Brecht started with the same

assumption that experimental science as conceived by Francis Bacon and
practiced by Galileo Galilei led to the development of modern technology, which exploited nature and was manipulated by governments and
big business. In the opening paragraph of the *Dialectic of Enlightenment*
Adorno and Horkheimer announce that "the wholly enlightened earth
is radiant with triumphant calamity" (1). This statement appears to
point toward the atomic bomb, but they did not follow through with this
idea; they only mention the dive-bomber as a more effective form of artillery. To be sure, it was impossible for the authors of the *Dialectic of
Enlightenment* to know about the construction of the atomic bomb in
1944, but they could have added a paragraph to the 1947 publication,
as they included another thesis in the chapter "Elements of Anti-
Semitism." With his *Galileo* of 1947, Brecht carries the argument to its
logical conclusion when he asserts that science that surrendered knowledge to the authorities to use it as it suits their needs has betrayed its mission. The news of the nuclear devastation of Hiroshima and Nagasaki
undoubtedly had a much stronger impact on him than on Adorno and
Horkheimer.

Brecht had an intense interest in Francis Bacon that may have been
even stronger than that demonstrated by Adorno and Horkheimer in the
first chapter of *Dialectic of Enlightenment*. After Marx and Hegel no
other philosopher influenced Brecht more than Bacon. As Ralph J. Ley
has shown, "no examination of the technique of *Verfremdung* [alien-
ation, that is, the breaking of illusion] could attempt to do full justice to
a proper understanding of the Brechtian methodology without coming
to grips with the influence exerted by the English philosopher" (174).
Brecht utilized Bacon's works when he wrote *Galileo*. Scholars have
shown that some of the seminal statements of Brecht's Galileo can be
traced back to quotations from Bacon (Ley 181; Schumacher, *Drama
und Geschichte*, 40–41). In scene 4, for example, when he declares that
" 'Truth is the daughter of Time, not of Authority,' " the citation is
clearly indicated by quotations marks, although the source is not listed
(GBA 5: 137). Similarly, in scene 13 he states that "the intent of science
is to ease up human existence" (GBA 5: 180).

In 1939 Brecht wrote a short story with Francis Bacon as the protagonist. Entitled "The Experiment" ("Das Experiment"), the story shows
obvious parallels between Bacon's life and that of Galileo (Ley 186–87).
Brecht's *Short Organum for the Theater (Kleines Organon für das Theater)* of 1949, the summary of his concept of theater, was modeled not
only on Aristotle's *Organum,* but also on Bacon's *Novum Organum.*

With his *Short Organum,* Brecht followed in Bacon's footsteps as he tried to establish "the theater of a scientific age" (GBA 23: 66). By calling his treatise an "organum," he placed it, as Ley says, "squarely within the philosophical tradition of the two most influential works in the history of Western epistemology" (187).

Brecht's Galileo figure of 1947 is persuasive evidence of the dominance of dialectics in exile modernism. On the one hand, Galileo is depicted as the first modern scientist to turn the scientific theory of his age upside down by showing that the earth revolves around the sun; on the other hand, he renounces his findings under the threat of torture and remains a prisoner of the Inquisition until his death. He liberates science from the influence of the Church and from superstition, but he also betrays science to the political interests of the ruling class. His retraction appears as a clever subterfuge, but it is also denounced as evidence of cowardice and moral corruption. On the one hand, science appears to be conducted for the sake of truth alone; on the other hand, an argument is made for its moral and social responsibility. If one focuses on the search for truth under conditions of repression, then the subterfuge of the recantation is justified, but if the focus is on the servitude of science to power politics, then the protagonist woefully neglects his responsibility to mankind. Brecht's *Galileo* is an exploration of the dialectics of the protagonist's life and work. On the one hand, he is an ideal scientist; on the other hand, his moral collapse is shown as a scientist's failure of historic proportion.

But *Galileo* is a dialectical play not only in terms of its contents, but also in terms of its structure. In the early 1930s and 1940s Brecht wanted to clarify his concept of theater by changing its name from "epic theater" to "dialectic theater." Brecht had formulated his ideas for a theory of dialectic theater in an essay of 1931, entitled "Notes on Dialectic Dramatics" ("Notizen über die dialektische Dramatik"), and in his "Dialectic and Alienation" ("Dialektik und Verfremdung") of early 1940. As Ernst Schumacher summarizes, "antitheses are an essential structural element in the dramatic. *Galileo* is antithetical in its parts and its entirety; and these antitheses are in turn transcended through the dialectical nature of its relationships, characters, and language" ("Dialectics" 123).

The American version of Brecht's play is much shorter than the Danish and German versions, comprising only sixty-four pages as compared to the more than one hundred pages of the other two versions as published in the Berlin edition of Brecht's works. The original of the American version is available only in the Berlin edition. All other American editions of the play, as, for example, the 1966 edition by Eric Bentley, are based on earlier or later versions.

The prologue, written in 1945, outlines the play's message, emphasizing the dialectical moral that addressed the modern audience:

> Respected public of the street called Broadway
> Tonight we invite you to step on board
> A world of curves and measurements, where you'll descry
> The newborn physics in their infancy.
> Here you'll see the life of the great Galileo Galilei,
> The law of falling bodies versus the gratias dei
> Science's fight against the rulers, which we stage
> At the beginning of a brand-new age.
> Here you'll see science in its blooming youth
> Also its first compromises with the truth.
> It too must eat, and quickly get prostrated
> Takes the wrong road, is violated—
> Once Nature's master, now it's no more
> Than just another cheap commercial whore.
> The Good, so far, has not been turned to goods
> But already there's something nasty in the woods
> Which cuts it off from reaching the majority
> So it won't relieve, but aggravate their poverty.
> We think that such sights are relevant today
> The new age is so quick to pass away
> We hope you'll lend a charitable ear
> To what we say, since otherwise we fear
> If you won't learn from Galileo's experience
> The Bomb might make a personal appearance.
>
>   (GBA 27: 235–36)

This prologue was not used for the Los Angeles performance, but it was for the New York production, since it addresses the Broadway audience. The German editor's comment that "Breite Straße" (Broadway) could also refer to Wide Street near the Coronet Theatre is an obvious mistake, because there is no such street in Beverly Hills (GBA 27: 511).

The American version has thirteen scenes. (A fourteenth scene, "1637. Galileo's Great Book the *Discorsi* Leave Italy," which was written before 1947, was omitted from the premiere production in Los Angeles). Most of the scenes have introductory doggerel verse, as, for example, scene 1:

> In the year sixteen hundred and nine
> Science's light began to shine.

At Padua City, in a modest house
Galileo Galilei set out to prove
The sun is still, the earth is on the move.

(GBA 5: 119)

Lines such as these were assigned to a group of singers who presented
them at the beginning of most of the scenes in front of the Brechtian half-
curtain. The Curtain Boy then opened the half-curtain from left to right
and then left the stage before the dramatic action began. In contrast to
the Danish version of 1938–39, which had conventional directions, the
scenario for the American version of 1947 was carefully laid out and obviously designed for an "epic" or "dialectic theater" production. For
each scene a title appeared in rear-projections, as, for example, for scene
1, "1609. GALILEO GALILEI, A TEACHER OF PHYSICS AT THE UNIVERSITY
OF PADUA, HEARS OF A NEW INVENTION." The titles and the introductory
verse summarize the action that is to follow, thus eliminating the suspense of Aristotelian drama and providing a Brechtian "alienation effect," that is, breaking the illusion for the audience. The German version
of 1955–56 uses the verses as mottos for its scenes, but it omits the
Singers and the Curtain Boy from the list of dramatis personae. But for
the Berlin production of 1957, directed by Erich Engel, the Singers were
reintroduced for a prologue and epilogue.

The first few scenes of the American version introduce Galileo at both
his best and his worst: he is enjoying the comforts of life, constantly questioning established doctrines, showing concern for the common people,
and prostituting his science to the rich and to the government. The conflict of astronomical theories is also introduced in dialectical fashion. An
astrolabe in Galileo's scantily furnished study represents the traditional
Ptolemaic system, which Galileo ridicules by teaching Andrea, his housekeeper's son, a lesson on the movement of the earth by moving a chair
around a washstand. Galileo's struggle toward a synthesis is the plot of
the drama: will he use the new science to serve the government, or will
he use it to help mankind? The first two scenes show him on the wrong
path, but since he hoodwinks the authorities, his failure appears as a
rogue's fun-loving trick. In order to make money, Galileo builds a telescope based on information received from Holland. Pretending that it is
his own invention, he presents the telescope to the leaders of the Republic
of Venice. His fraudulent invention, which earns him a tidy sum, then as-
sists the Venetian Republic in navigation and trade as well as in warfare.
Countering Francis Bacon's prediction that "kings with their treasure

cannot buy [knowledge], nor with their force command" (DE 1), Galileo serves the interests of the ruling class. Although these scenes emphasize the comic aspects of his clever deception, it shows nevertheless that scientific discovery goes hand in hand with capitalistic exploitation and imperialist expansion. The parallels between Brecht's *Galileo* and Adorno and Horkheimer's *Dialectic of Enlightenment* are nowhere as obvious as here. The science of optics is applied to the technology of the telescope, which can then be mass-produced and used by the Venetian Republic for its merchant marine (commerce) and naval warfare (imperialism).

That the telescope can also serve pure research is shown when Galileo demonstrates to one of his colleagues that the moon is a body similar to the earth. In scene 3 his observation of the behavior of the moons of Jupiter leads to the conclusion "that there are only stars and no difference between earth and heaven." But Galileo fails to consider the political implications of his research. The theological conclusions of his discovery are that heaven is abolished and God is "within ourselves—or nowhere" in this new system of the universe (GBA 5: 132). Although Galileo believes in the power of scientific proof, his colleague is afraid of the political consequences of such a discovery. He envisions Galileo tied to the stake, like Giordano Bruno in 1600. Hearing that Galileo has applied for a position as mathematician at the court of Florence, his colleague warns him of "leaving a republic for a principality under the influence of the monks" (GBA 5: 134), but Galileo rejects his warning.

The scenes at the Florentine court show Galileo encountering the open contempt of the courtiers, the ridicule and outrage of the clerics, and the disdainful arrogance of his colleagues. He finds unexpected support, however, from a papal astronomer who confirms his discovery of the four moons of Jupiter. On a visit to Rome, though, Galileo is informed of a church edict against his teachings. Cardinal Barberini, who shows sympathy for Galileo, tells him "to research to his heart's content," but to be careful of conclusions: "Science is the legitimate and beloved daughter of the Church and she must have confidence in the Church" (GBA 5: 146). Galileo heeds this clear warning. For eight years, he abides by the strictures of the Church (scenes 4–8).

Brecht wanted to see modern science practiced to serve mankind. His Galileo assembles a research team of members of the lower classes: Andrea, the son of his housekeeper; Federzoni, a lens grinder, who did not understand Latin, the language of medieval science; and the Little Monk, who is very much aware of science's social impact. His parents are poor peasants who have grown old and frail from stooped labor. Their only comfort is the Bible. which promises them that their hard work and suffering will be rewarded. The Little Monk, however, is afraid that science will prove the Bible to be full of mistakes and reveal to his parents that their suffering is in vain. Therefore, the Little Monk has decided to "abandon science for the sake of his simple parents' peace of mind" (GBA 5: 148). Although Galileo is determined to improve the living conditions of the lower classes, he has no patience for their suffering. Annoyed, he asks, "How can new machinery be evolved . . . , if we physicists are forbidden to study, discuss and pool our findings?" (GBA 5: 149–50). He is especially critical of the authorities, who use the Bible to consolidate their political power and keep the lower classes in their place. In the end, the Little Monk "succumbs to the thirst of knowledge" and joins Galileo's team (GBA 5: 148).

Brecht's Galileo is fully aware of the political implications of his research and prepared to risk his daughter's happiness for the sake of science. Ludovico, his future son-in-law, calls off his wedding to Galileo's daughter, Virginia, because Galileo has resumed his research in the field of astronomy. Ludovico's family will not tolerate teachings that are condemned by the Church because such defiance might unsettle their peasants: Ludovico's "mother has had to have a dog whipped in front of [the peasants] to remind them to keep their place" (GBA 5: 158). Ludovico's marriage to the daughter of a heretic could thus endanger his family's social position.

The play shows that during the next ten years Galileo's teachings have spread, and pamphleteers and ballad singers have picked up his new ideas. On All Fools' Day in 1632, many towns in Italy selected astronomy as the theme of their carnival processions. A performance by a ballad singer and his wife demonstrates that the common people have seized upon the political implications of Galileo's teachings. If the earth is no longer the center of the universe, neither is the pope nor the emperor at the center of the political world. Everyone is free to act on his own: "It feels good, just for a change to do just as one pleases!" Galileo is celebrated as "the Bible killer" (GBA 5: 160–64).

Modern science emerged at the threshold of modernity, but, as a conversation between Matti, an iron founder, and the astronomer reveals, Galileo maintains a medieval point of view in political matters. He turns down support from a representative of the rising bourgeoisie, preferring the patronage of his prince and the new pope. Galileo fails to understand the emerging political situation. There is a new progressive class on his side, ready to help him escape to Venice where he can defend himself (scene 10). The Florentine court, on the other hand, is no longer in a position to protect Galileo but instead submits to the request of the Inquisition to interrogate him in 1633. Galileo also learns that his trust in Cardinal Barberini is also misplaced: although he is elected pope as Urban VIII, his intervention in Galileo's case amounts to no more than a warning against torture. He tells the Grand Inquisitor that Galileo "is not to be tortured. . . . At the very most, he may be shown the instruments [of torture]!" (GBA 5: 169).

Galileo's recantation is introduced by a verse, entrusted to the Singers, that suggests the far-reaching significance of the action to follow:

> June, twenty-second, sixteen thirty-three,
> A date momentous for you and me.
> Of all the day that was the one,
> The age of reason could have begun.
>
> (GBA 5: 170)

In no uncertain terms the verse pronounces the radical change that did not take place. For a moment, however, the suspense is upheld. Andrea, Federzoni, and the Little Monk, who are assembled in the gardens of the Florentine ambassador in Rome, are led to believe for a brief time that Galileo has resisted the Inquisition. As they rejoice, envisioning the arrival of a new age, the official announcement of the recantation is read to the public. Devastated by his teacher's betrayal of modern science, Andrea resorts to censure and blame: "Unhappy is the land that breeds no hero." To this accusation Galileo can only answer, "Incorrect: 'Unhappy is the land that needs a hero'" (GBA 5: 173).

The conclusion of *Galileo* shows the most radical changes in comparison to the Danish version of 1938. Galileo is no longer conceived as an underground fighter who saves the results of his research for a better time. The slyness and cunning he demonstrates in writing the *Discorsi* and smuggling them out of the country for publication are no longer an excuse for his recantation. When Andrea, his favorite student, visits him in the country house where he is kept as a prisoner of the Inquisition, he offers this excuse:

> *Andrea:* We lost our heads. With the crowd at the street corners we said: "He will die, but he will never surrender!" You came back: "I surrendered but I am alive." We cried: "Your hands are stained!" You say: "Better stained than empty." (GBA 5: 178)

While Andrea seeks to justify Galileo's failure as a tactic to allow him to continue his research, Galileo demolishes this argument with a reference to his fear for his well-being:

> *Galileo:* I recanted because I was afraid of physical pain.
> *Andrea:* It was not a plan?
> *Galileo:* It was not. (GBA 5: 178)

Trying to bolster his mentor's self-confidence, Andrea reminds Galileo of his work on the *Discorsi* that he has kept concealed from the Inquisition:

> *Andrea:* Science has only one commandment: contribution. And you have contributed more than any man in a hundred years.

Galileo, however, does not accept this excuse and brutally accuses his student of unethical behavior:

> *Galileo:* Contributed to whom? Welcome to my gutter, brother scientist and fellow traitor. I sold out, you are a buyer. The first sight of the book [the *Discorsi*]! His mouth watered, and the scoldings were drowned. Blessed be our bargaining, white-washing, death-fearing community! (GBA 5: 179)

Galileo ends the debate in dialectical fashion. Andrea has come to him as an enemy, but when the student hears about the *Discorsi* he again becomes Galileo's friend and recants his accusation, praising his mentor's "recantation as a wise move, showing the scientists a new and realistic way of dealing with the authorities" (GBA 5: 178). Galileo, however, rejects this gesture of reconciliation. He shows his former student "how to think really scientifically by submitting his own case to logic" (GBA 5: 179) and explains that science is abused when it is withheld from the people. His response is the final synthesis of the dialectic of the play:

> *Galileo:* I take it the intent of science is to ease up on human existence. If you give way to coercion, science can be crippled. Your new machines may simply suggest new drudgeries. You may in time discover all there is to be discovered, but if you yield to coercion your progress must be a progress away from the bulk of humanity. The gulf between you and humanity might even grow so wide that the sound of your cheering at some new achievement could be echoed by a universal howl of horror. (GBA 5: 180)

While the last sentence is an obvious reference to the discovery of nuclear fission and its application to warfare in the form of the atomic bomb, it also reveals an argument similar to one developed in *Dialectic of Enlightenment.* Adorno and Horkheimer, however, never refer to the atom bomb; their analysis of the development of modern technology does not go further than the dive-bomber of the early 1940s (DE 2).

In the end, Galileo concludes with the most devastating self-indictment of his career:

> Galileo: As a scientist I had an almost unique opportunity. In my day as-
> tronomy emerged into the marketplaces. At that particular time,
> had one man put up a fight, it would have had wide repercussions.
> I have formed the opinion, [Andrea], that I was never in real dan-
> ger; for some years I was as strong as the authorities, and I surren-
> dered my knowledge to the powers that be, to use it, abuse it, just
> as it suits their ends. I have betrayed my profession. Any man who
> does what I have done must not be tolerated in the ranks of sci-
> ence. (GBA 5: 180)

Although Andrea wants to shake Galileo's hand and responds that his "savage analysis" cannot be the last word on the matter, it was Brecht's intention that the protagonist end up as a coward and trai-tor. Galileo does not allow Andrea to shake his hand, "since it is the hand of a traitor to science" (GBA 5: 180). If Andrea wants to be a true scientist, he cannot be Galileo's friend. The last lines of the text of the Los Angeles production are a warning by Galileo, directed at the audience:

> Galileo: May you now guard science's light
> Kindle it and use it right
> Lest it be a flame to fall
> Downward to consume us all. (GBA 5: 181)

The play was written to confront the audience with the conclusion that "if Galileo had not given in to the Pope and the Inquisition, the modern world would have been spared the horror of the atomic bomb" (Cook 177). Brecht placed great trust in his audiences (sometimes even overes-timating their reasoning power), and confronted them with the central problem of his time and the century to come: the existence and control of weapons of total destruction. The nonclosure of Brecht's *Galileo* un-dermines, as Russell Berman argues, "the stability of realistic mimesis" and emphasizes the "unresolved problematic" of modern science (282). That was the significance of "epic theater," or "dialectic theater," as Brecht preferred to call it at that time. To make this argument against sci-ence in the service of government even stronger, Brecht adds a statement to Galileo's speech that was originally drafted for the American version but later omitted (see Schumacher, *Drama und Geschichte* 243, 307). It was reinserted in 1955 and reads as follows in the English translation of the German version of 1955–56:

> *Galileo:* Had I resisted, scientists could have established a credo for science as Hippocrates did for medicine, a credo to use their knowledge only for the benefit of mankind. (GBA 5: 284)

During the 1950s, a great number of physicists pleaded for a moratorium on nuclear research and the enforcement of international guidelines controlling the development of nuclear energy. In 1988, scientists introduced the Oath of Buenos Aires, which provided ethical guidelines for modern scientists and their research. It reminded scientists of their social responsibility and asked them to conduct only research that furthered the interests of society and peace.

The contract submitted for the Los Angeles production of *Galileo* listed both Brecht and Charles Laughton as authors (Lyon, *Brecht in den USA*, 213), but the program notes clearly identify Brecht as author and attribute only the adaptation of the play to Laughton. On the basis of Brecht's recollection in his foreword to "Building Up a Part: Laughton's Galileo," an analysis of the actor's achievements, scholars agree that the translation and adaptation was a collaborative effort. Brecht recorded in his diary December 10, 1944, as the beginning of their collaboration (GBA 27: 212). They used to work in Laughton's small library in his house above the Pacific Ocean in Pacific Palisades. Describing their collaboration as most congenial, Brecht reports that when he arrived in the morning, Laughton would often "come and meet me in the garden, running barefoot in shirt and trousers over the damp grass, and would show me some changes in his flowerbeds, for his garden always occupied him, providing many problems and subtleties. The serenity and the beautiful proportions of this world of flowers influenced our work in a most pleasant way" (GBA 25: 13).

Laughton consulted his thesaurus and dictionaries to find similar passages in other literary texts, such as Aesop, the Bible, Molière, and Shakespeare, in order to study their rhetorical style or research specific linguistic gestures (GBA 25: 11). Brecht characterized their collaboration as "awkward" since "one translator knew no German and the other scarcely any English," although Brecht may have been downplaying his knowledge of English. The circumstance that compelled them "to use acting as their means of translation" may simply have been Laughton's profession as an actor. They did what, according to Brecht, "better equipped translators should do too: . . . translate gestures." For language, Brecht argued, was "theatrical in so far as it primarily expresses the mutual attitude of the speakers." He related that he "acted out everything in bad English or even in German," and Laughton "repeated it in different ways in correct English, until [Brecht] would say: 'That's it.'" Laughton would then write down the results (GBA 25: 11). For Brecht, this method had the advantage that it made discussions about psychological motivation—anathema to epic theater—unnecessary. The only disagreement that Brecht recorded was Laughton's disinterest in the final authorized book. He was only interested in a script for performance. Brecht wrote:

> In a striking and occasionally brutal way L. showed his lack of interest in the "book," to an extent that the author could not always share. What we were making was just a text, the performance was all that counted. It was impossible to persuade him to translate passages which the author was prepared to delete for the performance, but wanted to save for the "book"! [For Laughton] the most important was the evening of the performance, the text existed only for the sake of the performance; the text was consumed by the performance, it was spent like the explosives that generate fireworks! (GBA 25: 12).

There was, however, no apparent conflict or even irritation between actor and the playwright. Brecht respected Laughton's professionalism and was prepared to put aside his ego as an author for the sake of the project. The collaboration that began in December 1944 continued, with interruptions due to Laughton's movie commitments, for almost a year. On December 1, 1945, Laughton read the "final" text of the play to a group of guests and family members assembled at Brecht's house (GBA 27: 235).

Laughton negotiated with Orson Welles, who was eager to direct the play on Broadway in 1946, with Mike Todd as a producer, but these negotiations broke down because of the other commitments of the persons involved. Because of this, Brecht and Laughton welcomed the opportunity in early 1947 to produce the play in Los Angeles. Especially attractive was the promise to bring *Galileo* to Broadway in the fall, since it was rare that theater productions that originated in the cinema community moved to New York. The producer, T. Edward Hambleton, and the company, Pelican Productions, founded by John Houseman and Nor-

FIGURE 9. Coronet Theatre, 366 North La Cienaga Boulevard, Beverly Hills,
2005. Photograph by Juergen Nogai, Santa Monica.

man Lloyd, rented the Coronet Theatre at 366 North La Cienega Boulevard in Beverly Hills to introduce the Los Angeles audience to the latest
developments in modern drama. The company's first production was
Thornton Wilder's *The Skin of Our Teeth,* with *Galileo* following as the
second play and Jean Paul Sarte's *No Exit* as the third play.

    Galileo opened on July 30, 1947, with Laughton in the title role. The
stage director was Joseph Losey, who had been selected because he had
been involved in left-wing theater in New York in the 1930s (Brecht,
however, directed and produced the play, for all practical purposes).
Losey later directed the 1951 remake of Fritz Lang's *M,* and in 1975 he
directed the British film version of *Galileo.* The settings and costumes of

the production at the Coronet Theatre were by Robert Davison, the music by Hanns Eisler, and the choreography by Lotte Goslar. A cast of fifty players, headed by Hugo Haas as Cardinal Barberini / Pope Urban VIII and Frances Heflin as Galileo's daughter, appeared in support of Laughton. The program notes have July 24 as the date for the "world premiere," but the opening performance had to be postponed by a week because rehearsals took longer than expected.

The play ran for seventeen days and was also performed for six days at the Maxine Elliott Theatre in New York in December 1947, but Brecht had already left the country by that time. What made this production so noteworthy was the following: 1) it was the performance of an original exile drama; 2) with the exception of Laughton, it employed American actors exclusively; 3) the actors were directed according to Brecht's concepts of epic theater; and 4) it provided the model for the later production by the Berliner Ensemble, the Brecht repertory theater in East Berlin.

Before 1947 exile theater in Los Angeles had relied on Shakespeare and the German classics. In 1934, Max Reinhardt had directed Shakespeare's *Midsummer Night's Dream* at the Hollywood Bowl with great success, and in 1939 Leopold Jessner had put Friedrich Schiller's *Wilhelm Tell* in English translation on the stage at the El Capitan Theatre on Hollywood Boulevard. While Reinhardt relied on Hollywood actors, Jessner had employed German exile actors. Due to the actors' difficulties with the English language, the production was a dismal failure and had to be cancelled. Walter Wicclair's Freie Bühne, which specialized in German-language productions in Los Angeles from 1939 to 1949, relied on lowbrow comedies and did not stage a single exile drama.

The casting for the English-language production of *Galileo* was in the hands of Brecht and Laughton. With the exception of the major roles, they selected young and inexperienced American actors for a cast of about fifty characters. Brecht preferred young actors who had not yet been exposed to Stanislavski's theory and practice of method acting so that he could direct them according to the principles of his epic theater. According to the accounts available, Brecht did not lecture the players on epic acting but advised them repeatedly that they were not to impose their personal feelings on the characters they were representing. In general, he emphasized that he did not want sentimentality on the stage but intelligent acting. Since they were all Americans—with the exception of Charles Laughton—Brecht did not have to worry about language barriers.

On the basis of the program, the photographs and film made by Ruth Berlau, Brecht's close friend and collaborator, and the notes that Brecht published in "Building Up a Part: Laughton's Galileo" ("Aufbau einer Rolle—Laughton's Galilei") and his *Short Organum for the Theater (Kleines Organon für das Theater)*, it is not difficult to reconstruct the production. The program notes instructed the audience that the social responsibility of modern science was the central theme of the play:

> While Brecht was living in Copenhagen in 1938, the Bohr Institute, headed by the great Nobel scientist, Niels Bohr, revealed the full potential of the fission of uranium. Impressed by the awesome announcement and the trepidation of the scientists themselves about the possible misuse of this tremendous force, Brecht harked back to an earlier discovery of cataclysmic proportions—Galileo's determination that the earth revolved about the sun—and saw in this a drama which would highlight the enduring struggle between those who discover monumental truths and others who, through fear or selfish purpose, would suppress or distort these. (Lyon, *Brecht in den USA*, 218)

This message was visually reinforced by a display of the names of famous modern scientists. Ruth Berlau's film shows that the proscenium had the following names inscribed: Galileo, Newton, Marie Curie, Lise Meitner, and Einstein.

Brecht and Laughton had agreed on a number of principles guiding the production. Judging from the photographs, Joseph Losey, the token director, implemented these guidelines faithfully. As Brecht had recorded in "Building Up a Part":

1. The stage sets must not convey the impression to the audience that they are transported into a room in medieval Italy or the Vatican. The audience must always be aware of the fact that they are in a theater.

2. The background must show more than the immediate surroundings. It should indicate the historical space in an imaginative and artistically attractive manner,

3. Furniture and props must be realistic (including the doors) and must above all have a social-historical appeal. The costumes must be individually distinguishable and show signs of wear and tear. The social differences are to be stressed, since we cannot easily recognize them in historical fashions. The colors of the costumes should be coordinated.

4. The groupings of characters must have the quality of historical paintings. . . . The production will achieve this by providing historical titles for each action.

5. All action must be governed by composure and grand design. Constant change of position without significant gestures of characters is to be

    avoided. . . . At the same time, all stage action must be absolutely natu-
    ral and realistic.

6. The casting of the church dignitaries must be realistic. This production
   does not intend to ridicule the Church, but the refined way of speech
   and educated manner of the princes of the church of the 17th century
   must not influence the director to cast them as intellectuals. The
   Church in this play represents mainly the powers that be; as types these
   church dignitaries must resemble our bankers and senators.

7. Galileo's stage business must not be designed to establish sympathetic
   identification and compassion by the audience; it should rather enable
   the audience to assume an attitude of astonishment, critique and careful consideration.

8. The more profoundly the historical aspects of the production are established, the more extensively humor can be used. (GBA 25: 19–20)

In general, Brecht was greatly impressed by Laughton's performance. In
the thirteenth and final scene, however, Brecht was not satisfied with
Laughton's expression of cynicism when Galileo exclaims, "Welcome to
my gutter, brother scientist and fellow traitor. I sold out, you are a
buyer." According to Brecht, this was one of the few passages with
which Laughton had difficulties: "[Laughton] doubted that the audience
would understand the meaning of this passage, quite apart from the fact
that the text here did not follow the vocabulary of Galileo's otherwise
purely logical discourse" (GBA 25: 64). The discussion between Galileo
and Andrea in the last scene was Brecht's dialectical challenge not only
to his audience, but also to his leading actors. None—neither Charles
Laughton in Beverly Hills and New York nor Ernst Busch in East
Berlin—was able to meet this challenge. They wanted to play Galileo as
a hero, not a criminal. Laughton failed to understand Brecht's dialectical argument "that there must be a gesture that indicated the self-
condemnation of the opportunist by the condemnation of those who accept the rewards of opportunism" (GBA 25: 64). It was Brecht's
intention to have Galileo teach Andrea a lesson in the ethics of science,
but to do so by humiliating his favorite student and showing off his own
brilliant intellect. The audience was supposed to realize that Galileo was
condemned to "a kind of hell that was more frightful than that of Dante,
a kind of hell, where those reside who have gambled away the gift of
their intellect" (GBA 25: 65). Later, in East Berlin in 1956, Brecht elaborated on this problem of playing the part of Galileo when he said that
it was one of the role's great difficulties to extract the criminal from the
hero: "Galileo is shown as a man who is right, one of the great heroes of
the next five-hundred years, who will overcome all resistance—but then

he regresses and becomes a criminal. . . . In spite of everything: he is a hero—and in spite of it: he becomes a criminal" (Rülicke 121). The actor should not leave it to the audience to solve this contradiction, but he must demonstrate it and hope that the audience understands it.

In his *Short Organum for the Theater,* which was begun in exile but readied for the press in Switzerland in 1948 and finally published in East Berlin in 1949 (White 184–90), Brecht refers in detail to the Los Angeles production. He found the principles of epic or dialectic theater realized in Laughton's kind of acting: Laughton had made it perfectly obvious that he was acting as "a double persona" on stage, "as Laughton and as Galileo, so that the explaining *[zeigend]* Laughton did not disappear behind the explained *[gezeigt]* Galileo" (GBA 23: 83). Brecht praised Hanns Eisler for matching the events of the carnival procession in scene 9 with "music that was both triumphant and frightening." The music represented "the revolutionary turn that the lower classes associated with Galileo's theories" (GBA 23: 95). With regard to the sets, Brecht remembered that they were not designed to produce the illusion of a particular room or a landscape, but were limited to "presenting historical allusions by placing Galileo in front of projections of maps, documents and works of art of the Renaissance" (GBA 23: 95–96).

For the rehearsals in Los Angeles Brecht had instructed Ruth Berlau to create a so-called "Modell-book," a visual record of the production. She took photos of both the Los Angeles and New York productions and even had some phonograph records made of the New York production (the records were found in Switzerland in 2004). The visual record served as the basis for the rehearsals in 1956 of the third version of *Galileo,* performed by the Berliner Ensemble in 1957. In addition to the California "Modell-book," Brecht relied on the photographs and the 16 mm film that Ruth Berlau had made of the Los Angeles production. They provided the model for the Berlin production that premiered in January 1957, almost half a year after Brecht had died on August 14, 1956. It is noteworthy that Brecht ran into the same problem with Ernst Busch, the actor of the title role in Berlin, as he did with Charles Laughton in Los Angeles. Both actors wanted to generate sympathy for Galileo rather than condemnation of his cowardice. Brecht could never fully convince either actor of his interpretation.

The production of *Galileo* at the Coronet Theatre in 1947 was a critical success. More than half of the reviewers responded positively and expressed an appreciation of Brecht's epic theater. Almost all noticed the play's characteristic elements: a single, changeable set, back-stage projections, short poems at the beginning of each scene, and the Brechtian half-curtain to indicate the changes of scenes. The review in the *Los Angeles Daily News* of July 31 showed a clear understanding of the play's indictment of modern science and commented positively on its unconventional staging. The *Los Angeles Times* of the same day spoke of the play's "pioneering character," praising *Galileo* as a revolutionary production. The *New York Times* of August 1 noted the "abbreviated . . . Shakespeare mode" of the settings, while the West Coast edition of *Variety* reported that the European staging techniques of the epic theater, new to Los Angeles, heightened the presentation. The *Hollywood Reporter* of August 1 was right on target comparing both the staging and the dialogue to the "Shakespearean style of presentation, wherein scenery is but illusionary and the actors move the props around themselves." The reviewer was perceptive in comparing epic theater to the Elizabethan mode of performance. When proponents of the illusionist tradition complained about the modernist production, John Houseman came to Brecht's defense in a column of the *Los Angeles Daily News* on August 25, pointing out that Brecht had developed his epic theater in Weimar Germany for the very purpose of escaping from the drama of realistic detail:

> Certain very capable members of our acting and writing community have taken Pelican Productions to task for its presentation of *Galileo*. They have been in the main exponents of the naturalistic theater—the stage of realistic detail which Brecht thought to escape when he founded his Epic Theater in Germany in the late 1920's. We of Pelican have no quarrel with these critics. We appreciate their interest, and we are grateful for their passion. As a matter of fact, some members of the Pelican organization esteem the theater of Odets and of O'Casey above that of Brecht or Wilder. Nevertheless, they will support, to the death, the thesis that the Coronet stage must be a platform for all that is exciting and important, no matter, how it rates in their personal catalogue of dramatic values. (quoted from Lyon, *Brecht in America*, 199–200)

The majority of the reviews confirmed that the production achieved what the author had intended, although Brecht himself complained about the small number of people who saw the production. He estimated an audience of barely 10,000 for both the Los Angeles and New York productions. James Lyon's estimate for Los Angeles was approximately 4,500, but higher numbers could not be expected with a capacity of 260 seats at the Coronet Theatre and a run of only seventeen performances (Lyon, *Brecht in America*, 201). The New York production with Laughton in the title role and Joseph Losey as director had a run of only six days, from December 7 to 14, 1947.

Brecht's *Galileo* of 1947 was one of the earliest and most thought-provoking literary protests against the nuclear age. Although most critics classified the playwright as a left-wing modernist, the label does not apply to this play, and especially to the last scene. Although *Galileo* raises many arguments in favor of class warfare against the autocratic society of the seventeenth century that smack of a Marxism before its time, this emphasis shifts toward the end of the play. The play's final indictment and conclusion address the welfare of all mankind, not that of a particular class. These arguments regarding the responsibility of modern science toward mankind are developed along similar lines as those of Adorno and Horkheimer in *Dialectic of Enlightenment,* although Brecht's conclusions and recommendations are perhaps more radical. Most remarkable is his valorization of individual decision making. The future depends on the decisions of individuals with insights like those of Galileo in his last scene. In this context, it is most revealing that in 1955 Brecht had planned a sequel, "Life of Einstein" ("Leben des Einstein"). There are no more than three pages of text extant (GBA 10.2: 984–86; see Peter D. Smith 310–11), but they show that during the research Brecht rephrased his assessment of modern science in the twentieth century: "The goal of the scientist is supposed to be pure research, but the final product of research is less pure. The formula $E = mc^2$ is conceived for eternity, not obliged to anything. Thus, others are able to use it for their purposes: the city of Hiroshima has suddenly become very short-lived" (quoted from Wizisla N3). Because of its appeal to the ethics of the individual scientist, Brecht's *Galileo* of 1947 must be characterized as belonging to the "modernism of social individuality" (Berman). The dialectics of the play were to produce a new audience with social responsibility.

Among Brecht's exile plays written in Los Angeles and New York, only *The Caucasian Chalk Circle (Der kaukasische Kreidekreis)* of 1944 qualifies as "leftist modernism," not only because its setting is the Soviet Union, but also because the play illustrates the socialist notion of property. The action of the prologue takes place in 1945 in a war-ravaged Caucasian village, where two Soviet collectives meet to decide the future of a valley. They are told an old story, set in feudal Georgia, which constitutes the play proper. There is a dispute between a farm collective that is eager to plant fruit trees in the valley and a shepherds' collective that wants to use the valley as pasture as before. The farm collective argues that their members would put the land to better use than the shepherds'

collective. The play provides an argument to the farm collective to im-
plement their project as better suited to the welfare of the community
than that of the shepherds. The argument is based on the story of
Solomon's judgment in I Kings 3: 16–28, in which the real mother re-
linquishes her child rather than see it harmed. While in the biblical version the child is threatened with division by a sword, in another version,
based on an old Chinese story, the child is placed in a chalk circle and
both women are instructed to pull the child by its arms out of the circle.
A modern dramatization of the Chinese story, written by Klabund (a
pseudonym for Alfred Henschke) and staged in Berlin in 1925, was familiar to Brecht. Most critical, however, is the fact that Brecht reverses
the outcome: the biological mother, the governor's wife who abandoned
the child during a palace revolution, would rather see it hurt than relin-
quish her claim, while the peasant woman who rescued and raised the
child is willing to let it go to save it from suffering. Like Solomon, the
judge of the play awards the child to the motherly woman who wants it
protected from any pain. Motherhood is defined "socially rather than bi-
ologically," as Brecht states (*Collected Plays* 7: 296). The implied conclusion is that the land should go to the collective that would make better use of it. Legal title to possession is replaced by potential
productivity. Eric Bentley, the best-known translator of Brecht's works
into English, called the prologue of the *Caucasian Chalk Circle* "un-
American," although he did so tongue-in-cheek. Until 1965 the prologue
was always omitted from American productions. Bentley made a pitch
for it, though, when he said that the play suggests the possibility of a new
age: "there is the ultimate inversion: that the Golden Age should be en-
visaged, not in the past, but in the future, and not in fairyland or
Heaven, but in Georgia. The Russian Georgia, that is. But ours is included, at least in the sense that the play is about our twentieth-century
world" (Bentley, "Un-American Chalk Circle," 211). Brecht himself argued against the notion that the story was "told in order to clear up the
argument about who owns the valley," but he admitted that the story
displayed "a particular kind of wisdom, a potentially model attitude for
the argument in question." For him, the prologue provides "the background which locates the practicability and also the evolution of such
wisdom in an historic setting" (*Collected Plays* 7: 297). This leaves the
moral to be applied at the discretion of the audience, but the play ends
with the following lines, which do not leave much room for ambivalence
or nonclosure:

And you who heard the story of the chalk circle
Bear in mind the wisdom of our fathers:
Things should belong to those who do well by them
Children to motherly women that they may strive
Wagons to good drivers that they may be well driven
And the valley to those who water it, that it may bear fruit.

(*Collected Plays* 7: 229)

The play is not only about collectives, but also about creating a collective agreement among the members of the audience.

CHAPTER 5

Epic Theater versus Film Noir

*Bertolt Brecht and Fritz Lang's Anti-Nazi
Film* Hangmen Also Die

When American newspapers reported the assassination of SS-Obergruppenführer Reinhard Heydrich in Prague in May of 1942, Brecht and Fritz Lang immediately seized upon the idea of writing a script for a hostage film. In the *Los Angeles Times* of May 28, 1942, they found the headline "Assassin Bombs Hitler's 'Hangman'" and were informed of the event as follows:

> A bomb, either planted in his automobile or thrown as it passed at high speed along the road to Berlin inside Greater Prague, exploded, killing the driver, wrecking the car and seriously injuring the Nazi secret police chieftain, notorious throughout Europe as "the hangman."

Little did they know that the article would provide them with the key word for the title of their film. From the first day that the story broke the headlines referred to Heydrich as "the hangman." On May 28, he was reported in grave condition. The story also related that a manhunt had begun immediately after the assassination plot, and that the threat of swift reprisals hung heavy over the country: "Czech blood bath looms." As Brecht recorded in his diary on May 28, 1942, the news story first prompted them to think about the hostage film while they were on the beach in Santa Monica. A few weeks later they had completed an outline, an abbreviated version of the story that they were able to sell to Arnold Productions, an organization run by Arnold Pressburger, an exile producer from Hungary. The outline, entitled "437!! A Hostage Film"

("437!! Ein Geiselfilm"), was found in 1997 and published in 2003. The number in the title refers to the number of hostages shot by the German secret police. The typescript is thirty-nine pages long, at least twice as long as the average outline. As James K. Lyon has commented, the text "includes more material and makes it easy to identify elements in the final film that were conceived in this first round of work" ("The Original Story" 2).

The surprisingly detailed outline shows that the plot was fully developed at this stage. Although eventually a few names were changed and the new Nazi governor of Czechoslovakia was given different lines at the ending, the outline otherwise has the same plotline and denouement as the final film. The thirty-two-page English translation of the outline was registered by the Hollywood agent Sam Jaffe as an original story with the Screen Writers Guild on June 30, 1942. The English-language treatment, a more detailed version of the outline, has been preserved as a ninety-five-page typescript. Entitled "Never Surrender!" it was registered by the same Hollywood agent ("The Original Story" 2). Brecht and Lang also wrote a treatment of approximately one hundred pages in German, although this version has been lost. Published in 2005 (*Brecht Yearbook* 30, 7–60), the English-language treatment shows the basic plotline of the film in considerable detail. The only major difference between the treatment and the film version of the story is the treatment's happy ending—"Through the streets of Prague the liberated hostages walk home, silent and victorious, while the song of freedom rings out triumphantly" (*Brecht Yearbook* 30, 60)—which was abandoned in the film.

The movie was released through United Artists because Pressburger and Lang wanted the film to be independent from the Hollywood studio system. Originally founded by Mary Pickford, Douglas Fairbanks, Charlie Chaplin, and D. W. Griffith in 1919, United Artists in the 1940s had become primarily a distributor and financial backer of independent productions. This arrangement with United Artists boded well for a film that was motivated by the idea of avoiding the conventions of the Hollywood culture industry. It was to be expected that the director and his crew would have greater artistic freedom under Pressburger than in a studio production. The hiring of Hanns Eisler, who composed the music, of Alexander Granach as Gestapo inspector Alois Gruber, of Hans von Twardowski as Reinhard Heydrich, of Reinhold Schünzel as Inspector Ritter, and, last but not least, of Brecht as screenwriter and Lang as director appear to confirm that the production was not subject to the in-

FIGURE 10. Fritz Lang. Photograph courtesy of University of Southern
California Cinema-Television Library, Los Angeles.

tervention of the Hollywood studio system (Aurich, Jacobsen, and
Schnauber 352–56).

In the meantime, the *Los Angeles Times* had reported on the death of
Reinhard Heydrich on June 5, on his state funeral in Berlin on June 10,
on the total destruction of the Czech village of Lidice and the execution
of its male population on June 11, and on the shooting of the men accused as the assassins on June 19, 1942. The information from occupied
Europe was promptly relayed to the United States, and was fairly accurate, considering the censorship expected during a war. The German secret police was reportedly working on the theory that parachutists
dropped from British planes had carried out the assassination and that
the Czech population participated only by sheltering the conspirators.

Only two months after the assassination, Brecht pasted into his diary
a newspaper clipping of July 28 that announced the production of
Never Surrender, a film with a Czechoslovakian locale. The film, to be

produced by Arnold Pressburger and directed by Fritz Lang, would prominently feature the character of Heydrich the Hangmen. Lang's engagement was described as "a coup since he directed the notable offering, *Man Hunt,* during his sojourn at Twentieth [Century Fox], as well as *Return of Frank James* and *Western Union.*" It was also reported that Lang directed *Fury* for MGM, but in Hollywood this was seen as a film from "an earlier era." Brecht's name was also known well enough to be mentioned in the article. The story reported that Lang had been "collaborating on the story for the new picture with Bert Brecht, famous for his *Beggar's Opera*" (GBA 27: 117). The title *Never Surrender* had to be replaced because of copyright conflicts and was later changed to *Hangmen Also Die,* selected from the names submitted by studio employees during a contest to develop a new title.

Fritz Lang (1890–1976) arrived in Los Angeles earlier than most German exiles. Born in Austria in 1890, he had acquired German citizenship because he was working as a movie director in Germany, but after the Nazis came to power he left the country. His films *Die Nibelungen* (1923–24) and *Metropolis* (1925–26) had attracted the attention of the Nazis. In *Die Nibelungen,* presenting the story of Siegfried, Lang had put the German national myth on the screen, while in the modernist *Metropolis* he had presented in its final scene an ideology that was close to the Nazi resolution of the conflict between the working class and capitalism. In his history of Weimar film, Siegfried Krakauer refers to this ending as the "sham alliance between labor and capital," establishing an analogy between the movie's industrialist and Joseph Goebbels, the Nazi propaganda minister in charge of film production and censorship (164). According to Lang's "Autobiography," a six-page fragment published by Lotte Eisner (9–15), the Nazis were willing to overlook his implicitly anti-Nazi film *Das Testament des Dr. Mabuse,* and Goebbels supposedly offered him a leading position in the German film industry, but Lang declined and left for Paris the same evening he was offered the job, at the end of March or in early April. As Lang reported, "The 'interview' with Goebbels had lasted from noon to 2:30 P.M., by which time the banks had already closed and I could not withdraw any money. I had just enough at home to buy a ticket to Paris, and arrived practically penniless at the Gare du Nord" (Eisner 15). But since this meeting with Goebbels cannot be independently verified and Lang's passport shows July 31, 1933, as the date of his final departure from Germany, there is doubt about Lang's story (McGilligan 174–81; Aurich, Jacobsen, and Schnauber 215–18), and it was probably Lang's fabrication. The story, which he repeated again and again in interviews starting in 1943, had a cinematic quality and read like the treatment of a typical Langian movie (Gunning 8–9).

In Paris Lang made the film *Liliom*, which was released in 1933. He then left France because he had been offered a contract to work for Metro-Goldwyn-Mayer in Hollywood. By 1942 he had directed six films in the United States, among them *Fury* (1936), a film about an alleged lynching and mob hysteria, and was considered a successful American movie director. For Brecht, the collaboration with Lang was a unique opportunity to break into the movie business, which he had been unsuccessful in achieving so far. Lang was a friend of the Brecht family, and had supported Brecht's immigration with an affidavit and raised funds for his support (Aurich, Jacobsen, and Schnauber 335–40).

The entry of the United States into World War II had presented Hollywood with the opportunity to participate in the war effort by producing anti-Nazi films. Before 1941 the American movie industry had avoided such films, because the studios did not want to antagonize Nazi authorities and risk losing the profitable German market. For that reason Charlie Chaplin had to finance *The Great Dictator* (1940) out of his own pocket. But after Germany's declaration of war, the situation changed. The German market was lost, but anti-Nazi films formed a profitable new direction.

The report of Heydrich's assassination was welcome news to the movie industry, as it offered producers and directors a true story to depict. Judging from the newspaper report of July 28, 1942, Lang's project was not the only one in the making. The new production company Angelus Pictures claimed priority on the title *Heydrich the Hangman*, but their movie was never made. As chief of the Nazi security police and the highest-ranking Nazi official in German-occupied Czechoslovakia, Heydrich was a fascinating figure for movie and mythmakers alike. What was not known at the time was that Heydrich had also been the mastermind behind the Final Solution, which he had introduced at a conference in the Wannsee suburb of Berlin in January 1942.

In retrospect, Heydrich's assassination was a great success for the Czech government in exile, but the Czech residents paid a heavy price, as the men of Lidice were executed, the women were sent to concentration camps, and the children were put into orphanages because the villagers were suspected of harboring the assassins. The village's buildings were set on fire and the ruins bulldozed so that no trace of them would remain. According to Gestapo reports, 199 men were executed and 195 women arrested, and of the ninety-five children, eight were selected for "Germanization," while the rest disappeared. Although there was no hard evidence that the villagers had sheltered the parchutists responsible for Heydrich's death, this mass murder took place on the day of Heydrich's funeral, on June 9, 1942. In the end, there were more than 5,000 victims of Nazi reprisals in retaliation for the assassination (MacDonald 185–99).

Although Heydrich's car was bombed on May 27, 1942, he was not instantly killed. It was a week later, on June 4, 1942, that he died from his injuries. On June 9, 1942, an elaborate state funeral was staged for him in Berlin. Through its informers the Gestapo had collected information that pointed toward parachutists from Britain as the attackers rather than members of the Czech resistance. Nazi security forces were finally able to track down the team of four parachutists—two of them had carried out the attack—in the crypt of an Orthodox church in Prague on June 18, 1942, but all four committed suicide before they could be arrested. For propaganda reasons, it was in the Nazis' interest to blame British intelligence for the assassination rather than the Czech people, who were considered pacified by the Germans and were essential to the German war effort, especially in the armament industry. The parachutists were soldiers of the Czech army in exile and were trained by British intelligence, but they could not have operated in Nazi-occupied Czechoslovakia without the assistance of the local Czech resistance. Since the German government could not keep the assassination a secret, they tried to manipulate the information about the event, coloring the assassination as the result of intervention by British rather than Czech agents, but their massive reprisals against the Czech population contradicted their own fabrications.

Brecht and Lang, however, preferred to present the assassination as the action of a local resistance group that was supported by the Czech population because they wanted to provide evidence of popular uprisings in Nazi-occupied Europe. It is not clear whether Brecht and Lang followed their own intuition or directions by the Czech government in exile, which they had contacted for information. Concerned about the potential victims of Nazi reprisals, the Czech government in exile had denied responsibility for the assassination and claimed that the attack had been carried out by the underground without any instructions from London (MacDonald 207). Brecht and Lang obviously preferred the idea of local resistance, since it agreed with their first hunch that this was a story about civilian hostages. Therefore, they disregarded the historical events when they completed their film treatment. There are no parachute agents in their treatment or in the final movie. The assassination is presented as an action by the Czech underground that was carried out by a single assassin, a doctor from a local hospital.

On June 29, Brecht reported that he was working with Lang on the story from nine in the morning until seven in the evening. When they discussed the logic of events or continuity, Brecht often disagreed with Lang's arguments, which were based on audience reaction. Brecht found Lang more interested in surprises than in building suspense (GBA 27: 109). On July 20, Brecht wrote, "With Lang all the time, working on the hostage story to earn my bread. Supposed to get $5000, plus $3000 for further collaboration" (GBA 27: 115). By July 27, Brecht was complaining that the film was a "dismal fabrication," with hackneyed situations and false notes. He realized that the film's story belonged strictly to the framework of a bourgeois-national uprising and not of a proletarian revolution (GBA 27: 116).

Brecht continued to work on the script in August and September of 1942, now in collaboration with John Wexley, an American screenwriter, in an office of United Artists on Las Palmas Street in Hollywood. Wexley was hired because he wrote idiomatic English yet was fluent in German. Furthermore, he had written the screenplay of the first anti-Nazi film, *Confessions of a Nazi Spy* (1939), and was known to be a left-winger. On September 14, Brecht recorded that he had gained Wexley's support in writing "a totally new ideal script" at his home in the evening, a script that Brecht intended to present to Lang later. Brecht wanted the script to concentrate on the people. His preferred title for the film at that stage was therefore Trust the People. In October, both Wexley and Brecht asked for a raise. The raises were granted, but the writers were admonished by Lang to finish the main script. As a result, Wexley ceased to cooperate with Brecht in working on the "ideal script," which consisted of only seventy pages at that stage (GBA 27: 125). The "ideal script" was, however, never found among Brecht's papers, and there is some doubt whether it ever existed.

Brecht's diary entry of October 18, 1942, shows his approval of the final script, as he considered including some of the scenes from the movie in the projected publication of his works. He mentions the scene in which Heydrich meets with the Czech industrialists to show them evidence of sabotage:

> This is an intelligent presentation of modern tyrant: the terror is set in motion because Czech workers are sabotaging production destined for Hitler's war in the east. Thus the German terror has the same impersonal character as the Czech assassination.—then there are several scenes with

the hostages where class differences in the camp are shown. Just five minutes before the Nazis take the hostages for execution, there are displays of
anti-Semitism in their midst. (GBA 27: 129)

The scene with Heydrich appears in the final version of the movie as it is
described by Brecht. One may question Brecht's characterization of the
scene as "impersonal," but not his basic outline of the film. Most revealing, however, is Brecht's comment that the film was constructed in
the manner of epic theater, "with three stories that succeed one another,
the story of an assassin, the story of a girl whose father is taken hostage
and who knows something, and the story of a quisling, who is finished
off by [the people of] an entire town. That, for example, is not bad; nor
is the bit about the underground movement making mistakes which are
corrected by the broad mass of the people" (GBA 27: 129). From this
entry it is clear that Brecht not only approved the film's story and its
structure, but he also believed that at that stage the film met his expectations of "epic construction." What he did not anticipate was the fact
that Lang's ideas, formed by the principles of film noir, sometimes appeared to be identical with those of epic theater and at other times radically diverged from them. What has been considered a personality conflict between Brecht and Lang, or the quarrel of a European intellectual
with a representative of the Hollywood culture industry, was in fact a
clash between epic theater and film noir. And film noir won in *Hangmen
Also Die,* to the benefit of the movie.

Although the term *film noir* was coined in France between 1938 and
1939 (O'Brien 7–21), it became prevalent only after 1946, when French
moviegoers and critics discovered a new genre of American films being
screened in Paris (Naremore 9–39; Dimendberg 4–20). The term, when it
is compared to Brecht's term "epic theater," helps to explain the conflict
between Brecht and Lang. The films mentioned by the French critics as
film noir at that time were John Huston's *The Maltese Falcon* (1941),
Otto Preminger's *Laura* (1944), Edward Dmytryk's *Murder, My Sweet*
(1944), Billy Wilder's *Double Indemnity* (1944), and Fritz Lang's *The
Woman in the Window* (1944). But since some of the beginnings of film
noir can be traced back to the films of the Weimar Republic during the
early 1930s, especially to Lang's masterpiece *M* (1931), the use of the
term may be justified.

Too much has been made of the disagreements between Brecht and
Lang (see Cornelius Schnauber and Wolfgang Gersch, among others).
Brecht's October diary entries provide evidence of the frustrations he felt

as a result of changes in the script and the fact that Lang did not cast Fritz Kortner, a German exile actor, Oskar Homolka, an Austrian exile actor, or Brecht's wife, Helene Weigel, in the film. Lang argued that all the Czech characters should be played by actors who spoke English as their first language and only the German characters should be played by actors with a German accent, "in order to demonstrate more vividly to American audiences what an occupation was like" (Eisner 237–38). Indeed, the introductory scene of the film, in which Heydrich is at the Hradshin, the seat of government in Prague since the Middle Ages, was filmed almost entirely in German.

One probable reason for the alienation between Brecht and Lang was that Brecht was not treated as an equal during the later stages of the production, but only as part of the team that was responsible for the screenplay. Brecht was also out of the loop when Lang was ordered by Pressburger to start shooting the film three weeks earlier than planned. At that moment Lang realized that the script was far too long and he brought in a third writer to cut it by about 30 percent. Of course, Brecht was furious when he found out that scenes that he considered essential had been deleted.

After Brecht had not heard from Lang for two weeks, he was finally invited to the filming of the movie, which had begun on November 2, 1942. Brecht's diary shows his frustration with scenes that Lang had cut or changed and that were now filmed without his input. On December 13, Brecht recorded the "Solidarity Song" in his diary, in order to preserve it for the record:

> brother, it is time
> brother, be prepared
> pass on the invisible flag now!
> in dying you'll still be the same as you were in your life
> you will not, comrade, surrender to them.
> today you're defeated, which makes you a slave
> but the war only ends when the last battle is fought
> but the war will not end till the last battle is fought.
>
> brother, it is time
> brother, be prepared
> pass on the invisible flag now!
> violence or war, it's still in the balance
> but when slavery's day is done, a new day will follow,
> today you are defeated, which makes you a slave
> but the war only ends when the last battle is fought
> but the war will not end until the last battle is fought.

(GBA 27: 145–46)

FIGURE 11. Still photo from *Hangmen Also Die,* circa 1943, audience at the Hradshin with Hans von Twardowsky as SS-Obergruppenführer Reinhard Heydrich and Arthur Loft as Czech general Vortruba. Photograph courtesy of University of Southern California Cinema-Television Library, Los Angeles.

The "Solidarity Song," the inspiration of the Czech resistance in the movie, was central to the controversy between Brecht and Lang because Brecht believed that the song was trivialized in the English translation, commissioned by Lang. This Brecht text of the film is verifiably by Brecht; all other identifications are conjecture. The screenplay is not included in Brecht's collected works, but James K. Lyon has argued that it should be added to his corpus on the basis of the outline and treatment. On the basis of comparisons with some of Brecht's plays, Lyon attributes the screenplay to Brecht "with assistance by Wexley" ("Hangmen Also Die" 457; *Brecht plus minus Film* 35; *Brecht Yearbook* 30 [2005]: 1–6).

The tune that Hanns Eisler composed for the "Solidarity Song" resembles the melody of a song of the Communist International (Comintern), which would have been familiar to left-wing listeners but not to the general audience. Brecht was unhappy with the translation of the song, calling it "a piece of incredible crap" on December 17. The term "comrade" had been dropped and the "invisible flag" had been changed into an "invisible torch." Due to the difference in meaning of "torch" in American and British English, Brecht misunderstood the phrase "invisible torch" as "invisible flashlight." Instead of the "invisible flag" *(die unsichtbare Fahne),* it was now an "invisible torch" that was to be passed on from brother to brother, and Brecht commented that "invisible lightbulbs" were not an obvious symbol (GBA 27: 145–46). He also protested the plotline that involved the writing of the song by a worker in the hostages' camp:

> He reads it to a famous poet. He thinks for a second whether he should correct phrases like "invisible torch," then lets it stand as adequate and worth recording. Now Lang has cast the poet not as a fat alcoholic . . . but as a Ganghofer-type (kind, pale, vain) and he now has to find that same phrase "invisible torch" wonderful. In this way the scene becomes almost realistic: a proletarian expresses himself in the bourgeoisie's cast-off clichés, and the bourgeoisie swallows them with feeling! (GBA 27: 146)

Ludwig Ganghofer (1855–1920) was a popular novelist who liked to be photographed in the pose of a creative genius. According to the last sentence of this diary entry, Lang was unaware of the irony of this scene, which almost found Brecht's approval because of the dialectics of the class struggle involved in the production and approval of the song.

In the following months Brecht's irritation with Lang disappeared from his diaries, perhaps because Brecht had found more inspiring work in his collaboration with Lion Feuchtwanger. He did not even record the premier of *Hangmen Also Die,* on March 26, 1943. The only other outburst against Lang and his crew occurred on January 20, 1943, when Brecht wrote that "the sight of spiritual mutilation" of the film made him sick: "It is almost impossible to stand being in the same room with these spiritual cripples and moral invalids" (GBA 27: 148). Brecht went before the Screen Writers Guild to protest that he was denied screen credit as coauthor of the script. In spite of Lang's and Hanns Eisler's support, the Screen Writers Guild decided against Brecht and in favor of John Wexley as sole author of the screenplay. According to Lang, he yielded his own rights as author of the original story in order to allow the sole credit to go to Brecht after the decision in favor of Wexley. The final version of the film, however, shows both Lang's and Brecht's names for adaptation and the original story, with Brecht's name appearing first. The placement of his name was suggested by Lang, although Brecht was apparently not informed of Lang's gesture. At least, he never recorded the results of the arbitration before the Screen Writers Guild in his diary. According to

Lang, the arbitrators found in favor of Wexley on the grounds that Brecht would be returning to Germany in due course and could therefore do without the credit. One member of the arbitration panel later said that "Wexley got away with a credit he didn't deserve" (McGilligan 302).

The last entry on *Hangmen Also Die* in Brecht's diary, on June 24, 1943, was a reflection on the money that he had received for the film: it gave him "enough breathing space for three plays *(The Visions of Simone Machard, The Duchess of Malfi, Schweyk)*" (GBA 27: 152). The work that had occupied Brecht in the meantime was his collaboration with Lion Feuchtwanger on *The Visions of Simone Machard*, a Jean d'Arc play set in contemporary France. He found this collaboration more satisfactory than his work for the movies. Feuchtwanger developed the plot into a novel of his own, entitled *Simone,* and sold the story to Metro-Goldwyn-Mayer in 1944, sharing the honorarium with Brecht. The project was, however, never realized, although the financial arrangements were much more acceptable to Brecht than the haggling about the screen credits for *Hangmen Also Die.*

This is not the place for another telling of the controversy between Brecht and Lang, but rather for a discussion of the clash between the aesthetic principles involved on both sides. In many ways, epic theater and film noir aimed for similar effects, but they were radically different in terms of spectator reaction. While film noir tries to involve the spectator emotionally in the action, epic theater wants the spectator to be a rational observer who makes intelligent decisions. Brecht placed film noir in the category of the "culinary," considering it an art form that is designed to satisfy the emotional needs of entertainment. But if one compares Brecht's distinction between "culinary theater" (or, rather, "culinary opera") and epic theater and looks at the chart comparing the dramatic and epic forms of theater he drew up in 1930 (White 50–73), it will become clear that film noir cannot be written off as completely "culinary":

"DRAMATIC FORM OF THEATER"	"EPIC FORM OF THEATER"
the stage "reincarnates" events	it narrates events
it involves the spectator in the action and uses up his energy	it makes him an observer, but rouses him to action
gives him experience	gives him knowledge
the human being is a given factor	the human being is object of inquiry
eyes on the finish	eyes on the course
one scene in relation to others	every scene independent of others
the world as it is	the world as it will be

| human instincts | human motivation |
| thought determines existence | social existence determines thought. |

(GBA 24: 78–79)

Lang never established such a binary list, but it is obvious that some of the features of film noir are similar to those of the epic form, such as the fact that "the human being is the object of inquiry," the emphasis on "human motivation" and the idea "that social existence determines thought." As Anton Kaes says about Lang's film *M*, which is often classified as a film noir, the movie's "structure in its presentational gestus and epic sweep . . . resembled Brecht's Epic Theatre," but Lang's project was "ultimately a different one" (36; see also Gunning 263–64). Brecht put his finger on the problem when he protested against the " 'surprises,' which consist in impossible things happening," and against the " 'moments of suspense,' which consist of withholding information from the audience" (GBA 27: 130). The latter—withholding information—especially was a feature of film noir, whereas epic theater informed its audience beforehand of the events to take place on the stage. The common denominator was that both were dialectical. What complicated the matter even further was the fact that Lang considered himself "a 100% Brechtian" (Bonnaud 38).

As the French critics Raymond Borde and Étienne Chaumeton argue, the main objective of film noir was to "disorient . . . the spectator." The resulting confusion and alienation were an intellectual dilemma that had to be solved. As Borde and Chaumeton explain, "The moviegoer [was] accustomed to certain conventions: a logical development of action, a clear distinction between good and evil, well-defined characters, sharp motives, scenes more showy than authentically violent, a beautiful heroine and an honest hero" (Borde and Chaumenton 24). In film noir, however, the moviegoer was confronted with a world that did not conform to his expectations: there were "likeable killers and corrupt cops. Good and evil go hand in hand to the point of being indistinguishable. Robbers become ordinary guys. . . . The victim seems as guilty as the hitman who is just doing his job" (Borde and Chaumenton 25). It was the moviegoer's task to sort out this confusion—a task similar to that of the observer of epic theater. But while epic theater forced its spectators to make decisions as outside observers, film noir involved the moviegoers emotionally in the action and inspired "that state of tension . . . in the spectator when the psychological reference points are removed" (Borde and Chaumenton 25).

Lang had incorporated aspects of film noir in his celebrated movie *M* (1931) and in his Mabuse cycle (1922, 1932), and he employed them now in *Hangmen Also Die*. The film's story was characterized by a reversal of the standard values of society, but, in contrast to the manner in which it would be handled in epic theater, this reversal was constructed not in terms of rational dialectics, but rather in terms of dialectics of emotional suspense and ambiguity. Like *M*, Lang's masterpiece about a serial child murderer on the loose whom the police were unable to apprehend, his anti-Nazi film was also about a killer and incompetent cops, but in this case the killer was a member of the Czech resistance and the cops were Gestapo agents.

What makes *M* a film noir—besides the camera work and the sound effects—is the ambiguity of values. The murderer is presented not as a monster, but as a retarded person with a certain degree of childlike amiability. Film historian James Naremore describes this film noir feature as generating "sympathy for the devil" (63). The audience feels empathy with the pedophile, especially when he admits in despair that he cannot help his actions because of a curse inside him. As Lang explained, he counted on audience identification with "the outlaw who defies society and exults in cruelty" (quoted from Eisner 112). For a brief moment, the moviegoers are supposed to feel some sympathy for the criminal and want him to get away with murder.

In *M*, a gangster organization offers to assist the police in their search for this "abnormal" criminal because they cannot pursue their "honest crimes" because of unpredictable police raids. In his detailed interpretation of *M*, Tom Gunning shows that the operations of the underworld are presented as a direct reflection of "the legal structures and official codes of power" of the police. The mobster chief and "his gang organize to restore 'normal' order to the city" in exactly the same fashion as the chief of police and his police force (Gunning 181). The gangsters manage to apprehend the murderer and bring him before a gangster court, where he confesses that he is a victim of his drive to kill. The trial, conducted by outlaws, follows the same procedures as a regular court, including the use of a presiding officer, testimony, and a defense attorney (Gunning 193). The murderer's confession elicits some understanding or empathy from the audience. Kaes identified the murderer as a film noir hero who takes "a perverse pleasure in the act of retelling his crime" (68). The mobsters are outraged by his pathological crime and are ready to lynch him, but in the end he is handed over to the regular courts. Although a judge proclaims "In the name of the people," no sentence is pronounced. The film leaves the final verdict open.

The same aesthetic principles were applied to the anti-Nazi plot of *Hangmen Also Die:* the audience is required to reverse its value system because of the exceptional situation created by a foreign occupation. The hunt for Heydrich's assassin is presented like the search for a regular criminal in a mystery movie, but in this case the crime has to be understood as a heroic act. The authorities are the criminals, while the murderer was motivated by a noble cause. Lang makes it relatively easy for his audience to perform this reversal. The introductory scene shows Heydrich at a conference announcing his determination to put an end to the sabotage and slow-downs by Czech workers in the Skoda armament industry. The audience is left with no doubts about Heydrich, who displays arrogance and cruelty as he prepares to give orders for mass executions. On the other hand, his assassin, Dr. Franz Svoboda, is shown as the attractive leading man in a developing love story. Although he is on the run from the Nazi security forces, he is impeccably dressed with hat and tie, as if he were going on a date. To gain the trust of the family of Professor Novotny, he invents a fictitious amorous encounter with the professor's daughter, Mascha, in order to cover up his involvement in the assassination. In the beginning Mascha plays her part as if she were the leading lady in a love triangle involving Svoboda and Jan Horek, her fiancé. She supports Svoboda's ruse without hesitation, but the audience is made aware, together with Mascha, that there must be more to Svoboda's white lie than is obvious. Professor Novotny offers Svoboda an invitation to stay at their apartment when the Nazi curfew is announced, but he refuses to listen to any explanation by either Mascha or the doctor.

After this seemingly straightforward exposition, Lang sets the ambiguities of film noir into motion again: Svoboda becomes a villain in Mascha's eyes because he does not give himself up when the Nazis arrest four hundred hostages, including her father. The Nazis announce that until the assassin is found, they are going to execute a certain number of hostages in rapid succession. What Mascha does not know is that Svoboda is ready to sacrifice his life but is not allowed to surrender because of orders from the resistance. His expertise is still needed for other underground operations. Not aware of these facts, and out of love for her father, she goes to the local Gestapo headquarters intending to denounce Svoboda and obtain the release of her father.

At this moment, as Tom Gunning points out, "the Prague in *Hang-*

men, like Berlin in *M,* possesses a dual power system, both the official Nazi authorities and the shadowy institution of the Czech underground." The underground appears as ruthless as the Nazi terror because it does not prevent the arrest and execution of hostages: "The underground [creates] a system of terror as much as the Nazis in this film" (Gunning 295). Without realizing it, Brecht came across this principle of film noir when he observed that in the film's presentation the German terror had the same impersonal character as the Czech assassination (GBA 27: 129).

Once at the Gestapo headquarters, Mascha realizes that she has become involved on the wrong side. Although she does not reveal any of Svoboda's secrets, she is suspected of having contacts with the assassin. After her release by the Nazis, she is closely observed by Gestapo agents under the direction of Inspector Gruber. The Gestapo men are portrayed not as brutal thugs, but as dangerous police agents and bureaucrats who know their trade. Gruber, who was played by Alexander Granach, a well-known exile actor, is presented as an especially unscrupulous but highly intelligent detective. As Reynold Humphries observes, Inspector Gruber was much closer to the "positive hero" than the other Gestapo men who tortured Czech prisoners (89). Again and again, Gruber sets ingenious traps for Mascha and Svoboda, but they are always one step ahead of him and manage to escape.

Meanwhile, the resistance movement is under great pressure to surrender the assassin in order to stop the execution of the hostages. Because of the increasing number of innocent victims, popular opinion turns against them. Furthermore, based on information leaked to the Gestapo, Emil Czaka, the owner of a brewery, is suspected of being an informer or double agent. The resistance plots to deliver Czaka into the hands of the Germans as the alleged assassin. They test his claim that he does not know any German, but Czaka gives himself away when he laughs at a Hitler joke told in German by a waiter. Convinced of his double-dealing, the resistance is able to mobilize the Prague population and to use fabricated evidence to frame Czaka as the assassin of Heydrich and the murderer of Gruber. This plan is put into action in typical film noir fashion, with the audience left in the dark about plan's details. Totally surprised by the turn of events, the audience sees a perfect chain of evidence assembled against Czaka as alleged assassin. Even the revolver used in Heydrich's assassination turns up in Czaka's desk. Although a turncoat, Czaka is innocent of this particular crime. Duped by the evidence, the Gestapo men swiftly execute him in gangster style. He is driven to a deserted part of town, set free, and then gunned down in front of an open church door. Although the Nazis are fully aware that Czaka is the wrong man, the Gestapo does not hesitate to announce that they have captured and punished the assassin. The new governor who replaces Heydrich reports to Berlin that the occupying German authorities are compelled to save face and "choose the lesser evil by accepting Czaka as the assassin— and thus close the case" (text of letter in *Hangmen Also Die*). The truth does not matter to the Nazis in the propaganda war waged to keep the Czech population under control.

Inspector Gruber is on the right track when he closes in on Svoboda at the local hospital, but he does not take into account the popular support Svoboda enjoys. When Gruber tries to hold Svoboda and his colleague in check with his revolver, he is attacked from behind by Mascha's fiancé, Jan Horek, who until that moment has been jealous of Svoboda and uninvolved in politics. Horek then strangles Huber under a pile of sheets. The resistance is thus able to keep the identity of Heydrich's assassin a secret, and the Nazis have to continue coping with never-ending rumors about the conspiracy of the people of Prague.

Lotte Eisner reports that different versions of the ending were filmed. According to Eisner, "in the original version of the film the fact of the shooting of [Professor Novotny] was shown, followed by the flower-decked graves of the hostages, to indicate that the Nazis in fact broke their promise after the (apparent) surrender of the assassin" (230). According to Patrick McGilligan, the mass-grave scene was filmed and photographed for publicity purposes, but Lang thought better of it and deleted it from the final film (296). James K. Lyon, however, insists that the premiere edition of the film showed as one of the final scenes the execution of the remaining hostages, including Professor Novotny ("Hangmen Also Die" 462).

Most of the video versions now in circulation do not include these final scenes. Instead the audience sees the outline of the Hradshin as Brecht's solidarity song, "Never Surrender!" is delivered. The end of the movie is left open in the style of film noir: instead of the expected end title, the audience sees as the last frame the words: "NOT The End." This nonclosure is evidence of the link between film noir and modernism. Its message, however, is not ambiguous: the popular resistance is to continue. There will be new members to whom the resistance can "pass on the invisible torch." At the beginning and end of the film, the Hradshin, an assembly of medieval churches and baroque palaces overlooking the city, figures as "the shining city on the hill," symbolizing past and future freedom, while Prague under German occupation shows throughout the movie the terrifying aspects of the "centripetal urban space" that Edward Dimendberg associated with early film noir (6–17): dark alleys, dinky lodgings, smoke-filled back rooms, tawdry taverns, dark movie houses, conspiratorial meeting places in warehouses, prison cells, interrogation rooms, Gestapo offices, and barracks for the Czech hostages. Even the rooms of Professor Novotny's apartment are dark.

The artistic freedom associated with a production independent from the Hollywood studios was not fully realized in *Hangmen Also Die*. The film had to compete in a market that was controlled by the culture industry, and Lang felt that he had to make certain concessions to the American audience. While Lang and Brecht were still working on the story in June 1942, Brecht noticed that Lang's criterion for including certain events or adhering to a certain logic was whether "the public will accept that." Brecht sarcastically commented, "The public accepts the mastermind of the resistance hiding behind a curtain when the Gestapo searches a house." Listing some other improbable events, such as corpses falling out of wardrobes and mass meetings during a period of Nazi terror, Brecht contemptuously concluded that "Lang 'buys' that kind of thing," employing one of his favorite metaphors for Hollywood dealings: selling and buying (GBA 27: 109).

On October 16, 1942, Brecht recorded an altercation between Lang and John Wexley that revealed the pressure to conform to audience expectations. Behind closed doors Lang screamed at his scriptwriter, saying that he wanted to make a "hollywoodpicture" [*sic*] and that he "did not give a shit" about scenes that showed the people (GBA 27: 126). Financial pressures by the banks had forced the producer Arnold Pressburger to order Lang to begin shooting three weeks earlier than planned. The screenplay of about 280 pages also had to be reduced to shooting length within a short time. Most of this work was done by Wexley, according to Lyon ("A Qualified Winner" 65).

Due to the increased demand for anti-Nazi films, *Hangmen Also Die* was successful at the box office. It was also popular with most of the critics, especially those writing for the German exile papers in the United States (Horak 323–24). *Hangmen* also made the list of the best films of 1943 in the balloting of the New York Film Critics Circle, but it failed to win any Oscars at the 1943 Academy Awards (it was nominated for best sound recording and for best scoring). Best picture that year was awarded to *Casablanca* with Humphrey Bogart and Ingrid Bergman.

Film historians disagree about the merits of *Hangmen Also Die*. Tom

Gunning considers the political scenes with the hostages "unimaginative and unoriginal, especially the intoning of the resistance poem, and most of the leads, with the exception of Granach, give wooden, uninspired performances" (295), while Jürgen Schebera calls it one of the best anti-Nazi films to be produced during the early 1940s (218). For Jan-Christopher Horak, the film's emphasis on parallels between democratic traditions in Czechoslovakia and the United States is most significant. The Czech traditions were represented by Professor Novotny, whose character was based on Czechoslovakian statesmen such as Tomáš Masaryk and Edward Beneš. Otherwise, Horak ascribes a liberal, democratic ideology with leftist tendencies to the film (338–40). Reynold Humphries mentions the intimate relationship between *Hangmen Also Die* and the gangster film on the level of both dialogue and representation: "Surely it is a perfect example of one discourse—the gangster film—taking over another discourse—the anti-Nazi film—via tactics of repetition and memory destined to satisfy audience demands for the same" (89). French critics Jean Comolli and François Géré, however, go too far when they conclude that within the film noir structure of *Hangmen Also Die* even the spectators are condemned: they lose their desire for truth and their hope for justice. Although they have "to submit to the law of deceit" and seem to "have no more choice than the characters" (376), there can be no doubt that in the end they find themselves on the side of the underground and their hatred is directed unequivocally against the Nazi occupation. Gerd Gemünden, who also thought that the manipulation of falsehood was one of the main features of Lang's style, concludes that the "representations of false appearances that hide the truth" (74) in *Hangmen Also Die* is perhaps more dialectical than the anti-illusionism of Brecht's epic theater.

CHAPTER 6

California Modern
as Immigrant Modernism

*Architects Richard Neutra
and Rudolph M. Schindler*

Between the 1930s and 1940s immigrant modernism and exile modernism overlapped in Southern California. The representatives of immigrant modernism had arrived here during the 1920s. Many of them were working in the film industry, as, for example, William Dieterle, Ernst Lubitsch, Josef von Sternberg, and Erich von Stroheim; others, such as Richard Joseph Neutra (1892–1970) and Rudolph Michael Schindler (1887–1953), established careers in architecture. Both Neutra and Schindler had designed and built their signature examples of modernist architecture in Southern California before the first exiles from Nazi Germany arrived in Los Angeles. Therefore, Neutra and Schindler were, strictly speaking, immigrants rather than exiles. But comparing their type of modernism with that of the exiles of the 1930s and 1940s helps us to understand German exile culture *ex negativo* and render a more detailed profile of exile modernism. Such a comparison also establishes the general background for Weimar culture in Los Angeles, which began before 1933 and exerted its influence beyond the 1970s.

When Schindler and, a few years later, Neutra came to Los Angeles in the 1920s, they had been hired to work for Frank Lloyd Wright, the most famous architect of that period. Both were students of the architectural modernism emerging in Austria, but when they came to Southern California they adapted their modernism to their new homeland. Their European background placed them in close proximity to the exiles of the 1940s, but their experience was different. Neutra and Schindler witnessed the collapse of the Weimar Republic and the Austrian Repub-

FIGURE 12. Rudolph M. Schindler. Photograph courtesy of R. M. Schindler Collection, Architecture and Design Collection, University Art Museum, University of California, Santa Barbara.

lic from the West Coast. Both Neutra and Schindler were Austro-American Jews and tried to help relatives to escape to America from German-occupied Austria. The Nazi *Anschluss* of 1938 and the implementation of the Nuremberg laws prevented them from visiting their home country. The Neutras were in contact with Albert Einstein when he was a visiting professor at the California Institute of Technology in Pasadena in 1932; with Emil Ludwig, the author of popular biographies of Goethe and Bismarck; with Otto Klemperer, conductor of the Los Angeles Philharmonic; with the actress Luise Rainer and her husband, the American playwright Clifford Odets; as well as with Arnold Schoenberg, Ernst and Lilly Toch, and Lion and Marta Feuchtwanger (see Hines, *Richard Neutra,* 186–87).

But these experiences did not make either Neutra or Schindler exiles, as the British architectural critic Reyner Banham argued in his seminal book of 1971 on the architecture of four ecologies in Los Angeles. He claimed to detect in Neutra's and Schindler's buildings "the nervous feel-

FIGURE 13. Richard Neutra and Julius Shulman at the Tremaine House, Los Angeles, California, 1947. Photograph courtesy of Julius Shulman. © J. Paul Getty Trust. Used with permission of the Julius Shulman Photography Archive, Research Library at the Getty Research Institute, Los Angeles.

ing of creative angst" of European modernism, but he had to admit that they were "Californiated" (189). Not only were Neutra and Schindler not exiles, but there were tensions, or at least a certain distance, between them and the exiles who arrived in Los Angeles somewhat later. Neutra's wife Dione expressed strong reservations about the exiles of the 1940s and criticized them for wanting to go back to Europe and finding fault with everything in the United States. For this reason, she maintained, the Neutras did not cultivate contact with the exile community. And, as Dione reported in her oral history, she and her husband even stayed away from the German and Swiss immigrants who were already in Los Angeles in the 1920s, because they wanted to become Americans.

Any comparisons between the work of Schindler and Neutra and the Bauhaus are misleading insofar as both Schindler and Neutra were students of Otto Wagner and Adolph Loos, the major representatives of Viennese modernism, and, except for Neutra in 1930, they did not have much contact with German modernism, developed at the Bauhaus school for architecture in Weimar, then in Dessau, and finally in Berlin. But the Bauhaus style was associated with the International Style in the United States, and Neutra was perceived as being committed to this International Style. As curators of the landmark 1932 exhibition "Modern Architecture" at the Museum of Modern Art in New York, Henry-Russell Hitchcock and Philip Johnson had coined the term "International Style" in order to characterize the simultaneous development of similar trends in architecture in several different countries and their worldwide distribution. While this designation fit Neutra, it did not sit well with Schindler, who argued against its functionalism, which he considered monotonous and out of date. The term that best characterizes the styles of both Neutra and Schindler is California modernism.

Neutra's and Schindler's reactions to the crisis of modernism were quite different from those of the exiles of the 1940s. Because they were immigrants of the 1920s, they wanted to become successful in the United States. They manipulated modernism to adapt it to their new home country, on the one hand, and to incorporate indigenous ideas and local materials, on the other. Therefore, their example offers an instructive contrast to the attempts by the other group from Central Europe that was wrestling with a totally different problem after being expelled from their homelands after 1933. Neutra and Schindler wanted to reshape modernism in order to establish it in California, while the exiles of the 1940s wanted to redirect modernism because it had failed to combat fascism in Central Europe. The exiles' asylum in Los Angeles provided them with an opportunity to revise modernism in view of the present and future forms of totalitarianism.

Schindler's had trained in Austria under the modernists most representative of Austrian architecture, such as Otto Wagner and Adolph Loos. The latter was an admirer of America and encouraged Schindler to find employment there. Schindler had come to the United States in 1914 in order to work with an architectural firm in Chicago, but his ambition was to join Wright's studio. Both Schindler and Neutra had discovered Wright through the 1910 publication of his work in a deluxe edition by Ernst Wasmuth, a Berlin publisher well known for books on architecture. Both were deeply impressed by Wright's designs. It took Schindler three years in the United States before he was able to meet with Frank Lloyd Wright, who offered him his Chicago office to complete a project for his previous employer. Afterwards he joined Wright at Taliesin in Wisconsin to work on his new commission, the Imperial Hotel in Tokyo. While Wright was in Japan, Schindler supervised the offices in Chicago and Taliesin.

Wright built eight houses commissioned in Los Angeles and Pasadena during the 1920s, among them the Hollyhock House, a home he designed for oil heiress Aline Barnsdall in 1921, and the Freeman House, a concrete-block house built in 1924 (Sweeney, *Wright*). While he was working on contracts in other parts of the world, Wright sent Schindler in 1920 to supervise the construction of the Hollyhock House. Without Wright's assignment, Schindler probably would never have come to Los Angeles. In 1925 Schindler was joined by his friend Richard Neutra, who had emigrated to the United States in 1923. Neutra's training in Vienna had been similar to that of Schindler. After working for some firms in Chicago and New York, Neutra had also been invited by Frank Lloyd Wright to work at his Taliesin studio in Wisconsin. In addition to his Austrian training Neutra had previously worked with Erich Mendelsohn, one of the best-known modernist architects in Berlin, from 1921 to 1923. He had also become acquainted with the new ideas and designs of the Bauhaus at exhibitions in Berlin.

In 1925 Neutra moved to Los Angeles and rented an apartment from the Schindlers in their house and studio on Kings Road. Schindler had built this innovative combination of home and office in West Hollywood in 1921–22. It was designed to accommodate two artist/architect couples in separate studios and living quarters, with a communal kitchen, a two-car garage, and an additional unit earmarked as a separate guest studio with its own bath and kitchen. In the beginning, Schindler and his wife, Pauline Gibling Schindler, lived there with Clyde Chace, who helped in constructing the house, and his wife, Marian. After the Chaces left for Florida to join the family's construction business in 1924, Richard Neutra and his wife moved in. Today's so-called "Schindler House" is located at 835 North Kings Road and is open to the public. It serves as the MAK Center for Art and Architecture, L.A. of Vienna's Museum for Applied Art (*Museum für angewandte Kunst*, abbreviated as MAK) in Los Angeles and is administered by MAK in cooperation with the Friends of the Schindler House, a nonprofit organization. The house is the most accessible example of California modernist architecture during the 1920s.

For a while the house served as home for Schindler's and Neutra's families and as an office for their architectural firm, but by 1927 tensions had developed between the two architects over theoretical issues and the commission for the Lovell Health House. Schindler claimed that Neutra had taken the commission away from him, while Neutra said that Philip

Lovell gave him the commission because he was dissatisfied with Schindler's designs. But there were also other reasons for the conflict: it was difficult to raise children in this house, and both the Schindlers and the Neutras soon had to take care of newborn sons. In addition, there were tensions in the Schindler marriage that ultimately led to their divorce in 1940. Pauline Schindler left the Schindler House for the first time in 1927, returning intermittently for short stays, while the Neutras left for good; in 1930 Neutra traveled to Asia and then to Europe, where he was joined by his wife, after which they never returned to the house. When they came back to Los Angeles the architectural partnership was finally dissolved, and Neutra set up his new home and studio on Douglas Street in Echo Park in 1931.

Neutra had become famous during the late 1920s. During his visit to Europe in 1930 he taught for a month as a visiting professor at the Bauhaus. His designs were featured, along with those of Ludwig Mies van der Rohe, J. J. P. Oud, Charles-Édouard Jeanneret (Le Corbusier), and Frank Lloyd Wright in the historic "Modern Architecture" exhibition at the Museum of Modern Art in New York in 1932. Schindler's work, on the other hand, was rejected. Alfred Barr, the museum's director, dismissed Schindler's designs while calling Neutra "the leading modern architect of the West Coast" (Drexler and Hines 8). As Schindler's wife commented, Neutra had become "the prominent figure in town among modern architects, . . . while [Schindler] remained the mysterious and romantic [artist]." Although there was some truth to this statement, Schindler reacted defensively, associating Neutra with functionalism and the International Style and calling him a "sterile go-getter type" and "racketeer" (Sweeney, "Life," 103).

The Schindler House was the embodiment of Schindler's architectural philosophy and his wife Pauline's idea of an "ideal lifestyle" (Sweeney, "Life," 87). She dreamt of a bungalow "near a crowded city, which shall be open just as some people's hearts are open, to friends of all classes and types." She wanted "it to be as democratic a meeting-place as Hull-House, where millionaires and laborers, professors and illiterates, the splendid and ignoble meet constantly together." Hull House in Chicago was a private social welfare program run by Jane Addams, who attracted to her project many progressive intellectuals and artists, including Pauline Gibling Schindler, who had taught music there. When the Schindler House was originally built, it was located in an open field, as aerial photographs of Beverly Hills and West Hollywood of the early 1920s show. Today it is totally enclosed by the city, and neighboring apartments crowd the one-story building.

FIGURE 14. Schindler Studio House (designed by Schindler in 1921–22), 833 North Kings Road, Hollywood, 2005. Photograph by Juergen Nogai, Santa Monica.

Schindler's architectural philosophy was directed against the functionalism of the International Style. In his manifesto "Modern Architecture: A Program" of 1913, which was translated into English in 1932 when he submitted it to a Japanese architectural journal, he declared that attempts "to make form a symbol of construction or to give construction an artistically expressive form are dead," adding in italics: *"There are no more constructional styles"* (Schindler, "Modern Architecture," 11). He considered any modern style predicated upon construction and new materials, as, for example, reinforced concrete and steel, which are devoid of any artistic basis. Schindler writes, "The architect's instinct 'to build constructionally' has become a hollow slogan in an age that wants to give its artists the strangely necessary exhortation: Build with all the mental and technical resources that your culture offers you" (11). The reason for this conclusion Schindler gave was that, in his opinion, construction had "become monotonously perfect." For Schindler, the genuine task of modern architecture was "the shaping of space" (Mallgrave 15–17). Tracing the architectural history of man from the cave to modern dwellings, Schindler concluded his program with an argument that foreshadowed the *Dialectic of Enlightenment,* insofar as "civilized man has progressed from the fear of the elements to their domination." But Schindler did not perceive the domination of nature as alienation, as Adorno and Horkheimer did, but as a chance to return to nature: "His [civilized man's] home is no longer a timid retreat; his power has enabled him to return to nature." The significance of a dwelling no longer resided "in its formal development, but in the possibility of controlling within its confines light, air, and temperature" (Schindler, "Modern Architecture," 12). Perhaps nowhere is Schindler's program better expressed than in his Kings Road House.

Kathryn Smith, the historian of the Schindler House, may have exaggerated when she claimed that it "was the first executed realization of a new kind of residential architecture for the modern world," but she was correct when she argued that it broke decisively with tradition "in every one of its key elements—its program, its plan, its materials, its construction system, and especially, in its spatial relationships" (Smith, *Schindler House,* 7). For comparison, the "Experimental House am Horn" in Weimar, the first Bauhaus construction, designed by Georg Muche in 1922 for the first Bauhaus exhibition, was built in 1923. Muche (1895–1987) later distinguished himself as abstract painter rather than as an architect.

Schindler's intent for his house, as he stated in an article of 1932, was that it be a "cooperative dwelling for two young couples." The couples were conceived as a group of individuals with a common purpose, and the goal was that each member would be an artist who would contribute to the household's shared ambitions and goals. The layout abolished the "ordinary residential arrangement providing rooms for specialized purposes." The house combined three separate units of living quarters and studios with a shared kitchen under one roof. The plan was that the kitchen be used by both couples. Schindler thought that the wives would "take alternate weekly responsibility for dinner menus, and so gain periods of respite from the incessant household rhythm." Each person had "a large private studio, each couple a common entrance hall and bath," with the plumbing fully exposed to provide a sculptural effect. Open porches on the roof were "to be used for sleeping," but they proved to be too cold for comfort during the winter. The enclosed patios with outdoor fireplaces, one for each couple, were to serve "the purposes of an ordinary living room." Blurring the division between internal and external space, the garden was also divided "into several such private rooms."

There was also a separate guest apartment, with its own bathroom and garden (Schindler, "Cooperative Dwelling," 81).

The building plan consisted of three L-shaped arms that were arranged around a double fireplace. Each L-shaped arm contained the studio space for one couple (in addition to the guest room apartment). The house was constructed using the tilt-slab method, or, as Schindler preferred to call it, the "slab-tilt system." He adopted this practice from Irving Gill, a Los Angeles architect who had developed this "method of constructing walls by pouring concrete into molds and tilting the pre-fabricated sections into place after they cured" (Smith, *Schindler House,* 18). This method resulted in reinforced concrete walls that were "finished on both sides with a minimum of form work" (Schindler, "Cooperative Dwelling," 81). This close cooperation with local talents and the adoption of local methods were characteristic of both Schindler's and Neutra's modernism, and this particular collaboration between Schindler and Irving Gill is only one instance among many that distinguishes their contribution to the architectural style called California modern.

The one-story house was built on a reinforced concrete slab that served as the floor and had a flat composition roof. Sliding doors opened into the individual patios, which had an outdoor fireplace for each unit. The rooms were large studios "with concrete walls on three sides, the front open (glass) to the outdoors—a real California scheme," as Schindler described them (letter to Mr. and Mrs. Edmund J. Gibling). The ceilings, partitions, and patio walls were made of exposed redwood timber, the latter filled with glass and canvas. The clerestory windows allowed the residents to control the light, air, and temperature within the confines of the house, as Schindler had postulated in his program of 1913. Located throughout the house, the clerestory windows provided "a cooling air current right under the roof and [permitted] the sunlight to enter from all sides" (Schindler, "Cooperative Dwelling," 81).

The architectural theme that Schindler envisioned for the house was that of "a camper's shelter: a protected back, and open front, a fire place, and a roof." In October 1921, the Schindlers had spent several weeks camping at Yosemite National Park. During this vacation they decided that Schindler would open his own architectural office in Los Angeles and that they would build their own studio-residence in the city. The design of the Schindler House transferred their Yosemite experience to Los Angeles, enabling them to live in the city yet stay in contact with nature. As Schindler described the rooms, he emphasized again and again that each of them had "a garden front with a large opening fitted with slid-

ing doors." He firmly believed that with the shape of the rooms, their relation to the patios, and the alternating roof levels he had achieved in creating "an entirely new spatial interlocking between the interior and the
garden" ("Cooperative Dwelling" 81).

Richard Neutra's design of the Lovell Health House (1927–29) was
in striking contrast to the Schindler House because it embodied the functionalism that Schindler had declared obsolete. The steel, glass, and concrete residence, built into a steep hill near Griffith Park, was an example
of the overcoming of nature that Schindler abhorred. Schindler doubted
that the machine was a promising model for modern architecture, and in
a 1928 speech he declared the "Machine Age—not Human" (Wilson
117). But he did not reject the advantages offered by steel and concrete,
as his design of the Lovell Beach House in Newport Beach in 1926
showed. It was an intricate structure supported by five reinforced concrete frames that provided both views and privacy for the owners, but
stood out as a commanding structure on the beach.

Neutra called his architectural philosophy "nature-near" (*Nature
Near* 56), but he also believed in machine modernism. He considered his
client for the Lovell Health House, a popular health guru, to be the man
"who could see 'health and future' in a strange wide-open filigree steel
frame, set deftly and precisely by cranes and booms into this inclined
piece of rugged nature" (*Life and Shape* 221). In order to realize his vision, Neutra had to cut into the hillside just below the street to furnish
"the base for the main middle level." Another cut, one level down, provided the base for the "bottom half-floor that housed the laundry, utility, recreation, and dressing rooms, opening onto the pool" (Hines,
Richard Neutra, 79).

Philip Lovell, born as Morris Saperstein in New York, had renamed
himself when he moved to Los Angeles. He had picked up a degree from
a chiropractic college in Kirksville, Missouri, and presented himself as a
holistic doctor who advocated "natural" methods of healing and pre-
ventive health care with an emphasis on exercise, heat and water cures,
open-air sleeping, nude sunbathing, and vegetarianism. He wrote a
widely read column in the *Los Angeles Times* entitled "Care of the
Body." Although he had originally commissioned Schindler to design
and build three houses for him, after some vacillation and some soul-
searching among the architects themselves, he chose Neutra for this
project.

Neutra's Lovell Health House was a bold design that opened the
canyons of Los Angeles, Beverly Hills, and Hollywood to modern archi-

FIGURE 15. Lovell House, designed by Richard Neutra 1927–29, 4616 Dundee Lane, East Hollywood (Los Feliz), in 1950. Photograph by Julius Shulman. © J. Paul Getty Trust. Used with permission of the Julius Shulman Photography Archive, Research Library at the Getty Research Institute, Los Angeles.

tecture. Few had dared to build on such precarious sites before, but with the use of entirely steel-framed construction, used by Neutra for the first time for a private residence in the United States, such ventures became feasible without much difficulty. The light steel frame was able to support a building that jutted out of the hillside into the open air and established the prototype of Southern California hillside buildings. Pierre Koenig (1925–2004) in particular learned from Neutra's venture. His spectacular Case Study House No. 22 of 1960, built upon a steel structure that was anchored in concrete, would have been impossible without Neutra's design of 1927. Immortalized in a photo by Julius Shulman, the well-lighted living room of this house hovered like a spaceship over the city of Los Angeles at night. Without the Lovell Health House, this spaceship of the Hollywood Hills would perhaps never have taken off.

As Richard Neutra described the construction process, the steel frame was prefabricated in portable sections and transported to the building site. It took less than forty work hours to assemble the bolted steel frame. Casement windows were slipped into place as parts of the surface skin. For enclosures where there was no glass, concrete gunite was sprayed onto the wire lath using a 250-foot hose extending from mixers on the hillside road. In two days a thin shell of concrete enveloped the bolted steel frame. Open-web steel flooring and ceiling joists harbored plumbing pipes and electric wiring (*Life and Shape* 220–25).

The frame, filled and covered with light concrete and glass, "became the essence of the building," as architectural historian Thomas S. Hines concluded in 1982. "Rhetorically echoing its Chicago School origins [Louis Sullivan, Frank Lloyd Wright], the frame was the house, the house was the frame. Structurally and esthetically, it gave the house its meaning" (*Richard Neutra* 84).

Another innovative design feature of the Lovell Health House was that one entered the house at the rooftop, which was at street level and contained three bedrooms with sleeping porches and a study. Then one descended to the middle level, which contained the living room, dining room, kitchen, and library, and finally down to the bottom level, with the utility and recreation areas, including the pool, playground, gym court, and nursery porch. The house was, in a way, turned upside down to provide the different levels of the conventional living areas.

The landscaping, also supervised by Neutra, demonstrated his architectural philosophy of "building with nature" as well. Successive rows of low retaining walls followed the shape of the hillside. Planted with lush foliage, the walls provided an effective counterpoint to the rectangular lines of the house. Neutra drew on the natural landscape of the hills and made it habitable. As he said, "vista and landscape . . . permeated inward when the continuous but dividable drapes [in the house] were slid aside" (*Life and Shape* 123). Thomas Hines emphasized in 1982 that Neutra "surpassed all major twentieth-century architects" in his "knowledge of botany and his landscape design skills" (*Richard Neutra* 86).

Lovell was enthusiastic about the house and devoted a special article in his weekly column to describing the design and celebrating its features:

> For years I have periodically written articles telling you how to build your house so that you can derive from it the maximum degree of health and beauty. . . . Always at the end of each article was the thought, 'If I could

ever build a home myself—. At last the day has arrived. We have built such
a home—a home premised on the fundamental health principles and construction ideas which I have presented in my writings. (*Los Angeles Times
Sunday Magazine*, Dec. 15, 1929, 26; quoted from Hines, *Richard Neutra*, 86 ff.)

Lovell expressed the hope that Neutra's example would "introduce a
modern type of architecture and establish it firmly in California." For
that purpose on four successive afternoons he arranged public tours of
his house that attracted thousands of curious Angelenos. Lovell and
Neutra were available to explain the building's design features. The Automobile Club of Southern California conducted the traffic up and
down on steep, narrow Dundee Lane. The tours were a great success in
promoting modernist architecture, and the Los Angeles newspapers promoted the Lovell house without reservation, attracting national and international attention.

In his final analysis, Thomas Hines used Leo Marx's concept of the
"machine in the garden" to summarize Neutra's achievements, saying
that he and his cohorts "exploited the machine to achieve a minimalism
of structure and form that framed and emphasized and highlighted nature, almost, at times, to the downplaying of architecture—at least in its
more traditionally formal elements. Nowhere in the history of modern
architecture was the modernists' ideal of the 'machine in the garden'
more convincingly realized than in Southern California" ("Machines in
the Garden" 298).

Another lasting contribution by Neutra was the design of a prototype
for public school buildings in Southern California. Until his arrival, public schools followed the model of East Coast architecture. Examples of
these three- or five-story buildings of brick and stone, designed to take
up limited space and to withstand the harsh climate of the East Coast and
Midwest, can still be seen at the various high schools in Beverly Hills,
Hollywood, Santa Monica, and Venice. Neutra realized that in California public land was not at a premium as it was in the east, and public
schools could expand over a wider space. In addition, heavy construction was not required because of the milder climate. With this in mind,
he designed a new type of school that became the model for the area. The
first school that he designed according to these insights was an addition
to the Corona Avenue School in the district of Bell in southeast Los Angeles in 1934. The one-story L-shaped wing of the addition consisted of
a kindergarten and five elementary classrooms, all connected by an outdoor hallway. Each classroom had a sliding-glass wall that opened to

garden patios. The patios provided outdoor class space that was divided by hedges. Ventilation and lighting were provided by high clerestory windows on one side of each classroom, and by the outdoor hallway and the sliding glass wall on the opposite side. In addition, there were shade trees, adjustable awnings, and an overhanging roof that protected the classrooms and the outdoor hallways from the sun and the rain. Movable chairs and desks replaced the bolted-down furniture traditional in classrooms.

The school, called the "test-tube school," was widely publicized in the international press. Doyt Early, the chief state architect in the Division of Schoolhouse Planning, gave the design his unqualified endorsement:

> I think that the absence of historic romancing in design is both pleasing and honest. . . . There is better light in the classrooms than in any I've ever seen. The out-of-door possibilities lend freedom, variety and interest to the program, not to mention the health factors. There are some delightful color effects. I feel that you have made some fresh and inspiring contributions to the art, or shall I say science, of school planning. I will use it as a wedge, if I may, to encourage other districts to venture a little from the traditional. (Hines, *Richard Neutra*, 164–65).

The school's principal, Georgina Ritchie, submitted the first professional assessment in her official report to the Board of Education in 1936, asserting that "a school has at last been built which is a distinct improvement from the standpoint of health, safety, and educational opportunity, on the antiquated type of buildings, to which we have so stubbornly adhered in face of a steadily changing philosophy of education." Fourteen years later, she maintained her conviction when she wrote that she had "yet to find in Los Angeles or anywhere else, a building which can measure up to the primary grade buildings at Corona" (Hines, *Richard Neutra*, 165).

The Corona Avenue School revolutionized the design of public schools and became an important model for school buildings in California. Neutra followed the same principles of open-air classrooms with sliding doors for his design of buildings for the California Military Academy, a private preparatory school, in 1935, and for the Emerson Junior High School on Selby Avenue in Westwood in 1937. The latter, however, required a two-story structure because of the large number of students in the area. The movable wall–and–patio scheme could be implemented only on the ground floor, of course, but Neutra also provided open rooftop terraces wherever possible. During the 1950s Neutra designed additional school buildings that followed his prototype of 1934: the

FIGURE 16. Kester Avenue Elementary School Building, 5353 Kester Avenue, Van Nuys, designed by Richard Neutra in 1951. Photograph by author in 2005.

Kester Avenue Elementary School in 1951 and the UCLA Kindergarten and Elementary School in 1957, commonly known as the University Elementary School (UES). Portions of the latter, consisting of a string of classrooms arranged along the curves of a creek, were razed in the early 1990s to make way for UCLA's Graduate School of Management. In the early 1960s, Neutra provided the design for Palos Verdes High School, which had to adapt to code specifications for pitched red-tile roofs. The architect complied with these requirements, but he also insisted on implementing his one-story classroom wings connected by covered walkways. In a design for the Lemoore Naval Air Base, near Fresno, California, Neutra arranged the classrooms and the covered walkways in two half circles. This design dated back to his Ring Plan School of the 1920s, but it was now more successfully realized in California stucco, and the circular building complex was appropriately named the Richard J. Neutra School.

  Neutra was familiar with the problem of urban density, not only from his childhood in Vienna, but also and especially because he experienced the urban sprawl of Los Angeles in the 1930s and 1940s. He called densification "tumorous" and a major challenge for large, crowded cities.

On the other hand, he was convinced "that high-density design could succeed in a fully human way." He believed that human beings could be "brought together in close proximity" and "accommodated in very satisfying circumstances," if "that precious amenity called privacy" was considered (*Nature Near* 79, 81). In the 1930s Neutra designed four apartment complexes in Westwood that were intended to achieve a balance between density and privacy: the Landfair Apartments (1935–37), the Strathmore Apartments (1937), the Kelton Apartments (1942), and the Elkay Apartments (1948). Of the four, the Landfair and Strathmore apartments were outstanding, while the other two were less committed to modernism. The Landfair Apartments consisted of one building with two one-story flats on one side and a row of six two-story apartments, with staggered setbacks on the other side. The first floor contained living, dining, and kitchen areas and the second floor baths and bedrooms. All kitchens had separate service entrances. Each apartment had access to the roof-garden sun decks, and all occupants shared the common back garden. While the setbacks ensured individuals' privacy, the sun deck and garden provided space for community activities. Classifying it as a "masterwork," Hines called it an "urbane essay on the reciprocal imperatives of density and privacy" (*Richard Neutra* 167). Unfortunately, its unique design was disfigured when the complex was converted into a UCLA student co-op building.

In the Strathmore Apartments, Neutra incorporated style principles of the megastructures of the Southwest Pueblo Indians and the bungalow courts of Southern California. Six two-bedroom apartments and two one-bedroom flats were staggered atop each other over the hillside in pueblo fashion, while each unit had its own entrance facing a central garden in the manner of the traditional California bungalow court. Again Neutra managed to combine urban density with individual privacy. The success of the Strathmore Apartments can be measured in terms of their attraction to many famous tenants, including film stars Dolores Del Rio, Orson Welles, and Luise Reiner, and playwright Clifford Odets.

For architects whose major designs were for residential homes, there was little opportunity to build "houses against Hitler," so to speak, except by creating public housing during and after World War II. In the late 1930s, Neutra developed plans for Amity Village, an innovative community of low-income housing in Compton. Although this development was never built, Neutra used the Amity Compton plans for his Channel Heights projects of the 1940s. Neutra was also intimately involved in designing other public housing projects, the majority of which were built between 1940 and 1945 to house workers in the defense industry. During that time, the city's Housing Authority built more than 4,250 units. Because of the great number of visionary architects in the Los Angeles area, the public housing built in Los Angeles between 1940 and 1950 ranked, according to architecture critic Nicolai Ouroussoff, "among the country's most progressive" (*Los Angeles Times Calendar*, Nov. 4, 2001, 7). Neutra was involved in the planning of three of these public housing projects. Hacienda Village and Pueblo del Rio in South Central Los Angeles, sponsored by the Los Angeles Housing Authority, housed largely black and Mexican-American populations. Both were team efforts in which Neutra participated with other architects, but Channel Heights was exclusively his own design. Ouroussoff singled out Neutra's Channel Heights Housing Project as the best of these works (*Calendar*, Nov. 4, 2001, 7).

The Channel Heights project was funded by the Federal Works Agency and, like Hacienda Village and Pueblo del Rio, was coordinated by the Los Angeles Housing Authority. It was built for San Pedro shipyard workers who had moved to Los Angeles in large numbers to work in the national defense industry in 1942. The project consisted of three large clusters of stucco-and-redwood houses scattered in rows over a gently sloping 150-acre site on the south end of the Palos Verdes Hills. There were 222 residential units that provided housing for 600 families. All the houses were built at a forty-five-degree angle to their streets to afford the occupants a better view of the Los Angeles harbor and the ocean. Neutra developed the site as an "anti-urban space" by providing ample recreation spaces between the housing clusters that "provided both privacy and a sense of community" (Hines, *Richard Neutra*, 179). There were two types of housing available, as Hines described them, "one-story duplexes [alternating] with two-story, four-family units" (179). All were built of the ubiquitous local building materials, "stucco and redwood, with interiors painted in soft blues, greens, and yellows." Hines quoted one critic who noted the "sturdy simplicity and cheerful color" as the "keynote of the interiors" (180). The four-family units "featured upstairs balconies. All units contained a living and dining room, kitchen, bath, and utility and storage areas, with bedrooms ranging from one to three. . . . the project had an average cost per living unit of approximately $2600." Instead of building blocks of "rental barracks" *(Mietskasernen)*, as he was familiar with in the slums of Berlin, Vienna, New York, and Chicago, Neutra arranged individual housing clusters over the landscape. In addition, he offered the inhabitants a community life with a market building, a craft center, and a combined nurs-ery school and community center. According to Hines, "all [buildings] were well utilized and were deemed highly successful. In contrast to the slight pitch of the roofs of the houses, the community center featured a contrasting array of more steeply pitched roofs" (180). But Neutra made no concessions to antimodernist taste and strictures, and instead com-bined the best of the local materials and techniques with his typically modernist ideas and execution. "Throughout the development, Neutra utilized glass to its maximum possibilities and emphasized the interac-tion between inner and outer space" (Hines, *Richard Neutra,* 180).

By the 1950s, the lobbies of private real estate business were able to put a stop to public housing in Los Angeles, charging "creeping social-ism" as inspiration behind the projects. The government sold Channel Heights to large-scale developers who allowed the rental units to deteri-orate. The units were finally demolished to make room for private resi-dential housing. David Gebhard's architectural guide to Los Angeles de-clares that it was "a matter of public shame that this project has been allowed to disintegrate and for all practical purposes disappear" (Geb-hard and Winter xxii).

But Channel Heights was not the last public housing project in which Neutra was involved. He fought still another battle for low-income hous-ing in Los Angeles in the late 1950s. The "Battle of Chavez Ravine" was a ten-year struggle over the redevelopment of a 315-acre slum in an area called Chavez Ravine near downtown Los Angeles that was a Mexican-American neighborhood. The area was enveloped by Elysian Park on the north and west and bordered by the Pasadena Freeway, the oldest free-way in Los Angeles, on the east and south. Neutra described the site as "a hilly place, cleft with deep valleys, [which] had long attracted a large community of Mexican-American immigrants. Their ramshackle houses, thrown together out of whatever materials they could afford or find, [were] admittedly picturesque, but the standard of living was extremely low" (*Nature Near* 140).

Chavez Ravine was the largest site in Southern California to meet the requirements for public housing under the terms of the National Hous-ing Act of 1949. Endorsed by Los Angeles mayor Fletcher Bowron, the redevelopment program was unanimously approved by the city council in October 1950. A contract between the city and the housing authority for eleven projects, including Chavez Ravine, provided for 10,000 hous-ing units at a cost of $110 million. Neutra and his partner, Robert Alexander, were awarded the contract for the redevelopment of Chavez

Ravine, which had been renamed Elysian Park Heights by that time (see Hines, "Housing, Baseball," 123–30). Neutra considered the commission "an opportunity to create something truly outstanding, improving the lives of these poorer citizens, and to put in place a vibrant bellwether for urban revitalization across the country" (*Nature Near* 140).

Restricted by rigid guidelines and density requirements, Neutra and Alexander designed 24 thirteen-story high-rise towers and 163 two-story low-rise structures to house the approximately 3,360 families allocated for this development. The high-rise towers that were necessary to meet the density requirements constituted the major problem of the design. Neutra planned the high-rise towers to "be spaced great distances apart and in spacious groups, separated by several valleys" (Hines, "Housing, Baseball," 134–35), but regardless of how imaginatively the towers were designed, the planned density was the cause of much criticism. Whether Neutra and Alexander would have been able to overcome this criticism became a moot point, because Elysian Park Heights was never built. While the old houses in Chavez Ravine were demolished and the population was relocated, the same charges of "creeping socialism" were raised against Elysian Park Heights as were raised against Channel Heights, even though there was an extreme housing shortage in Los Angeles after World War II.

During the McCarthy period and Korean War such charges constituted a powerful argument that only a few dared to oppose. The Home Builders Association, the lobby of the California real estate business, the Chamber of Commerce, CASH (Citizens Against Socialist Housing), and the *Los Angeles Times* successfully attacked the public housing projects. Urban planner Donald Craig Parson documented in detail how red-baiting became an effective tool as the Los Angeles City Housing Authority (CHA) was at the center of a "Red Scare" campaign that destroyed public housing programs on both the national and local level (Parson 103–35, 199–200). To make a long story short, most of the larger housing projects were finally cancelled in 1953, and the unused land acquired by the federal government was sold to the city of Los Angeles at a major loss. In selling Chavez Ravine the federal government lost $4 million, but not before a valiant effort to defend low-cost housing was made by Mayor Fletcher Bowron, the Los Angeles unions of the AFL and CIO, the NAACP, the League of Women Voters, and various church and veterans' groups. The California Senate Committee on Un-American Activities investigated the Los Angeles City Housing Authority (CHA) and engineered the dismissal of three of its members for taking the Fifth Amendment. Conservative Republicans, such as U.S. senators William F. Knowland and Richard Nixon, campaigned against public housing and introduced legislation that allowed city governments to cancel contracts for public housing. In December 1951 the Los Angeles city council reversed its unanimous decision of 1950. In spite of decisions by the California Supreme Court and the U.S. Supreme Court that required the city council to honor its original contracts, the coalition against public housing turned the 1953 election for the mayor of Los Angeles into a test case for or against public housing. Running on an antihousing platform, Congressman Norris Poulson defeated Mayor Bowron, the champion of Los Angeles public housing. Poulson was able to negotiate the city's withdrawal from the major projects, including Elysian Park Heights. In 1957, the city was eager to give the land to Walter O'Malley, the owner of the Brooklyn Dodgers, in order to attract a major baseball team to Los Angeles. There was a pro forma exchange of real estate, but in reality the city gave the land away: the Dodgers got 315 acres in exchange for nine-acre Wrigley Field, which O'Malley had bought in 1957 in another part of Los Angeles. The Dodgers moved to Los Angeles in 1958. After the team had played four years at the Los Angeles Coliseum, it opened its season in the newly built Dodger Stadium at Chavez Ravine in April 1962. This give-away of the taxpayers' land to private interests was achieved by machinations that involved the FBI and the House Un-American Activities Committee. The California as well as the U.S. Supreme Court sanctioned the deal. Real estate interests had mobilized public opinion against public housing as anti-American (Cuff 277–309; Parson 170–86).

Neutra later listed as one of the most striking aspects of his experience with the Elysian Park Heights project "that the project was never doubted on its intrinsic merits as a framework for revitalization. This surely would have been justified, seeing as how it was such a large undertaking and one of the first major projects to be approved under the federal housing act of 1949." He saw the project as a prototype, generating all kinds of useful information and perspective, which he imagined would help other projects down the line. "In the beginning all of the parties had surmised that the quality of the planning, its technical provisions, functional diversity, and the architectural interpretation we had worked out would produce an ennobling beautiful situation for urban life" (*Nature Near* 142). Instead, there was "creeping selfishness," as Neutra described it. Urban sprawl was much more profitable to the local real estate business than federally subsidized low-cost housing with qualitative guidelines that were carefully monitored (*Nature Near* 141).

Richard Neutra designed and built more than one hundred residential houses, six apartment complexes, eight schools, and many commercial and public buildings in the Los Angeles area. In addition, he was involved in the planning and design of four of the most important public housing projects in Los Angeles. Rudolph Schindler was not quite as productive, but in Los Angeles there are about fifty single-family houses that he designed, as well as a great number of homes he remodeled. He also designed a number of apartments and commercial buildings, but he worked on no schools, except for some that were never built. In 1938–39, Schindler designed the music room for the legendary "Evenings on the Roof" series, which in the 1940s featured the premieres of works by composers such as John Cage and Arnold Schoenberg. For a long time Neutra's fame overshadowed that of Schindler—Neutra's photo appeared on the cover of *Time* magazine in 1949—but Schindler's reputation as a highly imaginative architect who made a great impact on residential architecture was revived by an exhibition at the Museum of Contemporary Art in Los Angeles in 2001.

The legacy of both Schindler and Neutra was that they were trying to meet the character of the locale when they built new houses in Southern California. They did not impose their European concepts of modernism upon their new environment, but instead adapted their style to Los Angeles. Eager to learn from indigenous talents such as Louis Sullivan, Frank Lloyd Wright, and Irving Gill, they developed the new California modern style. The secret of their success was that they introduced, as Schindler put it, "features which seemed to be necessary for life in California." These features included, for Schindler, "an open plan, flat on the ground; living patios; glass walls; translucent walls; wide sliding doors; clerestory windows; shed roofs with wide shading overhangs" (Smith and Darling 175). For Neutra we would have to add steel constructions on hillsides, open-air hallways for schools, and a balance of density and privacy for group housing. These design features became generally accepted as the basis for California houses and schools of their period and beyond. Architectural historian Sylvia Lavin has shown that Neutra reworked his concepts of modernism and expanded them "in the face either of new developments, such as World War II, or of previously underrecognized conditions, such as the impact of consumer culture on design" (3). She called him "a founder of environmental design," aligning him with the category of "contemporary architecture" of the 1950s

(7). Characterizing Neutra's style as a "second modernism," she describes him as "a pioneering regionalist who nurtured modernism in America and saw in the nation untapped strengths" (14). While it is difficult to ascribe a single style or system of modernist architecture to either Schindler or Neutra, it is safe to say that the latter worked mostly in the "rationalist" mode, whereas the former preferred the "expressionist" mode.

Schindler's and Neutra's houses are still highly desirable properties on the Los Angeles real estate market, and children, teachers, and administrators still appreciate Neutra's school buildings. Schindler's and Neutra's works have become iconic items of Southern California culture, and in this respect, they are different from the exiles that came to Los Angeles in the 1940s. While most of the exiles had their eyes focused on Europe, Neutra and Schindler contributed to the building of modern California.

There was not an unbridgeable gulf between the German-speaking immigrants and exiles in Los Angeles, as Neutra's social contacts show. Some immigrants identified closely with the exiles and their situation. Director William Dieterle and screenwriter Salka Viertel, for example, immigrated to Los Angeles before 1933, but Dieterle was instrumental in setting up the European Film Fund, which supported the exiles without income, and Salka Viertel opened her home as a haven to exiles and immigrants. On the other hand, Brecht rejected the term "emigrant" (or immigrant) for himself in his often-quoted poem "Concerning the Label Emigrant":

> we
> Did not leave, of our own free will
> Choosing another land. Nor did we enter
> Into a land, to stay there, if possible for ever.
> Merely, we fled. We are driven out, banned.
> Not a home, but an exile, shall the land be that took us in.
>
> (*Poems* 301; GBA 12: 81)

Whether to return to their home countries after the war was an issue that divided the exiles (see Suvin 107–23). Thomas Mann, who wanted to stay in the United States, argued that this issue should not divide them in a speech at the 1943 Writers' Congress at UCLA. The exiles had a common responsibility to support the war against Nazi Germany, he claimed. The question of returning home, however, could "only be answered individually, and the answer would vary according to personal circumstances" ("The Exiled Writer's Relation" 343).

FIGURE 17. Thomas Mann's house, 1550 San Remo Drive, Pacific Palisades, circa 1941. Photograph courtesy of J. R. Davidson Collection, Architecture and Design Collection, University Art Museum, University of California, Santa Barbara.

If one considers the relationship between immigrant and exile modernism, it is perhaps not surprising that Thomas Mann preferred to have his house designed by J. R. Davidson (1889–1977), whom Mann considered more moderate in his modernism than Neutra. Richard Neutra had presumed that he would be the logical choice for the German novelist when he planned to build a house in Pacific Palisades in 1941. Mann had taken a tour of new houses in Los Angeles with Neutra as his guide when he visited Los Angeles in April 1938, but he did not reveal his intense dislike of modern architecture. In his diary, however, he recorded his aversion to the "cubist glass-box style," which he found so "unpleasant" (April 18, 1938). When the Manns seized upon the idea of building a house in Los Angeles in 1941, they decided against the California modern style and chose a more conservative architect. Hines attributes Mann's choice to a reaction against Neutra's overzealous salesmanship, referring to a party given by the writer Vicki Baum, at which Neutra tried to win Mann's favor. According to witnesses, the novelist was so annoyed by the architect that he muttered to someone, "Get that Neutra off my back" (Hines, *Richard Neutra,* 186). But it was probably Neutra's modernism that was too avant-garde for Thomas Mann, who preferred a more conservative design for his house. It is noteworthy that J. R. Davidson was also an immigrant who had come from Berlin to Los Angeles in 1924 and was one of the city's leading architects in the 1930s.

In 1994, the architectural guide to Los Angeles described the Mann House as a "stucco and glass two-story Modern image house" (Gebhard and Winter 18). This description shows that immigrant modernism in architecture was not uniformly functionalist, but offered a variety of design solutions so that even Mann was able to find an acceptable version for himself. Davidson called the Mann House "nostalgic German" (Wefing 566) in its design. Neutra and Schindler, however, represented a modernism that was decidedly avant-garde and optimistic. Their signature houses "could never have been built anywhere except California" (Gebhard and Von Breton 99).

CHAPTER 7

Between Modernism and Antimodernism

Franz Werfel

For the Prague poet and novelist Franz Werfel (1890–1945), the year 1933 was not the occasion of a definite rupture, as it was for the other artists, writers, and intellectuals from Germany. This was in part because he was a citizen of Czechoslovakia who had opted to live in Vienna, and he was not affected by events in Germany until 1938, when Austria was annexed. The other reason was that Werfel had made his accommodation with re-actionary conservatism and was vacillating between modernism and an-timodernism. His conflicted position dated back to the early 1920s. Before 1923 Werfel had belonged to the Expressionist avant-garde, and his early poetry had attempted to combine aesthetic modernism and engagement in political action. The young Werfel's emotional address to mankind in his programmatic poem "To the Reader" ("An den Leser") had found an enthusiastic response among the young intellectuals in Central Europe (Sokel 141). Like the poet, they desired to be related to the prototypical new human being: "My only wish is to be related to you, Oh Mensch!" ("Mein einziger Wunsch ist, Dir, O Mensch verwandt zu sein!").

Werfel was so important as an avant-garde poet that some literary his-torians date the beginning of German Expressionism from the reading of "To the Reader" at a Berlin coffeehouse in mid-December 1911. In No-vember 1918, after the collapse of the Austro-Hungarian Empire, Wer-fel rushed to the barricades in Vienna. He was arrested for inciting vio-lence, but no charges were filed against him (Pfeifer 194). The idea of revolution informed Werfel's work during the early 1920s. By 1923,

FIGURE 18. Franz Werfel, circa 1945. Photograph courtesy of Bildabteilung, Deutsches Literaturarchiv, Marbach/Neckar.

however, Werfel had abandoned political activism as well as formal experiments in literature and turned, as Walter H. Sokel criticizes, "to the most conventional and 'popular' forms of writing" (228). His novel *Verdi: A Novel of the Opera* (1924) marked the end of his Expressionist phase and the culmination of his antimodernism. Some of his dramas of the period between 1918 and 1923 could be classified as modernist, but they are only further proof of his vacillation between modernism and antimodernism.

Walter Sokel's final verdict on Werfel in his classic study of German modernism, *The Writer in Extremis* (1959), was devastating, identifying Werfel's "spiritual anchorage" as "a happy and profitable blend of commercialism and Judaeo-Christian sentiments" (228). Werfel, who had been Alma Mahler Gropius's lover since 1917, wanted to keep up with her upper-class lifestyle and those who were in the increasingly conservative social circles that she preferred. Werfel went so far as to resign from the Jewish community in order to marry her in 1929 (Jungk 122, 273). His novel *The Pure in Heart (Barbara oder Die Frömmigkeit)*, written in 1929, reflects the intellectual sacrifices he made to accommodate his new lifestyle as a popular Viennese novelist who appealed to his readers from the politically conservative Catholic majority in Austria. In its barely disguised autobiographical episodes, Werfel's novel condemns his own revolutionary activism and issues a stern warning against the pervasive mode of modern rationalism.

Sokel's criticism was directed especially against Werfel's work in exile. Singling out his novel *The Song of Bernadette (Das Lied der Bernadette)* of 1941 as a "facile best-seller" and the basis for a Hollywood movie that made "millions of shop girls from Zurich to California" weep and rejoice, Sokel made Werfel the prime example of the abandonment of modernism by a former Expressionist writer (Sokel 227–30). Sokel's assessment of 1959 was so harsh because he felt, as many of Werfel's readers did, that the author had betrayed the revolutionary enthusiasm of his youth and had become "a eulogist of the Austrian restoration" (Politzer 57).

A critical reading of Werfel's literary production in exile, which culminated in his California works, must take into account his vacillation between modernism and antimodernism. Although he was not directly affected by the measures against modernist artists and writers implemented by the Nazi regime in 1933, Werfel nevertheless was exposed to the threat of exile. In May 1933 he was expelled as a corresponding member of the Prussian Academy of Arts in Berlin, and in February 1934 his novel *The Forty Days of Musa Dagh (Die vierzig Tage des Musa Dagh)* was banned from Germany at the request of the Turkish government. Thus Werfel became an exile author even before he was de facto exiled from Austria in 1938 by the *Anschluss*. Werfel's public and private statements as well as his literary production between 1933 and 1938 cannot simply be explained as a shift to the right, but perhaps can be understood as an attempt to fight Hitler's fascism with Dollfuß fascism, thereby creating a temporary sanctuary for spirituality and the creative arts in Austria. German fascism appeared to Werfel as materialist and technological modernism. He had no illusions about Austrian chancellor Engelbert Dollfuß, yet expressed his unconditional support for Dollfuß, even though he realized that the violent suppression of Austrian workers and the Austrian Social Democratic Party in February 1934 would eventually benefit only the Nazi Party. He saw Dollfuß marching "blood-stained into the future," and considered the ideology of the rightwing Heimwehr, the paramilitary organization of Austrian fascism, "as stupid as the face of [its leader Prince Rüdiger von] Starhemberg." Werfel considered Bolshevism the worst possible fate, and right-wing radicalism, "this bolshevism of the petit bourgeois," the second worst. Yet, these opinions were no obstacles to Werfel's admiration for Mussolini, nor for his acceptance of the award of the Austrian Medal for Arts and Scholarship, conferred to him by Chancellor Kurt von Schuschnigg in March 1937 (Steimann 62, 206). The conservatism of Austro-fascism seemed to offer Werfel the temporary sanctuary that he hoped would enable the regeneration of the arts and a new supranationalism, inspired by the "Habsburg myth" of a multination state of peace and prosperity (Magris 265–71).

Written between July 1932 and November 1933, Werfel's novel *The Forty Days of Musa Dagh (Die vierzig Tage des Musa Dagh)*, which deals with the Turkish genocide of the Armenians in 1915, can be considered the first work of Holocaust literature in German (Buch 107–17). The letters Werfel wrote while he was on a lecture tour in Germany in November 1932 show that he was fully aware of the historical parallels between racial violence in Turkey and Germany, even if he did not have a premonition of the Holocaust (Davidheiser 14). Werfel's identification of biomedical ideology as the driving force behind modern genocide is one of the major achievements of the novel, and nowhere was this ideology as early and as clearly denounced as in this work. "There can be no peace between human beings [i.e., the Turks] and plague germs [i.e., the Armenians]," General Enver Pascha explains to a representative of the German Orientgesellschaft who tries to intervene on behalf of the Armenians (*Musa Dagh* 139). This biomedical ideology was also behind Nazi anti-Semitism. Werfel was correct when he found this new mentality expressed in the features of the general in charge of the persecution of the Armenian population:

It was no sneering cruelty, no cynicism, that transfigured the boyish look on this war-lord's face. No. What [the representative of the Orientgesellschaft] perceived was that arctic mask of the human being who "has overcome all sentimentality"—the mask of a human mind which has got beyond guilt and all its qualms, the strange, almost innocent naiveté of utter godlessness. (*Musa Dagh* 142).

The German representative wished that the man were malicious, that he were Satan: "But he had no malice, he was not Satan; this quietly implacable mass-murderer was boyishly charming" (*Musa Dagh* 143). Within a few years after the publication of the novel, this new character type, represented by Enver Pascha, would become the norm in Central Europe. As a well-researched historical novel, *Musa Dagh* was unmistakably a departure from *The Pure in Heart,* but its narrative stance and its conventional closure disqualified it as a modernist novel. While an international squadron of British and French ships arrives to rescue the Armenians from the Musa Dagh, the "Moses Mountain," where they have defended themselves for forty days against the superior forces of the Turkish army, the protagonist, Gabriel Bagradian, who was their leader, stays behind. The assimilated French Armenian, who had returned to the Middle East to save his people, dissociates himself again from his fellow countrymen. He returns to the graveyard on the Musa Dagh where his son is buried. Killed by a Turkish bullet, Bagradian manages to die at his son's grave: as he clings to the wood, "his son's cross lay upon his heart" (817). The religious allegory at the end of the novel—the son's cross redeeming his father—erased the dialectical tension between the protagonist and his people and ensured a perfect closure.

Perhaps concerned about the future of *Musa Dagh* in Germany, Werfel requested from the president permission to sign the declaration of loyalty issued by the president of the Prussian Academy of Arts in March 1933. He must have been aware that Alfred Döblin and Thomas Mann had refused to sign it and had resigned from the academy in protest. Werfel, nevertheless, signed the declaration of loyalty, which, however, did not prevent his expulsion from the academy in May 1933 or the banning of his novel from Germany in 1934. In December 1933 Werfel had even applied for membership in Joseph Goebbels' Reich Organization of German Authors *(Reichsverband Deutscher Schriftsteller),* but to no avail. Werfel wanted to be officially recognized as a German author to ensure that his books would be sold in Nazi Germany, but his application was rejected because members had to be "of German blood" (Jungk 144).

Werfel considered himself a German author but was able to adjust to the new situation in Central Europe. He participated in the Hebrew Renaissance in German letters with his biblical drama *The Eternal Road (Der Weg der Verheißung)* in 1935 and his biblical novel *Hearken unto the Voice (Jeremias: Höret die Stimme)* in 1937. Exile authors were responsible for the other works of the Hebrew Renaissance, such as Thomas Mann's *Joseph and His Brothers (Joseph und seine Brüder)* of 1933–43 and Lion Feuchtwanger's trilogy on the Jewish historian Flavius Josephus of 1933–45. In view of Werfel's flirtation with Catholicism in his 1929 novel *The Pure in Heart (Barbara oder Die Frömmigkeit)*, his commitment to Jewish topics in the 1930s constituted a political statement. When he attended the rehearsals of *The Eternal Road (Der Weg der Verheißung)* in New York in 1936 (the play was performed at last in 1937), he told a Jewish audience that he felt at home among them: "I do not belong to those who needed a Columbus to discover their own Jewishness." He declared that nobody, neither Christians nor Jews, could drive him away from Judaism. Condemning the recent persecution of Jews in Germany, he proclaimed the "old truth" that "Israel cannot be destroyed by any persecution" (*Zwischen Oben und Unten* 544–45).

When the German army invaded Austria in March 1938, Werfel happened to be in Italy. In a diary entry Werfel admitted his intense grief, yet he avoided complete identification with the fate of Austria: "This Sunday, March 13, my heart is almost breaking with pain, although Austria is not my homeland" (quoted from Jungk 170). Complete despair and a total identification with the victims, however, overwhelmed Werfel in August 1938, when German troops entered the Sudetenland: "today on August 23, 1938 the climax of terror and shame! I identify more with Bohemia than I ever thought" (quoted from Jungk 174). Werfel and his wife, Alma, fled to Zurich, then via Amsterdam to London, but in the end they settled in France, first in Paris, then in St. Germain-en-Laye outside Paris, and finally in Sanary-sur-Mer on the Mediterranean coast, where many of the exiles from Germany, Austria, and Czechoslovakia had assembled. After the German conquest of France, the Werfels were caught up in the turmoil of the defeat. They fled to Lourdes because it was situated in the unoccupied part of France where they felt safe from immediate arrest by the German authorities. Here Werfel made his famous vow to write a book in honor of Saint Bernadette Soubirous if he were successful in escaping to the United States. With the assistance of Varian Fry and the American Emergency Rescue Committee the Werfels were able to escape together with Heinrich Mann, his wife Nelly, and Thomas Mann's son Golo via Spain and Lisbon to New York. In De-

FIGURE 19. Franz Werfel's house, 610 North Bedford Drive, Beverly Hills, 2005. Photograph by Juergen Nogai, Santa Monica.

cember 1940, the Werfels moved to Los Angeles, where they first lived at 6900 Los Tilos Road in Hollywood and later lived at 610 North Bedford Drive in Beverly Hills.

The best of Werfel's work in exile in France, "Cella or the Survivors" ("Cella oder die Überwinder: Versuch eines Romans"), remained unfinished and therefore unpublished during his lifetime. The other texts Werfel wrote in France were two dramatic sketches in the style of Brechtian theater, "The Doctor of Vienna: A Monodrama" ("Der Arzt von Wien: Ein Monodrama") and "The Actress" ("Die Schauspielerein"). All three of these texts reflect the events of the *Anschluss* in 1938. While the two dramatic sketches appeared in the *Pariser Tageszeitung* in 1938, "Cella or the Survivors," a novel dealing with the persecution of Jews in Vienna in 1938 and ending with the escape of the protagonist to Switzerland, was not published in its entirety. Instead, it appeared as a novella entitled "The Priest's Tale of the Restored Crucifix" ("Die wahre Geschichte vom wiederhergestellten Kreuz"), published by the Pazifische Presse in Los Angeles in 1942. It took until 1954 for the novel—without a doubt one of the best portrayals in German literature of the *Anschluss* and the subsequent pogrom— finally to be published.

In 1939 Werfel returned to his favorite topic, naïve Catholicism, with his novel *Embezzled Heaven (Der veruntreute Himmel: Die Geschichte einer Magd)*. This novel harks back to *The Pure in Heart (Barbara oder Die Frömmigkeit)* and clearly anticipates *The Song of Bernadette,* his American best seller of 1942 (the German edition of *Bernadette* was published in Stockholm in 1941). Nostalgia for a peasantlike religiosity is the dominant theme of all three novels. Their message is a clear warning against the Enlightenment project, but in contrast to Adorno's concept of literature and art, it is devoid of any dialectic. The story of *Embezzled Heaven* is loosely connected to the exile situation of the narrator, but the central plot reflects neither exile nor modernism. Although Werfel considered this novel one of his "most architectonic books," this observation does not account for the rupture between the frame and the central story. The novel changes abruptly from a first-person to a third-person narrative without a distinct narrator after chapter four, while the first-person narrator reappears without explanation in chapter twelve. Werfel did not make use of this obvious rupture in the perspective of the narration to emphasize the experience of exile. Instead, he employed naïve allegory and sentimental closure to drive home his conservative message.

The protagonist of the story is Teta Linek, a Czech cook who spends all her savings on her nephew's education for the priesthood in order to attain her own salvation. Although she does not even like her nephew, she responds to all his requests for money, considering her payments a good insurance policy. The nephew turns out to be a grifter who succeeds in receiving financial support from his aunt for more than thirty years. When he is finally exposed as a fraud, Teta Linek realizes that it was a sin to finance her own "mediator." On a pilgrimage to Rome, she confesses her sin to a chaplain and receives a special blessing from the pope. She dies within the walls of the Vatican, thus obtaining redemption. The epilogue reveals the novel as a simple allegory: Teta Linek is the soul of humanity, yearning for immortality. Although it is deceived and defrauded by modern rationality, the soul eventually finds its way back to heaven. As the first-person narrator explains, "Our souls refuse to believe any longer in their indestructibility, and hence their eternal responsibility. The Embezzled Heaven is the great deficit of our age. Because of it our accounts cannot be balanced, either in the realm of politics or in that of economics" (*Embezzled Heaven* 423).

At the end of the novel, the narrator believes that he sees the protagonist in a park outside Paris. The narrator realizes that the person is an old French woman, but against his better judgment he insists that the black figure and gait are those of Teta Linek and decides to follow her example. The narrator expresses his faith in the absurd, valuing it more highly than rational action. What makes this faith even more questionable is the fact that this novel was written as an exile novel. The narrator, who tells his story in exile, feels linked to his homeland by Teta's story. Nevertheless, the English translation of the novel became a best seller, and it was selected by the Book-of-the-Month Club soon after Werfel arrived in New York in 1940.

Werfel's novella *April in October (Eine blaßblaue Frauenhandschrift)* was his last work written in Europe, though it was not published until 1941 in Buenos Aires. Although it has a highly sentimental plot, the novella deals effectively with anti-Semitism in Germany and a similar attitude that was gaining strength in Austria in 1936. In the novella Leonidas, an Austrian civil servant in the ministry of education, is afraid that his relationship with a German Jewish woman eighteen years earlier, at the beginning of his marriage to a wealthy Austrian woman, resulted in a child, his only son. The Jewish woman is forced to leave Germany, but she recommends a young student to his care and future schooling in Austria. When Leonidas finds out that the student is not his son, he is relieved rather than disappointed and continues his life full of lies.

Werfel wrote *Song of Bernadette* as fulfillment of a personal vow he made when he was waiting for rescue from Nazi-occupied France. As he wrote in the "Personal Preface" to the novel:

> It was . . . a time of great dread. But it was also a time of great significance for me, for I became acquainted with the wondrous history of the girl Bernadette Soubirous and also with the wondrous facts concerning the healings of Lourdes. One day in my great distress I made a vow. I vowed that if I escaped from this desperate situation and reached the saving shores of America, I would put off all other tasks and sing, as best as I could, the song of Bernadette. (*Bernadette* 6)

The novel was a huge commercial success as a selection of the Book-of-the-Month Club in 1942, and it was made into a successful movie in 1943. Jennifer Jones won an Academy Award for best actress in the role of Bernadette Soubirous despite competition from Ingrid Bergman, who was nominated for her part in *For Whom the Bell Tolls*.

According to Werfel's biographer Peter Stephan Jungk, *The Song of Bernadette* was "one of the greatest hits in American publishing history." By July 1942, "sales of the American edition had reached 400,000 copies" (Jungk 199, 203). Yet, in spite of—or perhaps because of—its commercial success, Werfel's novel was considered a scandal by his loyal readers who had followed him into exile. They considered the novel's success a commercial exploitation of a religious vow and interpreted the subject matter as evidence of Werfel's defection from Judaism to Catholicism (Reisch 190–99). Although Werfel had clearly announced himself as a Jew who "dared to sing the song of Bernadette" (*Bernadette* 7), this personal announcement did not appease his fellow exiles. At the bottom of this disaffection was the perception that Werfel had betrayed modernism. This novel was, as Sokel declares, "as far from modernist spirit and Expressionist form as anything could be" (223).

In spite of the novel's lyrical title, *The Song of Bernadette*, the narration follows the conventions of the historical novel, beginning with the day of her first vision on February 11, 1858, and ending with her canonization in 1933. As Werfel explains in the preface to the novel:

> In our epoch an epic poem can take no form but that of a novel. *The Song of Bernadette* is a novel but not a fictive work. In face of the events here delineated, the skeptical reader will ask with better right than in the case of most historical epic narratives: "What is true? What is invented?" My answer is: All the memorable happenings which constitute the substance of this book took place in the world of reality. Since their beginning dates back no longer than eighty years, there beats upon them the bright light of modern history and their truth has been confirmed by friend and foe and by cool observers through faithful testimonies. My story makes no changes in this body of truth. (*Bernadette* 6–7)

The conventions of the historical novel are, however, countermanded by the religious structure of *The Song of Bernadette*, which is modeled on the divisions of the Catholic rosary. The novel is divided into five parts that are clearly marked in the table of contents (*Bernadette* 11–12). Each part consists of ten chapters, each chapter responding to one bead of the rosary. This structural arrangement makes each chapter into a sort of prayer (see Rostinsky 243–48; Weissenberger 139–41).

Bernadette's visions are reported in the auctorial voice of a historical narrator. The day and place of her first vision are clearly fixed: February 11, 1858, at the Massabiele grotto near Lourdes. Removing all doubts about the appearance, the narrator describes her first vision, as he observed it:

> There is no delusion possible now, for Bernadette rubs her eyes, closes
> them, opens them again, and repeats this process ten times. Nevertheless,
> what she sees remains. . . . [I]n the pointed niche of the rock in the cavern
> there dwells a deep radiance as though the old gold of powerful sunbeams
> had been left behind. And in this remnant of billowing light stands some-
> one who has come from the very depth of the world and issued here into
> the day after a long but painless and comfortable wayfaring. And this some-
> one is not at all an unprecise and ghostly or transparent and airy image, no
> changeful dream vision, but a very young lady, delicate and dainty, visibly
> of flesh and blood, short rather than tall, for she stands calmly and with-
> out touching side or arch in the narrow oval of the niche. (*Bernadette* 63)

Bernadette does not identify the "young lady" as the Virgin Mary, but
is overwhelmed by her beauty. She reacts to the appearance in a way that
she has been taught by her religious upbringing. Although Bernadette
feels paralyzed, she is able to cross herself with the lady's assistance and
recites the first decade of Aves of her rosary. The lady appears to supervise Bernadette's prayers:

> At the end of each Ave [the lady] lets a pearl glide between her index-finger
> and her thumb. But she always waits and lets Bernadette drop her little
> black bead first. Only when the decade is finished and followed by the in-
> vocation, "Glory be to the Father and to the Son and to the Holy Ghost,"
> does a strong breathing pass through the lady's form and does her mouth
> silently repeat the words. (*Bernadette* 70)

The rosary is described as the most powerful bond between Bernadette
and the apparition; it causes the lady to stay with her. The presentation
of the other visions—there were eighteen altogether—follows the same
method of factual observation. Later the lady speaks to Bernadette and
asks her to convey a message to the local dean that a chapel should be
built at the site of her appearance. The lady's self-identification as "L'im-
maculada councepciou" causes Bernadette some problems with the
clergy, but her ignorance of dogma that had been announced by Pope
Pius IX in 1854 saves her from further interrogations. At another meeting, the lady tells Bernadette to drink from a spring and wash herself, although there is no spring in sight. Bernadette obeys, digging a hole in the
dirt and smearing mud over her face. After this obvious humiliation in
front of the assembled crowd, a spring that has healing powers appears.
The first miracle that results is the reversal of the total paralysis of the
thighs of an infant, the so-called Bouhouhorts child. After this miracle,

the Virgin Spring at Lourdes becomes a place of pilgrimage for the sick and afflicted.

The novel accepts the visions as real, neither resorting to poetic language and invoking legend nor employing psychology as explanation. This stupendous naïveté of the novel in presenting Bernadette's visions as real caused much animosity among its critical readers, as documented by the comments of Thomas Mann in his diary (January 15, 1942) and in his *The Genesis of Doctor Faustus*. Mann found "something impure" in Werfel's "playing with miracles" (69). As Gottfried Reinhardt explained, Mann objected to Werfel's claim in the novel "that Bernadette had seen the mother of God. Why hadn't he said that Bernadette Soubirous had imagined that she had seen the Virgin? . . . And Werfel said: 'Because she saw her!' " (quoted from Jungk 296).

Throughout the novel the narrator identifies with Bernadette's religiosity, while his descriptions of the church and state hierarchies as Bernadette's antagonists show an obvious bias against modernity. The members of the state hierarchy—the mayor, the imperial prosecutor, the chief of police, the justice of the peace, and the municipal physician—assemble at the Café Français, whose owner would like his establishment to be known as the Café Progrès. He has installed the most recent lighting system, and all the progressive newspapers, including socialist papers, are to be found here. The narrator implies that the civil service is run by "disciples of Voltaire," while the population is "little influenced by modern nihilistic tendencies" (*Bernadette* 168). It is no surprise that Bernadette's visions are objectionable to the state authorities. The miracles are considered "a breach in the official deism and non-official nihilism of the age" (*Bernadette* 420). The authorities are afraid that Bernadette's visions are manipulated by the Church to stir up political unrest. Therefore, they try to suppress the news of her visions, and when that becomes impossible, they try to prevent the local crowds from visiting the grotto by injunctions and bans. The state authorities even resort to trickery, sending an agent provocateur to the impoverished Soubirous family. He pretends to be an English millionaire, offering to buy Bernadette's rosary and trying to persuade her parents to accept gifts of money. Although Bernadette and her parents refuse any gifts, they are arrested. The narrator comments that "the State had chosen a thoroughly indecent method for settling its score with the lady," and editorializes about the state's action: "But it is in the very nature of the State not to be fastidious in its choice of means when faced by real danger. And in an industrial age a miracle constitutes a real danger. It shakes to its foundations that social order which has shunted all metaphysical needs to the overgrown sidetracks of religion in order that the great arteries of traffic be not blocked by them" (*Bernadette* 279).

The state and its policies are represented by the imperial prosecutor, Vital Dutour. To protect the interests of the state, he is "obliged to prevent [the] triumph of the lady. . . . [N]o means toward this end was too despicable" (*Bernadette* 280), but he fails miserably when his trickery is exposed and he has to release Bernadette and her parents. The narrator's conclusion that "the self-inflicted hurt of the authority of the State was beyond measure" (*Bernadette* 282) reveals the author's prejudice. For Werfel, the state was evil. He did not differentiate between the nineteenth-century French empire and the modern totalitarian state, or even the modern democratic state. He accuses the "State," correctly capitalized in the English translation, of murder, theft, fraud, blackmail, and defamation, and he claims that the State performs these criminal acts "without a pang of conscience whenever it deems its stability threatened" (*Bernadette* 280). Later, when the devil appears to tempt Bernadette, it is not surprising that he resembles Vital Dutour, the imperial prosecutor, "with two goat's horns growing out of his bald skull" (*Bernadette* 525). The representative of evil is an incarnation of the state. This naïve conception of the relationship between religion and state as an opposition between good and evil is based on an outdated opposition that does not allow for any resolution by secular means (Taylor 649–52). Werfel must have realized that his rescue from German-occupied France was due at least in part to intervention by the Emergency Rescue Committee with support of the Roosevelt administration, and that his life in California was protected by a strong American military.

Werfel was among the first of the exile writers in Los Angeles to use a devil figure to represent evil; another was Alfred Döblin. But while Döblin's devil appears in various animal disguises, such as a lion, a rat, and a horse of hell, in *November 1918*, Werfel depicts "a very local and primordial sort of devil." He exposes Bernadette to "a devil with horns and tails," as the simple people of the region had imaged Satan throughout the centuries (*Bernadette* 524). Sometimes he appears in the shape of black sows and sometimes "in the most repulsive human forms and combinations. Sometimes he was but a painted jumping-jack who tried to singe her with a torch. Again he resembled Vital Dutour, the imperial prosecutor. . . . '*Apage Satanas!*' cried Bernadette, as she had been taught to do" (*Bernadette* 524–25).

Werfel's representation of the devil is quite conventional and naïve. In comparison, the devil in Thomas Mann's *Doctor Faustus* is but a feverish hallucination of the protagonist, envisioning not only the well-known pimp-master but also the more obscure music critic (Theodor W. Adorno) and a conventional theater devil. In Mann's novel the account of the encounter with the devil is contained in a transcript of a manuscript by the protagonist, and the narrator who transcribes it questions whether the devil even existed. But this makes it even more complex for the representation of evil than Werfel's narration. Mann's narrator realizes that it is "gruesome to think that the cynicism, the mockery, and the humbug likewise" come from the "stricken soul" of the protagonist, and not the devil (*Doctor Faustus* 237).

The provincial authorities in *The Song of Bernadette* are shown to view the crowds assembled at the Massabiele grotto as hostile toward Emperor Napoleon III and his government. The matter reaches the level of the imperial court: Empress Eugénie insists that the prince who appears to be sick be administered a glass of the spring water of Lourdes. When the prince gets well, the empress perceives his recovery as a miracle and demands that the grotto be opened to the public. The emperor reluctantly complies, sending a telegram to that effect to the provincial authorities. The spring of Lourdes signifies, as the narrator concludes, "a victory of the people . . . over the powers of both the Empire and the Church" (*Bernadette* 257).

The narrator is not as critical of the Church, however, and represents the clergy as interested in determining whether Bernadette is an impostor or a madwoman or has indeed been visited by special grace. The narrator presents her sufferings and her final disease as proof of that grace. The pastoral scenes of the lady's appearances, however, tend to displace Bernadette's later afflictions, and here the author misses an opportunity to emphasize that the state of grace included great pain and distress. Werfel had the opportunity to reach the level of the great Catholic novels of the twentieth century—those by Georges Bernanos, Graham Greene, and Elisabeth Langgässer—but Werfel missed the mark. On the other hand, he was not a Catholic writer, but a Jew who "dared to sing the song of Bernadette" (*Bernadette* 7).

Pope Pius XI removes all doubts about Bernadette's credibility in the novel's final sermon at the occasion of her canonization in 1933. The pope praises her "purity, simplicity, and the fearless fight she had fought for the genuineness of her visions against a whole world of doubters, mockers, haters. Not only in the beneficent miracles of Lourdes but in the whole life of the new saint there was contained a message of inexhaustible wealth" (*Bernadette* 573). Pope Pius XI speaks of the "confusion of demonic voices which had accompanied the visions of Bernadette." Since 1933 is also the year that Hitler came to power and Mussolini had ruled for more than a decade, it is natural for the pope to comment that the "confusion of demonic voices" has increased in recent times, as he says that the "fever of maniacal false doctrines was threatening to plunge the human spirit into bloody madness. In the battle against this, which man must win, not only did Lourdes stand like a very rock, but the life of Bernadette Soubirous retained its prophetic activity within time" (*Bernadette* 574). The pope places the saint's life in the center of the eternal conflict between rationalism and religion and submits the response of the Catholic Church as a challenge to mankind to win the battle against false doctrines.

The last chapter of *The Song of Bernadette,* entitled "The Fiftieth Ave," concludes with the prayers of the rosary, which are represented by the structure of the novel. This chapter deals with Bernadette's canonization in December 1933, some fifty years after her death in 1879. The Bouhouhorts child, the first beneficiary of a miracle at the Virgin Spring, now an old man in his seventies, visits Rome and whispers one Ave Maria after another during and after a service in Saint Peter's Cathedral. He turns "his soul not to the rosary of sorrows nor to that of joy but to that of glory which is to lift the thoughts of man to victory, glory, and the ascension into heaven" (*Bernadette* 575). The fiftieth Ave serves to close the novel: "After the fortieth Ave the smiling old eyes began to grow heavier and heavier and precisely during the fiftieth the Bouhouhorts child fell asleep. But great gladness was in his heart the while he slept" (*Bernadette* 575).

This ending conveys a clear religious message that allows no ambiguity. The narrative shows the victory of faith over modern rationalism, of the religious life over intellectual reasoning. The life of the charismatic saint was to inspire the readers and make them change their lives. Her "transfigurative grace" was to destroy the "rationalized bureaucracy" of the modern state and lead to a "renewed community" in faith (Berman 205). Werfel tapped into the growing religiosity or desecularization of wartime America. According to Adorno and Horkheimer's logic, his hagiography of Bernadette Soubirous was a "regress to mythology" (DE xviii, 20).

In his last two works, Werfel recovered some of the elements of modernism missing from his previous works, though the recovery was not total. Subtitled *Comedy of a Tragedy,* Werfel's play *Jacobowsky and the*

Colonel (Jacobowsky und der Oberst) of 1944 is an early representative of the "theater of the absurd," retelling the French defeat of 1940. Despite the threat of capture by the Germans, a Polish colonel on the run from his captors does not hesitate to exhibit his anti-Semitism toward a Polish Jew named Jacobowsky, who again and again comes to his rescue during their escape, providing a car and obtaining gasoline. Jacobowsky and the colonel share the same nationality, but as the former explains in his summary of recent history:

> Your people drove me from my home when I was only three years old. And then, in nineteen thirty-three, when this pest and this grief broke out over me in Germany, you Poles rubbed your hands and said: "Serves him right, this Jacobowsky!" And later on, when this pest and this grief broke out over me in Austria, you shrugged your shoulders and said: "What's that to us?" And not only you said: "What's it to us?" but all the rest of them said it too. Englishmen and Americans and Frenchmen and Russians! And then when this pest and this grief broke out in Prague, you still didn't believe that it was any of your business. . . . But when it finally came over you, this pest and this grief, you were very innocently surprised, and you weren't prepared at all, and you were done for in seventeen days. (II, i; *Jacobowsky* 49).

Although Colonel Stjerbinsky and Jacobowsky have in common the Germans as their enemy, they are engaged in an eternal metaphysical struggle with one another. Although the colonel sees their struggle as temporarily postponed by the German occupation of France, Jacobowsky confirms in the last act, "Our duel is eternal" (III, ii; *Jacobowsky* 120).

At the end, Jacobowsky confronts his opponent with the facts of the persecution and extermination that he faces: "The Jacobowskys are to be exterminated, with the overt or secret approval of the world. But they will not be exterminated, although millions die. God is punishing us. He probably knows why. He punishes us by unworthy hands, who make us stronger while they weaken us" (III, ii; *Jacobowsky* 118). Only when no other escape is possible does the colonel overcome his prejudice in order to save himself and his despised countryman on a boat to England. The colonel is even willing to let Jacobowsky go in his stead. But in the end it is not the colonel's grand gesture that saves Jacobowsky, but the latter's will to live. Jacobowsky throws the flask containing the poison for his suicide into the sea. Impressed by his courage, the British naval officer in charge of the rescue declares Jacobowsky eligible for the voyage to England. It is not a sentimental decision, however, because Jacobowsky is considered useful to the Allied war effort. As the British naval officer says, "You convinced me yourself! Your resoluteness and your will to live, you optimist! England can make use of you. The whole world needs you" (III, ii; *Jacobowsky* 119).

Although the plot was based on actual events—a Jewish banker from Stuttgart named S. L. Jacobowicz had told Werfel of his escape from France—the figures of Jacobowsky and the colonel were without doubt stereotypes, even during the 1940s. Tadeusz Boleslav Stjerbinsky is a courageous and chivalrous officer who led the legendary cavalry attacks against German tanks. Now he is entrusted with taking secret documents to the Polish government in exile in London. But Stjerbinsky is also arrogant and prejudiced, displaying an almost habitual anti-Semitism. According to him, Jews do not work with their hands, they only "clip coupons fr-r-rom bonds, carr-r-rry on long telephone conver-r-sations with Lisbon, New York, Buenos Aires, finance films with beautiful star-r-rs, and look for-r-r their-r-r names in the paper-r-r ever-r-ry day" (II, i; *Jacobowsky* 63). He does not hesitate to claim that Hitler is right: Jewish "existence is nothing but gr-r-rabbing, gr-r-rabbing, gr-r-rabbing" (II, ii; *Jacobowsky* 74). In contrast, Jacobowsky is portrayed in a positive light, even as his characteristics confirm anti-Semitic prejudices, as Egon Schwarz has shown (167–68). As victim of a pogrom in Poland, Jacobowsky fled to Germany, where he became successful as "President and Chairman of Boards of Directors." He admired, of course, German culture: "Goethe, Mozart, Beethoven!" And he founded a school for modern architecture, like the Bauhaus, and a chamber music society that perhaps played compositions by Arnold Schoenberg. As a capitalist, he had a bad conscience and funded a workers' library (I, i; *Jacobowsky* 15). Jacobowsky realizes that he has one advantage over the colonel: "I can never be Hitler, never, as long as the world lasts. But you could easily have been Hitler, and you could still be. At any time!" (II, i; *Jacobowsky* 49).

The realistic presentation of the crowded roads in France during the summer of 1940 convey an aura of historical authenticity, but this impression is defeated by situation comedy. The comedy resulting from the contrast between the war situation and the petty fighting between the main characters wears thin, and the jokes on the Polish and Italian accents of Stjerbinsky and Saint Francis and the Gestapo agent's speech impediment are offensive. While the figure of Marianne Deloupe as Madame la France can be dismissed as nonessential to the plot and a concession to dramatic shorthand, the allegorical figures of the Wandering Jew and Saint Francis of Assisi are a throwback to Werfel's penchant for naïve simplicity. The use of allegory undermines the sense of the absurd as well as the complexity of the relationship between Judaism and Catholicism. Furthermore, Werfel must have been aware that the Wandering Jew was a stock figure of Christian anti-Semitism. While the employment of the Ahasverus figure was not uncommon among Jewish writers in the 1920s, as, for example, by Franz Kafka, it was no longer legitimate after the persecution of Jews during the 1930s and 1940s. To place such a figure into a play at that time required a new characterization of Ahasverus that Werfel failed to supply. He depicted him as a Jewish intellectual who tells the same old Jewish jokes as Jacobowsky. To have this figure appear on a tandem bicycle with Saint Francis was not only a gross simplification, but also a denial of the failures of the Catholic Church during the Holocaust.

California's state historian Kevin Starr was on target when he criticized the play for using anti-Semitism as the central joke and raised the question whether Werfel was "pandering to anti-Semitism by making it seem humorous" (*Dream Endures* 393). This criticism was harsh, but it was also raised by other critics before him. A scene showing an exchange of identity between Jacobowsky and the colonel, however, has escaped the critics' attention. When the colonel's party is stopped by a German patrol, Jacobowsky tells the Germans that Stjerbinsky is the former husband of Marianne Deloupe and an inmate of an insane asylum. He escaped during a bombing raid and therefore has no papers. While the Gestapo agent believes he has discovered a "clinical case of the destruction of an Aryan by Juda," Jacobowsky explains that "loup is the French word for 'wolf.' Deloupe, fils de loup, son of the wolf, Wolfson. Even in France the Wolfs and the Wolfsons are not ordinarily Aryans" (II, ii; *Jacobowsky* 85). All members of the traveling party cooperate in the charade. Stjerbinsky is saved as a Wolfson. At this critical moment of mistaken identity he is the same as Jacobowsky, but as soon as the danger is over he denies his shared humanity. He insists on their difference, accusing Jacobowsky of "annihilating" him: "I feel like an unburr-ried corpse" (II, ii, *Jacobowsky* 87). Because of his prejudices, Stjerbinsky cannot rejoice over the fact that he has been saved from arrest by the Germans. The last line of the play reads: "END OF THE COMEDY," implying that the tragedy, announced in the subtitle, is to follow in film noir fashion.

Werfel had written the play in ten days in 1942 at the Biltmore Hotel in Santa Barbara, where he liked to withdraw to one of the bungalows on the grounds. He submitted the play to the New York Theatre Guild and it was revised and adapted for the stage by S. N. Behrman. In spite of Werfel's misgivings and furious protests against the changes, the Behrman's version, based on Werfel's original play in German, was quite successful when it premiered in March 1944 at the Martin Beck Theater in New York. Behrman's version was anthologized in the collection of *The Most Successful Plays in the History of the American Stage* later that year. The first translation of Werfel's original text, by UCLA professor Gustave O. Arlt, also appeared in 1944, while the German version, also edited by Arlt, was first published in a textbook for American students in 1945.

Werfel's *The Star of the Unborn (Stern der Ungeborenen),* which proved to be his last work, also signaled a return to modernism. He died on August 26, 1945, in his home in Los Angeles. It is important to note that he began to write this novel in the spring of 1943, at about the same time Thomas Mann started *Doctor Faustus.* Although Ruth Klüger called Werfel's novel "a poor cousin" of Mann's work, she confirmed that both novels shared traits of modernism with Hermann Broch's *The Death of Virgil (Der Tod des Vergil)* and Robert Musil's *The Man without Qualities (Der Mann ohne Eigenschaften).* These modernist traits accounted for their greatness: "In theme, a sense of doom and isolation, in form, a highly complex structure and a style that is not easily penetrable—hallmarks of works written for an ideal reader, not for a large and readily available public" (Angress [Klüger] 187).

The first chapter of *Star of the Unborn* reveals Werfel's renewed claim to modernism, showing a new application to literary experimentation as well as to dedicated opposition to the tendencies of his age. With an allusion to Romantic irony, the first chapter is but a prologue, while the plot begins with chapter two. In chapter one, the first-person narrator identifies himself with the initials F. W.; Franz Werfel appears to have been unable to invent any third person that could bear the burden of the plot for him:

> And so the "I" of this story is not a deceptive, novelistic, assumed, fictitious "I" any more than the story itself is the mere offspring of speculative imagination. It happened to me, as I must confess, quite against my will. Without the slightest preparation or premonition, contrary to all my habits and instincts, I was sent out one night as an explorer. (*Star* 4)

By means of this fictional device, the account of the narrator with the initials F. W. is introduced as a fact of reality—"What I experienced, I really experienced" (*Star* 4)—but the narrator must not be identified with the author Franz Werfel, as many critics have done. It is a case of self-reflective narration, as Bettina Englmann has shown (392–408). The narrator expresses his responsibility to his century and to his craft, admitting his failure in a long confessional statement that begins with his identification with exile and persecution:

> I have not forgotten that I, too, am persecuted. Nor have I become too deaf to hear the roar of the bombers, the clatter of the heavy machine guns, the death rattle of the mortally wounded, the cry of torment and the dying gasp of the ravished, the tortured, the massacred. The monstrous reality, the mad vision of a pain demon, constrict my throat by day and night, where I walk and stand, on the street and in my room, at work and at play. Of course, I am neglecting my duty. But this reality does not leave me even enough breath for an echoing groan to the cry of torment. (*Star* 6)

As if aware of Adorno's dictum that there can be no poetry after Auschwitz, the narrator feels unable adequately to express the horror of the events in Europe. Nevertheless, he devotes himself to his "travelogue" of the future (Mierendorff 480–88). Assuming the posture of a "historian of the future," the narrator presents his utopian tale by looking back on his present century from a future age.

The narrator in his persona as F. W. is transported from his house at 610 North Bedford Drive—Werfel's address in Beverly Hills—in April 1943 into the same region some hundred thousand years later, that is, California during the year 101,943. As he describes it:

> It is appropriately called a paradise, although certain snobs have been known to make disparaging remarks about this lovely spot and there are even some who claim to prefer the flat Florida landscape to the diversified West Coast. These snobs slanderously call California a desert covered with artificial luxuriance, whose rouged roses, bougainvilleas, poinsettias, and other flowers have no fragrance, whose fruits and vegetables have no savour, whose inhabitants are good-looking, but somehow Lemurian. That is because long before the beginnings of mankind as we know it, California was part of the submerged continent of Lemuria. That may have influenced the character of the Californians. The Lemurians seem to have been a shadowy, trifling race, whited sepulchers, in a word, actors, who deceived the world with gay and false pretenses with nothing true and tested behind them. There is a contemporary expression for this Lemurian characteristic, the word "phony." And so the snobs of today—I mean our own today or yesterday—turn up their noses at California, chiefly because a certain famous city in that state produces films, whose fantastic, photographic tales that have become the vogue of their time, although, or perhaps precisely because, they are Lemurian. (*Star* 16)

This amusing catalogue of twentieth-century clichés about Los Angeles and Hollywood sets the stage of the novel.

As a Dante of the twentieth century F. W. begins to explore the utopian culture of Southern California in the company of his childhood friend B. H. (Willy Haas, a critic from Prague), who serves as his Virgil. What he encounters is a subterranean urban civilization in California comprised of an endless city, named Panopolis. This highly developed civilization is characterized as "astromental," because its material as well as its mental needs are provided by stellar energy. The astromental civilization has abolished labor, technology, and economy, and has increased life expectancy to up to two hundred years. The astromental population has no body hair and wears no clothing, except for a delicate lace tissue that is cast over them by indirect light. Their dogs are so domesticated that they are able to converse with human beings in a kind of baby talk.

Since great significance is assigned to matrimony, marriages are arranged by the parents. Having only one child is the rule, and families with more children form the lower classes of society. Death has become a voluntary process of retrogenesis to a plantlike existence as a daisy in a region called the Wintergarden. The highest intellectual activity of the civilization is centered in the Djebel, an institution of micro- and macro-cosmological learning. The scholarship conducted at the Djebel has no practical application and functions as a kind of esoteric astronomical "glass-bead game," reminiscent of the titular symbol of Hermann Hesse's novel of 1943. The narrator participates in an elementary class at the School of Chronosophers, which takes him on a journey to inter-planetary and interatomic space. In this class, the narrator meets Io-Knirps, a gifted student who appears to be a reincarnation of his son with Alma Mahler. The authorities of the Djebel confirm the identity of this fictitious character with Werfel's son, Martin Carl Johannes, who died at age 10 months in 1919 after being born prematurely.

There is no gain without loss, however, in the astromental civilization. Elements of Adorno and Horkheimer's *Dialectic of Enlightenment* are implicitly inscribed into the novel. Because of the advanced standard of living, individuality is largely reduced, and the palms of the astromentals show no lines, suggesting the great uniformity in the society. Time is wasted in idle activities, as, for example, the mindless collecting of antiques that eligible bachelors parade as prize possessions at wedding parties. The narrator's visit to the Wintergarden shows that in spite of the lovely daisy fields, there are also failures in the retrogenic process that result in raving, gabbling turnip-manikins and in the so-called Catabolites, who remind the narrator of the victims of German extermination camps—Dachau and Majdanek are named in the text (*Star* 561). He also associates the attendants of the Wintergarden with SS doctors and "their murderous injections" (*Star* 580).

The only institutions of the past that have survived are the Catholic Church and Judaism, but their influence is marginal. The narrator reports encounters with representatives of both institutions who are still engaged in their mission as witnesses of transcendence. Representatives of both Catholicism and Judaism attend the funeral rites of Io-Knirps at the end of the novel. The narrator's last conversation with the Grand Bishop seems to suggest a commitment in favor of Christianity, but his assertions that the true shape of the universe is the shape of man and that self-correction is part of divine activity indicate that he has a cabbalistic or Gnostic commitment. (*Star* 361–63).

The intersection of three different eras—those of Werfel's childhood in Prague in the 1890s, his exile in Los Angeles in the 1940s, and the year 101,943, as well as the ensuing anachronism, contribute to the complex structure and style of *Star of the Unborn* as a utopian novel. The events of twentieth-century European history are reviewed as part of ancient history. According to the utopian informant, the Germans have taken the lead in humanitarianism and good will between World Wars II and III. Quoting a fictitious authority of the 1960s on the concept of the two Germanies, prevalent among the exiles during World War II, the Germans are divided into the Heinzelmännchen (the Brownies) and the Wichtelmännchen (the Imps). The Brownies are the good Germans, helpful, tireless, industrious workers who stubbornly appear everywhere, whether they are wanted or not, to atone for their guilt. The Imps, on the other hand, are the evil Germans, wicked, unregenerate hobgoblins who appear in hundreds of disguises. They are indistinguishable from the Brownies and worship an idol by the name of Heiltier or Hiltier—an obvious allusion to Hitler—who was, according to the guide, not "even a real German Imp, but was said to be a low-down mixed breed and a dirty border product of some sort" (*Star* 179). Although Werfel did subscribe to the theory of the two Germanies in 1939, he abandoned this theory in 1945 in his "Message to the German People." Like Thomas Mann in his speech "Germany and the Germans" of May 1945, Werfel refused to distinguish between a good and a bad Germany and declared that there was no other way for Germany and its population but that of moral regeneration.

The narrator F. W. has been summoned from the past in a séancelike procedure as a special gift for a young astromental couple on the occasion of their three-day wedding. The novel is divided into three parts, each covering one day of the event, until the narrator returns to the twentieth century. The narrator is invited to participate in the wedding because there is a great desire on the part of this highly developed culture for rejuvenation through the primitive past. The obvious analogy is the crisis of modernism at the end of the 1920s, when there was a similar desire for the renewal of civilization by means of primitivism or deliberate barbarization. Thomas Mann treated the same crisis in *Doctor Faustus* in his portrayal of the Kridwiß circle, a group of intellectuals in Munich during the 1920s who indulge in fascist table talk.

This desire for rejuvenation through rebarbarization finds additional motivation in *Star of the Unborn* through the juxtaposition of the astromental culture with a counterculture, represented by the so-called Jungle, which constitutes a threat as well as an object of fascination for the astromental population. This counterculture is still governed by labor and money, and by old-fashioned greed, violence, and raw sexuality, but it's also portrayed in a positive light as an agricultural economy in a sort of Balkan village setting. Some are reported to defect from the ranks of the astromentals to the other side, especially women who are attracted to the swarthy men of the Jungle. The exodus of the domestic cats from Panopolis constitutes one of the most memorable episodes of the novel. Standing at the edge of the Jungle, the narrator witnesses the cats that have successfully resisted any further domestication leave the realm of civilization. Their exodus is considered a general telluric omen. The first bloodshed among humans follows only a few pages further.

It is important, however, that the destruction of the astromental civilization is described as coming from within. A group of collectors of antique arms, among them the young bridegroom, destroy the astromental world order by pretending to defend it against the Jungle. The narrator, eager to establish a historical analogy, identifies this type of internal revolt as fascist. The neofascism of the future is shown to lead to a war between Panopolis and the Jungle. The majority of the astromental population prefers to avoid the conflict by mass emigration to the Wintergarden, that is, mass suicide. The majority of the neofascist rebels surrender, but a few manage to escape to inaccessible places from which they destroy the Djebel, the astromental temple of learning.

Returning to the ruins of the Djebel, the narrator loses his friend and guide B. H. to enemy fire. F. W. then witnesses the sacrifice of Io-

Knirps, one of the youngest and most gifted students at the Djebel, and, at the same time, the narrator's son in the twentieth century. Io-Knirps saves the Isochronion, an instrument that coordinates the atomic structures of micro- and macrocosm, from destruction, but he pays with his life for the daring rescue. By rescuing the Isochronion, which contains "the future of the human spirit" (*Star* 621), Io-Knirps ensures the continuity of the cosmos and the formation of a new culture. The heroic self-sacrifice of the boy child, however, also makes the beginning of a new future possible. This new future is the old past: pain and natural death are returned to their designated place in human life. The narrator is returned to his century and his Beverly Hills address by Io-Knirps, a kind of Goethean homunculus who has to return to the beginning of life in order to be reborn.

The boy child as the bearer of hope for a new century was a topos in the Judeo-Christian tradition from Isaiah to the New Testament and Virgil. This topos was also employed by many authors of Werfel's generation during the crisis of modernism, such as Hermann Broch in *The Spell (Die Verzauberung)* and *The Death of Virgil (Der Tod des Vergil)*, and Thomas Mann in *Joseph and His Brothers*. In *Doctor Faustus* the boy child, named Echo, dies as a victim of the protagonist's transgressions. It may have been tempting for Werfel to employ Io-Knirps as a redeemer figure, because such a device promised a neat closure, but Werfel invested the topos with so much pain and destruction that any facile solution is precluded. The narrator's belief in original sin is reconfirmed by his visit. The novel closes with an image of uncertainty and ambivalence. The narrator is confronted with a double vision:

> I could plainly see the face of the dead child. But it wasn't one face, there were two faces. Confounded astigmatism! Where are my glasses? . . . But there were really two boyish faces superimposed one over the other: a gray, dead face on top and a blooming, smiling one underneath. . . . The gray face became more and more indistinct and the smiling one more and more distinct, the closer I approached. (*Star* 644–45)

Of the two superimposed faces of Io-Knirps, the dead face slowly disappears, while the smiling face of the star dancer prevails. The narrator feels joy as he comes closer to the star dancer. The child's roguish smile suggests that he "had hoodwinked them all" before the narrator's memory loses strength and fades until he knows "nothing more" (*Star* 645).

The novel ends with the extinction of the narrator's consciousness. Werfel had planned to write a twenty-seventh chapter, a kind of epilogue to his utopian novel, but his early death in August 1945 prevented this final closure for the work that regained him some of his credibility as a modernist. In *Star of the Unborn* Werfel again combined literary experimentation, such as a new narrative form and perspective, with strategies that aimed for a critical review of established traditions and patterns of society. Thomas Mann in his obituary for Werfel praised the novel as "astonishingly creative," saying that the author had reached "the full height and dignity of his craft" in his last work (GW 10: 501).

With the exception of *The Song of Bernadette,* Walter H. Sokel did not include any of Werfel's works written in exile in his criticism of 1959. To be sure, Sokel's case against *Bernadette* was well founded, but it needed to be contextualized and expanded to include Werfel's other works. If one examines the history and politics in the texts of all his works in exile, Werfel emerges as an author who was painfully aware of the problem of his art in the twentieth century and used the haven of his California exile to renew the ability of modernist discourse to deal with the issues of his time. Werfel's production between 1933 and 1945 is a testimony to a modernism with a second chance. He did not succeed with all of his works, and some of his fragments suggest his potential better than his completed works. For the historian of modernism, Werfel's earlier novels *The Embezzled Heaven* and *The Song of Bernadette* were relapses into a pseudo-naïve Catholicism that was poorly suited for confronting the problems of the twentieth century. They cannot compare with the novels by Catholic authors such as Georges Bernanos, Graham Greene, or Elisabeth Langgässer, but are rather an example of the kitsch of Austrian Catholicism that Werfel found so hard to resist. Nevertheless, Werfel's work in exile was a powerful articulation of the crisis as well as the attempted renewal of modernism. Even though he was not completely successful, Werfel added a voice that demands critical respect to those of his fellow exiles in Los Angeles.

CHAPTER 8

Renegade Modernism

Alfred Döblin's Novel Karl and Rosa

Of all the German exile writers in Los Angeles, Alfred Döblin (1878–
1957) is the least known. The novelist, who had established himself as
the most avant-garde prose writer of the Weimar Republic with the publication of his novel *Berlin Alexanderplatz* in 1929, departed from modernism in his exile works in tandem with his conversion to Roman
Catholicism in 1941. As a Jew, a socialist sympathizer, and a member
of the avant-garde, he had been a target of the Nazis already during the
Weimar Republic. After the burning of the Reichstag in 1933, he immediately fled Germany via Zurich to Paris, where he lived relatively
comfortably until 1940, when France was invaded by German troops.
He had been able to transfer his funds from Germany to France, and his
new books were published by Querido in Amsterdam, a publishing
house devoted to German authors in exile. In 1936 Döblin obtained
French citizenship for himself and his family. The defeat of France in
1940, however, made it necessary for him and his family to leave the
country because it became obvious that his French citizenship would not
protect him from extradition to the German authorities, especially since
he had accepted a position in the French Ministry of Information,
where he was engaged in producing counterpropaganda against Nazi
Germany. He had sent his wife and youngest son ahead to southern
France, but when he tried to follow them on June 10, he got caught in
the masses of fleeing refugees. He spent two weeks in a refugee camp in
Mende in southern France, where he had his religious conversion expe-

FIGURE 20. Alfred Döblin, circa 1940. Photograph courtesy of Bildabteilung, Deutsches Literaturarchiv, Marbach/Neckar.

rience. Finally, on July 10, Döblin was reunited with his family and they left via Marseille, Madrid, and Lisbon for New York, where they arrived on September 9, 1940.

Through the efforts of the American Rescue Committee Döblin had obtained a one-year contract as a scriptwriter for Metro-Goldwyn-

Mayer, so he moved to Los Angeles in October 1940. Such contracts were a courtesy extended by the movie industry to some of the more prominent exiles, since such documents of prospective of employment, called "affidavits," were a requirement to obtain a visa into the United States. Numerous exiles, such as Heinrich Mann, Walther Mehring, and Alfred Polgar, received such one-year contracts, which were issued for the purpose of rescue and did not generally lead to long-term employment. In October 1941, Döblin's contract with MGM, like that of many other exiles, expired and was not renewed. After exhausting seven months of unemployment insurance, Döblin for the rest of his stay in Los Angeles, from 1942 to 1945, lived on the support of the European Film Fund, a financial aid committee funded and administrated by the exiles, and of private individuals. Unlike Lion Feuchtwanger, Thomas Mann, and Franz Werfel, he did not have an American publisher to put his books on the market in English translation. (although *Berlin Alexanderplatz* had been published by Viking Press in 1931). None of Döblin's works were published during his time in the United States, except for one chapter from his novel *Karl and Rosa,* entitled "Nocturno," which was published in 1944 as a separate volume by the Pazifische Presse, a small exile publishing house in Los Angeles, and two other short pieces, "The Chief" ("Der Chefarzt") in English translation and *Sieger und Besiegte* (1946), both published in *November 1918* (Meyer 46).

At the end of the war Döblin reestablished his connection with the French government, since he was a naturalized French citizen and had worked for the French Ministry of Information in 1939–1940. He was one of the first exiles to return to Europe, accepting in November 1945 a position as a cultural affairs officer in the French occupation zone in Germany. He was employed by the office of public education in the French military government and was in charge of reviewing literary manuscripts that required approval for publication. His position was equal in rank to that of a major or colonel in the French army, but, although Döblin wore a uniform, he never held a military rank. The Germans, however, saw it differently. His position and military uniform estranged him from a West German audience that was resentful of exile writers in general—and especially if they appeared in the uniform of the Allied armies. Döblin's new books did not find many readers, and he was unable to repeat the literary success that he had enjoyed during the Weimar Republic.

Döblin became embittered and demonstrated an almost pathological hatred of Thomas Mann. Although Mann, a traditionalist, and Döblin, a radical innovator, had been at opposite ends of the literary spectrum of the Weimar Republic, they had maintained a cordial relationship as members of the Prussian Academy of Arts and later as exiles in Los Angeles. But after his return to Germany, Döblin used his periodical *Das Goldene Tor* (The Golden Gate), which he had founded in 1946, to launch bitter attacks on Mann. He probably resented that he was not awarded the Nobel Prize, and he rejected Mann's exile novels as irrelevant, if not dangerous, for the reconstruction of literary life in postwar Germany.

In 1951, Döblin emigrated for a second time to France. Impoverished and in need of health care, he returned to West Germany in 1956; he died in a small-town public hospital in the Rhine valley, near the Black Forest, in 1957. Döblin was buried in France, in Housseras in the Vosges Mountains, beside his son Wolfgang, who was killed in action as a French soldier in 1940. Ten years after his death, Döblin's literary fame was reestablished when Günter Grass, one of the most creative writers of the postwar generation, praised Döblin as his teacher.

In California Döblin lived a fairly isolated life with his wife and youngest son in Hollywood, first in an apartment house at 1842 Cherokee Avenue, later in a house with a garden at 901 Genesee Avenue, and finally in a small house at 1347 North-Citrus Avenue, but he was not shunned by his fellow exiles in Los Angeles. On the contrary, he was welcomed upon his arrival in October 1940 by a reading of his works at the Jewish Club, a social and cultural organization of German-Jewish exiles in Los Angeles. Döblin was also celebrated in a public ceremony on the occasion of his sixty-fifth birthday in a little theater in Santa Monica in August 1943, a celebration that was attended by most of his fellow exiles. But his speech against moral relativism on that occasion and his confession of a turn toward religion offended many of his admirers. The speech offended Brecht's atheism, as he recorded in his diary of August 14, 1943, with hardly any empathy: "An awkward sensation came over the more rational of most of his listeners, something like the sympathetic horror felt when a fellow prisoner succumbs to torture and talks. The fact is that Döblin has been dealt some severe blows, the loss of two sons in France, a 2400-page epic *[November 1918]* that no publisher will print, [and] angina pectoris (that great saver of souls)" (GBA 27: 165).

Brecht was wrong about the two sons: only one was killed during the war in France, while the other escaped to Switzerland, but neither Brecht nor Döblin could know this at the time, and the agony Döblin felt about the unknown fate of his two sons left behind in France was real. Three

FIGURE 21. Alfred Döblin's house, 1347 North Citrus Avenue, Hollywood, 2005. Photograph by Juergen Nogai, Santa Monica.

months later Brecht himself lost a son—Frank Banholzer, an illegitimate child born when Brecht lived in Augsburg in 1919—who was killed in action as a German soldier in the Soviet Union in November 1943. Döblin had to wait until March 1945 until the death of his son Wolfgang was confirmed. He had died as a French soldier in June 1940, presumably committing suicide to avoid capture by the Germans.

When Döblin described at this celebration in August 1943 how, like many other writers, he, too, was to blame for the rise of the Nazis, Brecht was convinced that his former left-wing colleague would continue by saying "because I covered up the crimes of the ruling class, discouraged the oppressed, put off the hungry with songs," but to Brecht's great surprise, all that Döblin "did was to announce stubbornly, without repentance or regret, [it was] 'because I did not seek god' " (GBA 27: 166). Afterwards Brecht expressed his bitter disappointment in the poem "Embarrassing Incident":

> When one of my highest gods had his 10,000th birthday
> I came with my friends and disciples to celebrate
> And they danced and sang before him and recited poems.
> The people were moved. When the festivities came to an end,
> The celebrated god entered the stage that belongs to the artists
> And declared with a firm voice
> In front of my perspiring friends and disciples
> That he had suffered an epiphany and now had turned
> Religious and with obscene haste he donned a priest's
> Moth-eaten garb
> Indecently he knelt on his knees and without shame he intoned
> An impudent church hymn, thus violating the irreligious feelings
> of his audience, among whom there were juveniles.
>
> For three days I have not dared to face
> My friends and disciples, because
> I am so ashamed.
>
> (GBA 5: 91)

Although Döblin made a public confession of his turn towards religion in August 1943, he kept his conversion to Roman Catholicism a secret. His experience of the Christ figure that was crucial for his later conversion happened during his flight from Paris between June 22 and July 8, 1940, when he visited the cathedral of Mende in southern France again and again. As he relates in *Destiny's Journey (Schicksalsreise)*, his autobiography of 1949, he sat in the cathedral and looked at the crucifix: "The crucified Jesus will not let me be. I am fascinated by him and by the religion formed around. But I cannot manage to meld his image with what I feel is true" (*Destiny's Journey* 122). His was a conversion in stages. Döblin and his family were baptized in Los Angeles on November 30, 1941, and took Holy Communion on May 31, 1942, but he did not utter a word about his personal decision until 1945, when he returned to Europe. His silence has been attributed to his financial dependence on private welfare organizations and Jewish friends, such as Elvira and Arthur Rosin in New York, and on his solidarity with other Jews. He did not want to give the impression of deserting Judaism in a time of crisis, a dilemma that he shared to a certain degree with Franz Werfel, who, however, did not convert. As Döblin wrote in a letter of September 17, 1941, to his friends Elvira and Arthur Rosin:

If I would turn Catholic or Protestant today or tomorrow—which is not
the case—why shouldn't I—as long as I keep it secret "in my heart"? It has
become known that the philosopher Bergson, a Jew, as is well known, had
been a Catholic for many years; but he kept it a private matter and was
aware that an announcement of his conversion at this time would mean a
stab in the back of his people. (*Briefe* 1: 259)

He added, referring to the matter of betrayal, "If I would address the
public with some kind of Christian belief and a corresponding message,
especially at this time, then this would be a 'betrayal' of exactly that,
which I also represent, namely Judaism" (*Briefe* 1: 258).

Döblin's conversion to Catholicism was contradicted by the lecture he
delivered in London in June 1935 with the title, "I am not a Hitler Jew,"
that is, a Jew who had to be reminded of his roots by Hitler. He also declared that he had returned to his roots during a meeting of Jewish writers in Poland in 1921: "I . . . finally bound myself up with the Jewish
people, . . . I was one with these Polish Jews" (*Schriften* 311). During his
Paris exile, Döblin was actively engaged in the founding of the "Ligue
juive pour colonization," a branch of the international Freeland movement, which promoted overseas settlement of Jews threatened in Europe.
The Freeland movement differed from Zionism in that it considered
areas other than Palestine for emigration and insisted on Yiddish as a
common language. Not only did Döblin publish two major titles dealing
with Jewish renewal and emigration in German—*Jüdische Erneuerung*
(Jewish Renewal, 1933) and *Flucht und Sammlung des Judenvolks* (Exodus and Gathering of the Jewish People, 1935)—but he also wrote essays in Yiddish that appeared in Jewish journals. He was active as a lecturer and organizer for the Freeland movement until 1937 (Müller-Salget
233–46). Yet, in his *Reise in Polen,* his Polish travelogue of 1926, Döblin
wrote of his strong attraction to the crucifix in a church in Krakow in a
manner that appeared to foreshadow his experience in Mende in 1940
(*Reise in Polen* 237–48).

To be sure, the religious development and beliefs of a writer are not
criteria for literary quality. Every writer has the right to change his religion, or to abandon it, but literary criticism may examine to what degree
this private act affects an author's writings. This chapter will evaluate
Döblin's *Karl and Rosa* according to the criteria of exile modernism.

Döblin was quite productive during his years in Los Angeles, completing the first part of his autobiography, *Schicksalsreise: Bericht und
Bekenntnis* (translated as *Destiny's Journey*), as well as his novel *Karl
und Rosa (Karl and Rosa),* the last part of his tetralogy *November 1918*:

Eine deutsche Revolution (November 1918: A German Revolution). Before Döblin left for Europe in November 1945, he had started *Der Oberst und der Dichter* (The Colonel and the Poet), a didactic narrative, and his last novel, entitled *Hamlet oder Die lange Nacht nimmt ein Ende* (translated as *Tales of a Long Night*). It took ten years until his final novel, which was completed in Germany in 1946, was finally published in East Germany in 1956. It was published in West Germany one year later. The novel deals with the problem of guilt after World War II: a severely wounded British soldier returns home and is unable to resume his life as a civilian because of the what he perceives as the moral corruption of society, reflected in his own family. The novel shows its Los Angeles origins: the description of the protagonist's war injuries, caused by an attack of kamikaze planes on his warship, is based on details from an American newspaper story of damage to the U.S. battleship *Mississippi* in January 1945 (Meyer 483). Furthermore, the tales of Lord Crenshaw in the novel contain unmistakable references to the topography of Los Angeles. Gordon Allison, the father of the wounded soldier, is given this title by his friends who take it from "a Hollywood street and bus line of the same name, which, by a complex route, links La Brea Avenue with the endless Wilshire Boulvevard" (*Tales* 29). Crenshaw Boulevard is a main north-south thoroughfare that connects Wilshire Boulevard with Palos Verdes, and Döblin may have used the Crenshaw bus line to get to the MGM studios in Culver City. At any rate, he included in his novel a ludicrous story about the original Lord Crenshaw participating in a fake filming of a kidnapping scene in a film studio in the southern part of Los Angeles (*Tales* 30–31).

Döblin had begun *November 1918* in France in 1938 and completed the fourth volume in California in 1943. The names Karl and Rosa in the title of the final volume refer to the radical left-wing protagonists of the German Revolution of 1918, Rosa Luxemburg (1870–1919) and Karl Liebknecht (1871–1919), who were murdered by right-wing army soldiers and their officers during the so-called Spartacus revolt in Berlin in January 1919. They had been members of the Spartacus League, a group that was at the extreme left of the Independent Socialist Party, which was formed in opposition to the First World War in 1917. Both Liebknecht and Luxemburg supported the Spartacus revolt of January 1919 only reluctantly, but this did not save them from being heinously murdered when they were arrested by government troops. The revolt was brutally suppressed by the army and the so-called Free Corps, volunteer combat units under the direction of the transitional government, which was led by the Social Democratic Party. This reliance of the majority Socialist Party on the military and right-wing paramilitary forces caused the split between the Social Democrats and the Communists during the 1920s that, along with other factors, led to the collapse of the Weimar Republic, when the Communists considered the Social Democrats a greater evil than the Nazi party and called them *"Sozialfaschisten"* [socialist fascists].

Since *November 1918* was largely a historical novel, Döblin did a great amount of research at the Hollywood branch of the Public Library of the City of Los Angeles and probably at the UCLA library as well. He received advice from the university library at U.C. Berkeley and may also have contacted the Hoover Library on War, Revolution and Peace at Stanford University for interlibrary loans, but the archival evidence is ambiguous. There are some library tickets with titles and call numbers in Döblin's handwriting preserved in the archives at the Deutsches Literaturarchiv in Marbach, Germany, but they do not show the name of the library. It is important to note in this context that Döblin needed "libraries in order to write his books" (Auer 56). This was especially true of *November 1918*, the final edition of which lists more than fifty titles as sources. Döblin used Rosa Luxemburg's prison correspondence, published in 1929, and some of the writings of Karl Liebknecht for his portraits of the two politicians, as well as newspapers, historical accounts, memoirs, and analyses. For Döblin, copying sources was the first step in his writing process, and he later assimilated the material into the final version (Auer 56–57). Although the majority of the sources for *November 1918* have been identified, it is difficult to establish a close dependency, except for the most obvious texts, as, for example, Rosa Luxemburg's letters.

Initially the novel was an attempt to explain and commemorate the failure of the German Revolution of 1918 and to trace and explain the rise of National Socialism during the 1920s. The novel began as a panoramic representation of the events of November 1918, events that were expected to ensure the future of democratic socialism in Germany. The main players were the Social Democratic Party (Sozialdemokratische Partei Deutschlands, or SPD), that is, the majority socialists, under the leadership of Friedrich Ebert; the Independent Social Democratic Party (Unabhängige Sozialdemokratische Partei Deutschlands, or USPD), which split off from the majority socialists when the latter opposed World War I in 1917; and the extreme left-wing Spartacus League, loosely associated with the USPD. Members of the Spartacus League, including Karl Liebknecht and Rosa Luxemburg, founded the Communist Party of Germany at the end of December 1918.

On November 9, 1918, Prince Max of Baden, the last chancellor under Kaiser Wilhelm II, transferred the power of his office to Friedrich Ebert and declared that "the Kaiser and King has resolved to renounce the throne" and that a bill be drafted for the holding of immediate general elections "for a German Constituent National Assembly" (Ryder 151). This assembly would have the task of giving final form to the future constitution of the German people. Radical left-wing forces tried to postpone the elections and decide the outcome in favor of a socialist republic, but due to Ebert's efforts the elections took place on January 19, 1919, and the Constitutional National Assembly met at Weimar on February 6, 1919. The assembly elected Ebert president of the republic and approved a temporary constitution. The final constitution of the so-called Weimar Republic was promulgated at Weimar on August 11, 1919, and Ebert was formally elected president by a vote of the National Assembly.

Döblin planned *November 1918* to be a trilogy, but in 1942, when he determined the second volume would be too long, he divided it into two parts, turning the work into a tetralogy. It took a long time for it to be published in its entirety:

Volume I: *Bürger und Soldaten 1918* (Citizens and Soldiers in 1918, not available in English translation)

Volume II: *Verratenes Volk*, II:1 (available in English as *A People Betrayed*)

Volume III: *Heimkehr der Fronttruppen*, II:2 (available in English as *The Troops Return*)

Volume IV: *Karl und Rosa*, III (available in English as *Karl and Rosa*)

The debate about whether the work is a trilogy or a tetralogy was solved by Werner Stauffacher's edition in the *Ausgewählte Werke* (Selected Works), in which the text is offered in four parts, but it is numbered as three volumes, with volume two divided into II:1, *A People Betrayed*, and II:2, *The Troops Return* (Koepke 201). The English translation of 1983 combined both parts under the title *A People Betrayed*.

Although the first volume or "prelude," *Bürger und Soldaten 1918*, was first published in 1939, French censors did not approve it for republication after World War II because most of the plot takes place among German troops occupying Alsace. After 1945 the French were overly sensitive to the fact that this province had been part of the German Empire between 1871 and 1918 and had been annexed again in 1940 (Auer 57). Only volumes two through four were allowed to appear between 1948 and 1950. The tetralogy remained unpublished in Germany until 1978, when it finally appeared in its entirety in West Germany in a paperback edition. A four-volume East German edition followed in 1981. The final hardcover edition did not appear until 1990, when the text appeared in four volumes as part of Döblin's selected works *(Ausgewählte Werke)*. The English translation followed the French example, presenting only the last three parts in two volumes, *A People Betrayed* and *The Troops Return* in the first volume and *Karl and Rosa* in the second volume. In addition, all episodes dealing with Erwin Stauffer, a fictional dramatist who was to produce modern literature without religious conviction or providing moral guidance, were deleted from the English translation. Stauffer is not convincing as a burlesque counterfigure to Becker, and his absence is not crucial, but his deletion without editorial comment needs to be criticized.

The first volume, *Citizens and Soldiers in 1918,* begins on November 10, 1918, after Kaiser Wilhelm has been forced to abdicate and flee to Holland. It takes place among German soldiers and officers in a military hospital in an Alsatian garrison town and among the people in Strasbourg, the capital of the German imperial province *(Reichsland)* Alsace-Lorraine, which was to be returned to France. German troops withdraw from Strasbourg and French troops enter the city on November 22, 1918. Dr. Friedrich Becker, the central character of the novel, a highly decorated first lieutenant and *Studienrat* (high school teacher of Greek and Latin), recuperating from shrapnel wounds in the Alsatian military hospital, is returned by hospital train to Berlin in the company of his comrade, Lieutenant Johannes Maus. The second volume, *A People Betrayed*, begins with an attack by revolutionary sailors on the police headquarters in Berlin and culminates in the atrocities of December 6, 1918, in Berlin, when soldiers of an elite guard regiment shot and killed a great number of peaceful demonstrators. The third volume, *The Troops Return,* deals with the Versailles Treaty, the founding of the League of Nations, and the death of Woodrow Wilson. Döblin pays a special tribute to the American president, portraying him as a peacemaker who wanted to see the world governed by reason but failed to obtain the support of Congress and died a political and religious martyr: "The year 1620 lived in his soul, the year the proud Pilgrim fathers had pushed off from Europe, and three hundred years of unbroken and free growth of American humanity lived there too, as did the principles of Jefferson and Lincoln and his nation's dead, the men he had to cast into the maw of that Moloch that was Europe" (*A People Betrayed* 312). Döblin called Wilson "the great man of reason" (*A People Betrayed* 636). His eulogy was one of the tributes that the German-speaking exiles paid to American presidents, as Thomas Mann did for Franklin D. Roosevelt in his novel *Joseph and His Brothers* (1943) and Arnold Schoenberg did for George Washington and Roosevelt in his "Ode to Napoleon" (1942). In his 1948 foreword to the *Joseph* tetralogy, Mann said that Roosevelt's "New Deal [was] unmistakably reflected in Joseph's magic administration of national economy" (xiii).

The fourth and final volume, *Karl and Rosa*, describes in detail the counterrevolution of the Social Democrats, which culminated in the murder of Karl Liebknecht and Rosa Luxemburg in January 1919. The tetralogy ends with a religious postlude to the historical events: the salvation of Friedrich Becker, the war veteran and classical philologist who is fired from his job teaching at one of the elite high schools in Berlin. Döblin wrote this volume in Los Angeles between February 1942 and September 1943.

By selecting Liebknecht and Luxemburg as protagonists for his last volume, Döblin appears to endorse their radical left-wing position, or at least to commemorate them as martyrs of the revolution. As Sebastian Haffner, an exile journalist who wrote a critical account of the revolution, said about them, "they embodied the German Revolution in the eyes of both friends and enemies. They were its symbols, and who killed them, killed the Revolution" (Haffner 149). A similar assessment was offered by Döblin when he characterized Friedrich Ebert's opposition as "obstructionist." At the beginning of book two of *Karl and Rosa*, the narrator presents a radical left-wing interpretation of the German Revolution of 1918. Friedrich Ebert, the representative of the majority Social Democrats, Reich chancellor (for one day), and first people's deputy of the young republic, is called "the Obstructionist" who "was anxious not to disturb anything here. He was anxious to prevent anything from happening and to undo what had been done" (89). Modern German historians—Hans-Ulrich Wehler and Heinrich August Winkler, for example—have been much kinder to Ebert in their assessment of his role during the period from November 1918 to January 1919.

Döblin's narrator never changes his mind about Ebert, but there is an obvious shift in his evaluation of Karl Liebknecht and especially of Rosa Luxemburg between books two and eight. Although the narrator in the beginning endorses their socialist agenda and their pacifist stance during the First World War, his support of Karl's and Rosa's political activism during the so-called "Spartacus Week" of January 5 to 15, 1919, when the Berlin workers tried to regain what they had won on November 9 and 10, 1918, fades in the end. Their religious redemption becomes more important than the failure of the German Revolution.

Karl and Rosa, written in Los Angeles between 1942 and 1943, represents a rupture in the plot of the tetralogy and a new departure, transcending the historical framework of the work. Instead of returning to the events of December 1918 in Berlin, the novel consists of a book-length flashback to Rosa Luxemburg in prison in Breslau from 1916 to 1918. In November 1917 she hears that Lenin and his Bolsheviks have toppled the provisional government of Alexander Kerensky in St. Petersburg. But while "Lenin has his revolution," Rosa Luxemburg celebrates her "wedding in the cell" to her lover, Hannes Düsterberg, who has been killed in action and appears as a revenant. These chapters are the most controversial in the novel, as the critical reception has shown.

Rosa Luxemburg is known to have been an opponent of Lenin from her participation in debates; she did not approve of Lenin's liquidation of formal democracy in favor of revolutionary dictatorship. Yet her criticism of Lenin is mute in the novel until shortly before her release from prison at the end of book one, when she writes that "with the suppression of political life throughout the country, the political life of the Soviets must likewise languish. Without general elections, without unhampered freedom of the press and assembly, without free debate of opinions, life will die out in every public institution. It will only seem to live, while only one single effective pulse of life will remain—the bureaucracy" (*Karl and Rosa* 75). Rosa calls Lenin's bureaucratic dictatorship "a bourgeois dictatorship" and argues that a "real dictatorship, our dictatorship, consists in the application of democracy, not in its abolition" (*Karl and Rosa* 75). These sentences are an almost verbatim quotation from Rosa Luxemburg's famous treatise "The Russian Revolution" *(Die russische Revolution),* which was published posthumously in 1922 and shows her as a brilliant mind and political thinker.

But for most of her time in prison, Rosa is preoccupied with the news that her lover, Hannes Düsterberg, has been killed in action in Russia. The historical model for this figure is a man named Hans Diefenbach (1883–1917), who suffered the same fate, except that he was killed in France. Although Döblin used Rosa Luxemburg's *Briefe aus dem Gefängnis* (Letters from Prison), first published in 1920, as a source, the novel expands on this relationship far beyond its historical basis. While the depiction of the relationship makes Rosa Luxemburg more human in the novel, it also introduces a sadomasochistic aspect to her character that cannot be attributed to the historical figure, for which Döblin has been criticized (Tewarson 68–74). The novel presents Rosa indulging in visions of her lover visiting her in prison while Lenin deals with the political reality and accomplishes the goals of his revolution. Although Rosa explains her visions as "prison psychosis," she nevertheless believes in their reality: she has a wedding to her dead lover in her cell and goes on mysterious journeys with him around the world and to the Arctic.

At the beginning of the novel Rosa considers her visions an addiction. She feels "like an alcoholic who walks by a bar" and calls her prison cell her "den of iniquity," analyzing her state of mind as "prison psychosis" (*Karl and Rosa* 20). But then she indulges in her visions nevertheless, no longer worried about "crazy notions," "obsessions," and "hallucinations" (*Karl and Rosa* 23). On her forty-eighth birthday in prison, Rosa asks the revenant, Hannes, to marry her as a birthday present. They embrace, celebrating their marriage, and Rosa feels "something icy" touching her lips and breathing "against her teeth" and stroking her tongue: "It trickled down her throat, down her gullet. It dipped into her breast, into her body. She felt how it spread through her limbs down to the tips of her fingers and toes" (*Karl and Rosa* 25). A rhetorical figure, inverting their names as "Rosa Düsterberg / Hannes Luxemburg," symbolizes their union (ibid. 27).

In the chapter "A Fabulous Arctic Journey," the couple goes on their hallucinatory honeymoon trip, from the women's prison in Breslau to the North Pole. But Rosa realizes that this is not the honeymoon that they had been planning, a trip to Switzerland and Italy. It is a journey into "fantastic blackness" and deathlike coldness (63–71). She becomes aware of her grief as a sickness when her lover returns as a demonic spirit who attempts to assassinate her and tries to suck her blood like a vampire, and she is able to overcome her melancholia for the time being (81).

When Rosa Luxemburg is finally released from the Breslau prison on November 9, 1918, the action returns to Berlin. The People's Naval Division, the elite unit of the revolution, has occupied the Royal Palace and Royal Stables at the center of Berlin. On December 24, Ebert sends troops against the sailors to force their withdrawal, but the encounter ends with the defeat of the government troops. The use of the military against the revolutionary sailors is presented as a serious moral defect of the Ebert government, which relies on the generals of the High Command and the armed forces under their control to stay in power. Gustav Noske, a Social Democrat who has been successful in defusing the sailors' revolution in the German ports in early November, offers his services as commander in chief to lead the armed forces against the revolution with his infamous slogan, "Ultimately, someone has to be the bloodhound" (274).

But it is not only the flashbacks that signal the new departure of the tetralogy—there had been flashbacks in the books on Woodrow Wilson in volume three—but also the omnipresence of religion. In volume four there is the voice of Johannes Tauler (1300–1361), a medieval German mystic from Strasbourg who reminds Friedrich Becker of his salvation, and Satan also appears throughout, visiting Rosa during her visions in prison. Hannes is associated with Satan in a strange turn of events. Even Karl Liebknecht is confronted by the figure of Satan from Milton's *Paradise Lost* on the last night before his murder. And, at the end of the novel, the fictional protagonist, Friedrich Becker, who has concluded a wager with Satan, is saved to enter a heavenly Jerusalem.

Satan also appears in volume three, in this case as a mysterious Brazilian, a lion, and a rat (see the American edition of *A People Betrayed* 443–51, 452–59, 471–80), but these appearances cannot compare to the dominance of the religious struggle between good and evil depicted in volume four. The first edition of *Karl und Rosa,* in 1950, had as its subtitle *Eine Geschichte zwischen Himmel und Hölle* (A Story between Heaven and Hell). Because of production problems, however, Döblin was not able to add the subtitle to the title page of the first edition, and the final German edition of 1991 does not reproduce it either, except for a reference in the footnotes (Stauffacher 29; *Karl und Rosa* 773).

As a writer Döblin was prone to introducing religious symbols in support of his plots. His *Berlin Alexanderplatz: The Story of Franz Biberkopf* of 1929 is a case in point. In spite of its radical realism, the novel contains allusions and quotations from the Bible and church hymns. A whole chapter devoted to the biblical figure of Job is even inserted into the description of a Berlin slaughterhouse (*Berlin Alexanderplatz* 183–88). The other biblical references are to Adam and Eve in the Garden of Eden and to the sacrifice of Isaac by Abraham. The biblical passages provide, as Kathleen Komar has argued, "a framework and an interpretative tool for the main points in [Franz Biberkopf's] life story" (44). For this reason, the novel has been interpreted in terms of an allegorical *theatrum mundi.* The same applies to *November 1918*: the voice of Johannes Tauler, a medieval mystic who reminds Becker of his predestined salvation, appears for the first time in the first volume of the tetralogy (see German edition 139–40) and reappears in volumes two and three (see American edition *A People Betrayed* 417, 441–42).

Michael W. Jennings has shown that Döblin's style and technique changed from the first to the last volume of *November 1918.* While in the first volume Döblin still employed the montage technique that had made him famous and had become so familiar to the readers of *Berlin Alexanderplatz,* he developed new narrative devices for each of the following volumes. In volume two, *A People Betrayed,* there is a shift to a narrator's voice that claims universality and control over the material that is not justified by the confusing events portrayed in the novel. By the middle of the volume this narrative voice retreats "into an archaic sententious voice appropriated from eighteenth-century novels" (Jennings 145). In the last two volumes the narrator's voice is yielded to the voices of a series of characters, among them that of the fictional character Friedrich Becker.

Jennings interprets Döblin's concern for the individual as a concern for "the difficulty of identity formation—after the war and under fascism" (149). This concern is represented in *Karl and Rosa* by Döblin's shift to the traditional narration of the lives of his protagonists. Jennings perceptively argues that "Döblin's novel increasingly organizes itself around narratives devoted to figures in search of redemption" (149). What he implies, but does not pronounce, is that this final shift was a renunciation of modernism.

The characters of Karl and Rosa are interconnected with the historical figures of the time: Lenin, Friedrich Ebert, Philipp Scheidemann, and Gustav Noske. Their fates, presented in movielike scenes, run on parallel tracks. At the center of the novel is, however, the religious conflict—a struggle with Satan—that involves not only Friedrich Becker, the central fictional character of the novel, but also Rosa Luxemburg and, to a lesser degree, Karl Liebknecht. As Anthony W. Riley, one of the most astute critics of *Karl and Rosa,* has said, "The battle between the forces of good and evil, between Satan and the angels is the crux of the novel; in other words, the German Revolution of 1918 must be understood as the historical framework, the foundation, as it were, upon which Döblin constructs the edifice of his special concept of poetic truth—the timeless truth of faith" (Riley 103–4).

Riley defends Döblin's decision to privilege religion over politics in volume four, but Riley cannot refute the argument that the political dimension of the novel is at least diluted, if not compromised, in the work. *No-*

vember 1918 is, as Riley says, "in many ways the artistic summa of Alfred Döblin's philosophical, political, and religious views in his later years" (104), but this does not mean that his views were necessarily well suited to meet the challenges of a modernist presentation of the revolution.

While most of the tetralogy is an account of the months that ultimately failed to change the course of German history (November 1918 to January 1919), its final volume—in addition to treating the murder of Rosa Luxemburg and Karl Liebknecht in early January 1919—deals with Becker's futile attempt to save a young student from suicide and with the redemption of both Rosa Luxemburg and Becker. As Anthony W. Riley observes, "the paths of Friedrich Becker and Rosa Luxemburg never cross within the novel; thematically, however, their separate fates, their ultimate martyrdom, intertwine. Rosa Luxemburg's political struggles, and above all, her search for truth during her spiritual development, parallel those of Becker" (104). This is confirmed at the end of the novel, when the male protagonist is reminded by Satan that he has put on a "similar show," referring to the meeting between Hannes Düsterberg and Rosa. Both Becker and Rosa Luxemburg reveal their sinful pride in these encounters and experience their need to submit to divine mercy in their search for redemption (*Karl and Rosa* 541–42).

The narrative in books three through eight of *Karl and Rosa* alternates between Rosa's various encounters, Friedrich Becker's struggles, and the counterrevolution mounted by the majority socialists under the leadership of Friedrich Ebert. The first three chapters of book five show that even after her release from prison, Rosa is not through with the visions of her dead lover. They begin to haunt her again before January 6, the beginning of the Spartacus revolt. She resumes her secret talks with Hannes, who is taking her on another hallucinatory honeymoon trip, this time to Zurich and a fairy-tale castle. But her mysterious suitor turns out to be not Hannes, but Satan. In an erotic scene Rosa reveals her satanic disposition, admitting neither limits nor humility (265–66). Later, in book eight, major parts of the narrative are taken up by Rosa's dialogues with Satan, who has come with a message from Hannes, and by the visit of a cherub. Satan appears to her as the "liberator of mankind" to whom Rosa has sworn her allegiance. He invites her to the barricades to fight the enemy. She is not afraid to die and get rid of her "sad body"; for her, "the hour of liberation has come." She will not lead "a beggar's existence," as her lover Hannes does, living in a limbo of ghostlike figures (ibid. 434). But then a voice speaks to Rosa, a messenger from

Hannes, who regrets his "beggar's existence" and is looking for "justice and heavenly powers." First she is tempted to tell Hannes that he is making himself ridiculous, but then she silently agrees with his message, as angry and upset as she is (ibid. 435–37).

After this encounter a cherub with another message from Hannes appears to Rosa. She mocks the messenger and his message, but the cherub insists on communicating Hannes's call to eternal life. Hannes rhapsodically relates his pilgrimage to the silver-white gate of the heavenly garden. He tells Rosa through his messenger that a human being cannot know about freedom, but Rosa refuses to listen to his message; she wants to warm his ice-cold body and drive "that silly humbug" from his head: "This is what I want of you and what you still want of me, why should we pretend—you, a doctor of medicine and I a Marxist. I want to lie in your arms and on your breast. I want to melt away in you and not be able to find myself again for all eternity" (449). Her entreaties cause the appearance of Hannes, who mocks the cherub and is ready to make love to Rosa, but then she realizes that it is not Hannes but Satan whom she embraces. The cherub intervenes in hot pursuit of Satan and finally drives him away. Rosa resists the supernatural beauty of the cherub, but she finally yields and asks for his forgiveness: "If ever I was hungry, never did I eat and become filled as I am now. If I ever was thirsty, never did I drink and have my thirst quenched as now. . . . Like a child at its mother's breast, I cling to your glory and will not depart from it." When the cherub demands her soul as a price, Rosa invites him to take it, and when he demands repentance, she confesses that she feels it. She prays that the cherub does not desert her: "Have mercy upon me. I did not want to go back" (453). Her "proud soul" finally shows Christian repentance. This change of the historical Rosa Luxemburg into a fictional Christian is one of the most questionable features of the novel, as it has no basis in her biography and is clearly invented by the author, whose newly adopted religion required a shift from secular history to the history of salvation. As one critic has said, Rosa Luxemburg became "a true protagonist only when she emancipated herself as a Christian from her sexual and Jewish past" (Dollinger 208).

The title of *Karl and Rosa* leads the reader to expect an equal treatment of both characters, but the novel focuses more on Rosa. Because of her redemption, she is—with Friedrich Becker—the major figure of the novel. Karl is a lesser figure, perhaps because of his failure to redeem himself, as the chapter on his interpretation of Milton's *Paradise Lost* in book eight shows. He discusses the epic poem with Rosa the night before their murder. Karl places it "among the masterpieces of English literature." Concentrating on the figure of Satan, he concludes that they could learn from him how mankind needs to react in defeat (480). Praising Milton's "robust idea of God and Satan," Karl dismisses Goethe's version of this struggle in his Faust drama as pale humanism. While Rosa wonders about the existence of evil in God's creation, Karl identifies with Satan's "freedom of movement" that excited him to seduce Adam and Eve in paradise. Karl is attracted to Satan's "constant protest" and compares him to Spartacus in ancient Rome (483). Rosa tries to dismiss this analogy with the tongue-in-cheek suggestion that they now call themselves not Spartacists, but Satanists. But Karl takes the analogy seriously, exclaiming that Satan "can serve as an example for us" (ibid. 483). This statement seals his fate as a sinner who holds on to the world that Rosa has already abandoned in favor of her impending martyrdom and salvation.

The last two chapters of book eight describe in historical detail the arrest of Rosa Luxemburg and Karl Liebknecht in Berlin, their interrogation at the Hotel Eden, headquarters of the Guard Cavalry Rifle Division, on January 15, 1919, and their subsequent brutal murder. Karl is hit over the head with a rifle butt and later shot and killed under the pretext that he tried to escape. Rosa is mistreated with similar brutality: the soldier Runge, whom she had watched abusing draught oxen in the Breslau prison in January 1918, now smashes her head with a rifle butt (5–7, 489–90). The novel artfully makes this connection that did not exist in reality, although the facts of the murder and the name of fusilier, Otto Runge, are historically accurate. Rosa is shot and her body is tossed into the Landwehr Canal, where it is finally found in May. The statements of the soldiers reveal their extreme anti-Semitism: "Bloody Rosa, the red sow, there she lies. . . . And now you're dead, and that's what should happen to you all, all you swine and Jews, the whole tribe. Now you'll no longer be able to open that trap of yours and spit your poison, you snake" (490).

The text offers some estrangement in form of a naturalist imitation of the engine noise of the military automobiles used to transport the victims ("purr—purr—purr, went the motor"). Closure to the brutal murder is provided by a cruelly grotesque story. Two bums lose a rabbit that they want to roast near the bridge of the Landwehr Canal, where Rosa's body has been thrown into the water. A housemaid catches the rabbit and sells it to the restaurant on the corner, where it is finally roasted. The narrator's commentary that the rabbit in its present condition is "giving gladness to human hearts" conveys the message that life continues, banal as it is (486–93).

The Becker plot is resumed in book three, in which Becker is shown to have compassion for a young student, Heinz Riedel, who is studying Sophocles' *Antigone* in his class at the Berlin elite high school. In spite of his war injuries, Becker has volunteered to return to teaching before he is fully recuperated. Most of his students expect a war hero to appear before them, but he does not meet their expectations that he will regale them with war stories and confirm their male chauvinist ideology. When he instead presents a female protagonist, Antigone, as a model to follow, the students turn against him. They insist on calling Antigone a "girl" and argue that she breaks "the laws of the state, and during a war, moreover. And for a very private reason" (164). In that light they find her death sentence justified. Becker understands that "this debate [is] meant in his honor." The students find "it necessary to show off their manliness and [believe] they owe this attitude to him, the warrior returned home" (ibid. 164). But Becker disappoints them by insisting that Antigone has "a sisterly duty" to mourn and bury her brother. In doing so, "she challenges the king, and willfully, knowingly disobeys the law of the state" in order to honor a divine law (ibid. 170). He concludes, "Antigone is not following some blind impulse in doing this deed, but is governed by a universally recognized, moral and religious understanding. Antigone is not doing battle at all. She sees herself as an instrument. She is serving divine law. For good or evil she is bound up with it" (172). Becker impresses upon his students that Antigone does not stand in opposition to the state, as represented in the person of the king, but rather that she defends a principle that is at least as legitimate as that represented by the king (173). But this war generation of students rejects the tragedy as weak and sentimental. For them, the dead brother is a traitor who has assembled an army against his hometown. The citizens of Thebes are correct to let his body lie unburied on the battlefield. The students cite Heinrich von Kleist's drama *The Prince of Homburg* as a counterexample that provides the "German solution" to the problem. In their opinion, the prince recognizes the sovereignty of the state and his own duty to obey: "The Fatherland is for him, just as for his [ruler, the Grand Elector], the highest good" (192). Even when Becker invokes the dead of World War I and his personal duty to remember the many who died so young, he is unable to convince his students, with the exception of Heinz Riedel. The students are annoyed that they do not find Becker an ally for their nationalist cause, and they threaten to strike if the director who has invited Becker to teach dares enter their classroom again.

The Herr Direktor is involved in homoerotic relationships with some of his students, including Heinz Riedel. From the poems that he gives his disciples to read, it becomes obvious that the director is a follower of the poet Stefan George (1868–1933), a representative of the slogan "l'art pour l'art" who had assembled a homoerotic circle of young men around him. When the director's behavior becomes known and develops into a public scandal, students and parents mount a campaign against him. Riedel's father savagely beats the director, who dies from his wounds. Although Becker does not approve of the director's lifestyle, he follows "in the footsteps of Antigone," as one of the chapter headings reads (341), when he insists that the director receive a proper burial. Against official obstruction and parental condemnation Becker not only arranges the funeral, but he also attends the service at the grave site with his own mother, Heinz Riedel, and a colleague from the high school.

After the funeral, Heinz Riedel disappears. Becker suspects him of having joined the Spartacists, who have taken over the Berlin police headquarters. With the help of Johannes Maus, his former army comrade, Becker is able to join Heinz in the building that is occupied by the Spartacists and surrounded by government troops. Becker confesses that he does not want to become a Spartacist and has come to find Heinz and rescue him (411). He joins Heinz, however, in defending the building with their guns. Both are wounded in action. Becker is able to save Heinz and bring him to a first-aid station in the basement. On January 12, government troops move in on the police headquarters and the Spartacists are forced to surrender. Becker and Heinz are arrested. With the help of Maus, Becker manages to escape before the troops are able to execute him. He is saved from the "White Terror," as the mass executions conducted by the government troops are called in reference to the "Red Terror" of the revolutionaries. After the end of the White Terror Becker turns himself in and stands trial. He is sentenced to three years of prison, which he welcomes as a "stroke of luck," as it gives him time to reconcile with himself. As a minor, Heinz Riedel serves only a short sentence. Afterwards, he joins the revolutionaries in central Germany and is killed in a confrontation with government troops.

The plot of book nine is reserved exclusively for Becker. After he is released from prison in 1922 he wanders aimlessly through the Weimar Republic for several years with Satan on his heels. He has lost his position at the Berlin high school following a disciplinary hearing. Sitting at the graves of Heinz Riedel and the school director, he raises the question of whether he is obliged to assume the role of Antigone. Her name signifies that Becker has reached the ethical stage of his development and passed the aesthetic stage, represented by the period when he was a classical philologist and an admirer of Richard Wagner's *Tristan and Isolde*.

Critics have shown that Döblin was greatly influenced by Søren Kierkegaard's concept of the three stages of man, the aesthetic, ethical, and religious (Riley 95, 105). Döblin began reading *Either/Or* in Paris in 1935, and he continued his study of Kierkegaard in Los Angeles. His protagonist is now approaching the third stage, that of the religious man. Becker explains that since the time of Antigone "more light has come into the world." Christ's message is that "the curse has been taken from us. We can breathe. God is not malicious, and does not lead us to murder at the crossroads" like Oedipus (*Karl and Rosa* 504). This transition from the ethical to the religious stage, however, is not easy: there are snares laid for Becker. The first snare is women (508–12), the second is the temptation to live the life of a religious rebel storming the churches (ibid. 534–37), and the third and final snare is the wager with the devil (ibid. 537–42).

But before his final confrontation with Satan, Becker visits his friend and army comrade, Johannes Maus, who saved his life after the siege of the Berlin police headquarters. Maus is reintegrated into middle-class life, with a wife and a child. Living in southern Germany, he is studying to be an engineer. The most important aspect of Becker's encounter with his friend is Becker's ultimate repudiation of the aesthetic stage, which is symbolized here by the music of Richard Wagner's *Tristan and Isolde*. On the hospital train from Alsace to Berlin, he had introduced Maus to Wagner's opera. But even during the time on the train, after singing the *Liebestod* motif, Becker explains that life is different and attributes his recuperation to his transition to the ethical stage. This is an early example of identity formation as the moral responsibility of the individual. Almost a decade later, in the 1920s, Becker rejects Wagner's music because of its "total abrogation of the personality." He considers Tristan and Isolde poisoned, swimming "upon waves of lewd, moaning, languishing music" (527). The same holds true for Siegfried and Brunhilde in *Der Ring des Nibelungen*. As a final condemnation, Becker declares that Wagner's operas are representative of his time: "Love-death, alcohol-death, opium-death, war-death and all the other deaths to which men want to flee." With this statement Becker expresses his belief in individual life as God's gift that one cannot throw away: "You can't fool God. You can't escape him" (527–28). Döblin's repudiation of Wagner is one of the strongest among the exile writers in Los Angeles, especially compared to Adorno and Thomas Mann. It is also an example of exile modernism revising the canon of Weimar modernism: Wagner's time is over. At the end of the chapter, the pagan god Wotan is said to be leaving in his chariot above the clouds, with croaking "vultures flying before him" (ibid. 529).

Of the three snares that are laid to trap Becker, the least dangerous is that of women. He admits that he has fallen into the hands of some beautiful women. Speaking of their "baseness" that has infected him, he admits to "dancing the cancan on an altar" (510). It takes the intervention of Johannes Tauler to change Becker's way of life. The second snare is also not particularly difficult to escape. Becker disturbs church services, interrupting the preachers and accusing institutionalized Christianity of serving only the rich. Like Luther, he posts "messages on church doors, warning the congregation not to attend church and commanding them to starve out their pastors, so that the clergy too could learn what poverty was and then take their stand on the side of the common people" (535). Again and again, Becker is sentenced to prison for weeks or months at a time, but he has the full support of Johannes Tauler, who reveals the name of his guardian angel, Antoniel. In the end, it is a political event that causes Becker to recognize the futility of his behavior. Attending the rally of a nationalist party, Becker is booed when he takes the assembled masses to task for their nationalist pride. Becker charges that Christianity in Germany is no longer a religion but instead an attack on religion, opening "the door to a new paganism." After being accused of some instances of church arson, Becker is sentenced to prison again, but this does not change his mind that Christ is "the King over all the world" (536–37).

It is the final snare—a wager with the Devil—that finally entraps Becker. Tempted by Satan to demonstrate that all human beings are potentially good, he accepts the soul of a depraved bargeman into his inner self, becoming a Goethean Faust figure with "two souls, alas! residing in [his] breast." Satan transfers the bargeman's soul into Becker's while he is sitting in a shabby bar in Hamburg. But unlike Goethe's Faust, Becker is not able to prove the Devil at least halfway wrong. On the contrary, Becker surrenders himself entirely to this alien soul. His conduct sinks to the lowest level: he steals, utters obscene words and blasphemies, and participates in a robbery that leaves him severely wounded, like Franz Biberkopf. Not even Johannes Tauler can help him escape from this snare, but Tauler reminds him that it was pride that tempted him to resist Satan, thus to fall into the devil's trap. Tauler pronounces that he has lost the wager and that only the "unfathomable mercy of God" may save him (543–44). Indeed, Antoniel, Becker's guardian angel, does defend him against Satan and saves his soul in almost Goethean fashion. As in Goethe's *Faust, Part II*, in which Faust is finally rescued by the intercession of the Virgin Mary, Becker's soul is saved by Antoniel.

But Becker is not a Faustian man, neither in the manner of Goethe's Faust drama nor Thomas Mann's Faust novel (Busch 263–72). In Goethe's *Faust* the final salvation of the protagonist is not assured but instead left as an open question: in the very last scene Faust continues to strive, following a penitent Gretchen, who rises "to higher spheres." There is no such ambiguity in Döblin's novel. There is a fierce fight for his soul, a psychomachia between two lions and the horse of hell. The narrator employs animal allegory to show the battle between the forces of good and evil. The lions are smaller than the horse of hell, which symbolizes Satan. The horse tries to trample the lions to death, but they snap at its hooves and the horse is driven away, screaming in pain (546). Antoniel holds Becker and does not let him go, because he "cannot make it alone." Announcing Becker's admission to a heavenly Jerusalem, the angel praises God's mercy in ecstatic language:

> Do you hear them singing from the heavenly Jerusalem? The holy city, it lies afar, no man can take it by force. The holy city beyond the mountains, beyond the snowy peaks. It lies there, showered in flower petals. All the blood of the martyrs and saints rains down upon it. The city lies afar, the hovel of God. And he shall wipe away all tears, and there shall be no more death, neither sorrow, nor crying, neither shall there be any more pain. (547)

The end of the novel establishes a link between Becker and Rosa by repeating the motif of death by water. Becker's body endures a fate similar to that of Rosa's: his fellow criminals, fearing arrest by the police, slip his body into the water of the Hamburg harbor, as Rosa's body was thrown by soldiers into the Landwehr Canal. But Becker's physical destruction does not matter, since his soul has been saved from his "dungeon of a body" (546). In contrast to Döblin's novel, Mann followed the traditional model of condemnation provided by the chapbook in his *Doctor Faustus,* yet he left the question of redemption and grace deliberately open.

The close of Döblin's novel, with its religious psychomachia and vision, represents a radical change for the author, who, as a writer of the left-wing avant-garde of the Weimar Republic, had employed an extensive assembly of newspaper clippings, advertising, statistics, popular songs, weather reports, court records, and proverbs in his *Berlin Alexanderplatz* in order to reflect the metropolitan character of the city and achieve the greatest possible realism. Döblin had used also biblical references in his earlier novel, but the work did not depict a purely religious struggle for the soul of its protagonist, Franz Biberkopf. *Berlin Alexanderplatz* had no closure—Biberkopf marches on into the future—but *November 1918* has: Becker reaches his destination. As in Werfel's *Song of Bernadette,* the protagonists of *November 1918* have a charismatic function. Although they are sinners rather than saints, Friedrich Becker and Rosa Luxemburg are to inspire the readers so that they can learn from their examples. The message conveyed is a desire for a movement toward Christian religion.

In the end, *November 1918* deals exclusively with the redemption of its two protagonists, Friedrich Becker and Rosa Luxemburg. Some critics have interpreted *November 1918* as a continuation of *Berlin Alexanderplatz* because both take place in Berlin. To these critics, Friedrich Becker appears as an emancipated version of lower-class Franz Biberkopf. But such interpretations miss the point because *November 1918*, and especially its last volume, is a total departure from his earlier works. Döblin tried to combine secular history and a history of salvation to provide an explanation for the rise of Hitler and German fascism. Döblin's secular history of the revolution shows that Friedrich Ebert and the Social Democrats did not hesitate to use terror against the radical left, thus giving birth to Nazism. Sebastian Haffner argues that "the frame of mind and attitudes of the future SA and SS" were often directly inherited from the Free Corps, the volunteer battalions in the service of Ebert's government (Haffner 152). Döblin expressed the same idea in his outline of *Karl and Rosa*, which he submitted with his application for a fellowship from the Guggenheim Memorial Foundation in 1942. He criticized Friedrich Ebert for his alliance with the General Staff in order to repel the advance of Bolshevism represented by the Spartacus League. In his opinion, the officers used Ebert in order to return to power. The German bourgeoisie, devoted to the military, supported Ebert. Taking advantage of the fear of Bolshevism, Ebert succeeded in drawing to his side the majority of the Social Democratic Party with strongly bourgeois inclinations. Therefore, the fight of the revolution of 1919 was, according to Döblin, no longer, as it would have been a fight between the military right wing and the antimilitary left wing. Instead it separated the powerful block of the Social Democrats and the bourgeoisie, including the officers, from a tiny group of Spartacists and intellectuals. It was a tragedy that, after Ebert's death in 1925, Hindenburg, the leading German general of World War I, was elected president of the German Reich. It appeared no less logical to Döblin that Hindenburg was followed by Hitler, who denied the military defeat of 1918 and established total militarism that resulted in a war of aggression beyond the borders of the Reich of 1937 ("Plans for Work"; see German translation in *November 1918: Eine deutsche Revolution* 3: 800–803).

But Döblin did not follow his own outline of 1942, and the novel, completed in 1943, took a different turn. Its verdict was that "the revolution died a slow death" (*Karl and Rosa* 503). With this sentence Döblin abandoned the secular history of his novel that was to offer a political analysis of the German Revolution and present a new response to the crisis of Weimar modernism. This was a momentous decision because it rendered the secular history of the revolution in November 1918 meaningless. *Karl and Rosa* conveys the message that engagement in politics is evil. Instead of explicating secular history, the novel turns its attention to the history of salvation of two individuals, a Christianized Rosa Luxemburg and the fictional Friedrich Becker. The final message is that the "true" revolutionaries are those who seek God. The closure projects their final redemption, which is clearly defined by the image of the heavenly Jerusalem, invoked by Becker's guardian angel. In Adorno's and Horkheimer's terms, Döblin's novel is a "regress to mythology" (DE xviii, 20).

Karl and Rosa must be understood as Döblin's response to the crisis of modernism in exile. It was a response that signaled not only his conversion from Judaism to Roman Catholicism, but also, and more importantly, a turn toward religion that did not allow for dialectics or ambiguity. His new religious conviction superseded literature. "Human history appears as a religious story between heaven and earth," as Helmuth Kiesel concluded ("Döblin's November 1918" 230). In spite of his detailed description and analysis of the failure of the German Revolution of 1918, Döblin provided a conservative religious response to the political crisis. *Karl and Rosa* was a rejection of modernism (Kiesel, *Trauerarbeit*, 482–86). As Kiesel said, the final psychomachia obviously collided with the conception of modernism ("Döblin's November 1918" 228).

This rejection was perhaps not permanent, as his last novel, *Tales of a Long Night,* appears to show. At the suggestion of an East German critic Döblin rewrote its ending: instead of withdrawing into a monastery, the protagonist reenters life. This new ending challenges a strictly Christian interpretation of the novel (Auer 143–46). Döblin's other late texts, however—*Der unsterbliche Mensch: Ein Religionsgespräch* (Immortal Man: A Religious Dialogue) and the revised version of *Der Oberst und der Dichter* (The Colonel and the Poet), both of 1946, for example—demonstrate Döblin's continuing preoccupation with religion. For Döblin's work written in Los Angeles, however, the term "renegade modernism" applies without qualification.

CHAPTER 9

The Political Battleground
of Exile Modernism

The Council for a Democratic Germany

In July 1943 newspapers in the United States reported that the National Committee for a Free Germany had been founded by German exiles and German prisoners of war in the Soviet Union. The Soviet leadership appeared to be using the committee as, among other things, a political tool to attempt to bring about an early end to the war, even at the cost of a compromise peace with the German government. In July 1943 the opening of the second front by the Western Allies was still far in the future. In spite of the military successes since the battle of Stalingrad, the German enemy was still occupying a large territory of the Soviet Union, and the country had to reckon with heavy losses of troops and civilians before the war would end. On the other hand, after the defeat of Stalingrad numerous German prisoners of war had come to realize that Germany could no longer win the war. Therefore, with the support of the Soviet authorities, they had formed two organizations—the National Committee for a Free Germany and the League of German Officers—with the express intent of preserving Germany's national existence by overthrowing the Hitler regime (Scheurig 32–77). Their determination was echoed by Stalin's famous words of February 23, 1942, that "the Hitlers come and go, but the German people, the German state remains" (Scheurig 74). Since the Soviet Union had not yet won the war and Germany had not yet lost it, the Soviet and German interests could possibly be adjusted to a common ground.

The National Committee for a Free Germany was not conceived as a government in exile but as a representative of German interests recognized by the Soviet Union. The organization offered itself as an interim solution until a German countergovernment that was legally recognized to negotiate with the Soviet Union could be formed. If the National Committee were to succeed in convincing the German generals to cease hostilities and to withdraw the army in an orderly fashion to the German borders, a cease-fire was assured by the Soviets in return. Germany could achieve a favorable peace if the negotiations were based on the successful overthrow of Hitler. The Soviet Union would then be prepared to conclude a separate peace that would guarantee the German state within its 1937 borders, including Austria. A prerequisite for this would be a liberal democratic government that would be allied with the Soviet Union by pacts of friendship (Scheurig 61). The conclusion of the manifesto addressed to the German army and the German people expressed the program clearly:

> Put an end to the war immediately!
> The whole strength of the people against Hitler's war régime and for the saving of our nation from the impending catastrophe!
> Fight for a truly national government which will secure for our country liberty and peace! (quoted from Scheurig 220)

In response to its manifesto the National Committee received numerous sympathetic declarations from individuals in the United States, including Reinhold Niebuhr and German exiles such as Lion Feuchtwanger, Oskar Maria Graf, and Prince Hubertus of Loewenstein. Thomas Mann gave a statement to the Soviet news agency Tass that called the manifesto "a legitimate counterpart to the challenge by the Western powers to the Italian people to rid themselves of the fascist regime," as quoted in *Freies Deutschland,* the German exile paper in Mexico City, in November 1943.

The Western Allies were completely taken by surprise by the founding of the National Committee and responded negatively. In the *New York Times* of July 23, 1943, for example, the founding was described as a clever chess move by Stalin to establish a second front and was evaluated as dangerous to the anti-Hitler coalition of the Allies. The *Aufbau,* the leading paper of German-Jewish immigrants in New York, took up the phrase "Stalin's chess move" in its edition of July 30, 1943; and on August 13 the *Neue Volkszeitung,* an organ of the right wing of the Social Democratic Party (SPD) in exile, also decisively rejected the National Committee because of its cooperation with the German generals. Antimilitarism was too strongly established in both exile groups to allow for the alternative of a military coup instead of the continuation of the war.

FIGURE 22. Salka Viertel's house, 165 Mabery Road, Pacific Palisades, 2005. Photograph by Juergen Nogai, Santa Monica.

In addition, the German Social Democratic Party in exile refused to co-operate in any way with the communists because of their attacks on the SPD during the Weimar Republic.

Among the exiled writers on the West Coast the reaction was similar. At an often-mentioned meeting of August 1, 1943, held in the home of Salka Viertel, a well-known Hollywood screenwriter, the exiles were initially able to agree on an expression of sympathy with the National Committee. In addition to the hostess and her husband, Berthold Viertel, in attendance were Bertolt Brecht; Thomas and Heinrich Mann; Lion Feuchtwanger, an exile writer and friend of both Brecht and Thomas Mann; Bruno Frank, another exile writer; Ludwig Marcuse, who taught German literature at the University of Southern California; and Hans Reichenbach, originally a physicist, who taught philosophy at the University of California, Los Angeles, and had advised Brecht on questions of science when he was writing his play *Galileo*. Most attended the meeting with their wives, but the women had no influence on the wording. After a long debate, the following statement in English was adopted and read by Thomas Mann to the men and women assembled:

> At this moment when the victory of the allied nations draws nearer, the undersigned writers, scholars and artists of German origin consider it their duty to declare openly:
>
> We welcome the manifesto of German prisoners of war and exiles in the Soviet Union in which they call on the German people to force its suppressors to unconditional surrender and to fight for a strong democracy in Germany.
>
> We, too, consider it necessary to distinguish clearly between the Hitler regime and the social classes associated with it on the one hand and the German people on the other.
>
> We are convinced that there can be no lasting peace in the world without a strong democracy in Germany. (GBA 27: 161)

But, according to Brecht's diary, as early as August 2, 1943, Thomas Mann withdrew his signature from the document because the proclamation was "too patriotic" for his taste and he was afraid that it would therefore be considered a "stab in the back" by the Allies, as he told Lion Feuchtwanger on the telephone. Brecht's diary is the only record of that telephone conversation. Mann supposedly added that "he could not find it unjust if the Allies punished *[züchtigen]* Germany for ten or twenty years" (GBA 27: 163). Brecht's notes about what Thomas Mann said, including the offensive term *züchtigen,* which has a strong biblical connotation, were "at least secondhand" (Lehnert 187), but Brecht considered Mann's terminology typical and added with furious sarcasm:

> Once again the single-minded kowtowing of these "pillars of culture." . . . If the Hearst press takes them up, they will agree with Goebbels' assertion that Hitler and Germany are the same thing. . . . For a moment even I considered how "the German people" might live down having tolerated not only the crimes of the Hitler regime but also the novels of Herr Mann, especially when you think that the latter don't have the support of 20–30 SS-divisions behind them. (GBA 27: 163)

Mann's withdrawal from the carefully crafted declaration caused a bitter rift between Mann and Brecht. Its roots lay deeper, however, than the failure of the proclamation. While Brecht held fast to the belief that the first people whom Hitler oppressed were the Germans, Thomas Mann rejected this purposefully optimistic vision of an oppressed nation.

Brecht espoused the so-called "two Germanies theory," which posited that a good Germany was being suppressed by evil Nazi Germany, while Mann believed that there was only one Germany, both good and evil. Although Mann acknowledged the domestic German resistance movement in his radio broadcasts to Germany, he also pointed to the support of the Nazi regime by the German people who stood behind the regime and fought its battles. Thomas Mann insisted that the German people prove themselves moral by freeing themselves of Hitler. Only in their rejection of the collective guilt of Germans were Brecht and Mann in agreement, although they refused to admit even this common ground.

Brecht accused the novelist in a poem, unpublished at the time, of advocating the ten-year punishment of the German people. The poem, dated 1944, was finally published in 1965, many years after the deaths of both Brecht and Mann. Its lengthy title reads in translation: "When the Nobel Prize Winner Thomas Mann Acknowledged the Right of the Americans and the English to Punish the German People for Ten Years for the Crimes of Hitler's Government." Mann had never in fact done so, but poetic license gave Brecht the chance to vent his anger and frustration in this poem:

I
Punish the punished again and again!
Punish him in the name of immorality!
Punish him in the name of morality.

His hands resting in his empty lap
The exiled demanded the death of half a million people.
For their suffering he demanded
Ten years of punishment. The suffering people
Were to be punished.
The Prize Bearer asked the Cross Bearer
To attack his armed tormentors with his bare hands.
The papers did not publish a response. Now he feels offended
And demands the punishment of the crucified.

II
To win a hundred- thousand-dollar name
For the cause of the tormented people
The writer put on his Sunday suit
And approached the man of the propertied classes
With humble bows
In order to seduce him with glib words
To make a gracious statement about the people
In order to bribe him with flattery
To commit a good deed

In order to give him the false illusion
That honesty pays.

Full of distrust the celebrity listened.
For a moment he contemplated the opportunity
To be celebrated also in this case.
Write down, my friend, I consider it my duty
To do something for the people. Hurriedly
The writer wrote down the precious words, eager
To receive an additional statement, he saw only the back
Of the celebrity in the frame of the door. His attempt
Had backfired.

III
For a moment the petitioner
Also stood confused
Because the slave-like happiness
Caused him distress, wherever he encountered it.

But then reminding himself
That this immoral human being
Lived off his immorality, while the people
Only gain death, if they become immoral,
He left more calmly.

(GBA 15: 90–91)

Apart from the distortion of facts and the invectives heaped upon the
"Prize Bearer," who clearly represents Thomas Mann, this is not one of
Brecht's better poems. It appeals to the readers' left-wing ideology and
expects them to consider the German people in the collective singular as
a "cross bearer" and as a Christ figure who is asked by the Nobel Prize
winner to attack the Nazis with his bare hands. Since the Germans do not
respond to his absurd demand, the "Prize Bearer" is offended and demands that they be punished. The fact that the collective singular "cross
bearer" for the German people is related to the crucifixion renders the
metaphors of both the "cross bearer" and the "crucified" even less cred-
ible. Brecht's poetic self-portrait in part II is unconvincing in its self-
serving posture of humility and straightforward morality. The final stanza
of part III, expressing the total condemnation of the Nobel Prize winner,
contains "the most libelous statement in the poem," as Herbert Lehnert
called it (184). The Mann figure of the poem is characterized as "dieser
verkommene Mensch," which is translated here as "this immoral human
being." A literal translation would be "this degenerate man [or human
being]," but I translate it otherwise to avoid association with the term
used by the Nazis to defame modernist artists and writers, as, for exam-

ple, in the infamous exhibition of "degenerate art" in Munich in 1937. In Brecht's opinion, the Nobel Prize winner was "degenerate" because he had identified himself with the cause of the capitalist system. Furthermore, my translation misses the ambiguity of the adjective and verb *verkommen,* which means "to show moral decline" as well as "to perish." Herbert Lehnert therefore offers as a paraphrase of that last sentence that "the German people . . . if it perishes . . . wins only death" (184).

This poem is not a document of political analysis, but rather a poetic fantasy that articulates an immense frustration and rage. No invective was too cheap or slanderous to denounce Thomas Mann's withdrawal from what Brecht considered a common cause. What Brecht left out in his poem was the fact that the Soviet Union also might want to punish the German people after the war, but this did not fit into his vision of the future. The poem is, nevertheless, a document of the fierce discussion among the exiles about the future of Germany, and it belies the existence of any unity among the exiles. The future of Germany was a battleground of ideas and programs. This does not call into question the concept of Los Angeles as a center of antifascism. The exiles were in agreement about the removal of Hitler and his regime, but they were deeply divided about the future of Germany and Europe as a whole.

Regardless of the developments in Los Angeles, a steering committee for the formation of a "Free Germany Movement" was founded in New York in September and October 1943 in order to produce an American alternative to the National Committee for a Free Germany in the Soviet Union. Those involved undoubtedly wanted to forestall a purely communist initiative through the creation of an organization that stood above party differences. It was to be an independent body composed of "people who were [closely concerned with] different political persuasions, of liberals and the Catholic Center, of Social Democrats and Independent Socialists all the way to the Communists" (Paetel 289). But the FBI and the Office of Strategic Services (OSS) did not believe in the group's independence. They regarded it as the American branch of Moscow's National Committee for a Free Germany and monitored its activities very closely. All members of the group were under constant surveillance until its demise in October 1945 (Stephan 181–84).

The founders of the Free Germany Movement hoped to entice Thomas Mann to chair the organization since his name had a strong political appeal in the United States and his participation would assure that party differences among the bourgeois and Social Democratic exile groups would be overcome. On October 27 or 28, when Thomas Mann was on a lecture tour in New York, the representatives of the Free Germany Movement offered the novelist the leadership of their organization, but by that time Thomas Mann had already decided to become an American citizen and forgo a political role in postwar Germany. On November 2, 1943, he sarcastically noted in his diary: "In the course of the evening much about my future as Führer *[meine Führerzukunft]* in Germany, from which may God protect me." On November 4 Thomas Mann conferred with Paul Tillich, the exiled theologian from Frankfurt/Main, now at the Union Theological Seminary and Columbia University, Carl Zuckmayer, the exile dramatist, Paul Hagen, Siegfried Aufhäuser (SPD), Paul Hertz (SPD), and others in New York concerning the planned organization. The driving force behind the project was Paul Hagen, born Karl B. Frank, who could not be considered for the chairmanship because of his membership in the leftist-socialist group New Beginning. Thomas Mann declined the leadership offer, but he declared his willingness to intervene with the State Department to gain recognition for the Free Germany Movement.

Meanwhile, however, military and political developments made it doubtful that representative German exile groups could function in the Soviet Union and the countries of the Western Allies. The collapse of the German summer offensive at Kursk in July 1943 and the failure of mysterious Soviet peace feelers in Stockholm in September 1943 (Scheurig 75–76) led to a revision of the Soviet policy toward Germany, and the Soviet Union now aimed at defeating the German army and the German Reich. The agreement of the Western Allies to demand unconditional surrender was decisive for the adoption of this new policy.

At the Conference of Casablanca from January 14 to 26, 1943, the Western Allies established the criteria for unconditional surrender. At the Moscow Foreign Ministers' Conference, held on October 19–20, 1943, these criteria were also accepted by the Soviet Union. This rendered peace negotiations with a German government without Hitler meaningless. The danger of a separate Soviet peace with Germany, feared by the Western Allies, was banished. At the same time the significance of German exile organizations in the Soviet Union and in Western countries as well as of the German resistance movement was reduced. Their hope of attaining favorable conditions of peace for Germany through an early end to the war vanished. The demand of unconditional surrender meant that the Allies no longer differentiated between the German people and the Nazi regime and insisted upon the continuation of the war until the final defeat of the German armed forces.

The Conference of Teheran, at which Churchill, Roosevelt, and Stalin met from November 28 to December 1, 1943, led to a further coordination of the Allied war goals. They decided on the formation of the second front and on the western borders of the Soviet Union of late autumn 1939, as well as the territorial compensation of Poland with East Prussia and areas of Pomerania and Silesia, although a final decision with regard to the Polish borders was deferred. The new policy toward Germany also changed the function of the National Committee; it was no longer used to establish contacts with German generals in command of German troops on Soviet territory, but only for frontline propaganda intended to persuade German soldiers to defect. The promise of a negotiated peace in exchange for an ordered retreat onto German territory was replaced by the prospect of "rescue through defection" (Scheurig 131, 141).

Thomas Mann's intervention with the State Department on behalf of the Free Germany Movement took place in the context of these military and diplomatic decisions, which had already radically changed the meaning and function of the German exile groups in the Soviet Union and the countries of the Western Allies. In a letter dated November 18, 1943, to Adolf A. Berle, assistant secretary of state, Thomas Mann outlined the goals of the intended organization. The movement could "influence the people in Germany to support the political war waged," and, because of its members' "knowledge of the German mentality, [it] could prove useful in advising American administrators" (Bürgin and Mayer 2: 745). To Mann's relief, a discussion with Berle on November 25, 1943, in Washington, D.C., resulted in "a fortunately negative conclusion" regarding the group's recognition. Mann was divided. On the one hand, he considered the movement's recognition by the American government absolutely necessary for its operation. On the other, he hoped that the group would be denied such recognition, because the denial would give him an excuse to withdraw from active participation. Because of the state of American foreign policy at the time—the talk took place between the Foreign Ministers' Conference in Moscow and the Three Power Meeting in Teheran—it is not surprising that the State Department took a wait-and-see, if not negative, attitude toward the Free Germany Movement.

On November 26 in New York, Thomas Mann reported to Paul Tillich and the advocates of the Free Germany Movement about his conference with Berle. His diary entries clearly show a detached tone: "Gathering of the 'gentlemen' in my room. A fiery affair to inform them of the refusal and to comfort them." On November 29, at the suggestion of the State Department, Mann defended himself in a letter to the editor of the *New York Times* against rumors concerning his alleged participation in a "Free-Germany-Committee," and he designated the time as unsuitable for the formation of such a committee.

Mann's posture prompted a letter by Brecht, dated December 1, which Mann answered by return mail on December 10 by repeating his reservations. He reminded Brecht that Mann had used the same arguments "against equating what is Germany with what is Nazi" in his political lecture at Columbia University on November 16. He had also made the point that "we must take into account the democracies' grave complicity in the rise of Fascist dictatorship, in the growth of its power, and in all the disasters that have come down upon Europe and the world." He reminded Brecht that he had appealed to American liberals that "it was not Germany or the German people who must be destroyed and sterilized, . . . but the guilt-laden power combination of Junkers, army officers, and industrialists, which has been responsible for two world wars." Mann reconfirmed, however, that he considered the formation of a Free Germany Committee in America premature. Such a committee would be viewed as "a patriotic effort to shield Germany from the consequences of her crimes." He counseled Brecht to wait for the military defeat of Germany and for the moment when the Germans themselves would put all Nazi criminals on trial: "That will be the moment for us on the outside to testify that Germany is free, that Germany has truly cleansed herself, that Germany must live."

In his letter of December 1, Brecht had expressed concern that Mann's public statements would increase American doubts about the existence of considerable democratic forces in Germany. The victims of the Nazis, the inmates of the concentration camps, and the resistance movement were tying up—Brecht believed—fifty SS divisions in Germany and thus they deserved Mann's moral support. Brecht held dogmatically to the two Germanies theory, as his essay "The Other Germany" from 1943 shows. This essay, probably written for the Council for a Democratic Germany, survives in English only; the original in German was lost. Brecht identified the "other Germany" as the force that fought Hitler from within. Prominent refugees and foreign correspondents had confirmed the existence of this force: "At no time were even half the votes cast for the Hitler regime, and the existence of the most frightful instruments of oppression and the most frightful police force which the world has ever known, proved that the opponents of the regime were not inactive" (GBA 23: 24).

Brecht argued that Hitler had first "ravaged his own country before he ravaged other countries" and considered "the plight of Poland, Greece, or Norway . . . scarcely worse than that of Germany." He maintained that Hitler had "made prisoners of war in his own country," and, claiming that there were 200,000 inmates in German concentration camps in 1939, he compared their number to the smaller number of German soldiers taken prisoner at Stalingrad. In comparison, the 200,000 did "not comprise the whole of the other Germany. [The inmates were] only one detachment of its forces" (ibid. 24). Brecht conceded that the "other Germany" had not been able to stop Hitler and that the war, with its appeal to nationalism, had put an end to the smoldering civil war in Germany. For the exiles, there was nothing left but to hope now that all prognostication about the collapse of the regime had been proven wrong. Brecht argued that the war was in the interest of the ruling classes in Germany, the industrialists and the Junkers. The war was even in the interest of the German people, as long as they were not able to abolish the system under which they lived. According to Brecht, the German people supported the war because it provided "food, shelter, work," but he pointed out that there was "an enormous miscalculation" involved: "The regime had to choose war because the whole people needed war; *but the people needed war only under this regime and therefore have to look for another way of life*" (ibid. 28). Brecht concluded that a social revolution was the only way out of this dilemma. The Weimar Republic had been a failure. Although labor parties and small bourgeois parties had condemned the war, and "the arts, music, painting, literature and theatre flourished," the old power elites took back their positions and began the preparation of the next war (ibid. 28–29). Since Brecht was doubtful that the German people would be able to overthrow their government, he warned against a negotiated peace or leaving the former elites in charge of the economy. In that case, "it would be quite impossible to control Central Europe" (ibid. 29). He proposed that the occupation army of the Allies should provide food for the people and use military force against the Nazi government: "The foreign soldier with a gun in one hand and a bottle of milk in the other would only be regarded as a friend worthy of the great democracies that sent him *if* the milk were for the people and the gun for the use against the regime." On the other hand, Brecht was vehemently opposed to the Allied reeducation policies: "The idea of forcibly educating a whole people is absurd. What the German people have not learned when this war is over from bloody defeats, bombings, impoverishment, and from the bestialities of its leaders inside and outside Germany, it will never learn from history books" (ibid. 29–30). Although Brecht never clearly defined the relationship between the exiles and the Germans who stayed behind, he implied an identification of the "other Germany" with the cause of the German people under Nazi rule and advocated the total defeat of the Nazi regime.

Thomas Mann, on the other hand, developed the view of the dialectical identity of the one and the "other" Germany in both his political speeches after November 1943 as well as in his novel *Doctor Faustus*. This put him in close proximity to the Vansittart camp, which denied the existence of the "other Germany." Robert Gilbert Lord Vansittart, former British undersecretary of state for foreign affairs from 1930 to 1938, had campaigned against this concept of the "other Germany" in radio addresses and books since his retirement from office and called for the defeat of Germany in order to enable a future peace. Although his influence on the British Foreign Office was minimal, he made quite an impression on public opinion, especially in the United States after 1943. In his book *Lessons of My Life,* published by Alfred Knopf in New York in 1943, the former diplomat defined Vansittartism as the disarmament and reeducation of the German nation: "Every honest and reasonably informed man knows perfectly well that the Germans will do neither of their own accord, or without supervision. We have trusted them once— most unwisely. To do so again would be a crime against humanity. But there is no inhumanity in re-education" (22).

As for German militarism, Vansittart argued "that it must be *brought* to an end and by force. The end must be final but it need not be barbarous" (22). He advocated the total destruction of German militarism and "drastic control of Germany's heavy industry, coupled with the destruction of Germany's war-potential" (24). Taking the number of "good Germans" to be 25 percent of the population, he stated that Vansittartism did not require the persecution or extermination of the "bad Germans," even though he thought that 75 percent of Germans had "for seventy five years . . . been eager for any assault on their neighbours" (23). Vansittart's final criticism was targeted at the "myth" of the two Germanies and its defenders: "The Germany of their dreams is always just around the corner, and about to take charge. This childishness has conducted generations of us to our doom. Yet it is on this discredited myth that our propagandists base their output. The other Germany is *not* waiting round the corner. It has got to be created. If we cling to the old delusion, we shall lose the peace" (24).

From these excerpts it becomes obvious that Vansittart's use of the terms "good Germany" and "bad Germany" influenced Thomas Mann's 1945 speech "Germany and the Germans." The speech was a response to, among other things, the former diplomat's position. Although he did not share his views, Mann declared in his radio message to Germany of June 27, 1943, that Vansittart's position was represented "not without *esprit* in the Allied countries." In the same message, however, Mann dismissed Vansittart's thesis as untenable and declared that it would never be accepted. The facts did not support it, especially in view of the German students' resistance in Munich (GW 11: 1076). Mann's literary model for Germany was Robert Louis Stevenson's story *The Strange Case of Dr. Jekyll and Mr. Hyde,* as it was used by Sebastian Haffner in his 1940 book *Germany: Jekyll and Hyde.* Sebastian Haffner was the pseudonym of Raimund Pretzel, a German lawyer and exile journalist living in Britain. When he read Haffner's book in Princeton in May 1940, Mann was impressed by its analysis, and he adopted some of its ideas as he developed his own about Germany. But while Haffner stressed the duality of Germany, Mann expanded on the dialectics of this duality. It was not an accident that Mann returned to the study of Stevenson's story when he began to read sources and take notes for his novel *Doctor Faustus* in March of 1943 (Vaget, *"Germany: Jekyll and Hyde,"* 249–68).

The longer the war lasted, however, the stronger the support for Vansittartism became. Its supporters in the United States were William L. Shirer, Clifton Fadiman, and Emil Ludwig, as well as Rex Stout and his Society for the Prevention of World War III, which was founded to counter the opinion widely held during the early 1940s that there was an absolute difference between Germans and Nazis.

In 1944 the center of German exile politics in the United States shifted from the West Coast to the East. In May 1944 the founding committee of the Council for a Democratic Germany met, without the hoped-for participation of Thomas Mann, in New York. Heinrich Brüning, one of the last chancellors of the Weimar Republic and a member of the Catholic Center Party, had also refused the chairmanship of the council, stating that he would assume the position only if the American government specifically requested it. In the end Paul Tillich accepted the position. His political past as a religious socialist had shown Tillich to be above party politics. As a former SPD member he had proven himself to be on neither the extreme left nor the extreme right, and his opposition to the Nazi regime was well known. The Protestant theologian had been relieved of his teaching position at the University of Frankfurt in 1933 and had immigrated to the United States the same year. At the invitation of the American theologian Reinhold Niebuhr, he had taught at the Union Theological Seminary and at Columbia University in New York. Since 1936 Tillich had delivered numerous public speeches on German emigration, emerging as the spokesman of political exiles in the United States. From 1942 to 1944 he had written more than a hundred radio speeches directed at Germany for the Office of War Information, and he also maintained valuable contacts with American intellectuals and the White House, so that he seemed nearly as well suited for the office of chairman as Thomas Mann.

On May 15, 1944, the Council for a Democratic Germany turned to the American public with a founding manifesto that was signed not only by German exiles, but also by a group of American citizens who supported the program of the council. Members of the first group included Elizabeth Bergner, a former actress from Berlin, Bertolt Brecht, Oskar Homolka, Peter Lorre, and Erwin Piscator. The American group, which consisted of fifty-seven signatories and included Reinhold Niebuhr and Dorothy Thompson, called itself American Friends of German Freedom. Thomas Mann refused to sign the manifesto, but he never publicly opposed the council, even when he was challenged to do so.

The first public meeting of the council was held on July 17, 1944, in New York. Paul Tillich pointed to three issues that needed to be addressed: the composition of the council, its organization, and the reaction of the public. He emphasized the "balanced front" of the council: "We have taken great pain to insure that members of the so-called middle class, personalities who embraced the [Catholic] Center, Social Democracy, the New Beginning Group or Communism, as well as those who belong to no party are represented in suitable proportions on the Council." The council was not supposed to represent a "mirror image" of German exile groups in the United States, but rather "the forces expected to accomplish a democratic rebuilding in Germany" ("A Program for a Democratic Germany"). In contrast to the National Committee for a Free Germany in the Soviet Union, the council admitted active members by invitation only, and new members who were invited to join were under no circumstances to endanger the political balance of the council. The composition of the council was to resemble the distribution of seats in the last parliament of the Weimar Republic (Paetel 300). The council's "balance structure" demanded the consensus of all parties. No group could exert its will against the opposition of a minority group by means of a vote; instead, every party had veto power and could block the work of the council. This finally happened in the fall of 1945, when Commu-

FIGURE 23. Paul Tillich, circa 1954. Photograph courtesy of Harvard
University Archives, Call # UAV 605 Box 13 (F2327).

nist opposition prevented the council from functioning. The history of
the council during the following years is of no further relevance for the
political culture of the German exiles in Los Angeles, except for the
transcontinental participation of a few, such as Bertolt Brecht, Lion
Feuchtwanger, Leopold Jessner, Fritz Kornter, and Heinrich Mann.
With the exception of Brecht, however, these figures probably participated only in a token manner.

Between September 1944 and May 1945 the council published five issues of its *Bulletin of the Council for a Democratic Germany,* which
took a stand on problems that affected the future of Germany, such as
the so-called Morgenthau Plan of 1944 and the territorial agreements of

the Yalta or Crimean Conference of February 1945. Though these issues did not directly affect the lives of the German exiles in Los Angeles, they are nevertheless important to identify because they reflect the political discussion among German exile circles in the United States. The Morgenthau Plan called for the division of Germany into two autonomous states, the dismantling of the Ruhr industry, and Allied control of economic development for twenty years. Due to the opposition of the State Department, which considered German heavy industry essential for the rebuilding of Europe, Roosevelt withdrew his approval of the Morgenthau Plan at the end of September 1944. The council vigorously opposed the Morgenthau Plan in its *Bulletin* of October 1944, calling it "Hitler's plan in reverse" (No. 2 [Oct. 23, 1944]: 2).

The Crimean Conference, as the Yalta Conference was called in the United States, held February 3–11, 1945, caused a rift in the council, and the division created among council members was reflected in the fourth issue of the *Bulletin,* in February 1945. Churchill, Roosevelt, and Stalin had decided on a plan for the occupation and control of Germany and for the reparations to be paid once it was conquered. Poland was to be granted territorial gains in the west, although the final determination of the Polish border was tabled for a future peace conference. Because the council was unable to achieve a consensus for their response to the Crimean Conference, six different opinion statements were published in the *Bulletin*. A minority protested against the projected "semi-colonial status for Germany for an indefinite period, including territorial and industrial dismemberment," while the majority was willing to endure the decisions in the interests of a future democratic Germany. They preferred to stress the similarities between the Crimean declaration about "the eradication of the institutions and the spirit of Nazism and militarism" and their own point of view (No. 4 [Feb. 1945]). The last issue of the *Bulletin* of May 1945 dealt with the atrocities committed in the German concentration camps. It was not a surprise that the council unanimously condemned the camps and developed emergency measures for the elimination of Nazism and for the implementation of democratic reconstruction because many of the exiles had either been incarcerated in concentration camps or barely escaped them. The camps were among the most visible examples of Nazi brutality and terrorism before the discovery of the extermination camps in Poland.

The council existed until the fall of 1945, when it failed because of a protest against the agreements reached at the Potsdam Conference of July and August 1945. While the conference primarily just endorsed the implementation of the Crimean Declaration, it also added a few points that fueled the opposition of the German exile community. The new stipulations were the establishment of the Oder-Neiße line as western border of Poland until its adjustment by a peace treaty, the allocation of the city of Königsberg and the bordering areas to the Soviet Union, and the forced transfer of Germans from Poland, Czechoslovakia, and Hungary to Germany. Paul Tillich considered the Potsdam Accords to be the end of Germany as *Reich*. He was not wrong in this assessment of the goal of Allied policies, but he was incapable of envisioning Germany in any other form but as *Reich*. In a private letter to Friedrich Baerwald, the representative of the Catholic Center Party on the council, Tillich used the phrase "liquidation of Germany." For him the economic and territorial regulations of Potsdam represented a "radical acceptance of the Morgenthau Plan" (quoted from Baerwald 378–79). In a draft resolution Tillich opposed above all the economic decisions, which he considered intolerable. In his opinion they meant "either the extinction of a considerable portion of the German people or the necessity of nourishing it from outside for an unlimited period of time." He thus saw the establishment of a "viable democratic Germany" endangered. Tillich further sought to lodge a protest against "the methods of evacuation, of deportation and of forced labor" as well as against the "often quite favorable attitude of the occupation authorities toward former Nazis and their political allies" (quoted from Baerwald 381–82).

The Communists and some of the independent members of the council, however, refused to endorse a public censure of the Potsdam Accords and exploited the balance structure of the council to prevent further critical declarations. The same structure, however, also made it impossible to overcome Communist objections by means of a vote. As a result there were a number of resignations on both sides of the political spectrum represented in the council. Paul Hagen as representative of the left-socialist group New Beginning and Friedrich Baerwald as the main representative of the Catholic Center Party refused further cooperation under protest. The fate of the Council was thus sealed. Its last meeting took place on October 15, 1945 (Baerwald 377).

The Communists and the independent members of the council withheld their approval of the draft resolution authored by Tillich because they were adamantly opposed to public criticism of the Potsdam Accords. Their criticism of the resolution was not caused by the endorsement of the "other Germany," since this view was also held by the Communists, but by their opinion that any criticism of the Potsdam Accords would seem directed first and foremost against the Soviet Union and would prevent improvements suggested in the ongoing discussions of the Allies. Tillich's resolution seemed to be directed first and foremost against the Soviet Union. Although he was also against "the control by the stewards of the atomic bomb . . . for the maintaining of monopoly capitalism," his reservations about the Oder-Neiße border were by far more ideological. In a private letter to Friedrich Baerwald, Tillich revealed that he considered the Oder-Neiße border the annulment of "the thousand-year history of German eastern settlement" and a concomitant extermination of German Protestantism "with all the cultural forces that it had produced" (Baerwald 378–79). This private declaration was in total contradiction to the council's declaration of September 1944 and was an indication of vestiges of imperialist thinking among German political exiles of all factions. There prevailed a strong German *Reich* ideology among them, as they refused to accept the vision of a functioning German democracy that was not situated within the borders of 1937. The division of Germany was not only repugnant to them, but also incompatible with the reconstruction of a new democratic Germany.

At no time did the Council for a Democratic Germany declare itself a government in exile. Its first public statement, on May 15, 1944, declared that its members could not claim "a formal mandate from people now inside Germany." They believed, however, that they represented "some of the forces and tendencies which [would] be vitally needed in the creation of a new Germany within the framework of a free world." They therefore felt that it was their "duty in the interest of the United States and the United Nations to express [their] conviction about the future of Germany at a time when the German people [could not] speak for themselves" ("Program for a Democratic Germany"). The minimum goal of the Council was participation in the formation of the United States' policy toward Germany that was, however, never realized. Although President Roosevelt, members of Congress, and the American press were sympathetic to some prominent exiles, and some of them were employed by the Office of Strategic Services (OSS) or the Office of War Information (OWI), the council failed to influence American policy toward Germany. Historians have attributed this failure to the division among German exiles or to the deficits of political culture, but the main reason was the Allied demand for unconditional surrender that precluded any negotiations with representatives of the "other Germany" from the outset. From 1943 on, the State Department opposed, therefore, the formation of a German government in exile.

At the end of World War II Tillich described the original mission of the council as building a "bridge" between the democratic forces in Germany and "those circles in America which were in sympathy with the rebuilding of a democratic Germany." The group intended to prove that both inside and outside the fatherland there were representatives of the "other Germany" who could initiate the country's democratic reconstruction (Baerwald 382). Tillich's point of view was close to the official stance of the Social Democratic Party, or, at least, to the position of its right wing. Brecht's position was probably identical, with the exception of his opposition to criticism leveled against the Soviet Union, while Thomas Mann opposed both factions. As Herbert Lehnert has suggested, both Mann and Brecht had something in common beyond their ideological orientation: "They were both deeply concerned with the German problem during their years of exile. Both translated this concern into literature and approached each other in the process" (200). But Brecht's poem reproduced earlier in this chapter never made the transition from political invective to literature; it lacks the ambiguity of Mann's Faust novel, which has kept the German problem alive for all times.

CHAPTER 10

Evil Germany
versus Good Germany

Thomas Mann's Doctor Faustus

Before Thomas Mann was able to finish his novel *Doctor Faustus,* he delivered a lecture at the Library of Congress in Washington, D.C., in May 1945. This lecture was part of his contract as consultant for German literature at the Library of Congress, a position that Agnes E. Meyer, his patron and wife of the publisher of the *Washington Post,* had obtained for him in 1941. He had given two lectures before, and in early January of 1944 he consulted with the Library of Congress and Meyer about possible lecture dates for 1945. He chose the title for this lecture, "Germany and the Germans," as early as October 1944. He originally chose to deliver the lecture in early 1945, but it had to be postponed because of a painful tooth infection that Mann had in November. Now there were two dates looming that had to be considered: one was the end of the war in Europe, which was in sight, and the other was his seventieth birthday, on June 6, 1945. The lecture suddenly received a more momentous meaning because it symbolized the end of an era in terms of international as well as autobiographical history—a constellation that would have been most attractive to Thomas Mann under different circumstances, but now it could only be painful.

Mann's diaries show that he began writing his lecture on February 27, 1945, and that he completed it on March 18, 1945. He delivered the lecture to several of his friends and family members, made revisions, and finally had it translated. The lecture borrowed heavily from his novel—it was virtually a guide to *Doctor Faustus*—but it also elaborated an answer to the German question that was profound in the context of inter-

FIGURE 24. Thomas Mann in 1941. Photograph courtesy of
Keystone/Thomas-Mann-Archiv, Zurich.

national history and is significant for Mann's place in German literature.
In the fashion of exile dialectics, he proposed the "identity of the non-
identical," as he may have encountered it as principle in Adorno's *Dialectic of Enlightenment* and his other writings: "There are *not* two Germanys, a good one and a bad one, but only one, whose best turned into
evil through devilish cunning. Wicked Germany is merely good Germany
gone astray, good Germany in misfortune, in guilt, and ruin" (18). The
significance of Thomas Mann's conception of the German question was
never recognized, except by his brother Heinrich, who wrote to him on

May 19, after he had read the manuscript, that "to have discovered [this fundamental conception] in its unforgettable epitome, would justify any other author's whole life." Not only did Thomas Mann provide a convincing formula for his fellow exiles in their dogged pursuit of the two Germanies theory, but he also devised a concept that could have been a guide for the two Germanies to follow in their assessment of the Nazi era after 1945.

Mann delivered his lecture in the Coolidge Auditorium of the Library of Congress on the evening of May 29, 1945. Crucial political events, including the liberation of the extermination and concentration camps and the unconditional surrender of Germany on May 8, had taken place since the completion of the text of the lecture in March 1945. The lecture assessed not only the defeat of Germany, but also its shame as a civilized nation after the full extent of the atrocities in the extermination camps had been exposed. Mann stood as an American citizen before an American audience, but as a German-born writer he felt that he had "something in common with German destiny and German guilt" (2). His critical withdrawal was at the same time an act of identification: "The truth that one tries to utter about one's people can only be the product of self-examination" (3).

He began the lecture by talking about his roots in the medieval town of Lübeck, near the Baltic Sea, and its "unworldly, provincial, German cosmopolitanism" (3). The binary opposites that he established in his speech were perhaps an indication of the dialectical training he received from Theodor W. Adorno, but this was not recognized at that time when he spoke of "the combination of expansiveness and seclusiveness, of cosmopolitanism and provincialism in the German character" (3). Mann explained this combination as "a secret union of the German spirit with the Demonic"—a thesis that he hastened to defend by reference to his inner experience, although he admitted that it was "not easily defensible" (5). He cited the figure of Goethe's Faust, adding that "wherever arrogance of the intellect mates with the spiritual obsolete and archaic, there is the Devil's domain" (5). From the devil of the Faust legend Mann switched to the historical Martin Luther and his devil, who struck Mann "as a very German figure." A pact with the devil, "the Satanic covenant, to win all treasures and power on earth for a time at the cost of the soul's salvation," struck him "as something exceedingly typical of German nature" (5). Continuing this speculation, Mann wrote, "A lonely thinker and searcher, a theologian and philosopher in his cell who, in his desire for world enjoyment and world domination, barters his soul to the Devil—isn't this the right moment to see Germany in this picture, the moment in which Germany is literally being carried off by the Devil" (5). But as soon as Mann had turned his literary speculation into political analysis, he changed the topic by finding fault with part of the legend for not connecting Faust with music. This argument must have sounded strange to an audience that could not know of Mann's new conception of the Faust figure for his novel. What now reads as a defense of his literary invention must then have appeared as a most bizarre conclusion: "If Faust is to be the representative of the German soul, he would have to be musical, for the relation of the German to the world is abstract and mystical, that is, musical—the relation of a professor with a touch of demonism, awkward and at the same time filled with arrogant knowledge that he surpasses the world in 'depth' " (5). Mann identified this depth with what he called "the musicality of the German soul," elaborating on "its inwardness, its subjectivity, the divorce of the speculative from the socio-political element of human energy, and the complete predominance of the former over the latter" (6). Relating this musicality to the Faust motif, Mann argued "that such musicality of soul is paid for dearly in another sphere—the political, the sphere of human companionship" (6).

Mann then went on to list the forerunners of Nazi ideology from Martin Luther to Bismarck and to establish a countercanon that included the sixteenth-century sculptor and wood-carver Tilman Riemenschneider, Erasmus of Rotterdam, and Goethe, an admirer of Napoleon and an opponent of German nationalism. German Romanticism received Mann's severest criticism; he called the Germans "the people of the romantic counter-revolution against the philosophical intellectualism and rationalism of enlightenment—a revolt of music against literature, of mysticism against clarity" (15). He saw Romanticism disguised as Bismarckianism at the end of the nineteenth century. United with realism and Machiavellianism in the Germany of 1871, Romanticism formed, according to Mann, that "Unholy Empire of Prussian Nation" that "could never be anything but [a] war empire" (16). Finally reduced to the level of Hitler, German Romanticism showed its morbid nature by breaking "out into hysterical barbarism, into a spree and a paroxysm of arrogance and crime" during the 1930s and 1940s. This barbarism ended, according to Mann, "in a national catastrophe, a physical and psychic collapse without parallel" (18).

Even though the lecture sounded like a simplistic indictment of Romanticism, Mann presented a dialectical reading of Romanticism's history, calling it a "melancholy story" (18). He avoided the term "tragic," which was employed by fascist modernists to deny historical accountability. Romanticism was Mann's prime evidence for his thesis "that there are *not* two Germanys." Romantic Germany was "good Germany gone astray, good Germany in misfortune, in guilt and ruin" (18). Mann identified too much with German Romanticism to deny it as part of his heritage. Delivering a dialectical reading of its history, he found it impossible "to simply renounce the wicked, guilty Germany and to declare: 'I am the good, the noble, the just Germany in the white robe; I leave it to you to exterminate the wicked one' " (18). He admitted that it was "all within" him, he had "been through it all" (18).

Mann cited Goethe's wish for the Germans to be scattered over the world like the Jews and blamed nineteenth-century nationalism for Germany's decline: its "great good . . . could not come to fruition in the traditional form of the nation state" (19). He envisioned a global society that exceeded the bounds of bourgeois democracy and provided a home for a Germany of the future. In the end, he could not resist to referring to the "tragedy of human life" as a paradigm for what he called "the German misfortune" (20). In his final words, which were more appropriate for the ending of his projected novel than for this political speech, Thomas Mann invoked the biblical grace that Germany so sorely needed as a nation, as did his audience and himself.

The speech 1945 suggested the same parallel as the novel that awaited its conclusion on Mann's desk in Pacific Palisades: the story of Faust as an allegory of Germany's most recent history. In addition to the Faust theme, Adorno's principle of the "identity of the non-identical" informed both texts. In "Germany and the Germans" it undergirded the analysis of German identity; in *Doctor Faustus* it supplied the aesthetic theory for the composition of the novel as well as the history and concept of art presented within the novel. Thomas Mann welcomed Adorno's principle of "the identity of the non-identical" because it presented him with a solution that Nietzsche's aesthetic theory could not provide. Nietzsche's aesthetic theory, with its binary opposition of nature versus mind and life versus art, had dominated Mann's works since his early novellas around 1900. His turn toward Adorno in *Doctor Faustus* constituted the deconstruction of the binary opposition implemented as aesthetic principle for his earlier works. Adrian Leverkühn, the protagonist of *Doctor Faustus* and Thomas Mann's last artist figure, and his compositions were both Nietzschean in origin and makeup, but in their ultimate crisis and defeat they are marked by Adorno's concept of art. This is most significant for a novel that was, in Thomas Mann's own words, designed as a "Nietzsche novel" (*Story of a Novel* 33). The montage of Nietzsche's visit to a bordello and his later paralysis became crucial elements of the fictional life story (Bergsten 55–64). In an early note on *Doctor Faustus* Thomas Mann conceived of the novel in terms of the Nietzschean opposition of the Apollonian and Dionysian: "It is really a desire to escape from everything bourgeois, moderate, classical, Apollonian, sober, industrious, and dependable into a world of drunken release, a life of bold, Dionysian genius, beyond the bourgeois class, indeed superhuman" (Voss 16). In the end, *Doctor Faustus* proved to be the novel in which Thomas Mann overcame and transcended the Nietzschean dilemma of his art using Adorno's aesthetic theory. At the same time, Thomas Mann applied the same theory to a new problem: the ambiguity of modernist art.

During the 1920s Thomas Mann (1875–1955) was one of the most visible representatives of the Weimar Republic. When the Nazis came to power in 1933, Mann and his wife were abroad on a lecture tour in Holland, Belgium, and France, afterwards vacationing in Switzerland. Their children warned them not to come back to Munich, and Mann and his wife settled in Switzerland. For the first three years Mann abstained from making any political statements, but in 1936 he made a number of determinedly antifascist statements. The Nazi government declared his German citizenship null and void in December 1936, but Mann had already accepted a Czechoslovakian passport a month earlier. During the 1930s, Thomas Mann visited the United States four times on lecture tours. While traveling in the United States in February 1938, Mann decided to move there because of the annexation of Austria. In September 1938, he accepted a position as lecturer in the humanities at Princeton University, where he taught from 1938 to 1940. In 1941 Mann moved with his family to Pacific Palisades, a suburb of Los Angeles, seventeen miles west of downtown, near the ocean. They first lived in a rented house on 740 Amalfi Drive, and in 1942 they finally moved into their home on 1550 San Remo Drive that was custom built for them. In 1939 Mann completed *The Beloved Returns: Lotte in Weimar (Lotte in Weimar)*, a novel about the old Goethe. From 1941 to 1943 he worked on the completion of his tetralogy *Joseph and His Brothers*, a novel in four volumes on the biblical figure that was partially based on President Franklin D. Roosevelt and his New Deal. In 1944 Mann and his wife became U.S. citizens. He went on numerous lecture tours throughout the United States to warn Americans about Hitler's imperialism and his persecution of Jews. From 1940 to 1945, Mann wrote a regular radio commentary that was recorded in his own voice in an NBC studio in downtown Los Angeles and broadcast by the BBC from Great Britain to Germany. In January 1942 he protested the murder of more than four hundred Dutch Jews in human experiments with poison gas in Germany. In September 1942, Mann informed his German listeners of the extermination policies against European Jews and that 700,000 Jews had already been murdered or tortured to death by the Gestapo.

After he completed *Joseph and His Brothers* in January 1943, Mann began working on *Doctor Faustus* on March 17, 1943, based on his old "3-line plan of the Doctor Faustus from the year 1901" (*Story of a Novel* 17). The date in Mann's diary was wrong—the plan was actually from the year 1904—but his memory regarding its contents was not. The plan was an outline for a novel about a syphilitic artist: "For the novel. Driven by longing, the syphilitic artist becomes close to a pure, sweet young girl, carries on an engagement with the unsuspecting girl and shoots himself before the wedding" (quoted from Kurzke 462). Another outline provided the legendary name for the protagonist:

> Figure of the syphilitic artist: as Dr. Faust and one who has sold himself to the Devil. The poison works as intoxication, stimulus, inspiration; in ecstatic enthusiasm he can create genial, wonderful works; the Devil directs his hand. But finally the Devil takes him: paralysis. The affair with the pure young girl, with whom he carries on up to the marriage, proceeds. (quoted from Kurzke 462)

The outlines of 1904 dealt with Mann's concept of the artist and his guilt about homoerotic involvements, but they lacked the historical and political dimensions that Mann developed in the novel in the 1940s.

By the end of the nineteenth century the figure of Faust had come to represent the German character, and Goethe's *Faust* was considered the German national drama par excellence. Any German writer of rank felt challenged by Goethe's work. While the figure of the "pure young girl" in Mann's notes of 1904 showed the influence of Goethe's Margarete from his Faust drama of 1808, the master narrative for Mann's 1947 novel was provided by the chapbook that Mann began to read in April 1943, *Historia of D. Johann Fausten,* whose author is unknown but was published by Johann Spies in Frankfurt/Main in 1587. The chapbook tells the story of the peasant boy Johann Faust, who studies theology and obtains the degree of Doctor Theologiae. Faust makes a pact with a devil named Mephostophiles, giving him his soul in exchange for the devil's services on earth for twenty-four years. After a life of travel adventures and miraculous feats, Faust is condemned and carried off to hell. The German chapbook was translated into English, but only a revised edition of 1592 survives. It was probably the first edition of the English translation, now lost, that served as a source for Christopher Marlowe's *Tragical History of D. Faustus*. The German version of *Historia of D. Johann Fausten* had a clearly Lutheran bias. Although its language was rather crude, it nevertheless provided a sophisticated example of Luther's theology of grace, explaining that Faust's major sin was his denial of grace. The chapbook compares Faust to Cain, declaring that "his sins were greater than could be forgiven him." Faust's conviction "that in making his written contract with the Devil he had gone to far" was considered sinful pride (223–24). The chapbook was designed to serve as a warning to every Lutheran Christian never to abandon faith in the grace of God.

Mann followed Faust's life story as it appears in the chapbook: his Faust figure also grows up on a farm, studies theology, makes a pact with the devil, and is implicitly condemned at the end. Yet Goethe's Faust drama, published in two parts between 1808 and 1832, is not totally absent from Mann's novel. Goethe's Margarete returns in dialectical fashion as a prostitute named Esmeralda, who later turns up as the artist's patron, Madame de Tolna. Although the question of grace is prefigured in the chapbook, it is ultimately the alliance of divine grace with female love that links Mann's Faust novel to Goethe's drama. Esmeralda warns him against her body because she is afraid of infecting him with her syphilitic disease. As Zeitblom comments, "the hapless woman warned the man who desired her against 'herself'—and that means an act of the soul freely elevating itself above her pitiful physical existence, a humane act of distancing herself from it, an act of compassion, an act, if I may be permitted the word, of love" (DF 165; GW 6: 206). Leverkühn's damnation at his syphilitic collapse in 1930 and his death in 1940 (see chapter XLVII and the epilogue) is not as certain as Faust's damnation in the chapbook of 1587. The reader of Mann's work is told that human love is but "a reflection of the everlasting grace" (DF 474; GW 6: 600). The whole Esmeralda subplot, as Hans R. Vaget has shown, "is of central importance to the theological discourse of the book. It foreshadows the grace of which the [protagonist]—not unlike Goethe's Faust—is deemed worthy after all" ("Mann" 187).

On May 23, 1943, a Sunday morning, Mann began writing his *Doctor Faustus*. As the subtitle of the work, *The Life of the German Composer Adrian Leverkühn, as Told by a Friend,* indicates, the story is presented as a biography of a fictional composer narrated by his fictional friend, Serenus Zeitblom. This device enabled him as author to begin his narrative on the same day as Zeitblom, his fictional first-person narrator who puts his first lines on paper in his small study in Freising on the Isar, a small town in Nazi Germany, in May 1943. Interposing "the medium of the 'friend'" between himself as author and his subject allowed Mann to write the novel as a biography. As Mann explained,

> This strategy was a bitter necessity in order to achieve a certain humorous leavening of the somber material and to make its horrors bearable to myself as well as to the reader. To make the demonic strain pass through an undemonic medium, to entrust a harmless and simple soul, well-meaning and timid, with the recital of the story, was itself a comic idea. It removed some of the burden, for it enabled me to escape the turbulence of everything direct, personal, and confessional . . . , to steer it into indirection and to travesty as I depicted it through the eyes of this good and unheroic soul. (*Story of a Novel* 31)

Zeitblom completes the life story of his friend with a prayer in May 1945, after Germany's unconditional surrender, while Mann finished his novel—after many interruptions by lecture tours and a life-threatening but successful operation for lung cancer in 1946—finally on February 6, 1947.

The interposition of Serenus Zeitblom as a narrator living in Nazi Germany between 1943 and 1945 made it possible "to tell the story on a dual plane of time," to combine the everyday events that move "the writer as he writes with those that he is recounting, so that the quivering of his hands is . . . explained both by the vibrations of distant bomb hits" during the Allied air raids on Munich "and by his inner consternation" (*Story of a Novel* 31). From this perspective, *Doctor Faustus* provides also a history of the Weimar Republic and World War II. At the end of the novel, Zeitblom reports that in late April 1945 an American general "has the inhabitants of the city of Weimar file past the crematoria of [Buchenwald] and declares . . . that they, citizens who went about their business in seeming honesty and tried to know nothing, though at times the wind blew the stench of burned human flesh up their noses—declares that they share in the guilt of these horrors that are now laid bare and to which he forces them to direct their eyes" (DF 505; GW 6: 637).

It is surprising that Zeitblom does not mention the Jewish victims of Buchenwald, because Mann was well informed of the German genocide of the Jews, as his radio broadcasts to Germany confirm. It is one of the astounding and serious shortcomings of the novel that it portrays "a Germany without anti-Semitism" (Vaget, "'German' Music," 238). In

addition, there are two negatively drawn Jewish figures, Dr. Chaim
Breisacher, a prefascist intellectual in the Kridwiß circle in Munich, and
Saul Fitelberg, a concert agent from Paris who tries to lure Leverkühn
to a life as an internationally famous pianist and conductor of his music.
As Ruth Klüger points out, Breisacher is "at the very least . . . a case of
almost perversely bad taste, at worst . . . a whitewash of German intellectuals" (162; see also Darmaun 236–43). With regard to Fitelberg,
family members had warned the author about the anti-Semitic under-
tones in his description, but Mann insisted that this character stay for
comic effect (Darmaun 243–50, 290–91; Marquad 564–80). The author's misunderstanding of his own work is particularly embarrassing
in view of his "full knowledge of the Jewish catastrophe" (Angress-
Klüger 162).

According to Mann's diary, when the novel was completed in 1947,
there was a "champagne dinner in celebration . . . of Faustus and the
reading of the Echo chapter [chapter XLIV]." The child Echo, who was
modeled on Mann's beloved grandson, Fridolin Mann, dies in the novel
because Leverkühn disregards the devil's injunction that he must not
love. In the author's opinion, this was "doubtless the best and most poetic [chapter] of the book." After the reading, "more champagne" was
served.

When Mann first began planning the book, it was not obvious that his
Faust figure would be a composer. There had been artist figures—musi-
cians and writers—in his short stories and novels, but never a composer.
Mann consulted some musical sources in March and April of 1943—
Igor Stravinsky's memoirs, letters of Hugo Wolf, Paul Bekker's history of
music as a history of the change of musical forms (*Musikgeschichte als
Geschichte der musikalischen Formwandlungen,* Stuttgart 1926)—but
he also read books on Luther and Nietzsche. On April 11, 1943, however, Mann recorded in his diary, "Decided to study books on music."
On April 13 he wrote, "Made extracts of Lamentation of Faust and
mockery of the 'spirit' (intended as a symphony)." Then Mann connected music with the German national character, an idea that was typical for his generation and also appears in Schoenberg's writings. In a letter to Alma Mahler at the beginning of World War I, Schoenberg called
the French, English, Russians, Belgians, Americans, and Serbians bar-
barians on the basis of their musical productions:

> For a long time, this music has been a declaration of war, an attack on Ger-
> many. And if someone in a foreign country had to show apparent respect
> to us, . . . there was nevertheless an element of arrogance with it. . . . But

now comes the reckoning. Now we shall send these mediocre purveyors of kitsch back into slavery, and they shall learn to honor the German spirit and to worship the German God. (*Schoenberg Reader* 126; cf. Randol Schoenberg 27–30)

In 1921 Schoenberg was reported to have said to his student Josef Rufer about the twelve-tone music he had been developing, "I have made a discovery thanks to which the supremacy of German music is ensured for the next hundred years" (*Schoenberg Reader* 159).

As Pamela M. Potter explains in *Most German of the Arts,* "music has come to represent one of Germany's most important contributions to Western culture, impressing the rest of the world with a reputation for superior achievement and serving as a source of national pride, especially in times of low morale and insecurity" (x). As Potter elaborates, one such low point was reached at the end of World War I, when Thomas Mann praised German culture as superior to Western civilization in his *Reflections of a Nonpolitical Man* (*Betrachtungen eines Unpolitischen,* 1918) and Arnold Schoenberg allegedly made the above statement about "the supremacy of German music." One must add the unconditional surrender at the end of World War II as another low point of German self-esteem. In the light of this idea that music is the "most German of the arts," it is not surprising that Mann would turn to the subject of Germany's claim to musical hegemony not only for solace, but also for a comprehensive critique of German ambitions of world domination. Mann realized that "Germany's fateful turn to Nazism happened, not despite its idolatry of music, as the naïvely humanistic cliché would have it, but rather because of it" (Vaget, "National and Universal," 159).

On April 16, 1943, Mann referred to "thoughts on the way the subject [presumably music] was identified with things German, with German solitude in the world in general." In a letter to the conductor Bruno Walter on May 6, he revealed to his friend that he was writing a "novel on a pathological illegitimate inspiration, whose protagonist was to be finally a real musician (composer)." He felt uneasy, however, because he was not well informed about the training of a composer and asked for Walter's assistance. He inquired whether he should read a textbook on composition. On May 8, 1943, Mann mentioned Leverkühn's name for the first time in his diary. In his *Genesis of Doctor Faustus* he wrote, "His given name to be Anselm, Andreas, or Adrian" (*Story of a Novel* 29). As Mann summarized the central idea of the novel at that time, it was "the flight from the difficulties of the cultural crisis into the pact with the devil, the craving of a proud mind, threatened by sterility, for an unblocking of inhibitions at any cost, and the parallel between pernicious euphoria ending in collapse with the nationalistic frenzy of Fascism" (*Story of a Novel* 30).

In spite of his highly developed musical interests, Thomas Mann was aware that he needed a "helper, adviser, and sympathetic instructor" (*Story of a Novel* 42). Mann recorded consulting with Theodor W. Adorno for the first time while working on the novel on July 6, 1943 (they had met socially at Max Horkheimer's house in Pacific Palisades in 1942 and earlier in 1943). Adorno had brought him Julius Bahle's book on inspiration in musical creation entitled *Eingebung und Tat im musikalischen Schaffen* (Leipzig 1939). Reading Adorno's manuscript "On the Philosophy of Modern Music" two weeks later, Mann concluded that "here indeed was something important," as it dealt with modernist art:

> The manuscript dealt with modern music both on an artistic and on a sociological plane. The spirit of it was remarkably forward looking, subtle and deep, and the whole thing had the strangest affinity to the idea of my book, to the "composition" in which I lived and moved and had my being. The decision was made of itself: this was my man. (*Story of a Novel* 43)

Adorno's impact on *Doctor Faustus* is a matter of record (see Abel, *Musikästhetik*, 163–91; Kurzke 473–77; Tiedemann 9–33; Cobley 59–106). It has been acknowledged by Thomas Mann in *The Story of a Novel: The Genesis of Doctor Faustus* of 1949, as well as in his letters and diaries, and it has been the topic of numerous interpretations. Hermann Kurzke has argued that *The Story of a Novel* was written "mainly to honor the participation of Theodor W. Adorno" (461), although Mann's wife Katia and his daughter Erika sought to minimize Adorno's influence and Mann finally deleted a series of passages that praised his consultant. These passages, now available in volume 7 of Mann's diaries, confirm the close cooperation between the novelist and his "privy councillor" *(Wirklicher Geheimer Rat),* as he liked to call Adorno *(Tagebücher 1946–1948 948–53).*

Their relationship was intense and not exempt from Mann's malicious irony. He slipped Adorno's suppressed Jewish patronym "Wiesengrund" into the text of the novel, when Wendell Kretzschmar illustrates a passage in Beethoven's Piano Sonata in C Minor, opus 111, no. 32, by singing "Wiesengrund" (Meadowland) (59; GW 6: 75; *Story of a Novel* 48). Adorno had entered the United States as Theodor Wiesengrund, but

was naturalized as Theodor Adorno. Furthermore, Mann unsympathet-
ically furnished one of the devils of the pact scene with the philosopher's
features and arguments. Most interpretations cite Adorno's *Dialectic of
Enlightenment* of 1947 and his *Philosophy of Modern Music* of 1949 as
having had an impact on *Doctor Faustus*. As a matter of fact, *Dialectic
of Enlightenment* was available to Mann in its mimeographed version,
"Philosophical Fragments," while he was writing his novel, and so was
the typescript of Adorno's first chapter on Schoenberg in the *Philosophy
of Modern Music* (*Story of a Novel* 42–43). Mann admitted that the
analysis of the row system that appears in the dialogue in chapter XXII
of *Doctor Faustus* was "entirely based on Adorno's essay" (*Story of a
Novel* 46). In addition, Adorno supplied Mann with extensive notes
about works that a musician like Leverkühn would compose. There are
four such sketches now available in print: for Leverkühn's violin concerto for Rudi Schwerdtfeger in chapters XXXIII and XXXVIII; for two
chamber music compositions, an ensemble for three strings, three wood-
wind instruments, and piano, and a string quartet, in chapter XLIII; and,
finally, for the cantata, *The Lamentation of Doctor Faustus,* in chapter
XLVII (see *Adorno/Thomas Mann Briefwechsel* 158–61).

In a letter to Adorno of December 1945, Mann tried to justify his penchant for such uncredited borrowings by referring to his "inclination in
old age to regard life as a cultural product, hence a set of mythic clichés
which I prefer, in my calcified dignity, to independent invention." Mann
realized that in the case of *Doctor Faustus* this inclination was "more difficult—not to say more scandalous, [because] real literary borrowing
[was] involved, performed with an air that what has been filched [was]
just good enough to serve one's own pattern of ideas." He did not hesitate to call his behavior "brazen," although he hoped he was "not all together doltish," referring to his use of bits from Adorno's essay on
Schoenberg in the *Philosophy of Modern Music*. As Mann admitted,
"These borrowings cry out all the more for apology since for the time
being the reader cannot be made aware of them; there is no way to call
his attention to them without breaking the illusion (Perhaps a footnote:
'This comes from Adorno-Wiesengrund'? It won't do!)."

There are also good arguments for adding Adorno's *Aesthetic Theory*
to the list of works from which Mann borrowed. Although it was published posthumously in 1970, it is safe to assume that its central ideas
were existent, at least in embryonic form, at the time Thomas Mann
wrote *Doctor Faustus* and that its ideas formed part of the two authors'
discussions in the 1940s. While *Dialectic of Enlightenment* offered the

philosophy of history of *Doctor Faustus,* and *Philosophy of Modern Music* provided the history of modernist music used in the novel, it was Adorno's *Aesthetic Theory* that may well have served as the overall artistic foundation of the novel.

Adorno's well-known formula about the dual essence of art as that of "autonomy and *fait social*" (AT 229) certainly applies to Mann's novel *Doctor Faustus,* which has as its main topic the creation of a musical work during a century of social revolutions, two world wars, and genocide. In particular, the historical development of art's function from solace to "consciousness of suffering," which is fundamental to Thomas Mann's *Doctor Faustus,* can be traced back to Adorno's aesthetics. Mann's protagonist, Adrian Leverkühn, has a vision of art as it once used to be and will become again in the future: "An art without suffering, psychologically healthy, that confides without solemnity, that trusts without sorrow, an art that is on a first-name basis with humanity" (DF 339; GW 6: 429). But Leverkühn is presented as scrupulously aware of the historic situation of art and aware that for his century, an art "with stable warmth, cow warmth," as he calls it (DF 76; GW 6: 94), has not only become impossible but needs to be renounced. As Leverkühn declares after the death of his beloved nephew Echo, who has to die because of his satanic pact, "The good and noble, . . . what we call the human, although it is good and noble[, that is not to be]. What human beings have fought for and stormed fortresses for, what the people filled with joy have proclaimed—that is not to be. It is taken back. I will take it back. . . . The Ninth Symphony" (DF 501; GW 6: 634).

Thomas Mann has his protagonist renounce Beethoven's choral symphony because it could no longer provide the redemption that it promised at the beginning of the nineteenth century. To pretend that it still did was fraudulent. Even the novel's narrator, Serenus Zeitblom, realizes at the end of World War II that "a hymn of exultation, a *Fidelio,* a *Ninth Symphony*" is no longer a legitimate consolation to the German population: "Only this can benefit us, only this will be sung from our souls: the lament from the son of hell, the most frightful human and divine lament ever begun on earth, coming from a subject, but spreading further, and grasping Cosmos itself, as it were" (DF 509; GW 6: 643).

The symphonic cantata that Leverkühn produces as his final composition, *The Lamentation of Doctor Faustus,* is the legitimate artistic response to the historical situation and is explicitly presented as an "Ode to Sorrow," a negative counterpart to Beethoven's "Ode to Joy." Adorno did not conceive of art explicitly in historical terms, as Thomas Mann did, but rather thought of it in terms of its opposition to a reality to which it refuses to submit. Most of his examples demonstrating the principle points of his *Aesthetic Theory* were taken from modern art. Although he did not deny the solace of art during earlier centuries, Adorno had to insist on art's "memory of accumulated suffering" as its only redemptive quality in the twentieth century (AT 261).

This conception provided the theoretical foundation for Thomas Mann's *Doctor Faustus;* in the novel's central theme as well as its form, art serves as historiography and as the "memory of accumulated suffering." Mann traces Adrian Leverkühn's career as a composer and the development of his art as a historiography of modern music in terms of Adorno's *Philosophy of Modern Music* (see Sauerland, " 'Er wußte noch mehr,' " 130–45, and many others). Leverkühn was for Mann a representative not only of the German soul and its musicality, as he explained in his lecture "Germany and the Germans," but also of the historical progress of European art during the twentieth century. Leverkühn was shown to be aware of the crisis of artistic illusion *(Schein)* that Adorno considered central to modern art. From the beginning of his career in 1910, Leverkühn has considered composition as artwork for the sake of illusion (DF 192–93; GW 6: 241–42), but he is troubled by the question whether at this stage of history "this little game" of producing artistic illusion for the sake of spontaneous and organic appearance is still intellectually honest, whether a work of art still stands in any legitimate relation to the societal situation, "whether all illusion, even the most beautiful, and especially the most beautiful, has not become a lie today" (DF 192; GW 6: 241). According to Leverkühn, every work of art had become a fraud.

The novel's narrator, Zeitblom, who records this discussion, concludes this event with a quotation from Leverkühn that seems to reflect Adorno's *Philosophy of Modern Music:* "Illusion and game have begun even today to have the conscience of art against them. Art wants to cease being illusion and game, it wants to become comprehension" (DF 193; GW 6: 242). Because of the historical situation of art, Leverkühn has scruples regarding the autonomy of art, and he believes that form has become "mere illusion and game" (DF 194; GW 6: 243). In the early Brentano songs that he composes, Leverkühn resorts to a parody of tonality that Zeitblom characterizes as a "travesty of innocence" (DF 193; GW 6: 242). Later, however, Leverkühn renounces parody as a legitimate art form in his century.

In his next conversation with Zeitblom, when Leverkühn explains his new system of composing, he associates artistic freedom with sterility and theorizes that "complete organization" is the antidote to this dilemma (DF 204; GW 6: 255). It is noteworthy that everything that Leverkühn says the afternoon of this conversation has "the mark of suffering" (DF 208; GW 6: 259). Even though Leverkühn's suffering is nothing more than a hereditary migraine, his thoughts are explicitly related to suffering. Zeitblom emphasizes, although only tentatively at this early stage, that Leverkühn's suffering is a psychosomatic state. Nevertheless, it is most important that these offhand remarks place suffering at the center of Leverkühn's new aesthetics. The reader is to identify Leverkühn's suffering with that of mankind and to expect his successful compositions to give evidence of mankind's suffering in the twentieth century. The composer is not only to appear as "a 'hero of our time,' a person who bore the suffering of the epoch," as Mann called him (*Story of a Novel* 88), but his music is also to reflect the suffering of his century. Both the term "rational organization through and through" *(rationale Durchorganisation)* and the centrality of suffering constitute essential elements of *Doctor Faustus* that Mann took from Adorno's *Philosophy of Modern Music* and *Aesthetic Theory*.

As a Faust novel, Thomas Mann's work had to present a pact with the devil, and in this work the event is recorded by Leverkühn in a manuscript sent to Zeitblom. The credibility of his account is questionable, but it can be said to present Leverkühn's feverish imagination. During his conversation with Leverkühn, the devil changes his appearance four times. In one of his disguises the devil dons the mask of a music critic, an ironic gesture toward Adorno. Here Leverkühn characterizes the devil disparagingly as a "member of the intelligentsia, writer of art, on music for the ordinary press, a theoretician and critic, who himself composes, so far as thinking allows him" (DF 253; GW 6: 317). At the moment of the devil's pact, modern art is still represented in terms of the threat of artistic impotence and sterility. As Leverkühn records, art has become critique. The historical movement of the musical material has turned against the self-contained work of art: "Permissible is only . . . the undisguised and untransfigured expression of suffering in its actual moment" (DF 256; GW 6: 321). For historical reasons, certain things have become impossible in art: "The self-satisfied illusion of music itself . . . has become impossible and no longer tenable" (ibid). But Leverkühn rejects parody as a solution to the artistic dilemma of his time. What the devil promises is a "breakthrough" in Nietzschean terms: experience and feeling in antithesis to reason and critique. With a rhetorical gesture, the devil suggests that truth is experience and feeling: "What uplifts you, what increases your feeling of power and control, . . . that is the truth" (DF 258; GW 6: 323). What the devil offers is the Dionysian solution that Gustav von Aschenbach, another artist figure from Thomas Mann's *Death in Venice,* chose as a solution to the crisis of art. Aschenbach's choice, however, had fatal consequences. Leverkühn makes a different selection, yet with no less fatal results. Following Adorno's philosophy of art does not relieve him from suffering and death, but it does provide him at the end of his life with a work of modernist art that is able to deliver at the moment of greatest despair an answer to the crisis of his art and his age.

Thomas Mann's novel shows Leverkühn going through the stages of art that reflect the failures outlined in Adorno's *Aesthetic Theory* and that correspond to a certain degree to the stages of Schoenberg's career that Adorno described in *Philosophy of Modern Music.* Adorno criticizes the first phase of Schoenberg's music, the expressionism of his free atonality around 1910, for its lack of reflection, and he censures the second phase, during which he developed his twelve-tone compositions after 1923, for its complete domination of the musical material and its intolerance for the non-identical. Only in Schoenberg's late style does Adorno find a "new sovereignty" compatible with the subject in art and its treatment of the material. There would be more of Schoenberg in Adorno's *Philosophy of Modern Music* than Thomas Mann realized at the time. As he was genuinely surprised by Schoenberg's violent reaction to the musicological implications of his novel, the composer was equally justified as neighbor in exile in his protest against his fictional doppelgänger.

Adorno had originally identified the characteristics of this "late style" *(Spätstil)* in Beethoven's late works. It is well known that Adorno's interpretation of Beethoven's Piano Sonata, opus 111, was the model for the lecture delivered by Leverkühn's first music teacher, Wendell Kretzschmar, in chapter VIII. Early in October 1943, Adorno played the entire sonata for the novelist, who then rewrote parts of chapter VIII. According to Adorno, whose words are mouthed by the fictional Kretzschmar, the subjective and the conventional form a new relationship in this sonata. As Kretzschmar maintains in one of his lectures, "Where greatness and death meet, there arises a sovereign objectivity amenable to convention and leaving arrogant subjectivity behind, because the merely personal . . . supersedes itself again; it enters the collective and mythical ghostlike and gloriously" (DF 57; GW 6: 74). Thus Beethoven's piano sonata, with its dialectic between the conventional and the subjective, provides the typological model for Leverkühn's last composition, which is based on this kind of identity of the non-identical.

In *The Lamentation of Doctor Faustus* Leverkühn finally achieves the completion of the authentic work of art of his time, prefigured in Beethoven's Piano Sonata, opus 111, and foreshadowed in Leverkühn's conversation with Zeitblom in 1910. The dialectical process of the development of Leverkühn's art culminates at this point in the change from the strictest constraints to the free language of feeling without an abandonment to chaos or to the Dionysian frenzy that Nietzsche (or Leverkühn's devil) had advocated.

In Zeitblom's words, the "breakthrough" *(Durchbruch)* is achieved through a dialectical process that effects a "change from the strictest constraint into the language of feeling, the birth of freedom from constraint" (DF 510; GW 6: 644). This dialectical process, however, does not supersede rational organization but rather produces the coexistence of "extreme calculation" and the "purely expressive" (DF 512; GW 6: 647). The topic of the identity of the non-identical emerges early in the novel, in a conversation between Zeitblom and Leverkühn in 1910, when the composer explains his new system in which the subjective and the objective intermix to the point of being indistinguishable: "One brings forth the other and takes the character of the other, the subjective precipitates as objective and is awaked to spontaneity by genius" (DF 203; GW 6: 254). It is obvious that this reflects Adorno's concept of the "identity of the non-identical" *(Identität des Nichtidentischen)*. Zeitblom refers to the "substantial identity of the most blessed and the most heinous, the inner identity of the chorus of angelic children and hell's laughter" (DF 511; GW 6: 645). This "substantial identity" has already been characteristic of Leverkühn's oratorio *Apocalipsis cum figuris*, a composition that forms the stepping-stone for *The Lamentation of Doctor Faustus*. But what has been a formal utopia in the preceding work now becomes a universal theme in the Faust cantata.

It is well known that Thomas Mann owed his concept for Leverkühn's last composition and some crucial parts of its analysis to Adorno. Originally Mann had wanted his protagonist to die with the fragment of a composition in his hands, like Aschenbach, who left behind that famous "page and a half of exquisite prose" in *Death in Venice* (DF 46; GW 8: 493). But Adorno persuaded Mann to have Leverkühn complete his last composition. When Mann read the first version of chapter XLVI to his "privy councillor," Mann had to admit that it was a failure and that Adorno's criticism was not only justified, but most welcome. This realization required that Mann develop a detailed description and analysis of Levenkühn's last work and rewrite chapter XLVI, presenting the composition as a completed work of art that constituted an authentic "breakthrough" (*Tagebücher 1946–1948* 952–53).

Adorno also suggested making Faust's identity as "a bad and a good Christian" the general musical theme of the cantata. The words of the 1587 chapbook *Historia of D. Johann Fausten*—"For I die as both a wicked and good Christian"—form the general musical theme of the cantata (DF 511; GW 6: 646). The twelve syllables of this sentence ingeniously fit the composition, with twelve tones signifying in word and music the identity of the non-identical.

The biographical facts of the genesis of the novel, however, do not make Adorno into "a kind of co-author," nor can the modernism of Mann's novel be considered entirely equivalent with "Adorno's exegesis of modern music" (Vaget, "Mann," 176–77). It took Mann's abandonment of Nietzsche's antithesis of art and his serious engagement with Adorno's concept of the identity of the non-identical in art to produce the modernism of his novel. In chapter XLVI Mann demonstrates that the identification of the angelic choir with the hellish yelling that had already tentatively been employed by Leverkühn in his apocalyptic cantata had now become the universal principle of his final work: "That identity which exists between the crystalline angelic choir and the howls of hell in the *Apocalypse* has now become all-embracing . . . a formal arrangement of ultimate rigor that knows nothing that is unthematic, in which the ordering of the material is total, and within which . . . there is no longer any free note" (DF 512; GW 6: 646). These hellish howls are identified with the hellish "trills" and abominable "chirps" from the interrogation and torture cellars of the Gestapo, the very symbol of modern hell referred to by the devil in the pact scene in chapter XXV. By integrating this external horror, Leverkühn's art was able to oppose its society in part by identification with what art opposes. The Gestapo cellar was the non-art, so to speak, with which the modern work of art needed to identify in order to oppose it and maintain its autonomy and authenticity.

From a suppressed passage of *The Story of a Novel,* we know that Adorno advised Mann to introduce "the substantial identity of the laughter of hell and the angelic children's choir" (*Tagebücher 1946–1948* 951). Under pressure from his family, Mann decided to withhold from his readers the fact that he had received from Adorno this idea for the description of the Faust cantata in chapter XLVI. This fact is important for the argument that Adorno's concept of the "identity of the non-identical"—a central idea of this posthumous *Aesthetic Theory*—was already a part of his thinking in 1946 and that the novelist recognized it as the "most meaningful and fitting advice" for his chapter. The only thing Mann had to do was "to put it into verse" (*Tagebücher 1946–1948* 951).

The strict formal approach of the Faust cantata, which did not allow for anything unthematic and subordinated the material to total organization, resulted in the identification of music as total form and of music as free language: "Just by virtue of its character of absolute form, music is liberated as language" (DF 512; GW 6: 646–47). Technically speaking, *The Lamentation of Doctor Faustus* was to be Leverkühn's most rigid work—"a work of utmost calculation"—but it was simultaneously to be "purely expressive" (DF 512; GW 6: 647). The Faust cantata was classified by Zeitblom as a "late work" *(Spätwerk)* that had little in common with earlier works. In contrast to Leverkühn's previous compositions, it was written "without parody" (DF 513; GW 6: 648).

In his analysis, Zeitblom characterizes the Faust cantata as the inverse of Beethoven's *Lied an die Freude* (Ode to Joy), Leverkühn's *Lied an die Trauer* (Ode to Sorrow) "negating by its genius that transition of [Beethoven's] symphony into vocal jubilation" (DF 514; GW 6: 649). This negation of Beethoven's optimistic composition makes *The Lamentation of Doctor Faustus* into the ultimate revocation *(Zurücknahme)* of the solace of art that Leverkühn denounces after the death of his beloved five-year-old nephew Echo. His friend and interpreter leaves no doubt that Leverkühn conceives his last composition as the Ninth Symphony's "counterpart in a most melancholy sense of the word" (DF 514; GW 6: 649). Beethoven's symphony is negated by Leverkühn's work not only formally, but also thematically. The Faust cantata is "a negation of the religious," but not a denial of religion. The negation of the religious, "the only permissible chiffre of otherness," evolves as the identity of the non-identical that Adorno had suggested (Voss 199). Zeitblom further elaborates that a work dealing with the devil as tempter, with apostasy, and with damnation must be a religious work, but its religiosity can only be explained *ex nihilo* (DF 514; GW 6: 649). Leverkühn's Faust cantata does not allow any consolation, appeasement, or redemption until the very end. Then the dialectic of the identity of the non-identical—that is, the essence of art according to Adorno—finally produces, by analogy to the pure expressiveness resulting from extreme construction, the "hope beyond hopelessness" (DF 515; GW 6: 651), the solace of art in the Faust cantata. This solace is not a fraud or betrayal, but the proverbial "miracle that goes beyond faith" (DF 515; GW 6: 651).

With his detailed explication of *The Lamentation of Doctor Faustus*, Thomas Mann fulfilled Adorno's requirement that art function as historiography and as the memory of suffering. With the final note of his cantata Leverkühn overcomes the ambiguity of modernist art. The high G of a cello, vanishing in a *pianissimo fermata,* the dying note of sorrow, changes its meaning, "that tone, vibrating in the silence . . . , stands as a light in the night" (DF 515; GW 6: 651). The synesthesia of sound and light is to signal Leverkühn's victory in defeat. Mann provides the end of Leverkühn's last composition with a note of grace that is denied to the rest of his oeuvre and his entire life and career. It is this note of grace toward which Mann directed Zeitblom's prayer for his friend and his fatherland in the last words of the novel: "God be merciful to thy poor soul, my friend, my Fatherland" (DF 534; GW 6: 676).

While Gustav von Aschenbach's famous "page and a half of choicest prose" in *Death in Venice (Der Tod in Venedig)* was an Apollonian work of art derived from an Dionysian experience at the beach, Leverkühn's Faust cantata is the "breakthrough" toward a new work of art at the margin of modernism in which the identity of the non-identical is achieved: dissonance stands for beauty, and harmony and tonality for hell. In *Doctor Faustus,* the devil's Nietzschean advocacy of orgiastic freedom is rejected in favor of Adorno's concept of art as the identity of the non-identical. *The Lamentation of Doctor Faustus* is a work of agony that does not deny the suffering of its century. Conversely, the beauty of Aschenbach's completed work conceals the agony from which it originates. While its beauty renders the artist a victim to his Dionysian obsession, its *l'art pour l'art* stance is implicitly criticized by the narrator. Aschenbach's art had turned into the production of a beautiful illusion. He had failed to master the opposition of life versus art. Leverkühn, however, remains a master of his fate until his collapse in May 1930, after he has invited his friends and acquaintances to the fictional Bavarian village of Pfeiffering for his final farewell in imitation of the legendary D. Johann Faust, his typological model of the sixteenth century. His final work of art, however, does not secure his redemption—Adorno had warned Thomas Mann against such a simplistic solution of portraying Leverkühn "as if the archsinner had his salvation already in his pocket" (Voss 198). It is only the last tone of *The Lamentation of Doctor Faustus* that provides, in the words of the unreliable narrator, a faint promise of "hope beyond hopelessness, the transcendence of despair" (DF 515; GW 6: 651).

Thomas Mann designed his *Doctor Faustus* as an allegory of German history of the twentieth century. The dates of events in Leverkühn's life corresponded with critical moments in German history: his syphilitic infection in 1905 parallels the rise of Wilhelmine imperialism; the devil's pact takes place shortly before the outbreak of World War I; Leverkühn's collapse occurs in 1930, when the Nazi party became powerful in German politics; and his death takes place in 1940, one year after the beginning of World War II (Cobley 159–65; Robertson 142–44). With his speech "Germany and the Germans" Mann had explicitly endorsed such a reading, especially when he identified Germany with musicality and Faust and said that in May 1945, Germany was "literally being carried off by the Devil" (*Germany and the Germans* 5). In the novel, the narrator says on the last page that "Germany, . . . in the embrace of demons, a hand over one eye, with the other staring into the horror, was [plummeting] from despair to despair. When will it reach the bottom of the abyss?" (DF 534; GW 6: 676). But numerous critics pointed out that the allegory did not work. Even Thomas Mann seemed to abandon the allegorical reading of his novel when public criticism of his work began to haunt him. But his allegory of Germany was to be read as an antinomy, not as the equation Leverkühn = Germany. The antinomy of the allegory meant that the allegorical composer was not to be identified with imperialist or fascist Germany or with modernist art as such, but instead to be related dialectically against this background. Most of his critics failed to do so.

Thomas Mann got this idea from Walter Benjamin's book *Origin of the German Play of Mourning (Ursprung des deutschen Trauerspiels)*, which Adorno had given him as a birthday present in 1946 (*Story of a Novel* 187). The book, published in 1928, deals with German baroque tragedy, but it has wider implications for the reevaluation of allegory in modernism. For Mann, Benjamin's analysis of the baroque allegory served as a model for the allegory of Germany in *Doctor Faustus*. Under the subtitle "Antinomies of Allegory," Benjamin discusses the dialectical interpretation of modern allegory and declares:

> Any person, any object, any relationship can mean absolutely anything else: With this possibility a destructive, but just verdict is passed on the profane world: it is characterized as a world in which the detail is of no

great importance. But it will be unmistakably apparent, especially to anyone who is familiar with allegorical textual exegesis, that all of the things
which are used to signify derive, from the very fact of their pointing to
something else, a power which makes them appear no longer commensu-
rable with profane things, which raises them onto a higher plane, and
which can, indeed, sanctify them. (*Origin of German Tragic Drama* 175)

This concept of the antinomic allegory, as it was developed by Walter
Benjamin, informed Mann's treatment of Adrian Leverkühn and his art.
This treatment put the burden of interpretation on the individual reader,
who had to deal with the unresolved problems of the mythological material of Faust. There is no closure in *Doctor Faustus*. In Adorno and
Horkheimer's terms, however, myth in *Doctor Faustus* becomes history
and "recuperates," as Russell Berman argues, "its original role as enlightenment" (281). Benjamin's concept of the antinomic allegory satisfied a specific need for Mann as a novelist, as it precisely dovetailed
Adorno's idea of the identity of the non-identical that was essential to the
novel.

CHAPTER 11

A "True Modernist"

Arnold Schoenberg

Before Schoenberg was able to read Thomas Mann's new novel *Doctor Faustus*, well-meaning friends—among them Alma Mahler Werfel—told him the bare facts of the plot and informed him especially of the life and death of the protagonist and his method of composing music. Although he had received a personal copy of the German original with a handwritten dedication by the author, Schoenberg probably never read the entire novel because of his failing eyesight, but his assistant, Richard Hoffmann, recorded the sections of the book that dealt with musicology on a Dictaphone (J. Schmidt 163). Schoenberg was neither amused nor flattered because he thought that this fictional account of a modernist composer's career in Germany was a misappropriation of his intellectual property. In addition, he argued that the novel cast doubt on his own life and work. As Schoenberg argued in a public letter, "Leverkühn is depicted, from the beginning to end, as a lunatic. I am now seventy-four and I am not yet insane, and I have never acquired the disease from which this insanity stems. I consider this an insult, and I might have to draw consequences" (" 'Doctor Faustus' Schoenberg?" 22, reprinted by Carnegy 169).

Schoenberg never complained that the novel seemed to suggest that modern compositions must be demonic if they are to be successful. Most critics took issue with the novel's implicit claim that modern music— Germany's most characteristic art—was doomed to the same fate as the Nazi regime and its followers. Even Michael Mann, the novelist's youngest son, confirmed that the novel seemed to imply that Schoen-

FIGURE 25. Arnold Schoenberg, circa early 1940s (photographer: de Parua).
Photograph courtesy of Arnold Schönberg Center, Vienna.

berg's twelve-tone technique seemed to be related to a sick mind, or even
to National Socialism ("Musical Symbolism" 318).

What needled Schoenberg was that Mann had made his protagonist
the creator of Schoenberg's "method of composing with twelve tones"
(Carnegy 168). He protested first in a private letter to Mann in 1948, and
later in two public statements published by the *Saturday Review of Lit-*

erature and in *Music Survey,* both in 1949. Mann had already advised him that all future editions of the novel would have a postscript that advised the reader that "the form of composition delineated in Chapter XXII, known as the twelve-tone or row system, is in truth the intellectual property of a contemporary composer and theoretician, Arnold Schoenberg" (Lowe-Porter's translation of *Doctor Faustus* 511). Mann explained that he had "transferred this technique in a certain ideational context to the fictitious figure of a musician, the tragic hero of [his] novel," and that "the passages of this book that deal with musical theory are indebted in numerous details to Schoenberg's *Harmonielehre*" (ibid.)

As their private letters indicate, Mann and Schoenberg were reconciled in 1950, and the second public statement, published in *Music Survey,* was actually directed against Adorno rather than Mann (B. Schmidt). The controversy, however, was symptomatic of a problem of modernist literature: the montage of factual and historical data in a work of fiction were acceptable, as long as they were not personal. Individuals do not like to be treated as objects, a lesson that Mann apparently never learned, as other examples of his work demonstrate. Gerhart Hauptmann had not been amused to be used as the model for Mynheer Peeperkorn in *The Magic Mountain (Der Zauberberg).*

Arnold Schoenberg (1874–1951) was among the first of the famous exiles to come to Los Angeles. On March 20, 1933, he resigned as professor of composition at the Prussian Academy of Arts in Berlin. In May 1933 he left Berlin for France and then traveled to the United States in October 1933. Although the composer had converted to Protestantism as early as 1898, in Paris he reconverted to Judaism in July 1933, with Marc Chagall as his witness. His reconversion, which has been interpreted as an act of protest against the persecution of the Jews in Germany, had been brewing for many years. He had been committed to the Jewish cause long before 1933, as is indicated by the titles of some of his compositions, such as *Jacob's Ladder (Die Jakobsleiter)* (1917–22) and *Moses and Aaron (Moses and Aron)* (1930–51). The German title of *Moses and Aron* also revealed Schoenberg's obsession with the number twelve, as he intentionally misspelled the second biblical name in order that the title have twelve letters. In addition to his compositions, Schoenberg also wrote a utopian drama entitled *The Biblical Way (Der biblische Weg),* which advocated the establishment of a Jewish state in Africa. After his conversion in July 1933, Schoenberg occupied himself extensively with the political question of Jewish survival in Europe and wrote a draft platform for a Jewish Unity Party, which later became the basis for his "Four-Point Program for Jewry" of 1938 (Stuckenschmidt 368). This program left no doubt about his commitment, foresight, and militancy. The "four points" of his program were listed in capital letters as introduction and conclusion:

  I.   The fight against anti-Semitism must be stopped.
  II. A united Jewish party must be created.
  III. Unanimity in Jewry must be enforced with all means.
  IV. Ways must be prepared to obtain a place to erect an independent
       Jewish state. (Ringer 230–44; Randol Schoenberg 134–87)

By August 1933 Schoenberg regarded his participation in these efforts as more important than his art, and he wrote to Anton Webern, his friend and student, that he had decided "only to work in the future for the national state of Jewry" (Stuckenschmidt 370). Evidently Schoenberg was not cut out for such activity, and he returned to his music in November 1933, when he began teaching at the Malkin Conservatory in Boston. In December, however, he introduced aspects of his four-point program in speeches before Jewish organizations in Boston. Until the end of his life, Schoenberg was committed to the founding of an independent Jewish state. With great pride and satisfaction he accepted honors that were extended by institutions of the emerging state of Israel, such as the honorary presidency of the Israel Academy of Music.

Schoenberg and his family moved to California primarily for reasons related to his health. He taught composition first at the University of Southern California from 1935 to 1936, and then at the University of California, Los Angeles, from 1936 to 1944. In the United States he changed the spelling of his name from Schönberg to Schoenberg not only for pragmatic reasons—American typographers had difficulty with the German umlaut—but also for ideological reasons, to emphasize the fact of his exile. Schoenberg considered Southern California to be heaven: he felt "driven into paradise," as he said in a speech in Hollywood in October 1934. In contrast to the biblical snake that was driven out of paradise, he had arrived in a country where he did not have to crawl on his belly and eat dust all the days of his life: "Neither dust nor better food is rationed and . . . I am allowed to go on my feet, . . . my head can be erect, . . . kindness and cheerfulness is dominating, and . . . to live is a joy and to be an expatriate of another country is the grace of God" (*Style and Idea* 502).

To be sure, Schoenberg did not maintain this optimistic perspective throughout his stay in the United States, but he credited his long and pro-

FIGURE 26. Arnold Schoenberg's house, 116 North Rockingham Avenue,
Brentwood, 2005. Photograph by Juergen Nogai, Santa Monica.

ductive life to California's climate and ambience. He enjoyed playing ten-
nis with members of his family and new friends, among them George
Gershwin. In May 1937 his son Ronald was born, and in 1941 his second son, Lawrence, arrived.

In 1936 Schoenberg moved with his family to 116 North Rockingham
Avenue in Brentwood, not far from the campus of UCLA, where he was
a highly respected teacher. He devoted a great amount of time not only
to teaching, but also to the writing of textbooks on counterpoint, harmony, and composition. To the surprise of his students he did not teach
his twelve-tone method of composition, preferring to analyze the classics, from Johann Sebastian Bach to Johannes Brahms. In 1941 he became a U.S. citizen, and in 1944 he retired from UCLA. He continued to
compose until his death in 1951, and he continued teaching as well, as
he was forced to give private lessons to supplement his low retirement

income. (Among his private students in America was the avant-garde composer John Cage.) Because of his short tenure at UCLA, his pension amounted to an embarrassingly low sum of $29.60 per month. He once responded to a colleague who had inquired about his financial situation, "Unless I succeed in forcing exploiters of my works, publishers, performers, etc., to pay what they owe me, I would have to live on $29.60 with a wife and 3 small children (16, 11, 7). It has often enough occurred that I had for months no other income. There remains still the hope that my works might provide for us" (*Letters* 254). Schoenberg's application to the Guggenheim Foundation in 1945 for a grant that would enable him to devote himself exclusively to his creative work was rejected. At the time, his oratorio *Jacob's Ladder* remained unfinished, while his opera *Moses and Aaron* was complete except for the final act.

Schoenberg had one offer from the movie industry. Accounts vary as to why this offer never developed into a contract. In 1935, Irving Thalberg at Metro-Goldwyn-Mayer contacted Schoenberg about composing the music for the movie version of Pearl S. Buck's novel *The Good Earth*. Schoenberg asked for $50,000 and artistic control of the music. Not a single note was to be changed. The money did not seem to be a problem, but ceding him artistic control evidently was. Like Brecht, Schoenberg tried to justify his involvement with the movie industry as a means of supporting his creative work, as he wrote in a letter to Alma Mahler Werfel on January 23, 1936:

> I almost agreed to write music for a film, but fortunately asked for 50,000 dollars, which likewise fortunately, was much too much, for it would have been the end of me; and the only thing is that if I had somehow survived it, we should have been able to live on it—even if modestly—for a number of years, which would have meant at last being able to finish in my lifetime at least those compositions and theoretical works that I have already begun, even if not beginning any more new things. And for that I should gladly have sacrificed my life and even my reputation. (Stuckenschmidt 412–13)

Schoenberg was aware that working for Hollywood would inspire the contempt of his peers, yet, like Bertolt Brecht, he was tempted by the prospect of financial security and free time for working on his unfinished compositions.

From the beginning of his career, Schoenberg's modernist music was associated with isolation from the general audience. This isolation, which was characteristic of European modernism, was manifest in not only music but the other arts as well. It was evidenced by the secessionist art exhibitions in Paris, Berlin, Munich, and Vienna, and by the existence of private nonprofit societies such as Die Brücke (The Bridge) in Dresden and Der Blaue Reiter (The Blue Rider) in Munich, groups of Expressionist painters that enrolled members to support private exhibitions, the sale of original prints and paintings, and the publication of art magazines. Modernist literature was supported by similar special interest groups, like the Stefan George Circle, by journals such as *Der Sturm* (The Storm) and *Die Aktion* (The Action), and by small publishing houses such as Der jüngste Tag (The Youngest Day), which published Franz Kafka's short stories. Modernist poetry was recited at private readings before select audiences in private homes or special coffeehouses in Berlin, Munich, Vienna, and Zurich.

Similarly, private societies were founded to supply modernist composers with a receptive audience. Modernist music performed publicly frequently met with protest, which provided welcome publicity. Many of the premiers of Schoenberg's music in Vienna from 1902 to 1913 had resulted in publicity scandals that contributed to his fame. But such scandals proved counterproductive in the long run. For this reason, Schoenberg had instituted "private concerts" to protect his music from the demands of the public at large.

Twice, in 1904 and in 1918, Schoenberg founded private societies for the performance of modern music. The Verein der schaffenden Tonkünstler (The Society of Creative Composers) of 1904 attempted to reach a sizable and sympathetic audience by providing a location for the performance of modern music and informing the public about the state of the art. In 1918 Schoenberg went a step further when he founded the Verein für musikalische Privataufführungen (The Society for Private Musical Performances), which was open only to experts and supporters. The goal was not to win a larger audience, but rather to exclude it. Journalists and critics were not admitted, and neither applause or nor displays of displeasure were permitted. The program was not published before the concert in order to prevent selective attendance. The president of the society was Schoenberg himself, whose term of office was not limited and who had full authority in the direction of the organization (Smith 251). This elitist disregard of the audience at large can be described as "public isolation" (Dümling 164–67, 252–60). Positively speaking, the organization enabled the artists' emancipation from the culture industry, as Theodor W. Adorno was to describe it in *Dialectic of Enlightenment* in the 1940s. The modernist artist took possession of the means of production and kept them under his control. He kept his art independent from the consumer so that it did not become a commodity, as traditional art in modern society did. Negatively speaking, Schoenberg's society of 1918 was elitist and self-admiring.

This particular dilemma of modernism—its elitist self-isolation from society—was well recognized by its followers and its opponents. As early as 1923 Franz Werfel raised this subject in his Verdi novel, in which he introduces a fictitious composer, Mathias Fischböck, who declares that he composes neither for his age nor for posterity: "I simply realize in my compositions the essence of music," he said. "What the world does, or fails to do, with it, does not concern me" (*Verdi* 329–30). Werfel had modeled this figure on the Austrian composer Joseph Matthias Hauer (1883–1959), who, independently of Arnold Schoenberg, had developed a twelve-tone system. Werfel's novel was an indictment of modernism in favor of popular art and has rightly been criticized as a reversal in Werfel's career as a modernist, especially in view of the fact that Giuseppe Verdi was a much more sophisticated composer than Werfel would have his readers believe. But Thomas Mann also placed this dilemma of modernist art at the center of his novel *Doctor Faustus* of 1947, with the exception, however, that he considered it an inevitable historical development, as discussed in the previous chapter.

In the 1940s it became evident to the Weimar exiles that modernism had to develop an art that made no compromises yet was still able to reach society. This was the goal of modernist art in exile. It is in this domain that one can see what Schoenberg had in common with Bertolt Brecht, Alfred Döblin, Thomas Mann, and Franz Werfel, even if they had differing opinions about the forms of aesthetic experimentation or the means of reaching an audience. The task of reaching out to an audience without making compromises was easier in the 1940s than it had been during the 1920s, as the modernist exiles now had a political agenda in common, regardless of whether they were conservative or radical: the defeat of German fascism in Europe.

Schoenberg appears to have demonstrated a different attitude toward his audience while in exile than he had when in Europe, and a great number of his exile compositions were informed by a concern to obtain a wider audience than before without making concessions to public taste. Schoenberg showed a certain testiness about the infrequent performance of his works in Los Angeles and the United States in general. This attitude should be attributed not only to his need for recognition, fame, and money—although money must have been a concern for any exile with a large family and a small retirement salary—but also to his need to address a wider audience with his music. In November 1934 Schoenberg refused to attend a banquet in honor of Otto Klemperer, who had been appointed conductor of the Los Angeles Philharmonic, because he believed that the orchestra had been suppressing his works in Los Angeles for the last twenty-five years (*Letters* 192).

Schoenberg was sometimes "very disappointed" not to find society interested in his music, nor to find an appreciation for what he was doing to promote "the future state of musical culture" in Los Angeles. Although he was confident that his work would constitute an important chapter in the musical history of Los Angeles, Schoenberg did not hesitate to enlist people to create, as he said, "propaganda for his work in favour of the musical culture of Los Angeles" (*Letters* 196). On the occasion of a performance of his four string quartets at Royce Hall at the University of California, Los Angeles, in early 1937, he complained about the lack of publicity (*Letters* 200). Concluding that his music was "almost totally unknown in America," Schoenberg declared in 1949 that he would make it his task "to take every chance of enabling people to hear some of it." Even if the records made of his music were bad, he expressed satisfaction "that the largest possible number of people get to know at least that part of [his] work" (*Letters* 268). These letters indicate a complete reversal of his former elitist attitude toward his audience and demonstrate that he was approaching what Adorno considered one of the negative aspects of mass culture.

Of Schoenberg's works composed in exile, three stand out for combining the direct address of his new audience with his uncompromising method of modernist composition: the *Kol Nidre*, opus 39, of 1938, *Ode to Napoleon Buonaparte*, opus 41, of 1942, and *A Survivor from Warsaw*, opus 46, of 1947. It is noteworthy that Schoenberg did not compose for his private satisfaction. As he stated in a theoretical essay of 1937, he had to express "what was [historically] necessary to be expressed," and he knew that he "had the duty of developing [his] ideas for the sake of progress in music, whether he liked it or not" (*Style and Idea* 53). This concept of the historical necessity of the progress of art made Schoenberg attractive to Adorno. The Schoenberg chapter of *Philosophy of Modern Music*, which was written before Adorno came to Los Angeles and was published, together with the later Stravinsky chapter, in West Germany in 1949, was based on the same insight. It is extremely ironic that Schoenberg disliked Adorno and his analysis of modern music to such a degree that the major estrangement between Schoenberg and Thomas Mann was in part caused by Adorno's analysis of modern music and its influence on

the conception of *Doctor Faustus* (Stuckenschmidt 495, 508). Schoenberg sarcastically dismissed Adorno's contribution as "Leverkühn's
Twelve-Note Goulash" ("Further to the Schoenberg-Mann Controversy" 78).

The *Kol Nidre*, for speaker, mixed chorus, and orchestra, is based on
the traditional liturgy of the evening before Yom Kippur, the day of
atonement, the holiest Jewish holiday. The "Kol Nidre" (All Vows) deals
with the annulment of oaths and promises. As Steven J. Cahn explains
the significance of the service,

> *Yom Kippur* is associated with Israel's repentance for the sin of wor-
> shipping the golden calf and God's subsequent forgiveness of Israel for
> this sin. This act of forgiveness becomes manifest as Moses descends
> from Mount Sinai bearing the second tablets of the law marking the
> first *Yom Kippur*. The "Kol Nidre" service ushers in the evening service
> for *Yom Kippur*. It begins while there is still daylight, thus creating a
> bridge to the holy day of prayer and fasting that is about to begin.
> (Cahn 205)

Situating the "Kol Nidre" service within the history of the American
Jewish community, Cahn found that it had become controversial by the
1930s. As Schoenberg explained, "Nobody could understand why Jews
should be allowed to make oaths and vows and promises which they
could consider as null and void. No sincere, no honest man could understand such an attitude" (*Schoenberg Reader* 282). There was a movement among American Jews to drop the "Kol Nidre" from the Yom Kippur service because it was not mentioned in the Talmud or the Bible and
its text was considered out of date and out of place. However, the principal melodies of the "Kol Nidre" were so dear even to secular Jews that
the Central Conference of American Rabbis decided to keep the melodies
without the text. According to Stephen J. Cahn, Schoenberg's *Kol Nidre*
was an attempt to find "a creative solution to the embattled 'Kol Nidre'
at a time when the American Jewish Community had an urgent need to
coalesce culturally, religiously, and politically" (204). Schoenberg provided historical justification for the text when he referred to the oppression of Jews during the Spanish Inquisition:

> I assume that at the time when these words were spoken the first time,
> everybody understood them perfectly. Whenever under pressure of per-
> secution a Jew was forced to make oaths, vows, and promises counter

to his inherited belief in our religious principles, he was allowed to repent them and to declare them null and void. Thus he was allowed to pray with the community as a Jew among Jews. This seems to me the very idea of atonement: purgation through repentance. (*Schoenberg Reader* 282)

Schoenberg found a collaborator for rewriting the text in Rabbi Dr. Jacob Sonderling of the Fairfax Temple in Los Angeles, who also commissioned the work. It is noteworthy that this composition addressed the congregation of a synagogue, an audience that was not predisposed toward modernist music. The work was conceived not only for use in religious services, however, but also was intended to have universal appeal for a secular audience.

The beginning of the composition is orchestral. The speaker, representing the rabbi, delivers his text in *Sprechstimme,* a half-sung, half-spoken style developed and favored by Schoenberg for concert presentations, as for example in *Pierrot Lunaire,* opus 21, of 1912:

Rabbi: The Kabbalah tells a legend:
At the beginning God said: "LET THERE BE LIGHT."
Out of space a flame burst out.
God crushed that light to atoms.
Myriads of sparks are hidden in our world, but
Not all of us behold them.
The self-glorious, who walks arrogantly upright,
Will never perceive one;
But the meek and modest, eyes downcast, He sees it.
"All light is sown for the pious."

Only after this kabbalistic narrative about the divine creation of light does the speaker assume the rabbi's liturgical function in response to the choir:

Rabbi: All vows, oaths, promises and plights of any kind,
Wherewith we pledged ourselves
Counter to our inherited faith in God,
Who is One, Everlasting, Unseen, Unfathomable,
We declare these null and void.

We repent that these obligations have estranged
Us from the sacred task we were chosen for.

Choir: We repent.

Rabbi: We repent.

We shall strive from this Day of Atonement till the next
To avoid such and similar obligations,
So that the Yom Kippur to follow
May come to us for good.

Schoenberg himself considered the *Kol Nidre* to be "very effective both in the synagogue and in the concert hall" (*Letters* 213). The work was premiered on Yom Kippur on October 4, 1938, under Schoenberg's direction. The performance, however, was not in a synagogue but in a concert hall. The composition was never accepted into the liturgy because its orchestration was too lavish.

Rabbi Sonderling, who was an exile from Germany himself, selected Schoenberg as composer because he thought that as a Viennese Jew Schoenberg faced the future with courage and had "perfected an individual idiom" that had universal appeal (Sonderling, cited by Cahn 206). The new text (see Appendix III of this voume) was a collaborative effort by Sonderling and Schoenberg that combined modern concerns with the traditional function of the "Kol Nidre." Cahn, who attributed most of the changes to Sonderling, listed as significant innovations the incorporation of the kabbalistic legend of the creation of light at the beginning, the use of English rather than Aramaic, and the introduction of the "sacred task" or mission of Israel (209).

Schoenberg proceeded in a similar fashion as Rabbi Sonderling; he did not change the familiar liturgical melody, but rather subjected it to his method of composition, eliminating the sentimentality that the melody had acquired in previous adaptations by Max Bruch, among others. Schoenberg thus transformed the tonality of a familiar melody according to his method without sacrificing its liturgical tradition. This dialectical procedure confused many of his critics, who had difficulty classifying *Kol Nidre* as either tonal or atonal.

Schoenberg's *Ode for Napoleon Buonaparte*, opus 41, for string quartet, piano, and speaker, was based on a poem with the same title by Lord Byron, who wrote it when he heard the news of the emperor's abdication at Fontainebleau in 1814, after his defeat in Russia and in the battle of Leipzig (see Appendix IV). The ode, consisting of nineteen nine-line rhymed stanzas, employs the rhetoric of public denouncement to ex-

press the poet's contempt for his former hero, who had abused his power
and become a despicable tyrant:

> 'Tis done—but yesterday a King!
>   And armed with Kings to strive—
> And now thou art a nameless thing:
>   So abject—yet alive!
> Is this the man of thousand thrones,
> Who strew'd our earth with hostile bones,
>   And can he thus survive?
> Since he, miscalled the Morning Star,
> Nor man nor fiend hath fallen so far.

Byron introduced examples from the biblical and classical traditions
as well as from world history to characterize Napoleon's despotic rule
and celebrate his deserved fall from power. Modern audiences needed
explanations to understand the typological allusions that are listed here
according to their provenance and occurrence within the poem by the
number of the stanza in Roman numerals:

Bible: "Morning Star," reference to Lucifer and his fall (I), the overthrow of
    the king of Babylon (XV);
Classical tradition: death of Milo of Crotona (VI), Prometheus (IX), Diony-
    sios II of Syracuse, banished to Corinth (XIV), Prometheus (XVI);
History: abdication of the Roman dictator Sulla, 138–78 B.C. (VII), abdica-
    tion of Emperor Charles V, 1500–1558 A.D. (VIII), the despotism of
    Tamerlane, ruler of the Mongols, 1336–1405 A.D. (XV).

From March to June 1942 Schoenberg set the complete English text of the
poem to music. The text is delivered by a narrator in *Sprechstimme*, with ac-
companiment by piano and string quartet. The whole work was composed
according to Schoenberg's twelve-tone method, but there were tonal references to familiar works such as Beethoven's Fifth Symphony and "La Marseillaise," the song of freedom of the French Revolution. Some critics noticed that the last stanza ended with an unusual cadence in E-flat major, the
key of Beethoven's Third Symphony. Charles Rosen called it "a deliberate
quotation, a reference to that other great 'Napoleonic work,'" the "Eroica"
(93), reminding the audience of the composer's original dedication and his
change of mind, like Lord Byron's, caused by Napoleon's tyrannical rule.

The events of December 1941—the attack on Pearl Harbor and the
declaration of war—obviously influenced this composition. As Leonard
Stein, Schoenberg's assistant at UCLA, recalled, he had spent the afternoon of December 7 at Schoenberg's home discussing with him the im-

plications of the bombing of Pearl Harbor: "The next day we heard Roosevelt's 'day of infamy' speech, declaring war on Japan, broadcast in Royce Hall at UCLA. Perhaps it was at that moment that Schoenberg conceived the idea for what was to be his first musical statement on the war" (Stein 53). It was Stein who brought the text of Byron's poem to Schoenberg's attention in a local bookstore in Westwood. The parallels between Napoleon and Hitler had been explored by some German exile dramatists before, but Byron's poem made these parallels especially obvious in terms of the ethical and religious dimensions involved. These dimensions were also elements of Schoenberg's speculations on Nazi philosophy. He explained that he was extremely puzzled by "the relationship of the valueless individual being's life in respect to the totality of the community, or its representative: . . . the Führer. I could not see why a whole generation . . . of Germans should live only in order to produce another generation of the same sort, which on their part should also fulfill only the same task: to keep the race alive" (*Schoenberg Reader* 291).

He recognized that "all the sacrifices of the German *Herrenvolk* [master race] would not make sense, without a goal of world domination" (ibid. 291). Byron's poem condemned Napoleon as a scourge of God and reminded Schoenberg of the crimes against humanity by Hitler. The League of Composers had commissioned him to write a piece of chamber music for their concert season with the request that it employ only a limited number of instruments. As Schoenberg recalled, he at once had the idea "that this piece must not ignore the agitation aroused against the crimes that provoke[d] this war." He knew that "it was the moral duty of the intelligentsia to take a stand against tyranny" (*Schoenberg Reader* 291):

> Ill-minded man, why scourge thy kind
>   Who bow'd so low the knee?
> By gazing on thyself grown blind,
>   Thou taught'st the rest to see.
> With might unquestion'd,—power to save,—
> Thine only gift has been the grave
>   To those that worshipped thee;
> Nor till thy fall could mortals guess
> Ambitions less than littleness!

In the fourth stanza, with its reference to the "earthquake voice of Victory," Schoenberg inserted tonal material from Beethoven's Fifth Symphony and "La Marseillaise" to allude to freedom in the musical tradition:

The triumph, and the vanity,
　　The rapture of the strife—
The earthquake voice of Victory,
　　To thee the breath of life;
The sword, the scepter, and that sway
Which man seem'd made but to obey
　　Wherewith renown was rife—
All quell'd! Dark Spirit! What must be
The madness of thy memory!

For Schoenberg, Byron's poem even alluded to his former home country when it addressed "Austria's mournful flower." The original metaphor referred to Napoleon's second wife, Marie-Louise of Habsburg (1791–1847), whom he had married to gain access to one of the royal families in Europe and to establish the legitimacy of his rule as Emperor of France:

And she, proud Austria's mournful flower,
　　Thy still imperial bride;
How bears her breast the torturing hour?
　　Still clings she to thy side?
Must she too bend, must she too share
Thy late repentance, long despair,
　　Thou throneless Homicide?
If she still loves thee, hoard that gem,
'Tis worth thy vanished diadem!

Byron's metaphor of 1814 gained a new, poignant meaning within the context of the *Anschluss*. Annexed after the Nazi invasion of March 1938, Austria and its population, like the Austrian princess wed to Napoleon I in 1810, had to share the fate of Germany and its dictator.

The last stanza introduced the figure of George Washington as an exception, a modern Cincinnatus, referring to the proverbial patriot of Roman history who became a dictator to defend Rome against foreign armies, but resigned his dictatorship and returned to his farm as soon as the enemies were defeated:

Where may the wearied eye repose
　　When gazing on the Great:
Where neither guilty glory glows,
　　Nor despicable state?
Yes—one—the first—the last—the best—
The Cincinnatus of the West,
　　Whom envy dared not hate,
Bequeath'd the name of Washington,
To make man blush there was but one!

As president and commander in chief Washington symbolized the hope of progressive minds at the beginning of the nineteenth century, as did his modern counterpart, Franklin D. Roosevelt, in 1942. Adding a totally new dimension to Lord Byron's ode, which was set to music shortly after the news of the attack on Pearl Harbor, Schoenberg provided a composition that would remind the people of their fight against the new tyrant of the twentieth century. Yet Schoenberg's *Ode to Napoleon* was not a work of political propaganda, resorting to the tonal tradition of Beethoven and "La Marseillaise" in order to influence its audience, as some critics have suggested. It was a work that recalled the past with a difficult text and melody in order to reinterpret the present and the future in a composition that set high standards for the listener (Reich 212).

The third work of this group is *A Survivor from Warsaw*, opus 46, for narrator, male chorus, and orchestra (see Appendix V). The work's composition was prompted by the life histories of survivors from the Warsaw Ghetto Uprising of April 19, 1943. The text, written by Schoenberg and assigned to the narrator of the oratorio, was a condensed version of eyewitness accounts of the brutal suppression of the uprising, but the composer expanded the narrative to include scenes from extermination camps. Details of time and place were obscured in order to emphasize the symbolic character of the event. As David I. Lieberman, who has provided one of the most detailed analyses of Schoenberg's composition, observed, "Reference to Warsaw continues to function, however, as a symbolic reminder of the ghetto uprising. By placing the scene in an unnamed camp, then, Schoenberg gives the narrative a mythic status: through the shown but unnamed concentration camp Holocaust history becomes Holocaust trope" (Lieberman 213). The work was commissioned by the Koussevitzky Music Foundation in Boston, and Schoenberg dedicated it to the memory of Natalie Koussevitzky. He composed *A Survivor from Warsaw* within two weeks in the middle of August 1947. His failing eyesight forced him to work on large sheets of paper, the music later transcribed to regular staff paper to produce a conventional orchestral score.

Most commentators have remarked upon Schoenberg's use of various languages. During the approximately seven minutes of its performance the oratorio employs three different languages, beginning in English, then breaking into German, and finally ending in Hebrew. The linguistic frame is established in English, when the narrator in *Sprechstimme* tries to recollect the past in a stream-of-consciousness sequence:

I cannot remember ev'rything. I must have been unconscious most of the
time.—I remember only the grandiose moment when they all started to
sing, as if prearranged, the old prayer they had neglected for so many
years—the forgotten creed! But I have no recollection how I got to live underground in the sewers of Warsaw for so long a time.

The narrator evokes a scene from the Warsaw Ghetto Uprising in
which prisoners are rounded up to be transported to a German extermination camp:

The day began as usual: Reveille when it still was dark. Get out!
Whether you slept or whether worries kept you awake the whole night.
You had been separated from your children, from your wife, from your
parents. You don't know what happened to them—how could you
sleep? . . .
    Get out! The sergeant will be furious! They came out; some very slow:
the old ones, the sick ones; some with nervous agility. They fear the sergeant. They hurry as much as they can. In vain! Much too much noise,
much too much commotion—and not fast enough!

A shrill voice in German with the characteristic vulgarisms of the Berlin
dialect that Schoenberg knew from his stay in the German capital breaks
in upon the narrator's presentation in English, shouting an order that the
inmates be lined up and counted:

Achtung! Stilljestanden! Na wirds mal! Oder soll ich mit dem Jewehrkolben nachhelfen? Na jutt; wenn ihrs durchaus haben wollt!

[Stand at attention! Hurry up! Or do you want to feel the butt of my gun?
Okay, you have asked for it!]

The linguistic signifiers of the Berlin dialect are the substitution of con-
sonants in the following three words: -jestanden instead of -gestanden,
Jewehr instead of Gewehr, and jutt instead of gut. After beating the Jewish prisoners into submission, the sergeant wants to know how many he
has to send to the gas chamber:

Rascher! Nochmal von vorn anfangen! In einer Minute will ich wissen
wieviele ich zur Gaskammer abliefere! Abzählen!

[Quicker! Start again! In one minute I want to know how many I am going
to deliver to the gas chamber! Number off!].

The speaker reports that the counting started slowly, irregularly. It
was not fast enough. The counting began again, faster and faster, so that
it sounded to the narrator "like a stampede of wild horses." Then, all of
a sudden, silence, and "they all started to sing, as if prearranged, the old
prayer they had neglected for so many years." In an act of defiance and

faith they burst into singing the "Shema Yisroel," the old prayer and affirmation of the Jewish faith:

> *Male Choir*
> (*sung in hebrew*): Hear Israel:
>   The Lord our God is one Lord,
>   And you should love the Lord, your God,
>   With all your heart and with all your soul
>   And with all your might.
>   And these words, which I command you today,
>   Shall be in all your heart;
>   And you shall teach them diligently to your children and
>   talk of them
>   When you sit in your house
>   And when you walk along your way,
>   When you lie down and when you rise.

As the sergeant's text established his German identity, "the Hebrew
prayer inevitably points to Jewish identity, and the text of the prayer confirms the latter's absolute, irreconcilable opposition to the former"
(Lieberman 216). While German identity was distilled into savagery,
"Jewish identity, forcefully refusing confinement to the past, [insisted] on
the continuity of human civilization in general and Jewish mission in particular" (Lieberman 216). As Reinhold Brinkmann analyzed the work,
it is, "from the very beginning, directed toward the 'grandiose moment'
where the melody of the old prayer, the 'forgotten creed,' emerges out of
the holocaust and transcends this situation of bestiality and desperation
into a moment of political eschatology. The work ends with the hymn-
like prayer, sung in unison, and does not return to the narration"
("Schoenberg the Contemporary," 212). Brinkmann does not hesitate to
use the term *Durchbruch* (breakthrough) from Thomas Mann's account
of Leverkühn's career. He calls the composition a *Durchbruch* "with a
new and precise goal and statement. . . . Schoenberg takes the position
of the victim who will be victor" (ibid. 212).

Research has shown that the "Shema Yisroel" used as the final chorus in Schoenberg's work follows a "similar melodic contour" of traditional chants (Heller 69–74). The similarities are clearly audible to the
trained ear, but even a non-Jewish listener would realize that this composition in the twelve-tone method is based on a traditional liturgical
melody that transcends the historical event in a most powerful fashion.
Lieberman describes the dialectics of the musical composition that put

the survivor's narrative in opposition to the setting of the Hebrew prayer. The first part of the composition invoked a musical style that Schoenberg "had rejected as an artistic dead-end nearly thirty years earlier," while the latter part developed "a melodic line comprised of several statements of the serial row" (Lieberman 217–18). Schoenberg achieved a final synthesis by using "the melodic half-step, previously symbolic of the Jews' suffering," as "the foundation of their collective prayer" (218). Lieberman concluded, "it would be difficult to imagine a more compelling musical realization of Schoenberg's conviction that Jewish belief and Jewish suffering are intimately connected" (218).

There are numerous reports that members of the audience were moved to tears after hearing the work performed for the first time, and "others were so shocked that they could not even speak" (René Leibowitz, quoted by Reich 223). At the work's premiere by the Albuquerque Civic Symphony Orchestra in New Mexico on November 4, 1948, the audience demanded to hear the work again and the conductor and his ensemble complied: the entire composition was repeated. Similar reactions were reported from the European premiere in Paris in 1950.

It was left to Theodor W. Adorno to provide some tortuous comments on *A Survivor from Warsaw*. He praised the music of the concluding chorus "as the protest of mankind against myth" and argued that in this piece Schoenberg had suspended "the aesthetic sphere through the recollection of experiences which are inaccessible to art. Anxiety, Schoenberg's expressive core, identifies itself with the terror of men in the agonies of death, under total domination. . . . Horror has never rung as true in music, and by articulating it music regains its redeeming power through negation" ("Arnold Schoenberg, 1874–1951" 172). But later Adorno became concerned about the overwhelming aesthetic effect of the music, which appeared to undermine the terror of the men who were suffering the "agonies of death." He was afraid that "the victims are turned into works of art, tossed out to be gobbled up by the world that did them in. The so-called artistic rendering of the naked physical pain of those who were beaten down with rifle butts contains, however distantly, the possibility that pleasure can be squeezed from it" ("Commitment" 88).

Concerned that the solemn prayer sung at the end render suffering meaningful, Adorno identifies the aporia: "the unthinkable" of the Holocaust is made "to appear to have had some meaning." It became "transfigured, something of its horror removed" (ibid.). Adorno felt that "an injustice is done the victims, yet no art that avoided the victims could

stand up to the demands of justice" (ibid.). Yet, at the very moment when
art gives voice to their cries of desperation, it runs the risk of replacing
suffering with aesthetic affirmation. Adorno concludes with an attack on
the West German culture industry of the 1960s, arguing that "when even
genocide becomes cultural property . . . , it becomes easier to continue
complying with the culture that gave rise to the murder" ("Commitment" 88).

Schoenberg's commitment to Judaism, especially evident in his choral
music written in exile, raises the question of the "regress to mythology"
(DE 20) that has been associated with Alfred Döblin's and Franz Werfel's return to religion and their abandonment of modernism. But while
the works of Döblin and Werfel attempted to combat materialism and
atheism and to convert their readers to a life of faith, Schoenberg's music
uses Judaism in a commemorative function; history is used to elucidate
religion. Schoenberg searched for a historical explanation of the text of
the "Kol Nidre," which he found in its origin during the Spanish Inquisition. Only then did it make sense to him to set this text to music, combining traditional liturgy with modernism. The composition itself was
designed not exclusively for the synagogue, but also for the concert hall.
Similar motivations applied to *A Survivor from Warsaw*. The main reason for composing the oratorio was the commemoration of Jewish identity during a period of persecution. History served as enlightenment, not
as mythology. The nonclosure provided an unceasing reminder to future
listeners.

Schoenberg's instrumental music during this period follows a pattern
similar to that of his choral compositions: twelve-tone constructivism
is combined with tonal expressiveness. Most critics misunderstand the
dialectics of his compositions, characterizing this new combination as
alternating between two styles, "between the old and the new style,"
as Michael H. Kater puts it (192). He lists Schoenberg's works according to their tonal or atonal mold, placing into the first category the
String Quartet Concerto after Handel, the Suite for String Orchestra
that was not assigned an opus number, the Second Chamber Symphony, opus 38, the D minor Variations on a Recitative, opus 40, and
the Variations for Wind Band, opus 43A. Only the Violin Concerto,
opus 36, and the String Quartet No. 4, opus 37, qualify as serial compositions, according to Kater (192–93). The Piano Concerto, opus 42,
is characterized as a "serial work 'with quasi-tonal leanings'" (193).
These classifications are not necessarily correct, but even among musi-
cologists there is confusion about the tonal or atonal quality of some

of Schoenberg's compositions in exile. While Dieter Schnebel interprets them as "re-tonal" (Dahlhaus 161) and Jost Hermand speaks of "classicism" (110), Ethan Haimo finds his late twelve-tone compositions characterized by "the unabashed willingness to try to interleave elements of tonal syntax into the context of a twelve-tone serial composition" (175).

It was Adorno who coined the term "late style" *(Spätstil)* for Beethoven's late string quartets. He applied this term as well to Schoenberg's work in exile. Although the composer himself rejected Adorno's interpretation of his music, it is a useful term for understanding Schoenberg's dialectical combination of new expressiveness within the constraints of the twelve-tone method after 1933. This new expressiveness is related to the vision of a new world order after World War II that is communicated with the aid of a method that is based on formal experimentation. It is a return to modernism on a level that is higher than that of the 1920s, and an attempt to address the dilemma of isolation from a larger audience with a choice of topics that were central to the interests of mankind: the defeat of tyrants and the Holocaust. But even in his *Spätstil,* Schoenberg never went easy on his audience. It takes a trained ear to hear the ironic references to traditional motifs and melodies. With a few exceptions, such as Carl Dahlhaus and Hans Heinz Stuckenschmidt, European critics neglected Schoenberg's work in exile and relegated it to *engagierte Musik,* that is, music engaged in political and religious topics and that was not worth serious discussion. It took until 2001, when the first symposium on Schoenberg in America took place in Vienna, for this perception of the late Schoenberg to be corrected, although this reassessment was not by shared by all the symposium participants (see *Schoenberg in America*). His late music is perhaps the best example of the crisis of modernism and its renewal in exile.

Comparing Schoenberg to his fellow exiles, one can observe that Bertolt Brecht and Alfred Döblin likewise stayed the course of artistic experimentation and did not abandon their social visions. Döblin is perhaps more difficult to compare to Schoenberg because Döblin's life and work in Los Angeles must be placed at the conservative end of the spectrum of exile culture. Although Schoenberg and Döblin were fellow members of the Prussian Academy of Arts in Berlin, there is no record of close contact between the two in Los Angeles. Politically Schoenberg was a conservative, favoring the monarchy, and as a naturalized citizen he decided that he had "no right to participate in the politics of the natives" *(Style and Idea* 506). But this conservatism did not show in his music, whereas the religious closure of Döblin's novel *Karl and Rosa,* which reflected the author's conversion, put his previous experiments with the form of the novel into question.

In contrast, Brecht refined his theory and practice of modernist theater in exile. Schoenberg was familiar with Brecht's concept of epic theater or epic opera, from the latter's work in Berlin at the end of the 1920s. Brecht's *Short Organum for the Theater,* written in exile, fulfilled a function similar to that of Schoenberg's "Composition with Twelve Tones" of 1941. Both artists laid down the essentials of their craft in these short treatises. In July 1942, Brecht visited one of Schoenberg's lectures on composition, and in his diary he expressed his admiration for Schoenberg as a master craftsman, emphasizing his intellectual approach to music. Like Schoenberg, Brecht wanted to reach his audience in exile, and like Schoenberg he refused to make compromises to traditional expectations or demands (with the exception of his work for the movie industry). The production of his *Galileo,* based on the staging principles of the epic theater, did not endear him to his conservative critics, but Brecht held on to his principles of experimentation on the stage. The Los Angeles production became the model for the staging of the German version by the Berliner Ensemble in 1957.

A comparison of Schoenberg with Werfel is unnecessary because the latter's concessions to conventionality were obvious. Schoenberg must have realized that Werfel's *Song of Bernadette* was as far from modernism as anything could be, but this did not prevent him from counting Werfel and his wife Alma among his close circle of friends in Los Angeles (he knew them from his time in Vienna before World War I). It is doubtful whether Schoenberg read Werfel's last novel, *Star of the Unborn* (1946), and thus realized that it signaled a return to modernism, because his poor eyesight prevented him from reading longer texts by that time.

A comparison between Thomas Mann and Schoenberg yields different results. They were on friendly terms in Los Angeles. Many entries in Mann's diary record invitations to dinner and Viennese coffee at the Schoenbergs. Before 1933 they had been in contact on numerous occasions. Both were members of the Prussian Academy of Arts in Berlin, and both resigned in protest. But while Schoenberg had been a modernist in the 1920s, in this period Mann had still followed the models of the great novelists of the nineteenth century, with considerable success. In 1929 he was awarded the Nobel Prize for Literature, primarily as a result of his novel *Buddenbrooks* of 1901. During his California exile, however, Mann developed into a veritable modernist, especially in his novel *Doc-*

tor *Faustus* of 1947. It was to be, as Mann said, "a novel to end all novels," comparing it to James Joyce's famous modernist novel *Ulysses* (*Story of a Novel* 91). Whether Mann's novel ever fulfilled this promise is another question. He definitely experimented in the spirit of modernism and had none other than Theodor W. Adorno as his "privy councillor" in matters of modernism. It is another case of extreme irony that this modernist novel should be the cause for the infamous controversy and two-year estrangement between Schoenberg and Mann during the late 1940s.

In addition to complaining that his method of composition had been plagiarized in *Doctor Faustus*, Schoenberg considered the portrayal of the novel's protagonist an attack on his personal integrity, "since he was neither diseased nor mad, as Mann's character was" (Reiff 102). In defense of Mann, it must be emphasized that the model for Leverkühn was Nietzsche and not Schoenberg. But Mann had raised the issue of modernist art, in this case modernist music. In this respect, Thomas Mann's fictional composer had more in common with Schoenberg and the dilemma of modernist music than has been realized. As a composer, Adrian Leverkühn goes through the same phases of development as Schoenberg did. His dilemma is that in his striving for modernism he is forced to compose music that appeals to an ever-smaller audience. He becomes aware that he may finally reach a point where experimentation results in obscurity and communication with an audience ceases to exist. Leverkühn realizes that, for his century, "an art without suffering, psychologically healthy, that confides without solemnity, . . . an art that is on a first-name basis with humanity," is no longer an option (*Doctor Faustus* 339; GW 6: 429). An art with "stable warmth, "cow warmth," as he calls it (ibid. 76; GW 6: 94), has not only become impossible, but it needs to be renounced. Leverkühn intends to take back Beethoven's Ninth Symphony and its optimistic message. His last work, entitled *The Lamentation of Doctor Faustus,* is explicitly presented as an "Ode to Sorrow," a negative counterpart to Schiller's "Ode to Joy," which Beethoven put to music in the final chorus of his Ninth Symphony. There can be no doubt that *The Lamentation of Doctor Faustus* was conceived as a work of *Spätstil,* as Adorno had defined it. It shows a similar combination of extreme calculation and pure expressiveness.

Now it becomes obvious that Adrian Leverkühn's *Lamentation of Doctor Faustus* was not intended to disparage Schoenberg and his music but to praise them. Thomas Mann's novel was perhaps conceived as an homage to Schoenberg and to modernism. This interpretation makes

sense when we realize that in January 1948 Thomas Mann presented
Schoenberg with a copy of the German version of *Doctor Faustus* that
contained the following handwritten dedication:

> Arnold Schönberg,
> dem *Eigentlichen,* [the *true one,*]
> mit ergebenem Gruss [with sincere greetings]
> Pacific Palisades
> 15 Januar 1948 Thomas Mann. (Nono-Schoenberg, No. 1390)

Dem Eigentlichen is a characteristically German adjectival construction
that implies a noun that is not supplied. *Dem Eigentlichen* translates literally as "the real one" or "the true one." To suggest the noun that needs
to be supplied is the purpose of this chapter and will perhaps answer
some of the questions raised by this book. It is my contention that Adrian
Leverkühn is not identical with Schoenberg, but instead a negative counterfigure to the composer. Leverkühn had a "breakthrough" at the end
of his life, but he had to pay for it with his death, while his home country was plunging into hell. With his personal inscription to the composer,
I argue that Thomas Mann intended *dem Eigentlichen* to mean, as he
said in his letter to the *Saturday Review,* "Not Leverkühn is the hero of
this musical era, you [Arnold Schoenberg] are its hero." As Reinhold
Brinkmann confirms:

> [Schoenberg] is not "Adrian Leverkühn": he doesn't take back the 9th
> Symphony [see Thomas Mann's *Doctor Faustus:* "The good and noble—
> that is not to be. I will take it back, the Ninth Symphony."] We don't have
> the reversal of the ["Ode to Joy"] here, we have a statement of victory . . .
> in the Survivor from Warsaw. ("Denn mit mir ist es ein Hakenkreuz" 222)

Thomas Mann's dedication was, in his own words, "a bow, a compli-
ment" to "the uncompromising and bold artist." He had always addressed the composer "with the utmost respect" (Carnegy 172). *Dem
Eigentlichen* was dedicated to Arnold Schoenberg, the true modernist,
the composer who overcame the crisis of modernism in exile.

The Weimar Legacy
of Los Angeles

Los Angeles is often called a city without historical memory. Critics argue that people came here to escape history. They refer to the fact that most houses are built of wood and stucco and not of stone. According to their observations, the people here read, but only trade journals and magazines. Their shelves are filled with knickknacks and souvenirs rather than books. Most Angelinos allegedly get their political information from television. History for them is a Hollywood set that can easily be changed for the next production in a different country and a different century. These clichés about "Lotusland" and "Tinseltown" are predictable, but they cannot substitute for historical analysis.

It is true that there is no monument to Bertolt Brecht or Thomas Mann in Los Angeles as there is one of Goethe and Schiller in front of the Weimar National Theater. The Weimar legacy of Los Angeles is to a large degree hidden, but it is not difficult to trace. Historians of the twenty-first century are trained to read the city like a palimpsest. I have attempted in this study to identify the artifacts of Weimar culture and assess their influence and staying power, demonstrating that there was a specific exile culture in Los Angeles that revised and modified Weimar modernism to meet the challenges of the period between 1933 and 1958.

This culture did not disappear without a trace. Despite earthquakes, fires, and mud slides, the polemically discredited houses of wood and stucco—especially those designed by Richard Neutra and Rudolph Schindler— have survived remarkably well. Although these two architects did not belong to the exile generation and had developed their California modern style before the first refugees arrived in 1933, their architecture contributed to the visibility of the exiles. The common assumption in Los Angeles was that a modernist architect had to be "a refugee from the Nazi persecutions of the early 1930s" (Banham 179), even if he had arrived earlier and his designs were examples of immigrant modernism. But this misunderstanding paved the way for the recognition of genuine exile modernism in film, literature, music, and philosophy.

The residences of the exiles serve as another reminder of their presence in the 1930s and 1940s. Many of them are still standing and appear to serve their new inhabitants well. With Cornelius Schnauber's guidebook *Hollywood Haven* in hand, the modern historian can identify the residences of Theodor Adorno, Bertolt Brecht, Lion Feuchtwanger, Thomas Mann, Salka Viertel, Franz Werfel, and many others. Mann's residence displays a plaque reminding visitors of the novelist's stay in Pacific Palisades. Feuchtwanger's "castle on the sea," as Thomas Mann called it with an ironic allusion to a poem by Ludwig Uhland, a second-rate Romanticist, is now considered "a city landmark and a cultural monument to German exiles," according to the *Los Angeles Times* of March 20, 2005. The so-called Villa Aurora, owned and supported by the German government and the city of Berlin, now hosts European writers, composers, and filmmakers as artists in residence. Every year the Villa Aurora awards a fellowship for up to twelve months to a writer who is being persecuted or forced to live in exile. This program was created to keep alive the memory of the exiles from Weimar Germany who found sanctuary in Los Angeles.

Like the exiles' residences, the venues where exile theater was produced—the Hollywood Bowl of Max Reinhardt's *Midsummer Night's Dream* in 1934, the El Capitan Theater of Leopold Jessner's *William Tell* in 1939, and the Coronet Theatre of Brecht's and Charles Laughton's *Galileo* in 1947— have not been turned into sports arenas, ice-skating rings, or parking lots, but instead have continued to serve audiences of the twentieth and twenty-first centuries. Schoenberg Hall, on the campus of the University of California, Los Angeles, has reminded generations of faculty and students of the composer's tenure at their institution.

The presence of German exiles shaped the cultural life in Los Angeles, especially in the fields of music, theater, and film. The Hollywood movies that have been shown in retrospectives by the Academy of Motion Picture Arts and Sciences, the American Cinematheque, the local

FIGURE 27. Villa Aurora: Lion and Marta Feuchtwanger's house, 520 Paseo Miramar, Pacific Palisades, 2005. Photograph by Juergen Nogai, Santa Monica.

Goethe Institut, the Los Angeles County Museum of Art, and the UCLA Film and Television Archive have kept alive the memory of the German-speaking film colony. The contributions of the exile film directors to the industry were essential to Hollywood modernism (see Giovacchini 27–35, 45–47).

At the same time, Los Angeles theater developed a format that was similar to German repertory theater. The Mark Taper Forum, under the leadership of Gordon Davidson from 1967 to 2005, is not a commercial enterprise but instead a not-for-profit organization that presented six to eight productions per year. In 1989 the Mark Taper Forum merged with the Ahmanson Theatre at the Music Center, and in 2004 with the Kirk Douglas Theatre in Culver City as the Theatre Center Group of Los Angeles. Even though the actors rotated for each production, the artistic director, administrative staff, and costume shop were permanent. The same is true of the Odyssey Theatre Ensemble in West Los Angeles, which selected a Brecht play to celebrate its thirty-fifth anniversary in 2005. When the Berliner Ensemble came to perform *The Resistible Rise of Arturo Ui* at UCLA in 1999, critics referred to the visit as Brecht's homecoming.

A chamber music series called "Evenings on the Roof" (1939–54), organized by Peter Yates and his wife Frances Mullen, featured Schoenberg's music on a regular basis between 1940 and 1954. In 1948 they put on an all-Schoenberg program. Yates's programming was not unlike that of Schoenberg's Viennese Society for Private Performances, established after World War I (Crawford 282). Yates's series was succeeded by "Monday Evening Concerts" (1954–71), which continued the tradition under the direction of Lawrence Morton. In March 1970 the four Schoenberg string quartets were performed in consecutive programs at the "Monday Evening Concerts" (Crawford 238). The Los Angeles Philharmonic, under music director and conductor Esa-Pekka Salonen, is also dedicated to the performance of works by Schoenberg and other exile composers. Salonen placed Schoenberg's *A Survivor of Warsaw* together with Beethoven's Ninth Symphony on the season's opening program in 2000, indicating by this placement that Schoenberg's oratorio represents the Ninth Symphony of the twentieth century. In 2001–2002 the L.A. Philharmonic's season was dedicated to a four-part series of Schoenberg Prism concerts in memory of the composer. The Los Angeles Opera performed *Moses and Aaron* in 2001.

The critical theory of Theodor W. Adorno and Max Horkheimer was reimported to the United States in the late 1960s, when the students at the University of California at Berkeley, the University of Wisconsin, and Columbia University were searching for a theoretical explanation for their discontent and their opposition to American society and its politics. Leo Lowenthal and Herbert Marcuse, members of the Frankfurt School who stayed in America (Lowenthal at U.C. Berkeley and Marcuse at Brandeis University and then at U.C. San Diego), became the godfathers of the American student revolution. While American philosophy departments were dominated by analytic philosophy, critical theory found its home in departments of English, foreign languages, art history, film studies, and musicology in the 1990s. Although French structuralism and poststructuralist theory became serious competitors, critical theory maintained its position against attacks and opposition. While Peter Uwe Hohendahl questioned in 1991 whether the reception and integration of Adorno's and Horkheimer's works could be called complete, at least most of Adorno's writings—with the exception of his letters and unpublished materials—are now available in English ("Reappraisals" 198).

It is difficult to measure the impact and endurance of the German "mi-

nority literature" (Deleuze and Guattari) in Los Angeles from the 1930s
to the 1950s. However, there was an important witness, Susan Sontag,
who wrote a story of her visit to Thomas Mann's house in Pacific Palisades in 1947 for the *New Yorker* in 1978. As a fourteen-year-old she
had read Mann's *Magic Mountain,* but when her boyfriend called the
Mann house to request a meeting with the famous author and they were
invited for tea, she felt miserable and trapped. Susan Sontag was intim-
idated by the stature of her idol. The title of her story, "Pilgrimage," is
an indication of how the German novelist was revered at that time in the
United States:

> Mann, unlike the other exiles, was also a public presence. To have been as
> officially honored in America as Thomas Mann was in the late nineteen-
> thirties and early nineteen-forties was probably more anomalous than to
> have been the most famous writer in the world. . . . Mann had the stature of
> an oracle in Roosevelt's *bien-pensant* America, proclaiming the absolute evil
> of Hitler's Germany and the coming victory of the democracies. Emigration
> had not dampened his taste, or his talent, for being a representative figure.
> If there was such a thing as a good German, it was now to be found in this
> country (proof of America's goodness), embodied in his person; if there was
> a Great Writer, not at all an American notion of a writer is, it was he. (228)

During their conversation Mann talked mostly about *Doctor Faustus,*
which had been translated into English by Helen Tracy Lowe-Porter
by that time. What Thomas Mann said was not surprising and could
have been gleaned from his essays and *The Genesis of Doctor Faustus.* He mentioned Nietzsche and Schoenberg, revealing that his protagonist was not a philosopher but a composer, and that his composer's music was not like Wagner's music, but was "related to the
twelve-tone system, or row, of Schoenberg" (233). Mann concluded
the conversation with the confession that *Doctor Faustus* was the
book of his old age: "My *Parsifal,* . . . And, of course, my *Faust*"
(234).

More important than what was said during this exchange between the
German writer in exile and his teenage American visitors was the memory of this visit, which she suppressed because she found it so embarrassing. The man whom she admired as a writer delivered "only sententious formulas" and she "uttered nothing but tongue-tied simplicities,"
although she was "full of complex feeling" (238). Yet, this "memory of
embarrassment" made her a writer. It liberated her from her "childhood's asphyxiations": "Admiration set me free. And embarrassment,
which is the price of acutely experienced admiration" (239).

In addition to this intimate example of literary influence, there is a more objective indicator of the importance of German exile literature to American letters: the selections of the Book-of-the-Month Club. Six of the Los Angeles exile writers—Vicki Baum, Lion Feuchtwanger, Bruno Frank, Emil Ludwig, Thomas Mann, and Franz Werfel—had titles selected. Vicki Baum's titles were selected before 1933: *Grand Hotel* in 1931 and *And Life Goes On* in 1932. Thomas Mann had *Joseph the Provider* in 1944, *Doctor Faustus* in 1948, and *The Holy Sinner* in 1951, in addition to *Stories of Three Decades* and *Joseph in Egypt* as book dividends in 1936 and 1938. Books by Werfel selected included *The Forty Days of Musa Dagh* in 1934, *The Embezzled Heaven* in 1940, and *The Song of Bernadette* in 1942. Bruno Frank, Lion Feuchtwanger, and Emil Ludwig had one title each: *A Man Called Cervantes* by Frank in 1935; *This Is the Hour,* Feuchtwanger's historical novel about the Spanish painter Francisco de Goya, in 1951; and *The Nile* by Ludwig in 1937. The selections were no clear indication of their success among readers. According to Charles Lee, the Book Club's historian, Mann's *Doctor Faustus* sold the fewest copies, although it was paired with Somerset Maugham's novel *Catalina*. In the case of Werfel's *Song of Bernadette* in 1942, the religious sublime was made more attractive by an offer of a more pragmatic title, *Victory Through Airpower,* for only 40 cents extra (Lee 161–94). Nevertheless, the numerous selections were a significant accomplishment for Weimar on the Pacific, especially when one considers that only a few German exile writers from other cities or countries had their books selected during the same time: Erich Maria Remarque (New York), Anna Seghers (Mexico City), Arnold Zweig (Palestine), and Stefan Zweig (Brazil).

Finally, the exile writers of World War II in Los Angeles became almost mythical figures in Christopher Hampton's *Tales from Hollywood.* His play, which was commissioned by Gordon Davidson for the Mark Taper Forum, premiered in 1982. It was a takeoff on Ödön von Horváth's 1931 play *Tales from the Vienna Woods (Geschichten aus dem Wiener Wald).* The Austro-Hungarian playwright Horváth, who was killed in a freak accident in Paris in 1938 when a tree fell on him during a lightning storm on the Champs-Élysées, was revived in Hampton's play as an exile writer in Los Angeles. He serves to tell the story of Brecht, Thomas and Heinrich Mann, and the other literary greats. In the end, the Horváth figure drowns and is found at the bottom of a swimming pool, like the male protagonist in Billy Wilder's *Sunset Boulevard.* The plot revolves around Heinrich Mann and his younger wife, Nelly, who is driven by despair to alcoholism and finally suicide. The action integrates isolated events into a comprehensive story of the German-speaking exiles in Los Angeles, beginning with Brecht's arrival in San Pedro and ending with the HUAC hearings that sealed their fates, whether they stayed in Los Angeles or returned to Europe.

Although Weimar modernism had projected an image of the "new woman" *(die neue Frau),* the emancipation of women in Weimar Germany was in fact still incomplete, and many of the limited gains achieved during the Weimar Republic were lost during emigration. Traditional patriarchal culture resurfaced in exile, and women were not given the recognition that they deserved (Heinrichsdorff 1–20). Vicki Baum (1888–1960) was largely ignored, although she continued her success as a popular novelist in exile. Many critics have dismissed her genre, the mainstream novel dealing with current issues such as the emancipation of women and modern city life, as inferior, but recently more sophisticated critics have found her novels to reflect the experience of modern life as Walter Benjamin, Georg Simmel, and Siegfried Kracauer have analyzed it (Matthias 328). Baum's 1929 novel *Menschen im Hotel (Grand Hotel)* was also successful as a stage drama in Berlin and New York and was turned into the 1932 Oscar-winning film *Grand Hotel,* with Greta Garbo and Joan Crawford. The movie's sequel, *Hotel Berlin* of 1945, was based on her novel *Hotel Berlin '43* (1944). Baum was one of the very few exile writers who wrote her books in English after 1938. Dealing with characters living under the Nazi regime in the same Berlin luxury hotel as *Grand Hotel, Hotel Berlin '43* deserves to be included among the titles of German exile literature. Some characters, including members of the German military elite and students at the University of Leipzig, are part of the resistance movement, while others are collaborators of the Gestapo and SS: a British writer who broadcasts Nazi propaganda, a German poet who did not go into exile, a successful actress, a German air force ace on leave, a Jewish woman trying to obtain medicine for her ailing husband. The story of the student resistance is obviously based on the activities of the Munich student group Die weiße Rose (The White Rose), who distributed anti-Nazi pamphlets at the university and were executed in 1943. Thomas Mann had praised them in one of his radio addresses to Nazi Germany in June 1943 (GW 11: 1077). The characters assembled in the Berlin hotel are exposed to extensive Allied bombing raids that drive them into the hotel's air-raid shelter again and again. While German postwar literature has been faulted for not dealing with the Allied air raids, the destruction of German cities, and the fatalities among the civilian population, Baum's *Hotel Berlin '43* addressed these issues.

In general, women were more successful as screenwriters than their male colleagues, as the careers of Gina Kaus (1894–1985), Salka Viertel (1889–1978), and Victoria Wolff (1908–92) show. They generally become more proficient in English than their male counterparts, and better adapted to the teamwork involved in Hollywood productions. Ruth Berlau (1906–74), a Danish author who had followed Brecht into exile and filmed the theatrical production of *Galileo,* became a highly acclaimed photographer in exile (Meyer and Wizisla; see also *Brecht Yearbook* 30: 82–251). She teamed up with Brecht again in East Berlin, where she became—in spite of many interpersonal conflicts—an indispensable assistant as editor of the "Modell-books" of his productions. Berlau was also listed as coauthor of Brecht's *War Primer (Kriegsfibel)* and at least five of his plays. Brecht's wife, Helene Weigel (1900–1971), an acclaimed actress during the 1920s and 1930s, did not have a single role in American theater or film, except for a nonspeaking part in *The Seventh Cross,* a film based on a novel with the same title by Anna Seghers. Brecht had written a nonspeaking part for his wife in *Hangmen Also Die,* but Fritz Lang preferred an American actress for the role of a Czech shopkeeper. After her return to East Germany in 1949 she became director of the Berliner Ensemble and was a great success as an actress in some of Brecht's plays, such as *Mother Courage* and *The Caucasian Chalk Circle* (see Hecht).

Exhibitions at the Jewish Museum in New York and the Skirball Cultural Center in Los Angeles in 2005 gave some of these women their due. In the Skirball exhibition Vicky Baum was acknowledged as author of the novels that provided the stories for *Grand Hotel* and *Hotel Berlin,* while Salka Viertel was celebrated as screenwriter and a *salonnière* who was central to the German exile community in Los Angeles. The New York exhibition presented Viertel's home as the "poignant and bittersweet conclusion" of the history of Jewish salons, which were started by Rahel Levin Varnhagen (1771–1833) in Berlin and thereafter organized by Jewish women elsewhere in Europe (Eichler B36; Bilski and Braun 138–47, 209–11). That Salka Viertel's salon in Santa Monica represented the end of this illustrious period served to emphasize the importance of Weimar culture in Los Angeles. Salka Viertel, born Salomea Steuermann in Galicia, was a successful actress and a protégée of Max Reinhardt. She had arrived in Pasadena in 1928 with her husband, Berthold Viertel, who had been given a contract as a director in Hollywood. Viertel had a career as a successful screenwriter in Los Angeles, specializing in scripts for her close friend, Greta Garbo. Her salon attracted celebrated exiles such as Bertolt Brecht, Charlie Chaplin, Lion and Marta Feuchtwanger, Greta Garbo, Aldous Huxley, Thomas and Heinrich Mann, Arthur Rubinstein, and many others. Viertel offered her house for the celebration of Heinrich Mann's seventieth birthday in 1941, to which forty-five people were invited. Her home also served as the meeting place where the exiles issued the ill-fated political statement of solidarity with the National Committee for a Free Germany in the Soviet Union in 1943. As Jeremy Eichler argued in his review of the New York exhibition, the gatherings at Viertel's house at 165 Mabery Road "were life rafts in the form of a few cherished hours of speaking in a native tongue, commiserating with friends and compatriots. Ultimately, they were also a moving attempt to protect a liberal vision of German culture at the very moment it was so gruesomely perverted on the world stage" (Eichler B36). This assessment was a meaningful testimony to the role and achievements of the women in the exile community. At the same time, it reflected the dialectics of German exile modernism in Los Angeles, which tried to preserve and re-create a culture that was confronted with total destruction in Europe.

The return of five paintings by Gustav Klimt (1862–1918) by the Austrian government to the family of Maria Altmann in Los Angeles in March 2006 again drew attention to the German-speaking exile community of the 1940s. The paintings belonged to the collection of Ferdinand and Adele Bloch-Bauer in Vienna, but were confiscated by the Nazis in 1938 and withheld from the heirs by the Austrian government on the basis of a will that the Austrians interpreted in their favor. The Austrian government claimed Klimt's paintings, especially his famed portrait of Adele Bloch-Bauer (1907), an icon of Viennese Jugendstil (art nouveau) as part of the nation's cultural patrimony. After a legal dispute of seven years, the paintings were returned to their rightful owners and shown in an exclusive exhibition at the Los Angeles County Museum of Art from April to June of 2006. Maria Altmann was a niece of Adele Bloch-Bauer. As a refugee from Vienna she arrived in Los Angeles in 1942. The Los Angeles Times of April 4, 2006, used the occasion to mention the names of other illustrious exiles such as conductor Otto Klemperer, writers Thomas Mann and Brecht, theater director Max Reinhardt, movie director and screenwriter Billy Wilder, and actress Marlene Dietrich. But even more important, the article emphasized that Altmann's family attorney, who succeeded in securing the release of the

Klimt paintings, was E. Randol Schoenberg, the grandson of Arnold Schoenberg. This event reflected the local history of German-speaking exile in Los Angeles. Christopher Knight, the art critic of the Los Angeles Times, made an argument for Los Angeles's patrimonial claim to the paintings because of its mid-century prominence as a refuge for Central and Eastern European Jews fleeing Hitler (*Los Angeles Times,* 4 April 2006, E1, E5). The most famous of the Klimt paintings, the *Portrait of Adele Bloch-Bauer I,* was, however, sold to Ronald S. Lauder of the Neue Galerie in New York in June 2006. Yet this sale did not put an end to the history of Weimar on the Pacific, but confirmed once again that the memory of so many Austrian and German Jews who found a refuge in Southern California in the 1930s and early 1940s is still alive in the collective consciousness of the city.

Adorno had reservations about Weimar culture and called into question the "return to culture" in Germany after 1945 because he found it inseparably bound up with barbarism. As he declared in *Minima Moralia,* in an aphorism of 1944, there was hardly any culture of true value when the Nazis came to power: "The claim that Hitler has destroyed German culture is no more than an advertising stunt of those who want to rebuild it from their telephone desks. Such art and thought as were exterminated by Hitler had long been leading a severed and apocryphal existence, whose last hideouts Fascism swept out. . . . The whole span of German culture was languishing . . . for its Hitler" (MM 57). Adorno was opposed to the idea of rebuilding German culture after World War II if it were to be used as an alibi for German society: "The idea that after this war life will continue 'normally' or even that culture might be 'rebuilt'—as if the rebuilding of culture were not already its negation—is idiotic. Millions of Jews have been murdered, and this is to be seen as an interlude and not the catastrophe itself. What more is this culture waiting for?" (MM 55).

Adorno was quite familiar with the state of Weimar culture around 1933 and very perceptive with regard to the culture that Germans would want to institute after 1945. But there was a strange gap in his perception of German culture between 1933 and 1945. He wrote an article entitled "What National Socialism Has Done to the Arts" but no article on German exile culture, especially that in Los Angeles. He was an active participant in this culture and considered himself perhaps biased. But another reason for this omission was that in 1944 the major works of German exile culture in Los Angeles, such as Brecht's *Galileo,* Mann's *Doctor Faustus,* and Schoenberg's *A Survivor of Warsaw,* had not yet been

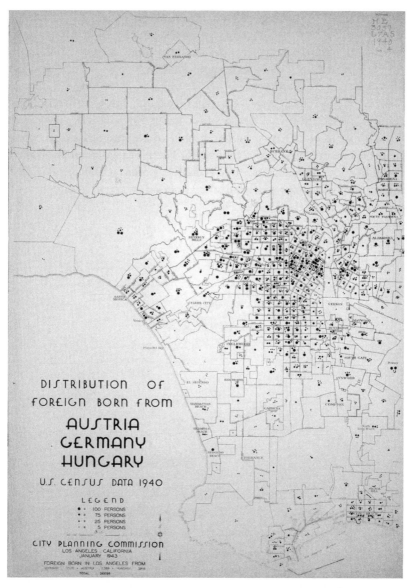

FIGURE 28. Census map of Los Angeles showing distribution of foreign-born residents from Austria, Germany, and Hungary, based on U.S. census data of 1940. Reproduction courtesy of Department of Special Collections, Charles E. Young Research Library, University of California, Los Angeles.

completed. When Adorno returned to Germany in 1949 his writings on aesthetics, literature, and music dealt with the redefinition of culture and its resistance to barbarism. They were clearly influenced by German exile culture in Los Angeles and its response to the crisis of modernism. For today's American observer it is obvious that Adorno owed a debt to Weimar on the Pacific. Its legacy was indispensable to his redefinition of culture.

If culture is, indeed, as Fredric Jameson said, "the space of mediation between society or everyday life and art as such" (177), then Weimar on the Pacific was unique. It was not simply a transplant of Weimar Germany to the West Coast of the United States, nor could its culture simply be returned to Central Europe after World War II. Weimar on the Pacific achieved its own identity between 1933 and 1958 and deserves its place among the global cityscapes of modernism.

Chronology

1933

January 30	Adolf Hitler becomes Reich Chancellor by invitation of President Hindenburg to lead a coalition government of nationalist conservatives and National Socialists.
February 15	Heinrich Mann emigrates to France.
February 27	The Reichstag building, housing the German parliament, burns down.
February 28	President Hindenburg signs an emergency decree that abolishes basic rights of association, assembly, and freedom of the press and enables the government to persecute opponents by legislative fiat.
	Bertolt Brecht, with his wife, Helene Weigel, and his son, Stefan, leaves for Prague.
	Alfred Döblin leaves Berlin for Switzerland, then moves to Paris, where he lives with his wife and youngest son until 1940.
March 5	The National Socialists gain 43.9 percent of votes in a national election. With the support of the Nationalists and the Catholic Center Party, they pass an emergency law, the so-called Enabling Law, giving Hitler dictatorial power.
March 12	Thomas Mann and his wife Katia, while on vacation in Switzerland after a lecture tour in Holland and Belgium, decide not to return to Germany. They settle in Küsnacht, near Zurich.

April 11	*Bauhaus* in Berlin is closed by the Nazis.
May 10	Joseph Goebbels, Nazi minister of propaganda, attends book burnings in front of the University of Berlin. Book burnings in other university cities follow. Works by Sigmund Freud, Heinrich Mann, and Erich Maria Remarque are among those burned.
May 17	Arnold Schoenberg leaves Berlin for Paris; here he formally rejoins the Jewish religion on July 24.
July 31	Fritz Lang leaves Berlin for Paris via Amsterdam (although there is some controversy about Lang's departure date, this date is verified by an exit stamp in his passport).
August 9	Bertolt Brecht settles in Denmark.
September 18	Arnold Schoenberg is dismissed from his position at the Prussian Academy of Arts, Berlin.
September 22	The Reich Chamber of Culture is established under the leadership of Joseph Goebbels to control all aspects of artistic activities within Germany.
October 25	Schoenberg and his family leave from Le Havre for New York. They move to Boston, where Schoenberg accepts a teaching position at the Malkin Conservatory. In 1934, Schoenberg and his family move to Los Angeles.

1934

May 3	Max Horkheimer arrives in New York.
May 19–June 9	Thomas Mann visits the United States for the first time.
June 12	Fritz Lang arrives in New York and moves to Los Angeles.
August 19	Hitler proclaims himself Führer and Reich Chancellor.

1935

June 9–July 13	Thomas Mann makes his second visit to the United States.
September 15	Anti-Semitic Nuremberg Laws are promulgated.

1936

July 1	Arnold Schoenberg is appointed professor of music at the University of California, Los Angeles (UCLA).
December 2	Thomas Mann, his wife, and children are deprived of German citizenship by decree of the German Ministry of the Interior. Mann had been awarded Czech citizenship on November 19, 1936.

1937

April 6–29	Thomas Mann visits the United States for the third time, upon the invitation of the New School of Social Research in New York.

1938

February 10–March 15	Mann delivers the lecture "The Coming Victory of Democracy" in cities across the nation on his fourth visit to the United States. The lecture at the Shrine Auditorium in Los Angeles is on April 1.
February 29	Theodor W. Adorno arrives in New York.
March 13	*Anschluss:* Annexation of Austria.
March 19	Because of the annexation of Austria, Thomas Mann decides to settle in the United States.
May 28	Thomas Mann accepts an appointment as lecturer at Princeton University.
September 14	Thomas Mann departs from Zurich.
September 20	Thomas Mann arrives in New York. He lives in Princeton from September 28, 1938, to March 15, 1941.
September 29	Munich Conference: Britain, France, and Italy agree to Germany's annexation of the Sudetenland, the German-speaking territory of Czechoslovakia.
October 1	Germany occupies Sudetenland.
November 9	Anti-Semitic pogroms, including the so-called Night of Broken Glass, take place in Germany.

1939

March 15	Germany occupies Czechoslovakia.
April 23	Brecht leaves for Stockholm, Sweden.
September 1	Germany invades Poland. World War II begins in Europe.
September 3	Britain and France declare war on Germany.

1940

April 9	The German army invades Denmark and Norway.
April 17	Brecht leaves with his family for Helsinki, Finland.
May 10	German troops start their invasion of France, violating the neutrality of Belgium and the Netherlands.

June 10	Alfred Döblin leaves Paris. His wife and youngest son had left Paris on May 26.
June 22	France signs armistice with Germany.
July 10	Döblin meets with his wife and youngest son in Toulouse, France.
September 3	Alfred Döblin leaves with his wife and youngest son from Lisbon for New York.
September 26	Walter Benjamin commits suicide at Portbou after he is turned back at the Spanish border because he does not have a French exit visa.
October 4	After escaping from France, fleeing by foot over the Pyrenees to Portbou, Heinrich Mann and his wife Nelly, Lion Feuchtwanger and his wife Marta, and Franz Werfel and his wife Alma Mahler-Werfel travel by train to Barcelona, Madrid, and Lisbon to sail to New York.
October 5	Lion Feuchtwanger arrives in New York after escaping from a French internment camp, illegally crossing the border across the Pyrenees, and traveling to Lisbon via Barcelona and Madrid.
October 13	Franz Werfel and his wife arrive in New York; they move to Los Angeles at the end of December 1940. Heinrich Mann and his wife are on the same boat.
October 26	Alfred Döblin attends his welcome celebration at the Jewish Club of 1933 in Los Angeles. Döblin has a contract to work for Metro-Goldwyn-Mayer.
November 1	Thomas Mann takes leave of his brother Heinrich, who travels with his wife, Nelly, from New York to Los Angeles, where he has a one-year contract working for Warner Brothers.

1941

January 25	Lion Feuchtwanger leaves New York for Los Angeles.
April 8	Thomas Mann moves to Los Angeles, where he lives in Pacific Palisades from 1941 to 1952.
May 15	Brecht leaves for the United States via the Soviet Union together with his family and his collaborators, Ruth Berlau and Margarete Steffin, who dies in Moscow. The rest of the group continues traveling by railway to Vladivostok, where they take a merchant ship to Los Angeles.
June 22	Germany invades the Soviet Union.
July 21	Brecht arrives in San Pedro, California, with his family and Ruth Berlau.

November 19	Theodor W. Adorno and his wife, Gretel, arrive in Los Angeles.
December 1	Thomas Mann is appointed as consultant in Germanic literature at the Library of Congress, as of January 1, 1942.
December 7	Japan attacks Pearl Harbor.
December 8	The United States declares war on Japan. Enemy aliens in the United States are required to have a permit to travel and are subject to a curfew from 8 P.M. to 6 A.M.
December 11	Germany and Italy declare war on the United States, and the U.S. Congress declares war on Germany and Italy.

1942

| January 20 | Wannsee Conference on "the Final Solution." |
| February 19 | President Roosevelt issues Executive Order No. 9066, which authorizes the internment of some 120,000 Japanese-Americans from 1942 to 1945. |

1943

| February 2 | German 6th Army surrenders at Stalingrad. |
| July 12–13 | National Committee Free Germany is founded in Krasnogorsk, Soviet Union. |

1944

May 3	Council for a Democratic Germany is founded in New York.
June 6	The Allies land in Normandy (D-Day).
September 13	Arnold Schoenberg retires from UCLA. Due to his short tenure, his retirement amounts to $29.60.

1945

February 3–11	The Yalta (or Crimean) Conference on Germany's borders and the future of Europe takes place.
April 30	Hitler commits suicide.
May 7–8	The German Armed Forces unconditionally surrender.
June 5	The Allied Control Commission assumes authority over the former German Reich within the borders agreed upon at Yalta.
July 17	The Potsdam Conference (Britain, the United States, and the Soviet Union) opens.
August 6	An atomic bomb is dropped on Hiroshima.

August 9	An atomic bomb is dropped on Nagasaki.
August 15	The Japanese emperor announces that Japan will accept the Allies' terms of surrender. President Truman declares the end of World War II.
August 26	Franz Werfel dies in Beverly Hills.
September 2	Representatives of Japan's government and its military sign the formal surrender document.
October 8	Alfred Döblin leaves the United States for Baden-Baden, Germany, to work as Chargé de Mission of Public Education of the French Occupation Forces.
November 20	The Nuremberg Trials of major war criminals begin.

1947

July 30	The first performance of *Galileo*, with Charles Laughton, is staged at the Coronet Theatre in Beverly Hills.
October 17	Thomas Mann's *Doktor Faustus* (in German) appears in Europe.
October 30	Thomas Mann challenges the House Committee on Un-American Activities (HUAC) by declaring his willingness to testify as a "hostile witness."
	Brecht testifies before the House Committee on Un-American Activities in Washington, D.C.
October 31	Brecht leaves by plane from New York for Paris.

1948

May 26	Max Horkheimer returns to Frankfurt to teach at the Goethe University. The Institute for Social Research, the so-called Frankfurt School, is returned to the university in 1949.
September	Thomas Mann's *Doctor Faustus* is published in English translation by Knopf, New York; 7,000 copies are printed.
November	Mann's *Doctor Faustus* appears as a Book-of-the-Month selection; 100,000 copies are printed.

1949

April 4	*Life* magazine lists Thomas Mann among "fellow travelers" and "dupes" of communism.
May 23	The Federal Republic of Germany (West Germany) is founded.

May 30	Bertolt Brecht and his wife, Helene Weigel, settle in East Berlin. Helene Weigel becomes managing director of Berliner Ensemble, a new theater company.
October 7	The German Democratic Republic (East Germany) is founded.
November 2	Theodore W. Adorno returns to Frankfurt to teach at the Goethe University.
November 12	The theater company Berliner Ensemble opens with *Mr. Puntila and His Hired Man, Matti,* staged by Bertolt Brecht.

1950

March 12	Heinrich Mann dies in Santa Monica.

1951

July 13	Arnold Schoenberg dies in Los Angeles.

1952

June 24	Thomas Mann leaves Los Angeles to return to Europe, where he settles in Kilchberg, near Zurich, Switzerland.

1953

August 22	Rudolph M. Schindler dies in Los Angeles.

1954

March 19	The Berliner Ensemble is given a location of its own, the Theater am Schiffbauerdamm, in East Berlin.

1955

August 12	Thomas Mann dies in Zurich, Switzerland.

1956

June 26	Alfred Döblin dies in Emmendingen, West Germany.
August 14	Bertolt Brecht dies in East Berlin.

1958

December 21	Lion Feuchtwanger dies in Los Angeles.

1960

August 29   Vicki Baum dies in Los Angeles.

1969

August 6   Theodor W. Adorno dies in Visp, Switzerland.

1970

April 16   Richard Neutra dies, during a visit of the Kemper house
                       that he designed in Wuppertal, West Germany.

1973

July 7   Max Horkheimer dies in Nuremberg, West Germany.

1974

January 15   Ruth Berlau dies in East Berlin.

1976

August 2   Fritz Lang dies in Los Angeles.

1978

September 20   Salka Viertel dies in Los Angeles.

1985

December 23   Gina Kaus dies in Los Angeles.

1987

October 25   Marta Feuchtwanger dies in Los Angeles.

1988

August 10   U.S. Civil Liberties Act, signed by President Ronald Rea-
                       gan, grants $20,000 and an apology to 82,000 former
                       Japanese American internees of World War II.

1992

September 16   Viktoria Wolff dies in Los Angeles.

Appendices

Döblin, Alfred   1842 Cherokee Avenue, Hollywood (1940)

                                  901 Genesee Avenue, Hollywood (1941)

                                  1347 North Citrus Avenue, Hollywood
                                  (1941–45)

Eisler, Hanns   869 Amalfi Drive, Pacific Palisades

Evenings on the Roof   1735 Micheltorena Street, Silver Lake
  (Peter Yates)

Feuchtwanger, Lion   2088 Mandeville Canyon Road, Brent-
  and Marta   wood (1941–43)

                                  520 Paseo Miramar, Pacific Palisades
                                  (1943–87)

Fischinger, Oskar   1010 Hammond Street, West Hollywood

Horkheimer, Max   13524 D'Este Drive, Pacific Palisades

Klemperer, Otto   924 Bel Air Road, Bel Air

Lang, Fritz   2141 La Mesa Drive, Santa Monica
                                  (1934–45)

                                  1501 Summit Ridge Drive, Beverly Hills
                                  (1945–76)

Laughton, Charles   14954 Corona Del Mar, Pacific Palisades

Lovell House   4616 Dundee Drive, East Hollywood

Ludwig, Emil   333 Bel Air Road, Pacific Palisades (1943)

                                  701 Amalfi Drive, Pacific Palisades

Mann, Heinrich   264 Doheny Drive, Beverly Hills (1940)

                                  481 South Holt Avenue, West Hollywood
                                  (1941)

                                  301 South Swall Drive, Beverly Hills
                                  (1942–48)

                                  2145 Montana Avenue, Santa Monica
                                  (1948–50)

Mann, Thomas   441 North Rockingham Avenue, Brentwood
                                  (1940)

                                  740 Amalfi Drive, Pacific Palisades
                                  (1941–42)

                                  1550 San Remo Drive, Pacific Palisades
                                  (1942–52)

Neutra, Richard	2300 East Silver Lake Drive, Silver Lake
Reinhardt, Max	15000 Corona Del Mar, Pacific Palisades
Scheyer, Galka	1880 Blue Heights Drive, West Hollywood
Schindler, Rudolph M.	833 North Kings Road, West Hollywood
Schindler Studio House	833 North Kings Road, West Hollywood
Schoenberg, Arnold	116 North Rockingham, Brentwood
Stravinsky, Igor	1260 North Wetherly Drive, West Hollywood
Viertel, Salka	165 Mabery Road, Pacific Palisades
Villa Aurora (residence of Lion and Marta Feuchtwanger)	520 Paseo Miramar, Pacific Palisades
Walter, Bruno	608 North Bedford Drive, Beverly Hills
Werfel, Franz and Alma Mahler Werfel	6800 Los Tilos Road, Hollywood (1941–42)
	610 North Bedford Drive, Beverly Hills (1942–45)

II. FILMOGRAPHY: *HANGMEN ALSO DIE*

Producer:	Arnold Pressburger, Fritz Lang, and T. W. Baumfield [Baumfeld]
Director:	Fritz Lang
Screenplay:	Fritz Lang, Bertolt Brecht, and John Wexley, based on a story by Lang and Brecht
Photography:	James Wong Howe
Art Direction:	William Darling
Music:	Hanns Eisler; Song, "No Surrender," by Sam Coslow
Sound:	Fred Law
Editor:	Gene Fowler
Assistant Production Manager:	Carl Curley Harriman
Assistant Directors:	Walter Mayo and Fred Pressburger
Cast:	Brian Donlevy (Dr. Franz Swoboda)

Walter Brennan (Professor Novotny)

Anna Lee (Mascha Novotny)

Gene Lockhart (Emil Czaka)

Dennis O'Keefe (Jan Horek)

Alexander Granach (Alois Gruber)

Margaret Wycherly (Ludmilla Novotny)

Nana Bryant (Mrs. Novotny)

Billy Roy (Beda Novotny)

Hans von Twardowski
(Reinhard Heydrich)

Tonio Selwart (Haas, Gestapo Chief)

Jonathan Hale (Dedič)

Lionel Stander (Cabby)

Byron Foulger (Bartos)

Virginia Farmer (Landlady)

Louis Donath (Schirmer)

Sarah Padden (Miss Dvorak)

Edmund MacDonald (Dr. Pilar)

George Irving (Necval)

James Bush (Worker)

Arno Frey (Itnut)

Lester Sharpe (Rudy)

Arthur Luft (General Vortruba)

William Farnum (Victorin)

Reinhold Schünzel (Inspector Ritter)

Filmed at Arnold Productions, United Artists, Hollywood, in 1942 in 52 days

Original length: 140 minutes. Some versions in distribution lack the last ten minutes.

Released on March 26, 1943.

Source: E. Ann Kaplan, *Fritz Lang: A Guide to References and Resources* (Boston: G. K. Hall, 1981), 86–87.

III. TEXT OF THE *KOL NIDRE*

As arranged by Schoenberg for his Composition for Reciter, Mixed Chorus, and Orchestra, opus 39 (1938)

Rabbi:
The Kabalah tells a legend:
At the beginning God said: "LET THERE BE LIGHT."
Out of space a flame burst out.
God crushed that light to atoms.
Myriads of sparks are hidden in our world, but
Not all of us behold them.
The self-glorious, who walks arrogantly upright,
Will never perceive one;
But the meek and modest, eyes downcast,
He sees it.
"All light is sown for the pious."
Bischiwo Schel Malo Uwishiwo Schel Mato [By the authority of the Heavenly Court above and of this court on earth]
In the name of God!
We solemnly proclaim
That every transgressor
Be it that he was unfaithful to Our People because of fear,
Or misled by false doctrines of any kind,
Out of weakness or greed:
We give him leave
To be one with us in prayer tonight,
A light is sown for the pious, a light is sown for the repenting sinner.
All vows, oaths, promises and plights of any kind,
Wherewith we pledged ourselves
Counter to our inherited faith in God,
Who is One, Everlasting, Unseen, Unfathomable,
We declare these null and void.
We repent that these obligations have estranged
Us from the sacred task we were chosen for.

Choir:
We repent.

Rabbi:
We repent.
We shall strive from this Day of Atonement till the next

To avoid such and similar obligations,
So that the Yom Kippur to follow
May come to us for good.

Choir:
All vows and oaths and promises and plights of any kind
wherewith we pledged ourselves
counter to our inherited faith in God
who is One, Everlasting, Unseen, Unfathomable,
we declare these null and void.
We repent that these obligations have estranged
us from the sacred task we were chosen for.
We repent.
We repent
that these obligations have estranged us from the sacred task
we are chosen for.
We shall strive from this day of atonement
till the next to avoid such and similar obligations
so that the Jom Kippur to follow
may come to us for good.

Rabbi and Choir:
Whatever binds us to falsehood
May be absolved, released, annulled, made void
And of no power.

Choir:
Hence all such vows shall be no vows,
And all such bonds shall be no bonds,
All such oaths shall be not oaths.
We repent.
Null and void be our vows.
We repent them.
All light is sown for the sinner.

Rabbi:
We give him leave to be one with us in prayer tonight.

Choir:
We repent.

Source: Pierre Boulez, *Schönberg: Das Chorwerk* (Sony
Classical), 46–50. See also Arnold Schönberg, *Sämtliche
Werke*, Section V, Series A., Vol. 19, 1–60. Used by
permission of Belmont Music Publishers.

IV. LORD BYRON'S "ODE TO NAPOLEON BUONAPARTE"

As used for Schoenberg's Composition for String Quartet, Piano, and Reciter, opus 41 (1942)

'Tis done—but yesterday a King!
    And armed with Kings to strive—
And now thou art a nameless thing:
    So abject—yet alive!
Is this the man of thousand thrones,
Who strew'd our earth with hostile bones,
    And can he thus survive?
Since he, miscalled the Morning Star,
Nor man nor fiend hath fallen so far.

Ill-minded man, why scourge thy kind
    Who bow'd so low the knee?
By gazing on thyself grown blind,
    Thou taught'st the rest to see.
With might unquestion'd,—power to save,—
Thine only gift hath been the grave
    To those that worshipped thee;
Nor till thy fall could mortals guess
Ambition less than littleness!

Thanks for that lesson—it will teach
    To after-warriors more
Than high Philosophy can preach,
    And vainly preach'd before.
That spell upon the minds of men
Breaks never to unite again,
    That led them to adore
Those Pagod things of sabre sway,
With fronts of brass, and feet of clay.

The triumph, and the vanity,
    The rapture of the strife—
The earthquake voice of Victory,
    To thee the breath of life;
The sword, the scepter, and that sway
Which man seem'd made but to obey
    Wherewith renown was rife—

All quell'd! Dark Spirit! What must be
The madness of thy memory!

The Desolator desolate!
    The Victor overthrown!
The Arbiter of others' fate
    A Suppliant for his own!
Is it some yet imperial hope
That with such change can calmly cope?
    Or dread of death alone?
To die a prince—or live a slave—
Thy choice is most ignobly brave!

He who of old would rend the oak,
    Dream'd not of the rebound;
Chain'd by the trunk he vainly broke—
    Alone—how look'd he round?
Thou in the sternness of thy strength
An equal deed hast done at length,
    And darker fate hast found:
He fell, the forest prowlers' prey;
But thou must eat thy heart away!

The Roman, when his burning heart
    Was slaked with blood of Rome,
Threw down the dagger—dared depart,
    In savage grandeur, home.—
He dared depart in utter scorn
Of men that such a yoke had borne,
    Yet left him such a doom!
His only glory was that hour
Of self-upheld abandon'd power.

The Spaniard, when the lust of sway
    Had lost its quickening spell,
Cast crowns for rosaries away,
    An empire for a cell;
A strict accountant of his beads,
A subtle disputant on creeds,
    His dotage trifled well:
Yet better had he neither known
A bigot's shrine, nor despot's throne.

But thou—from thy reluctant hand
  The thunderbolt is wrung—
Too late thou leav'st the high command
  To which thy weakness clung;
All Evil Spirit as thou art,
It is enough to grieve the heart
  To see thine own unstrung;
To think that God's fair world hath been
The footstool of a thing so mean;

And Earth has spilt her blood for him,
  Who thus can hoard his own!
And Monarchs bowed the trembling limb,
  And thank'd him for a throne!
Fair Freedom! We may hold thee dear
When thus thy mightiest foes their fear
  In humblest guise have shown.
Oh! Ne'er may tyrant leave behind
A brighter name to lure mankind!

Thine evil deeds are writ in gore,
  Not written thus in vain—
Thy triumphs tell of fame no more
  Or deepen every stain:
If thou had'st died as honour dies,
Some new Napoleon might arise,
  To shame the world again—
But who would soar the solar height,
To set in such a starless night?

Weigh'd in the balance, hero dust
  Is vile as vulgar clay;
Thy scales, Mortality! are just
  To all that pass away;
But yet methought the living great
Some higher sparks should animate,
  To dazzle and dismay:
Nor deem'd Contempt could thus make mirth
Of these, the Conquerors of the earth.

And she, proud Austria's mournful flower,
  Thy still imperial bride;
How bears her breast the torturing hour?

Still clings she to thy side?
Must she too bend, must she too share
Thy late repentance, long despair,
    Thou throneless Homicide?
If still she loves thee, hoard that gem,
'Tis worth thy vanished diadem!

Then haste thee to thy sullen Isle,
    And gaze upon the sea;
That element may meet thy smile—
    It ne'er was ruled by thee!
Or trace with thine all idle hand
In loitering mood upon the sand
    That Earth is now as free!
That Corinth's pedagogue hath now
Transferr'd his by-word to thy brow.

Thou Timour! In his captive's cage
    What thoughts will there be thine,
While brooding in thy prison'd rage?
    But one—'the world was mine!'
Unless like he of Babylon,
All sense is with thy scepter gone,
    Life will not long confine
That spirit pour'd so widely forth—
So long obey'd—so little worth!

Or, like the thief of fire from heaven,
    Wilt thou withstand the shock?
And share with him, the unforgiven,
    His vulture and his rock!
Fordoom'd by God—by man accurst,
And that last act, though not the worst,
    The very Fiend's arch mock;
He in his fall preserved his pride,
And, if a mortal, had as proudly died!

There was a day—there was an hour,
    While earth was Gaul's—and Gaul thine—
When that immeasurable power
    Unsated to resign
Had been an act of purer fame

Than gathers round Marengo's name
   And gilded thy decline,
Through the long twilight of all time,
Despite some passing clouds of crime.

But thou forsooth must be a kind
   And don the purple vest,—
As if that foolish robe could wring
   Remembrance from thy breast.
Where is that faded garment? Where
The gewgaws thou wert fond to wear,
   The star—the string—the crest?
Vain forward child of empire! say,
Are all thy playthings snatch'd away?

Where may the wearied eye repose
   When gazing upon the Great;
Where neither guilty glory glows,
   Nor despicable state?
Yes—one—the first—the last—the best—
The Cincinnatus of the West,
   Whom envy dared not hate,
Bequeathed the name of Washington,
To make man blush there was but one!

Source: Lord Byron, *The Complete Poetical Works,* ed. Jerome
J. McGann, vol. 3 (Oxford: Clarendon Press, 1981), 259–66.
See also *Schoenberg: Pierrot Lunaire / Herzgewächse / Ode to
Napoleon* with Christine Schäfer and Pierre Boulez (Hamburg:
Deutsche Grammophon, 1998), 37–47, and Arnold Schön-
berg, *Sämtliche Werke,* Section VI, Series A, Vol. 24, 97–166.

V. TEXT OF ARNOLD SCHOENBERG'S *A SURVIVOR OF WARSAW*

For Narrator, Male Chorus, and Orchestra, opus 46 (1947)

Narrator: I cannot remember ev'rything. I must have been unconscious most of the time.—I remember only the grandiose moment
when they all started to sing, as if prearranged, the old prayer they had
neglected for so many years—the forgotten creed! But I have no recollection how I got underground to live in the sewers of Warsaw for so
long a time.—

The day began as usual: Reveille when it still was dark. Get out! Whether you slept or whether worries kept you awake the whole night. You had been separated from your children, from your wife, from your parents. You don't know what happened to them—how could you sleep?

The trumpets again—Get out! The sergeant will be furious! They came out; some very slow: the old ones, the sick ones; some with nervous agility. They fear the sergeant. They hurry as much as they can. In vain! Much too much noise, much too much commotion—and not fast enough!

The Feldwebel [sergeant] shouts [in German]: "Achtung! Stilljes-tanden! Na wirds mal! Oder soll ich mit dem Jewehrkolben nach-helfen? Na jutt, wenn ihrs durchaus haben wollt!" [Stand at attention! Hurry up! Or do you want to feel the butt of my rifle? Okay, you've asked for it!].

The sergeant and his subordinates hit everybody: young or old, quiet or nervous, guilty or innocent.—It was painful to hear them groaning and moaning. I heard it though I had been hit very hard, so hard that I could not help falling down. We all on the ground who could not stand up were then beaten over the head.—

I must have been unconscious. The next thing I knew was a soldier saying: "They are all dead," whereupon the sergeant ordered to do away with us. There I lay aside—half conscious. It had become very still—fear and pain.

Then I heard the sergeant shouting: "Abzählen!" [Number off!]. They started slowly and irregularly: one, two, three, four—"Achtung!" the sergeant shouted again: "Rascher! Nochmal von vorn anfangen! In einer Minute will ich wissen, wieviele ich zur Gaskammer abliefere! Abzählen!" [Quicker! Start again! In one minute I want to know how many I'm going to deliver to the gas chamber! Number off!].

They began again, first slowly: one, two, three, four, became faster and faster, so fast that it finally sounded like a stampede of wild horses, and all of a sudden, in the middle of it, they began singing the Shema Yisrael.

> *Male Choir*   Hear Israel:
> *(sung in Hebrew):*   The Lord our God is one Lord,
> And you should love the Lord, your God,
> With all your heart and with all your soul

And with all your might.
And these words, which I command you today,
Shall be in all your heart;
And you shall teach them diligently to your
    children and talk of them
When you sit in your house
And when you walk along your way,
When you lie down and when you rise.
[Deuteronomy 6: 4–7]

Source: Pierre Boulez, *Schönberg: Das Chorwerk* (Sony
Classical), 88–92. See also Arnold Schönberg, *Sämtliche
Werke*, Section V, Series A, Vol. 19, 91–120, and
Schoenberg Reader, 319–20. Used by permission of
Belmont Music Publishers.

Bibliography

INTRODUCTION

Abel, Angelika. *Musikästhetik der Klassischen Moderne: Thomas Mann— Theodor W. Adorno—Arnold Schönberg.* Munich: Fink, 2003.

Albert, Claudia. "Ende der Exilforschung? Eine Überlegung anläßlich neuerer Veröffentlichungen zum Thema Exilliteratur." *Internationales Archiv für Sozialgeschichte der deutschen Literatur* 24 (1999): 180–87.

Bahr, Ehrhard. "Literary Weimar in Exile: German Literature in Los Angeles, 1940–1958." In Bahr and Carolyn See, *Exiles and Refugees in Los Angeles,* 3–27. Los Angeles: William Andrews Clark Memorial Library, 1988.

———. "Los Angeles als Zentrum der Exilkultur und die Krise des Modernismus." *Exilforschung: Ein internationals Jahrbuch* 20 (2002): 199–212.

Bander, Carol. "Exilliteratur und Exil im Spiegel der deutschsprachigen Presse der Westküste: 1933–1949." *Deutsche Exilliteratur seit 1933,* vol. 1: Kalifornien, part 1, ed. John M. Spalek et al., 195–213. Bern: Francke, 1976.

Barron, Stephanie, ed. *Exiles and Emigrés: The Flight of European Artists from Hitler.* Los Angeles: Los Angeles County Museum of Art, 1997.

Berman, Russell A. *The Rise of the Modern German Novel: Crisis and Charisma.* Cambridge, MA.: Harvard University Press, 1986.

Bracher, Karl Dietrich. *Die Auflösung der Weimarer Republik: Eine Studie zum Problem des Machtverfalls in der Demokratie.* 5th ed. Villingen: Ring-Verlag, 1971.

Davis, Mike. *City of Quartz: Excavating the Future in Los Angeles.* London: Verso, 1990.

Deleuze, Gilles, and Félix Guattari. *Kafka: Toward a Minor Literature.* Trans. Dana Polan, foreword by Réda Bensmaïa. Minneapolis: University of Minnesota Press, 1986.

Englmann, Bettina. *Poetik des Exils: Die Modernität der deutschsprachigen Exilliteratur.* Tübingen: Niemeyer, 2001.

Fine, David M. *Imagining Los Angeles: A City in Fiction.* Albuquerque: University of New Mexico Press, 2000.

Fine, David, ed. *Los Angeles in Fiction: A Collection of Original Essays.* Albuquerque: University of New Mexico Press, 1984; 2nd rev. ed., 1995.

Friedrich, Otto. *City of Nets: A Portrait of Hollywood in the 1940's.* New York: Harper & Row, 1986.

Gay, Peter. *Weimar Culture: The Outsider as Insider.* New York: Harper & Row, 1968.

Giovacchini, Saverio. *Hollywood Modernism: Film and Politics in the Age of the New Deal.* Philadelphia: Temple University Press, 2001.

Goethe im Urteil seiner Kritiker: Dokumente zur Wirkungsgeschichte Goethes in Deutschland. Ed. Karl Robert Mandelkow. Vol. 4. Munich: Beck, 1984.

Graevenitz, Gerhart von, ed. *Konzepte der Moderne.* Stuttgart: Metzler, 1999.

Gumprecht, Holger. *"New Weimar" unter Palmen. Deutsche Schriftsteller im Exil in Los Angeles.* Berlin: Aufbau Taschenbuch Verlag, 1998.

Heilbut, Anthony. *Exiled in Paradise: German Refugee Artists and Intellectuals in America from the 1930s to the Present.* New York: Viking Press, 1983.

Horak, Jan-Christopher. *Fluchtpunkt Hollywood: Eine Dokumentation zur Filmemigration nach 1933.* 2nd rev. and enlarged ed. Münster: MAkS, 1986.

Jackman, Jarrel C., and Carla M. Borden, eds. *The Muses Flee Hitler: Cultural Transfer and Adaptation 1930–1945.* Washington, D.C.: Smithsonian Institution Press, 1983.

Jameson, Fredric. *Late Marxism: Adorno, or, The Persistence of the Dialectic.* London: Verso, 1990.

———. *A Singular Modernity: Essay on the Ontology of the Present.* London: Verso, 2002.

Jay, Martin. "The German Migration: Is There a Figure in the Carpet?" In Barron, *Exiles,* 326–37.

Kesten, Hermann, ed. *Deutsche Literatur im Exil: Briefe europäischer Autoren 1933–1945.* Vienna: Desch, 1964.

Krohn, Claus-Dieter. *Intellectuals in Exile: Refugee Scholars and the New School for Social Research.* Trans. Rita and Robert Kimber, foreword by Arthur J. Vidich. Amherst: University of Massachusetts Press, 1993.

Krohn, Claus-Dieter, Patrick von zur Mühlen, Gerhard Paul, and Lutz Winckler, eds. *Handbuch der deutschsprachigen Emigration 1933–1945.* Darmstadt: Wissenschaftliche Buchgesellschaft, 1998.

Laqueur, Walter. *Weimar: A Cultural History, 1918–1933.* London: Weidenfeld and Nicolson, 1974.

Lunn, Eugene. *Marxism and Modernism: An Historical Study of Lukács, Brecht, Benjamin, and Adorno.* Berkeley: University of California Press, 1982.

Marcuse, Ludwig. *Mein Zwanzigstes Jahrhundert: Auf dem Weg zu einer Autobiographie.* Munich: List, 1960.

McClung, William Alexander. *Landscapes of Desire: Anglo Mythologies of Los Angeles.* Berkeley: University of California Press, 2000.

Mehlman, Jeffrey. *Émigré New York: French Intellectuals in Wartime Manhattan, 1940–1944*. Baltimore, MD: Johns Hopkins University Press, 2000.

Meyer, Michael A. "Refugees from Hitler's Germany: The Creative Elite and Its Middle Class Audience in Los Angeles in the 1930's and 1940's—Film Noir and Orders of 'Sunny-Side Up.' " In *Preußens Himmel breitet seine Sterne . . . Beiträge zur Kultur-, Politik- und Geistesgeschichte der Neuzeit*, vol. 1, Festschrift zum 60. Geburtstag von Julius H. Schoeps, ed. Willi Jasper and Joachim H. Knoll, 357–74. Hildesheim: Olms, 2002.

Middell, Eike, ed. *Exil in den USA mit einem Bericht "Schanghai—Eine Emigration am Rande."* Leipzig: Reclam, 1979.

Merrill-Mirsky, Carol, ed. *Exiles in Paradise: Catalog of the Exhibition "Exiles in Paradise," Hollywood Bowl Museum*. Los Angeles: Los Angeles Philharmonic Association, 1991.

Miller, Tyrus. *Late Modernism: Politics, Fiction, and the Arts between the World Wars*. Berkeley: University of California Press, 1999.

Mommsen, Hans. *The Rise and Fall of Weimar Democracy*. Trans. Elborg Forster and Larry Eugene Jones. Chapel Hill: University of North Carolina Press, 1996.

Naficy, Hamid. *The Making of Exile Cultures: Iranian Television in Los Angeles*. Minneapolis: University of Minnesota Press, 1993.

Nash, Gerald D. *The American West Transformed: The Impact of the Second World War*. Bloomington: Indiana University Press, 1985.

Nicholls, Peter. *Modernisms: A Literary Guide*. Berkeley: University of California Press, 1995.

Payrhuber, Franz-Josef. *Bertolt Brecht*, Literaturwissen. Stuttgart: Reclam, 1995.

Peukert, Detlev J. K. *The Weimar Republic: The Crisis of Classical Modernity*. Trans. Richard Leveson. London: Penguin Press, 1991.

Pfanner, Helmut. *Exile in New York: German and Austrian Writers after 1933*. Detroit: Wayne State University Press, 1983.

Rasmussen, Cecilia. "Nothing Sleepy about This Past." *Los Angeles Times*, 14 May 2006, B2.

Roden, Johanna W. "Der 'Jewish Club of 1933, Inc.'—ein deutsches Kulturzentrum am Pazifischen Ozean." *Deutschsprachige Exilliteratur seit 1933*, vol. 3, part 3, ed. John M. Spalek et al., 482–94. Bern: Saur, 2002.

Röder, Werner, and Herbert A. Strauss, eds. *Biographisches Handbuch der deutschsprachigen Emigration nach 1933 / International Biographical Dictionary of Central European Emigres 1933–1945*. 3 vols. Munich: Saur, 1980–83.

Said, Edward W. "Movements and Migrations." In *Culture and Imperialism*, 326–36. New York: Knopf, 1994.

———. " Reflections on Exile." In *Reflections on Exile and Other Essays*, 173–86. Cambridge, MA: Harvard University Press, 2000.

Schaber, Will, ed. *Aufbau/Reconstruction: Dokumente einer Kultur im Exil*. Introduction by Hans Steinitz. New York: Overlook Press, 1972.

Schnauber, Cornelius. *German-speaking Artists in Hollywood: Emigration Between 1910 and 1945*. Bonn: Inter Nationes, 1996.

———. *Hollywood Haven: Homes and Haunts of the European Emigres and Exiles in Los Angeles.* Trans. Barbara Zeisl Schoenberg. Riverside: Ariadne Press, 1997.

Spalek, John M., and Joseph Strelka, eds. *Deutsche Exilliteratur seit 1933: 1. Kalifornien,* parts 1 and 2. Bern: Francke, 1976.

Starr, Kevin. *The Dream Endures: California Enters the 1940s.* Oxford: Oxford University Press, 1997.

———. *Embattled Dreams: California in War and Peace, 1940–1950.* Oxford: Oxford University Press, 2002.

Steinitz, Hans. "Aufbau, Neubau, Brückenbau: Ein Geleitwort vom Chefredakteur des *Aufbau.*" In Schaber, *Aufbau/Reconstruction,* 11–20.

Stephan, Alexander. *Die deutsche Exilliteratur 1933–1945: Eine Einführung.* Munich: Beck, 1979.

Taylor, John Russell. *Strangers in Paradise: The Hollywood Emigres 1933–1950.* New York: Holt, Rinehart & Winston, 1983.

Ulin, David L., ed. *Writing Los Angeles: A Literary Anthology.* New York: The Library of America, 2002.

Verge, Arthur C. *Paradise Transformed: Los Angeles during the Second World War.* Dubuque, IA: Kendall/Hunt, 1993.

Vietta, Silvio. *Die literarische Moderne: Eine problemgeschichtliche Darstellung der deutschsprachigen Literatur von Hölderlin bis Thomas Bernhard.* Stuttgart: Metzler, 1992.

Vietta, Silvio, and Dirk Kemper, eds. *Ästhetische Moderne in Europa: Grundzüge und Problemzusammenhänge seit der Romantik.* Munich: Fink, 1998.

Völker, Klaus. *Brecht-Chronik.* Munich: Hanser, 1971.

Wagner, Anton. *Los Angeles: Werden, Leben und Gestalt der Zweimillionenstadt in Südkalifornien.* Leipzig: Bibliographisches Institut, 1935.

Walter, Hans Albert. *Deutsche Exilliteratur 1933–1950.* 4 vols. Stuttgart: Metzler, 1978–2003.

The Weimar Republic Sourcebook. Ed. Anton Kaes, Martin Jay, and Edward Dimendberg. Berkeley: University of California Press, 1994.Winkler, Heinrich August. *Weimar 1918–1933: Die Geschichte der ersten deutschen Demokratie.* Munich: Beck, 1973.

Weschler, Lawrence. "Paradise: The Southern California Idyll of Hitler's Cultural Exiles." In Barron, *Exiles,* 341–57.

Williams, Raymond. "When Was Modernism?" In *The Politics of Modernism: Against the New Conformists,* ed. and introduction by Tony Pinkney, 31–35. Reprint London: Verso, 1997 [1989].

Wolman, Ruth E. *Crossing Over: An Oral History of Refugees from Hitler's Reich.* Twayne's Oral History Series, noo. 21. New York: Twayne, 1996.

CHAPTER 1

Adorno, Theodor W. *Briefe und Briefwechsel.* Ed. Theodor W. Adorno Archiv. 5 vols. Frankfurt/Main: Suhrkamp, 1994–2003.

————. "Cultural Criticism and Society." In *Prisms*, trans. Samuel and Sherry Weber, 17–34. Cambridge, MA: MIT Press, 1983.

————. *Gesammelte Schriften in zwanzig Bänden.* Ed. Rolf Tiedemann in cooperation with Gretel Adorno, Susan Buck-Morss, and Klaus Schultz. Frankfurt/Main: Suhrkamp, 1973–86.

————. *Minima Moralia: Reflections from Damaged Life.* Trans. E. F. N. Jephcott. London: Verso, 1978.

————. *Nachgelassene Schriften.* Ed. Theodor W. Adorno Archiv. 16 vols. Frankfurt/Main: Suhrkamp, 1993–2003.

————. "Scientific Experiences of a European Scholar in America." In *Critical Models: Interventions and Catchwords*, trans. with a preface by Henry W. Pickford, 215–42. New York: Columbia University Press, 1998.

Bernstein, J. M. *Adorno: Disenchantment and Ethics.* Cambridge: Cambridge University Press, 2001.

Claussen, Detlev. *Theodor W. Adorno: Ein letztes Genie.* Frankfurt/Main: Fischer, 2003.

Dewey, John, and Horace M. Kallen, eds. *The Bertrand Russell Case.* New York: Viking, 1941.

Gros, Harvey. "Adorno in Los Angeles: The Intellectual in Emigration." *Humanities in Society* 2.4 (Fall 1979): 339–51.

Hohendahl, Peter Uwe. *Prismatic Thought: Theodor W. Adorno.* Lincoln: University of Nebraska Press, 1995.

Horkheimer, Max. *Gesammelte Schriften.* Ed. Alfred Schmidt and Gunzelin Schmid Noerr. 19 vols. Frankfurt/Main: Fischer, 1988–96.

Horkheimer, Max, and Theodor W. Adorno. *Dialectic of Enlightenment.* Trans. John Cumming. New York: Seabury Press, 1972.

————. *Dialectic of Enlightenment: Philosophical Fragments.* Ed. Gunzelin Schmidt Noerr, trans. Edmund Jephcott. Stanford, CA: Stanford University Press, 2002.

————. "Memorandum." Unpublished typescript of 11 December 1940, 1 page. Horkheimer-Archiv, Stadt- und Universitätsbibliothek, Frankfurt/Main.

Israel, Nico. *Outlandish Writing between Exile and Diaspora.* Stanford, CA: Stanford University Press, 2000.

Jäger, Lorenz. *Adorno: Eine politische Biographie.* Stuttgart: DVA, 2003. Trans. by Stewart Spencer as *Adorno: A Political Biography.* New Haven, CT: Yale University Press, 2004.

Jameson, Fredric. *A Singular Modernity: Essay on the Ontology of the Present.* London: Verso, 2002.

Jay, Martin. "Adorno in America." In *Permanent Exiles: Essays on the Intellectual Migration from Germany to America*, 120–37. New York: Columbia University Press, 1985.

————. *The Dialectical Imagination: A History of the Frankfurt School and the Institute of Social Research 1923–1950.* Boston: Little, Brown, 1973.

Kellner, Douglas. *Critical Theory, Marxism and Modernity.* Baltimore, MD: Johns Hopkins University Press, 1989.

Lowenthal, Leo. "Theodor W. Adorno: An Intellectual Memoir." *Humanities in Society* 2.4 (Fall 1979): 387–99.

Müller-Doohm, Stefan. *Adorno: Eine Biografie*. Frankfurt/Main: Suhrkamp, 2003. Trans. by Rodney Livingstone as *Adorno: A Biography*. London: Polity Press, 2005.

O'Connor, Brian, ed. *The Adorno Reader*. Oxford: Blackwell, 2000.

Sproul, Robert G. "Letter to Max Horkheimer of November 4, 1940." Unpublished letter, Horkheimer-Archiv, Stadt- und Universitätsbibliothek, Frankfurt am Main.

Wiggershaus, Rolf. *The Frankfurt School: Its History, Theories, and Political Significance*. Trans. Michael Robertson. Cambridge: Polity Press, 1994. German edition: *Die Frankfurter Schule: Geschichte, Theoretische Entwicklung, Politische Bedeutung*. Munich: Hanser, 1986.

CHAPTER 2

Adorno, Theodor W. *Adorno on Music*. Ed. Robert W. Witkin. London: Routledge, 1998.

———. *Aesthetic Theory*. Ed. Gretel Adorno and Rolf Tiedemann, newly trans., ed. and with a translator's introduction by Robert Hullot-Kentor. Minneapolis: University of Minnesota Press, 1997.

———. *Briefe an die Eltern 1939–1951*. Ed. Christoph Gödde and Henri Lonitz. Frankfurt/Main: Suhrkamp, 2003.

———. *The Culture Industry: Selected Essays on Mass Culture*. Ed. and introduction by J. M. Bernstein. London: Routledge, 1991.

———. *Essays on Music*. Trans. Susan H. Gillespie, with introduction, commentary, and notes by Richard Leppert. Berkeley: University of California Press, 2002.

———. "Farewell to Jazz." In *Essays on Music*, 496–500.

———. *Philosophie der neuen Musik*. 8th ed. Frankfurt/Main: Suhrkamp, 1997.

———. *Philosophy of Modern Music*. Trans. Anne G. Mitchell and Wesley W. Blomster. New York: Seabury Press, 1973.

Bernstein, J. M. *The Fate of Art: Aesthetic Alienation from Kant to Derrida and Adorno*. University Park: Pennsylvania State University Press, 1992.

———. "Introduction." In Adorno, *The Culture Industry*, 1–28.

Crawford, Dorothy Lamb. *Evenings On and Off the Roof: Pioneering Concerts in Los Angeles, 1939–1971*. Berkeley: University of California Press, 1995.

Dahlhaus, Carl. "Schoenberg's Late Works." In *Schoenberg and the New Music: Essays by Carl Dahlhaus*, trans. Derrick Puffett and Alfred Clayton, 156–68. Cambridge: Cambridge University Press, 1987.

Hohendahl, Peter Uwe. "Autonomy of Art: Looking Back at Adorno's *Aesthetische Theorie*." In *Reappraisals: Shifting Alignments in Postwar Criticial Theory*, 75–98. Ithaca, NY: Cornell University Press, 1991.

Israel, Nico. "Adorno, Los Angeles, and the Dislocation of Culture." In *Outlandish: Writing between Exile and Diaspora*, 75–122. Stanford, CA: Stanford University Press, 2000.

Jay, Martin. *The Dialectical Imagination: A History of the Frankfurt School and the Institute of Social Research*. Boston: Little, Brown, 1973.

Koepnick, Lutz. *The Dark Mirror: German Cinema between Hitler and Holly-wood*. Berkeley: University of California Press, 2002.

Roth, Joseph. "Berliner Vergnügungsindustrie [1930]." In *Werke* 3: Das jour-nalistische Werk 1929–1939, ed. Klaus Westermann, 211–15. Cologne: Kiepenheuer & Witsch, 1991.

Schmidt, James. "Mephistopheles in Hollywood: Adorno, Mann, and Schoen-berg." In *Cambridge Companion to Adorno*, ed. Tom Huhn, 148–80. Cam-bridge: Cambridge University Press, 2004.

Schoenberg, Arnold. *Style and Idea: Selected Writings*. Ed. Leonard Stein, trans. Leo Black. Berkeley: University of California Press, 1975.

Theodor W. Adorno-Archiv, ed. *Adorno: Eine Bildmonographie*. Frankfurt/Main: Suhrkamp, 2003.

CHAPTERS 3 AND 4

Armor, John, and Peter Wright. *Manzanar*. Commentary by John Hersey, pho-tographs by Ansel Adams. New York: Vintage, 1989.

Bentley, Eric. "An Un-American Chalk Circle?" In *Brecht*, ed. Erika Munk, 198–212. New York: Bantam, 1972.

Bentley, Eric, ed. *Thirty Years of Treason: Excerpts from Hearings before the House Committee on Un-American Activities, 1938–1968*. New York: Viking, 1971.

Bentley, Eric, presenter. *Bertolt Brecht before the Committee on Un-American Activities: House of Representatives 80ᵗʰ Congress, Oct. 20–30, 1947. An Historical Encounter*, Folkways Records no. FD 5531. New York: Folkways Records, 1961.

Bohnert, Christiane. *Brechts Lyrik im Kontext: Zyklen und Exil*. Königstein/Ts.: Athenäum, 1982.

Brecht, Bertolt. *Collected Plays*. Ed. Ralph Manheim and John Willet. Vol. 7. New York: Vintage Books, 1975.

———. *Galileo: A Play by Bertolt Brecht*. English version by Charles Laughton, ed. and introduction by Eric Bentley. New York: Grove Press, 1966.

———. "Galileo: English Adaptation by Charles Laughton." In *Werke: Große kommentierte Berliner und Frankfurter Ausgabe*, ed. Werner Hecht et al., 5: 117–86. Frankfurt/Main: Suhrkamp, 1988.

———. *Journals 1934–1955*. Ed. John Willett and Ralph Manheim. New York: Routledge, 1993.

———. *Poems 1913–1956*. Ed. John Willett and Ralph Manheim with the co-operation of Erich Fried. New York: Methuen, 1976.

———. *Werke: Große kommentierte Berliner und Frankfurter Ausgabe*. Ed. Werner Hecht et al. 30 vols. Frankfurt/Main: Suhrkamp, 1988–2000.

Brecht Handbuch in fünf Bänden. Ed. Jan Knopf. 5 vols. Stuttgart: Metzler, 2001–2003.

Ceplair, Larry, and Steven Englund. *The Inquisition in Hollywood: Politics in the Film Community, 1930–1960*. Berkeley: University of California Press, 1983.

Cook, Bruce. *Brecht in Exile*. New York: Holt, Rinehart & Winston, 1982.

Eisler, Hanns. *The Hollywood Songbook / Hollywood Liederbuch with*

Matthias Goerne and Eric Schneider, Piano. Music Suppressed by the Third Reich / Entartete Musik. London: Decca Records, 1998.

Englmann, Bettina. "Gestische Mimesis: Bertolt Brecht." In *Poetik des Exils: Die Modernität der deutschsprachigen Exilliteratur,* 98–119. Tübingen: Niemeyer, 2001.

Foucault, Michel. "Of Other Spaces." Trans. Jay Miskowiec. *Diacritics* 16.1 (Spring 1986): 22–27.

Frey, Erich A. "Thomas Mann and His Friends Before the Tolan Committee (1942)." In *Exile: The Writer's Experience,* ed. John M. Spalek and Robert F. Bell, 203–17. Chapel Hill: University of North Carolina Press, 1982.

Fuhrmann, Marion. *Hollywood und Buckow: Politisch-ästhetische Strukturen in den Elegien Brechts.* Cologne: Pahl-Rugenstein, 1985.

Hecht, Werner. *Brecht Chronik 1898–1956.* Frankfurt/Main: Suhrkamp, 1997.

Hermand, Jost. "Bertolt Brecht: Hollywood Elegien (1978)." In *"Das Ewig-Bürgerliche widert mich an": Brecht-Aufsätze,* 172–76. Eggersdorf: Theater der Zeit, 2001.

Hersey, John. " 'A Mistake of Terrifically Horrible Proportions.' " In Armor and Wright, *Manzanar,* 1–66.

Hohenwallner, Ingrid. *Antikerezeption in den Gedichten Bertolt Brechts,* Arianna, vol. 5. Salzburg: Bibliopolis, 2004.

Jameson, Fredric. *A Singular Modernity: Essay on the Ontology of the Present.* London: Verso, 2002.

Knopf, Jan. *Brecht-Handbuch: Lyrik, Prosa, Schriften: Eine Ästhetik der Widersprüche.* Reprint Stuttgart: Metzler, 1996. Cited as Knopf, *Brecht-Handbuch 2.*

———. *Brecht-Handbuch: Theater: Eine Ästhetik der Widersprüche.* Reprint Stuttgart: Metzler, 1996.

———. *Gelegentlich: Poesie: Ein Essay über die Lyrik Bertolt Brechts.* Frankfurt/Main: Suhrkamp, 1966.

Langemeyer, Peter, ed. *Bertolt Brecht: Leben des Galilei,* Erläuterungen und Dokumente, no. 16020. Stuttgart: Reclam, 2001.

Ley, Ralph J. "Francis Bacon, Galileo, and the Brechtian Theater." In *Essays on Brecht: Theater and Politics,* ed. Siegfried Mews and Herbert Knust, 174–89. Chapel Hill: University of North Carolina Press, 1974.

Lyon, James K. *Bertolt Brecht in America.* Princeton, NJ: Princeton University Press, 1980.

Lyon, James K., ed. *Brecht in den USA.* Frankfurt/Main: Suhrkamp, 1994.

Lyon, James K., and John B. Fuegi. "Bertolt Brecht." *Deutsche Exilliteratur seit 1933: 1. Kalifornien,* ed. John M. Spalek and Joseph Strelka, 268–98. Bern: Francke, 1976.

Mann, Thomas. *Tagebücher 1940–1943.* Ed. Peter de Mendelssohn. Frankfurt/Main: Fischer, 1982.

Mann, Thomas, and Agnes E. Meyer. *Briefwechsel 1937–1955.* Ed. Hans Rudolf Vaget. Frankfurt/Main: Fischer, 1992.

Materialien zu Brechts Leben des Galilei. Ed. Werner Hecht. Frankfurt/Main: Suhrkamp, 1963.

Mennemeier, Franz Norbert. *Bertolt Brechts Lyrik: Aspekte, Tendenzen.* Düsseldorf: Schwann-Bagel, 1982.

The Penguin Book of German Verse. Ed. Leonard Forster. Reprinted with revisions. Harmondsworth, Middlesex: Penguin Books, 1959.

Pike, Donald, and Roger Olmstedt. "The Japanese in California." In *Executive Order 9066: The Internment of 10,000 Japanese Americans,* ed. Masie and Richard Conrat, 17–23. Reprint University of California, Los Angeles, Asian American Studies Center, 1992.

Plagens, Peter. *Sunshine Muse: Art on the West Coast, 1945–1970.* Berkeley: University of California Press, 1999 [1974].

Rülicke, Käthe. "Bemerkungen zur Schlußszene." In *Materialien zu Brechts* Leben des Galilei, 91–152.

Schumacher, Ernst. "The Dialectics of Galileo." In *Brecht Sourcebook,* ed. Carol Martin and Henry Bial, 113–23. London, New York: Routledge, 2000.

———. *Drama und Geschichte: Bertolt Brechts* Leben des Galilei *und andere Stücke.* Berlin: Henschel, 1965.

Smith, Peter D. "Pure Science, Lethal Technology: Brecht's *Leben des Galilei.*" In *Metaphor and Materiality: German Literature and the World-View of Science 1780–1955,* 265–318. Oxford: European Humanities Research Centre, 2000.

Whitaker, Peter. *Brecht's Poetry: A Critical Study.* New York: Oxford University Press, 1985.

White, John J. *Bertolt Brecht's Dramatic Theory.* Rochester, NY: Camden House, 2004.

Wizisla, Erdmut. "Vortreffliches für verbildete Zeitgenossen. Galileo Galilei—Albert Einsteins Briefe an Bertolt Brecht." *Frankfurter Allgemeine Zeitung,* 15 September 2004, N3.

Wüthrich, Werner. " 'Hello, dear Brecht . . . ' Charles Laughton demonstriert Bertolt Brechts episches Theater." *Neue Zürcher Zeitung,* 27 February 2006, www.nzz.ch/2006/02/27/fe/articleDKGET.html.

CHAPTER 5

Alberts, Jürgen. *Hitler in Hollywood oder: Die Suche nach dem Idealscript.* Göttingen: Steidl, 1997.

Aurich, Rolf, Wolfgang Jacobsen, and Cornelius Schnauber, eds. *Fritz Lang: Leben und Werk. Bilder und Dokumente / Fritz Lang: His Life and Work. Photographs and Documents / Fritz Lang: Sa vie et son oeuvre. Photos et documents.* Berlin: Filmmuseum Berlin—Deutsche Kinemathek and jovis Verlag, 2001.

Bonnaud, Irène. "Widerstand in Widersprüchen: Bertolt Brecht und Fritz Lang im Streit um *Hangmen Also Die.*" In *Brecht plus minus Film,* 38–46.

Borde, Raymond, and Étienne Chaumeton. "Towards a Definition of Film Noir." In *Film Noir Reader,* ed. Alain Silver and James Ursini, 17–25. 6th ed. New York: Limelight Editions, 2001 [1996]..

Brecht plus minus Film: Filme, Bilder, Bildbetrachtungen, Recherchen 16. Ed. Thomas Martin and Erdmut Wizisla. Berlin: Theater der Zeit, 2003.

Comolli, Jean, and François Géré. "Deux Fictions de la Haine." *Cahier du Cinéma* 286 (March 1978): 30–48. English translation in E. Ann Kaplan, *Fritz Lang: A Guide,* 373–76.

Cook, Bruce. "Brecht and Fritz Lang." In *Brecht in Exile*, 78–96. New York: Holt, Rinehart &Winston, 1982.

Dimendberg, Edward. *Film Noir and the Spaces of Modernity*. Cambridge, MA: Harvard University Press, 2004.

Doherty, Thomas. *Projections of War: Hollywood, American Culture, and World War II*. New York: Columbia University Press, 1993.

Eisner, Lotte H. *Fritz Lang*. Reprint New York: Da Capo Press, 1986. Originally published: London: Secker and Warburg, 1976.

Gemünden, Gerd. "Brecht in Hollywood: *Hangmen Also Die* and the Anti-Nazi Film." *TDR. The Drama Review: A Journal of Performance Studies* 43.4 (1999): 65–76.

Gersch, Wolfgang. *Film bei Brecht: Bertolt Brechts praktische und theoretische Auseinandersetzung mit dem Film*. Munich: Hanser, 1975.

Grant, Barry Keith, ed. *Fritz Lang: Interviews*. Jackson: University Press of Mississippi, 2003.

Gunning. Tom. *The Films of Fritz Lang: Allegories of Vision and Modernity*. London: British Film Institute, 2000.

Haasis, Hellmut G. *Tod in Prag. Das Attentat auf Reinhard Heydrich*. Reinbek: Rowohlt, 2002.

Horak, Jan-Christopher. *Anti-Nazi-Filme der deutschsprachigen Emigration von Hollywood 1939–1945*. 2nd ed. Münster: MAkS Publikationen, 1985.

Humphries, Reynold. *Fritz Lang: Genre and Representation in His American Films*. Baltimore, MD: Johns Hopkins University Press, 1988.

Jenkins, Stephen, ed. *Fritz Lang: The Image and the Look*. London: British Film Institute, 1981.

Kaes, Anton. *M*. London: British Film Institute, 2000.

Kaplan, E. Ann. *Fritz Lang: A Guide to References and Resources*. Boston: G. K. Hall, 1981.

Koepnick, Lutz. *The Dark Mirror: German Cinema Between Hitler and Hollywood*. Berkeley: University of California Press, 2002.

Krakauer, Siegfried. *From Caligari to Hitler: A Psychological History of the German Film*. Princeton, NJ: Princeton University Press, 1974.

Lang, Fritz. "Autobiography." In Lotte H. Eisner, *Fritz Lang*, 9–15. New York: Da Capo Press, 1986.

———. *Fritz Lang's Masterpiece of Intrigue and Deception: Hangmen Also Die, Noir: The Dark Side of Hollywood*. U.S. 1943 B&W 134 Min. © Arnold Productions, Inc., © renewed 1970 Film Archives Trading Co.

Lang, Fritz, and Bertolt Brecht. "437!! Ein Geiselfilm." *Brecht Yearbook* 28 (2003): 9–30.

———. " *Never Surrender!*" *Brecht Yearbook* 30 (2005): 7–60.

Lyon, James K. "Hangmen Also Die." In *Brecht Handbuch*, ed. Jan Knopf, 3: 457–65. Stuttgart: Metzler, 2002.

———. "*Hangmen Also Die* Once Again—Dispelling the Last Doubts about Brecht's Role as Author." In *Brecht Yearbook* 30 (2005): 1–6.

———. "The Original Story Version of Hangmen Also Die—A Recently Discovered Document." In *Brecht Yearbook* 28 (2003): 1–8.

———. "A Qualified Winner—The Film *Hangmen Also Die.*" In *Bertolt Brecht in America,* 58–71. Princeton, NJ: Princeton University Press, 1980.

———. "Das hätte nur Brecht schreiben können." In *Brecht plus minus Film,* 26–36.

MacDonald, Callum. *The Killing of SS Obergruppenführer Reinhard Heydrich.* New York: Free Press, 1989.

Mews, Siegfried. "Hitler in Hollywood: Hangmen Also Die Revisited." In *Brecht Yearbook* 28 (2003): 33–46.

McGilligan, Patrick. *Fritz Lang: The Nature of the Beast.* New York: St. Martin's, 1997.

Naremore, James. *More Than Night: Film Noir and Its Contexts.* Berkeley: University of California Press, 1998.

O'Brien, Charles. "Film Noir in France: Before the Liberation." *Iris* 21 (Spring 1996): 7–21.

Schatz, Thomas, ed. *History of the American Cinema: Boom and Bust: The American Cinema in the 1940s.* New York: Scribner/Macmillan, 1990.

Schebera, Jürgen, ed. *Henker sterben auch (Hangmen Also Die): Drehbuch und Materialien zum Film.* Trans. Jürgen Schebera. Berlin-Ost: Henschel, 1985.

Schnauber, Cornelius."Brecht und Lang: *Hangmen Also Die.* Ein Bericht." In *Wenn wir von gestern reden, sprechen wir über heute und morgen: Festschrift für Marta Mierendorff zum 80. Geburtstag,* ed. Helmut G. Asper, 191–206. Berlin: Edition Sigma Bohn, 1991.

———. *Fritz Lang in Hollywood.* Vienna: Europaverlag, 1986.

Silver, Alain, and James Ursini, eds. *Film Noir Reader.* 6th ed. New York: Limelight Editions, 2001 [1996].

White, John J. *Bertolt Brecht's Dramatic Theory.* Rochester, NY: Camden House, 2004.

Whiting, Charles. *Heydrich: Henchman of Death.* Barnsley, South Yorkshire: Leo Cooper, 1999.

CHAPTER 6

Banham, Reyner. "Architecture III: The Exiles." In *Los Angeles: The Architecture of Four Ecologies,* 179–99. Harmondsworth: Penguin Books, 1973 [1971].

Clark, Robert Judson, and Thomas S. Hines. *Los Angeles Transfer: Architecture in Southern California.* Los Angeles: William Andrews Clark Memorial Library, 1983.

Cuff, Dana. *The Provisional City: Los Angeles Stories of Architecture and Urbanism.* Cambridge, MA: MIT Press, 2000.

Drexler, Arthur, and Thomas S. Hines. *The Architecture of Richard Neutra: From International Style to California Modern.* New York: Museum of Modern Art, 1982.

Gebhard, David. *Schindler.* Preface by Henry-Russel Hitchcock. New York: Viking Press, 1972.

Gebhard, David, and Harriette Von Breton. *Los Angeles in the Thirties:*

1931–1941. 2nd rev. and enlarged ed. Los Angeles: Hennessey & Ingalls, 1989.

Gebhard, David, and Robert Winter. *Los Angeles: An Architectural Guide*. Salt Lake City, UT: Gibbs Smith, 1994.

Hines, Thomas. "Housing, Baseball, and Creeping Socialism: The Battle of Chavez Ravine, Los Angeles, 1949–1959." *Journal of Urban History* 8.2 (February 1982): 123–43.

———. *Irving Gill and the Architecture of Reform: A Study of Modernist Architectural Culture*. New York: Monacelli Press, 2000.

———. "Los Angeles Transfer: Rationalism and Reintegration 1920–1980." In Clark and Hines, *Los Angeles Transfer: Architecture in Southern California 1880–1980*, 57–120.

———. "Machines in the Garden: Notes toward a History of Modern Los Angeles Architecture, 1900–1990." In *Sex, Death and God in L.A.*, ed. David Reid, 259–318. New York: Pantheon, 1992.

———. *Richard Neutra*. New York: Rizzoli; Enfield: High Marketing [distributor], 2005. Originally published as *Richard Neutra and the Search for Modern Architecture*. New York, Oxford: Oxford University Press, 1982.

———. *Richard Neutra and the Search for Modern Architecture*. Oxford: Oxford University Press, 1982.

Lamprecht, Barbara Mac. *Richard Neutra, 1892–1970: Survival through Design*. Cologne: Taschen, 2004.

———. *Richard Neutra: The Complete Works*. Ed. Peter Goessel, preface and editorial assistance by Dion Neutra, epilogue and principle photography by Julius Shulman. Cologne: Taschen, 2000.

Lavin, Sylvia. *Form Follows Libido: Architecture and Richard Neutra in a Psychoanalytic Culture*. Cambridge, MA: MIT Press, 2004.

Mallgrave, Harry Francis. "Schindler's Program of 1913." In *R. M. Schindler: Composition and Construction*, ed. Lionel March and Judith Sheine, 14–19.

Mann, Thomas. "The Exiled Writer's Relation to His Homeland." In *Writers' Congress: The Proceedings of the Conference Held in October 1943 under the Sponsorship of the Hollywood Writers' Mobilization and the University of California*, 339–44. Berkeley: University of California Press, 1944.

March, Lionel, and Judith Sheine, eds. *R. M. Schindler: Composition and Construction*. New York: Academy Editions, 1993.

Marmorstein, Gary. "Steel and Slurry: Dr. Philip M. Lovell, Architectural Patron." *Southern California Quarterly* 84 (2002): 241–70.

McCoy, Esther. *Five California Architects*. Reprint Los Angeles: Hennessy + Ingalls, 1987 [1960].

Neutra, Dione. "To Tell the Truth." Oral history transcript. Interviewed by Lawrence Weschler, 1978. Los Angeles: Oral History Program, University of California, 1983.

Neutra, Richard Joseph. *Amerika: Die Stilbildung des neuen Bauens in den Vereinigten Staaten*, Neues Bauen in der Welt, 2. Vienna: A Schroll, 1930.

———. *Life and Shape*. New York: Appleton-Century Crofts, 1962.

———. *Mensch und Wohnen. Life and Human Habitat*. Stuttgart: A. Koch, 1956.

———. *Nature Near: Late Essays of Richard Neutra.* Ed. William Marlin, foreword by Norman Cousins. Santa Barbara, CA: Capra Press, 1989.

———. *Naturnahes Bauen. Building with Nature.* Ed. Dione Neutra. New York: Universe Books, 1971.

———. *Survival through Design.* New York: Oxford University Press, 1954.

———. *Wie baut Amerika?*, Die Baubücher, 1. Ed. Dione Neutra. Stuttgart: J. Hoffmann, 1927.

Noever, Peter, ed. *Schindler by MAK: Prestel Museum Guide.* Munich: Prestel, 2005.

Ouroussoff, Nicolai. "Back to the Housing Lab: The restoration of L.A.'s Pueblo del Rio, built to acclaim in 1942, will say much about our society and its ideals today." *Los Angeles Times*, Calendar, 4 November 2001, 6–7, 71.

Parson, Donald Craig. *Making a Better World: Public Housing, the Red Scare, and the Direction of Modern Los Angeles.* Foreword by Kevin Starr. Minneapolis: University of Minnesota Press, 2005.

Polyzoides, Stefanos. "Space Architecture Inside Out." In *R. M. Schindler: Composition and Construction*, 196–205.

Sarnitz, August. *R. M. Schindler, Architect (1887–1953).* Trans. David Britt. New York: Rizzoli, 1988.

Schindler, R. M. "A Cooperative Dwelling. T-Square 2 (February 1932): 20–21." Appendix B in Kathryn Smith, *Schindler House*, 81.

———. "Letter to Mr. and Mrs. Edmund J. Gibling, Evanston, Illinois, November 26, 1921." Appendix A in Kathryn Smith, *Schindler House*, 80.

———. "Modern Architecture: A Program (1913): A New Translation of Schindler's Original Manuscript." In *R. M. Schindler: Composition and Construction*, ed. Lionel March and Judith Sheine, 10–12.

Sheine, Judith. *R. M. Schindler.* New York: Phaidon, 2001.

Smith, Elizabeth A. T., and Michael Darling, eds. *The Architecture of R. M. Schindler.* Los Angeles: Museum of Contemporary Art, 2001.

Smith, Kathryn. *Schindler House.* New photography by Grant Mudford. New York: Abrams, 2000.

Steele, James, Peter Gossel (editor), and Joachim Schumacher (photographer). *R. M. Schindler.* New York: Taschen, 1999.

Suvin, Darko. "Displaced Persons." *New Left Review* 20 (March/April 2003): 113–30.

Sweeney, Robert L. "Life at Kings Road: As It Was, 1920–1940." In *The Architecture of R. M. Schindler*, ed. Elizabeth A. T. Smith and Michael Darling, 86–115.

———. *Wright in Hollywood: Visions of a New Architecture.* New York: Architectural History Foundation; Cambridge, MA: MIT Press, 1994.

Wefing, Heinrich. "Das Haus des Zauberers: Thomas Manns Villa in Pacific Palisades." *Sinn und Form* 56 (2004): 562–69.

Wilson, Richard Guy. "Schindler's Metaphysics: Space, the Machine, and Modernism." In *The Architecture of R. M. Schindler*, ed. Elizabeth A. T. Smith and Michael Darling, 116–43.

Wright, Frank Lloyd. *Ausgeführte Bauten und Entwürfe.* Berlin: Erich Wasmuth, 1910.

CHAPTER 7

Angress [Klüger], Ruth. "The Christian Surrealism of Elisabeth Langgässer." In *The Vision Obscured: Perceptions of Some Twentieth-Century Catholic Novelists*, ed. Melvin J. Friedman, 187–200. New York: Fordham University Press, 1970.

Buch, Hans Christoph. "Ein Genozid, die offiziell nie stattgefunden hat. Über Werfels Die vierzig Tage des Musa Dagh." In *Waldspaziergang: Unpolitische Betrachtungen zu Literatur und Politik*, 107–17. Frankfurt/Main: Suhrkamp, 1987.

Davidheiser, James C. "From Premonition to Portrayal: Franz Werfel and World War II." In *Der Zweite Weltkrieg und die Exilanten: Eine literarische Antwort / World War II and the Exiles: A Literary Response*, ed. Helmut F. Pfanner, 13–22. Bonn: Bouvier, 1991.

Englmann, Bettina. " 'Je une autre'—Franz Werfels ironisches Spiel mit der auktorialen Identität in *Stern der Ungeborenen*." In *Poetik des Exils: Die Modernität der deutschsprachigen Exilliteratur*, 392–408. Tübingen: Niemeyer, 2001.

Jungk, Peter Stephan. *Franz Werfel: A Life in Prague, Vienna, and Hollywood.* Trans. Anselm Hollo. New York: Grove Weidenfeld, 1990.

Magris, Claudio. *Der habsburgische Mythos in der österreichischen Literatur.* Salzburg: Otto Müller, 1966.

Mann, Thomas. *The Story of a Novel: The Genesis of Doctor Faustus.* Trans. Richard and Clara Winston. New York: Knopf, 1961.

Mierendorff, Marta. "Spekulierende Einbildungskraft und historische Analyse: Franz Werfels Exilroman Stern der Ungeborenen." In *Die deutsche Exilliteratur 1933–1945,* ed. Manfred Durzak, 480–88. Stuttgart: Reclam, 1973.

Pfeifer, Josef. "Werfel und die politischen Umwälzungen des Jahres 1918 in Wien." *Etudes Germaniques* 26 (1971): 194–207.

Politzer, Heinz. "Prague and the Origins of R. M. Rilke, Franz Kafka and Franz Werfel." *Modern Language Quarterly* 16 (1955): 49–62.

Reisch, Terry. "Franz Werfel: Waiting for His Time to Come." In *The Fortunes of German Writers in America: Studies in Literary Reception,* ed. Wolfgang Elfe, James Hardin, and Gunther Holst, 185–210. Columbia: University of South Carolina Press, 1992.

Rosenthal, Regine. "Reinscribing the Other: Transfigurations of the Wandering Jew in Heym, Kafka, and Werfel." *Carleton Germanic Papers* 24 (1996): 127–54.

Rostinsky, Joseph N. "Number Symbols and Remnant Motifs in Franz Werfel's *Song of Bernadette*: A Pragmatic Interpretation." In *Unser Fahrplan geht von Stern zu Stern: Zu Franz Werfels Stellung und Werk,* ed. Joseph Strelka and Robert Weigel, 243–48. Bern: Lang, 1992.

Schwarz, Egon. " 'Ich war also Jude! Ich war ein Anderer!' Franz Werfels Darstellung der soziopsychologischen Judenproblematik." In *Franz Werfel: Neue Aspekte seines Werkes,* ed. Karlheinz Auckenthaler, 165–76. Acta Germanica, 2. Szeged: Jozsef-Attila University, 1992.

Sokel, Walter H. *The Writer in Extremis: Expressionism in Twentieth-Century German Literature*. Stanford, CA: Stanford University Press, 1959.

Starr, Kevin. *The Dream Endures: California Enters the 1940s*. Oxford: Oxford University Press, 1997.

Steimann, Lionel B. *Franz Werfel: The Faith of an Exile: From Prague to Beverly Hills*. Waterloo, Ontario: Wilfrid Laurier University Press, 1985.

Taylor, Rodney. "The Concepts of Reality and Transcendental Being in Franz Werfel's Das Lied von Bernadette." In *Autoren von damals und heute: Literaturgeschichtliche Beispiele veränderter Wirkungshorizonte*, ed. Gerhard P. Knapp, 639–63. Amsterdam: Rodopi, 1991.

Weissenberger, Klaus. "Franz Werfels Lied von Bernadette und die dichterische Darstellung des Wunders." *Colloquia Germanica* 25 (1992): 122–44.

Werfel, Franz. *Embezzled Heaven*. Trans. Moray Firth. New York: Viking, 1940.

———. *The Forty Days of Musa Dagh*. Trans. Geoffrey Dunlop. New York: Viking, 1934.

———. *Jacobowsky and the Colonel: Comedy of a Tragedy in Three Acts*. Trans. Gustave O. Arlt. New York: Viking, 1944.

———. *The Song of Bernadette*. Trans. Ludwig Lewisohn. New York: Viking, 1942.

———. *Star of the Unborn*. Trans. Gustave O. Arlt. New York: Viking, 1946.

———. *Der Weltfreund. Gedichte*. Charlottenburg-Berlin: Axel Juncker, 1911.

———. *Zwischen Oben und Unten: Prosa, Tagebücher, Aphorismen, Literarische Nachträge*, ed. Adolf D. Klarmann. Munich: Langen-Müller, 1975.

CHAPTER 8

Auer, Manfred. *Das Exil vor der Vertreibung: Motivkontinuität und Quellenproblematik im späten Werk Alfred Döblins*. Bonn: Bouvier, 1970.

Bartscherer, Christoph. "Robinson the Castaway: Döblin's Christian Faith as Reflected in His Autobiography *Schicksalsreise* and His Religious Dialogues *Der unsterbliche Mensch* and *Der Kampf mit dem Engel*." In *A Companion to the Works of Alfred Döblin*, 247–70.

Busch, Arnold. *Faust und Faschismus: Thomas Manns Doktor Faustus und Alfred Döblins November 1918 als exilliterarische Auseinandersetzung mit Deutschland*. Frankfurt/Main: Lang, 1984.

A Companion to the Works of Alfred Döblin. Ed. Roland Dollinger, Wulf Koepke, and Heidi Thomann Tewarson. Rochester, NY: Camden House, 2004.

Döblin, Alfred. *Berlin Alexanderplatz: The Story of Franz Biberkopf*. Trans. Eugene Jolas. New York: Continuum, 2000. Originally published as *Alexanderplatz Berlin*. New York: Viking, 1931.

———. *Briefe*. Ed. Heinz Graber. Olten, Freiburg im Breisgau: Walter, 1970. Quoted as *Briefe*.

———. "The Chief [Der Chefarzt]." In *Heart of Europe: An Anthology of Creative Writing in Europe*, ed. Klaus Mann and Hermann Kesten, with an introduction by Dorothy Canfield Fisher, 678–84. New York: Blakiston, 1943.

———. *Destiny's Journey*. Ed. Edgar Pässler, trans. Edna McCown, introduction by Peter Demetz. New York: Paragon House, 1992.

———. *Karl and Rosa. November 1918: A German Revolution*. Trans. John E. Woods. New York: Fromm International, 1983.

———. *Nocturno*. Los Angeles: Pazifische Presse, 1944.

———. *November 1918: Eine deutsche Revolution,* Ausgewählte Werke in Einzelbänden. Ed. Werner Stauffacher. Vols. 1–3 in 4 vols. Olten, Freiburg im Breisgau: Walter, 1991.

———. *A People Betrayed. November 1918: A German Revolution*. Trans. John E. Woods. New York: Fromm International, 1983.

———. "Plans for Work (Novel: "November 1918" 3rd vol)." Unpublished typescript, 5 pages. Deutsches Literaturarchiv / Schiller- Nationalmuseum, Marbach am Neckar. German trans. in *November 1918: Eine deutsche Revolution* 3: 800–803. Düsseldorf: Patmos Verlag GmbH & KG / Walter Verlag, 1991.

———. *Reise in Polen*. Ed. Heinz Graber. Olten, Freiburg im Breisgau: Walter, 1968.

———. *Schriften zu jüdischen Fragen*. Ed. Hans Otto Horch. Düsseldorf: Walter, 1995.

———. *Sieger und Besiegte*. New York: Aurora, 1946.

———. *Tales of a Long Night*. Trans. Robert and Rita Kimber. New York: Fromm International, 1984.

Dollenmayer, David B. *The Berlin Novels of Alfred Döblin:* Wadzek's Battle with the Steam Turbine, Berlin Alexanderplatz, Men without Mercy, *and* November 1918. Berkeley: University of California Press, 1988.

Dollinger, Roland. *Totalität und Totalitarismus im Exilwerk Döblins.* Würzburg: Königshausen & Neumann, 1994.

Haffner, Sebastian. *Failure of a Revolution: Germany 1918–1919*. Trans. Georg Rapp, foreword and afterword by Richard Bruch. Chicago: Banner Press, 1986.

Jennings, Michael W. "Of Weimar's First and Last Things: Montage, Revolution, and Fascism in Alfred Döblin's *November 1918* and *Berlin Alexanderplatz*." In *Politics in German Literature,* ed. Beth Bjorklund and Mark E. Cory, 132–52. Columbia, SC: Camden House, 1998.

Kiesel, Helmuth. "Döblin's November 1818." In *A Companion to the Works of Alfred Döblin,* 215–32.

———. *Literarische Trauerarbeit: Das Exil- und Spätwerk Alfred Döblins.* Tübingen: Niemeyer, 1986.

Koepke, Wulf. *The Critical Reception of Alfred Döblin's Major Novels.* Rochester, NY: Camden House, 2003.

Komar, Kathleen L. *Pattern and Chaos: Multilinear Novels by Dos Passos, Döblin, Faulkner, and Koeppen.* Columbia, SC: Camden House, 1983.

Kort, Wolfgang. *Alfred Döblin*. New York: Twayne, 1974.

Meyer, Jochen, and Bernhard Zeller, eds. *Alfred Döblin, 1878–1979: Eine Ausstellung des Deutschen Literaturarchivs im Schiller-Nationalmuseum, Marbach am Neckar.* Munich: Kösel, 1978.

Müller-Salget, Klaus. "Döblin and Judaism." In *A Companion to the Works of Alfred Döblin,* 233–46.

Riley, Anthony W. "The Aftermath of the First World War: Christianity and Revolution in Alfred Döblin's *November 1918*." In *The First World War in German Narrative Prose: Essays in Honor of George Wallis Field*, ed. Charles N. Genno and Heinz Wetzel, 93–117. Toronto: University of Toronto Press, 1980.

Ryder, A. J. *The German Revolution of 1918: A Study of German Socialism in War and Revolt*. Cambridge: Cambridge University Press, 1967.

Sander, Gabriele. *Alfred Döblin*. Stuttgart: Reclam, 2001.

Stauffacher, Werner. "Einführung." In *November 1918: Eine deutsche Revolution. Ein Erzählwerk in drei Teilen. Erster Teil: Bürger und Soldaten 1918*, 9–64. Olten, Freiburg im Breisgau: Walter, 1991.

Tewarson, Heidi Thomann. "Alfred Döblins Geschichtskonzeption in November 1918: Eine deutsche Revolution. Dargestellt an der Figur Rosa Luxemburgs in Karl und Rosa." In *Internationale Alfred Döblin-Kolloquien 1980–1983: Basel 1980—New York 1981—Freiburg i. Br. 1983*, ed. Werner Stauffacher, 64–75. Bern: Lang, 1986.

Wehler, Hans-Ulrich. *Deutsche Gesellschaftsgeschichte 1914–1949*, 348–71. Munich: Beck, 2003.

Weissenberger, Klaus. "Alfred Döblin." In *Deutsche Exilliteratur seit 1933: Band 1: Kalifornien, Teil 1*, ed. John M. Spalek and Joseph Strelka, 299–322. Bern: Francke, 1976.

Winkler, Heinrich August. *Der lange Weg nach Westen*, vol. 1: *Deutsche Geschichte vom Ende des Alten Reiches bis zum Untergang der Weimarer Republik*, 378–416, 456–58. Munich: Beck, 2000.

———. *Weimar 1918–1933: Die Geschichte der ersten deutschen Demokratie*. Munich: Beck, 1993.

CHAPTER 9

Baerwald, Friedrich. "Zur politischen Tätigkeit deutscher Emigranten im Council for a Democratic Germany." *Vierteljahrshefte für Zeitgeschichte* 28 (1980): 372–83.

Bahr, Ehrhard. "Paul Tillich and the Problem of a German Government in Exile in the United States." *Yearbook of German-American Studies* 21 (1986): 1–12.

Bulletin for the Council for a Democratic Germany, issued by the Council for a Democratic Germany, Nos. 1–5 (1 September 1944—May 1945).

Bürgin, Hans, and Hans-Otto Mayer, eds. *Die Briefe Thomas Manns: Regesten und Register*. 5 vols. Frankfurt/Main: Fischer, 1976–87.

Görtemaker, Manfred. *Thomas Mann und die Politik*. Frankfurt/Main: Fischer, 2005.

Krohn, Claus-Dieter. "Der Council for a Democratic Germany." In *Was soll aus Deutschland werden?* ed. Langkau-Alex and Ruprecht, 17–48.

Langkau-Alex, Ursula, and Thomas M. Ruprecht, eds. *Was soll aus Deutschland werden? The Council for a Democratic Germany in New York 1944–1945. Aufsätze und Dokumente*. Frankfurt: Campus, 1995.

Lehnert, Herbert. "Thomas Mann, Bertolt Brecht, and the 'Free Germany' Movement." In *Exile: The Writer's Experience*, ed. John M. Spalek and

Robert F. Bell, 182–202. Chapel Hill: University of North Carolina Press, 1982.

Paetel, Karl O. "Zum Problem einer deutschen Exilregierung." *Vierteljahrshefte für Zeitgeschichte* 4 (1956): 286–301.

Scheurig, Bodo. *Free Germany: The National Committee and the League of German Officers.* Trans. Herbert Arnold. Middletown, CT: Wesleyan University Press, 1969.

Stephan, Alexander. *"Communazis": FBI Surveillance of German Emigré Writers.* Trans. Jan van Heurck. New Haven, CT: Yale University Press, 2000.

Tillich, Paul. "A Program for a Democratic Germany." *Christianity and Crisis* 4, no. 8 (15 May 1944), reprinted with permission of *Christianity and Crisis*, 3 pp.

Vaget, Hans Rudolf. *"Germany: Jekyll and Hyde.* Sebastian Haffners Deutschlandbild und die Genese von *Doktor Faustus."* In *Thomas Mann und seine Quellen: Festschrift für Hans Wysling,* ed. Eckhard Heftrich and Helmut Koopmann, 249–71. Frankfurt/Main: Klostermann, 1991.

Vansittart, Robert Baron. *Lessons of My Life.* New York: Knopf, 1943.

CHAPTER 10

Abel, Angelika. *Musikästhetik der klassischen Moderne: Thomas Mann—Theodor W. Adorno—Arnold Schönberg.* Munich: Fink, 2003.

———. *Thomas Mann im Exil.* Munich: Fink, 2003.

Adorno, Theodor W., and Thomas Mann. *Briefwechsel 1943–1955.* Ed. Christoph Gödde and Thomas Sprecher. (Briefe und Briefwechsel, vol. 3). Frankfurt/Main: Suhrkamp, 2002.

Angress-Klüger, Ruth. "Jewish Characters in Thomas Mann's Fiction." In *Horizonte: Festschrift für Herbert Lehnert zum 65. Geburtstag,* ed. Hannelore Mundt, Egon Schwarz, William J. Lillyman, 161–72. Tübingen: Niemeyer, 1990.

Benjamin, Walter. *Ursprung des deutschen Trauerspiels.* Berlin: Rowohlt, 1928.

———. *The Origin of German Tragic Drama.* Trans. John Osborne, introduction by George Steiner. London, New York: Verso, 1977.

Bergsten, Gunilla. *Thomas Mann's* Doctor Faustus: *The Sources and Structure of the Novel.* Trans. Krishna Winston. Chicago: University of Chicago Press, 1969.

Carnegy, Patrick. *Faust as Musician: A Study of Thomas Mann's Novel* Doctor Faustus. New York: New Directions, 1973.

Cobley, Evelyn. *Temptations of Faust: The Logic of Fascism and Postmodern Archaeologies of Modernity.* Toronto: University of Toronto Press, 2002.

Dahlhaus, Carl. "Fiktive Zwölftonmusik: Thomas Mann und Theodor W. Adorno." *Jahrbuch der deutschen Akademie für Sprache und Dichtung 1982,* no. 1: 33–49.

Darmaun, Jacques. *Thomas Mann, Deutschland und die Juden.* Trans. Jacques Darmaun. Tübingen: Niemeyer, 2003.

Kurzke, Hermann. *Thomas Mann: Life as a Work of Art. A Biography.* Trans. Leslie Wilson. Princeton, NJ: Princeton University Press, 2002.

Mann, Thomas. *Briefe.* Ed. Erika Mann. 3 vols. Frankfurt/Main: Fischer, 1961–65.

———. *Death in Venice and Seven Other Stories.* Trans. H. T. Lowe-Porter. New York: Vintage, 1954.

———. *Doctor Faustus: The Life of the German Composer Adrian Leverkühn As Told by a Friend.* Trans. H. T. Lowe-Porter. New York: Alfred A. Knopf, 1948.

———. *Doctor Faustus: The Life of the German Composer Adrian Leverkühn As Told by a Friend.* Trans. John E. Woods. New York: Alfred A. Knopf, 1997.

———. " 'Doctor Faustus' Schoenberg?" *Saturday Review of Literature* 32.1 (1 January 1949): 22–23.

———. *Germany and the Germans.* Washington, D.C.: Library of Congress, 1945.

———. *Gesammelte Werke in dreizehn Bänden.* 13 vols. 2nd rev. ed. Frankfurt/Main: Fischer, 1974.

———. *Letters of Thomas Mann, 1889–1955.* Trans. Richard and Clara Winston, introduction by Richard Winston. New York: Knopf, 1971.

———. *The Story of a Novel: The Genesis of* Doctor Faustus. Trans. Richard and Clara Winston. New York: Knopf, 1961.

———. *Tagebücher.* Ed. Peter de Mendelssohn and Inge Jens. 10 vols. Frankfurt/Main: Fischer, 1979–95.

Marquad, Franka. "Der Manager als Sündenbock. Zur Funktion des jüdischen Impresario Saul Fitelberg in Thomas Manns *Doktor Faustus.*" *Zeitschrift für Germanistik* 14 (2004): 564–80.

Potter, Pamela M. *Most German of the Arts: Musicology and Society from the Weimar Republic to the End of Hitler's Reich.* New Haven, CT: Yale University Press, 1998.

Robertson, Ritchie. "Accounting for History: Thomas Mann, *Doktor Faustus.*" In *The German Novel in the Twentieth Century: Beyond Realism,* ed. David Midgley, 128–48. Edinburgh: Edinburgh University Press; New York: St. Martin's Press, 1993.

Röcke, Werner, ed. *Thomas Mann,* Doktor Faustus, *1947–1997,* Supplement to Zeitschrift für Germanistik, new series, vol. 3. Bern: Lang, 2001.

Sauerland, Karol. *Einführung in die Ästhetik Adornos.* Berlin: de Gruyter, 1979.

———. " 'Er wußte noch mehr . . .' Zum Konzeptionsbruch in Thomas Manns Doktor Faustus unter dem Einfluß Adornos." *Orbis litterarum* 34 (1979): 130–45.

Schmidt, James. "Mephistopheles in Hollywood: Adorno, Mann, and Schoenberg." In *Cambridge Companion to Adorno,* ed. Tom Huhn, 148–80. Cambridge: Cambridge University Press, 2004.

Schmidt-Schütz, Eva. Doktor Faustus *zwischen Tradition und Moderne: Eine quellenkritische und rezeptionsgeschichtliche Untersuchung zu Thomas Manns literarischem Selbstbild.* Thomas-Mann-Studien, 28. Frankfurt/Main: Klostermann, 2003.

Schoenberg, E. Randol. "The Most Famous Thing He Never Said." In *Arnold*

Schoenberg und sein Gott / and His God, ed. Christian Meyer, 27–30. Vienna: Arnold Schönberg Center, 2003.

A Schoenberg Reader. Ed. Joseph Auner. New Haven, CT: Yale University Press, 1993.

Schubert, Bernhard. "Das Ende der bürgerlichen Vernunft? Zu Thomas Manns *Doktor Faustus.*" *Zeitschrift für deutsche Philologie* 105 (1986): 568–92.

Schwarz, Egon. "Jewish Characters in *Doctor Faustus.*" In *Doctor Faustus: A Novel at the Margin of Modernism,* ed. Herbert Lehnert and Peter C. Pfeiffer, 119–40. Columbia, SC: Camden House, 1991.

Tiedemann, Rolf. " 'Mitdichtende Einfühlung': Adornos Beiträge zum *Doktor Faustus*–noch einmal." *Adorno-Blätter* 1 (1992): 9–33.

Vaget, Hans R. "Fünfzig Jahre Leiden an Deutschland: Thomas Manns Doktor Faustus im Lichte unserer Erfahrung." In *Thomas Manns* Doktor Faustus *1947–1997,* ed. Werner Röcke, 11–34. Bern: Lang, 2001.

———. " 'German' Music and German Catastrophe: A Re-Reading of Doctor Faustus." In *Companion to the Works of Thomas Mann,* ed. Herbert Lehnert and Eva Wessel, 221–44. Rochester, NY: Camden House, 2004.

———. "Mann, Joyce, Wagner: The Question of Modernism in Doctor Faustus." In *Thomas Mann's* Doctor Faustus: *A Novel at the Margin of Modernism,* ed. Herbert Lehnert and Peter C. Pfeiffer, 167–91. Columbia, SC: Camden House, 1991.

———. "National and Universal: Thomas Mann and the Paradox of 'German' Music." In *Music and National Identity,* ed. Celia Applegate and Pamela M. Potter, 155–77. Chicago: University of Chicago Press, 2002.

Voss, Lieselotte. *Die Entstehung von Thomas Manns Roman* Doktor Faustus. *Dargestellt anhand unveröffentlichter Vorarbeiten.* Studien zur deutschen Literatur, vol. 39. Tübingen: Niemeyer, 1975.

CHAPTER 11

Adorno, Theodor W. "Arnold Schoenberg, 1874–1951." In *Prisms,* trans. Samuel and Sherry Weber, 147–72. Cambridge, MA: MIT Press, 1983.

———. "Commitment." In *Notes to Literature,* trans. Sherry Weber Nicholsen, 76–94. Vol. 2. New York: Columbia University Press, 1992.

The Arnold Schoenberg Companion. Ed. Walter B. Bailey. Westport, CT: Greenwood Press, 1998.

Arnold Schoenberg in America: Report of the Symposium, May 2–4, 2001. Ed. Christian Meyer. Vienna: Arnold Schönberg Center, 2002.

Brinkmann, Reinhold. " 'Denn mit mir ist es ein Hakenkreuz.' Arnold Schoenberg: From Inner Emigration to Exile [Summary of Amherst Colloquium Paper by Susan L. Cocalis]." In *Wider den Faschismus: Exilliteratur als Geschichte,* ed. Sigrid Bauschinger and Susan L. Cocalis, 221–23. Tübingen: Francke, 1993.

———. "Schoenberg the Contemporary: A View from Behind." In *Constructive Dissonance,* 196–219.

Cahn, Steven J. " 'Kol Nidre' in America." In *Arnold Schoenberg in America,* 203–18.

Carnegy, Patrick. *Faust as Musician: A Study of Thomas Mann's Novel Doctor Faustus*. New York: New Directions, 1973.

Constructive Dissonance: Arnold Schoenberg and the Transformation of Twentieth-Century Culture. Ed. Juliane Brand and Christopher Hailey. Berkeley: University of California Press, 1997.

Crittenden, Camille. "Texts and Contexts of A Survivor from Warsaw, Op. 46." In *Political and Religious Ideas in the Works of Arnold Schoenberg*, 231–58.

Dahlhaus, Carl. "Schoenberg's Late Works." In *Schoenberg and the New Music: Essays by Carl Dahlhaus*, trans. Derrick Puffett and Alfred Clayton. Cambridge: Cambridge University Press, 1987.

Danuser, Hermann. "Composers in Exile: The Question of Musical Identity." In *Driven into Paradise*, 155–71.

Driven into Paradise: The Musical Migration from Nazi Germany to the United States. Ed. Reinhold Brinkmann and Christoph Wolff. Berkeley: University of California Press, 1999.

Dümling, Albrecht. *Die fremden Klänge der hängenden Gärten: Die öffentliche Einsamkeit der neuen Musik am Beispiel von Arnold Schönberg und Stefan George*. Munich: Kindler, 1981.

Freitag, Eberhard. *Schönberg*. Reinbek: Rowohlt, 1973.

Gervink, Manuel. *Schönberg*. Regensburg: Laaber, 2000.

Haimo, Ethan. "Schoenberg's Late Twelve-Tone Compositions." In *Arnold Schoenberg Companion*, 157–76.

Heller, Charles. "Traditional Jewish Material in Schoenberg's A Survivor from Warsaw, Op. 46." *Journal of the Arnold Schoenberg Institute* 3 (1979): 69–74.

Hermand, Jost. "A Survivor from Germany: Schönberg im Exil." In *Literatur und die Künste nach 1933*, ed. Alexander Stephan, 104–17. Bonn: Bouvier, 1990.

Kater, Michael H. "Arnold Schoenberg: Musician of Contrasts." In *Composers of the Nazi Era*, 183–210. Oxford: Oxford University Press, 2000.

Lieberman, David I. "Schoenberg Rewrites His Will: A Survivor from Warsaw, Op. 46." In *Political and Religious Ideas in the Works of Arnold Schoenberg*, 193–230. New York: Garland, 2000.

Mann, Michael. "The Musical Symbolism in Thomas Mann's Doctor Faustus." *Music Review* 17 (1956): 314–22.

McBride, Jerry. "Selective Discography." In *Arnold Schoenberg Companion*, 309–22.

McDonald, Malcolm. "In the Wilderness (1933–1951)." In *Schoenberg*, The Master Musician Series, 43–51. London: Aldine, 1976.

Muxeneder, Victoria. "Lebens(Werk)Geschichte in Begegnungen: Vorgespräche zu Arnold Schönbergs 'A Survivor from Warsaw, op. 46.'" In *Schoenberg & Nono: A Birthday Offering to Nuria on May 7, 2002*, ed. Anna Maria Morazzoni, 97–113. Venice: Olschki, 2002.

Nono-Schoenberg, Nuria, ed. *Arnold Schoenberg 1874–1951: Lebensgeschichte in Begegnungen*. Klagenfurt: Ritter, 1992.

Political and Religious Ideas in the Works of Arnold Schoenberg. Ed. Charlotte M. Cross and Russell A. Berman. New York: Garland, 2000.

Reich, Willi. *Schoenberg: A Critical Biography.* New York: Praeger, 1971. German edition: *Arnold Schönberg oder Der konservative Revolutionär.* Vienna: Molden, 1968.

Reiff, Jo-Ann. "Adrian Leverkühn, Arnold Schoenberg, Theodor Adorno: Theorists Real and Fictitious in Thomas Mann's *Doctor Faustus.*" *Journal of the Arnold Schoenberg Institute* 7 (1983): 102–12.

Ringer, Alexander L. *Arnold Schoenberg: The Composer as Jew.* Oxford: Clarendon Press, 1990.

Rosen, Charles. *Arnold Schoenberg.* Princeton, NJ: Princeton University Press, 1975.

Schmidt, Bernhold. "Neues zum *Doktor Faustus*—Streit zwischen Arnold Schönberg und Thomas Mann." In *Augsburger Jahrbuch für Musikwissenschaft* 1989: 149–79, and 1990: 177–92.

Schmidt, James. "Mephistopheles in Hollywood: Adorno, Mann, and Schoenberg." *The Cambridge Companion to Adorno,* ed. Tom Huhn, 148–80. Cambridge: Cambridge University Press, 2004.

Schoenberg, Arnold. *Briefe.* Ed. Erwin Stein. Mainz: B. Schott, 1958.

———. " 'Doctor Faustus' Schoenberg?" *Saturday Review of Literature* 32.1 (1 January 1949): 22.

———. "Further to the Schoenberg-Mann Controversy." *Music Review* 2.2 (1949): 78–79.

———. "Kol Nidre." *Sämtliche Werke,* Section V: Chorwerke, Series A, Vol. 19. Ed. Josef Rufer and Christian Martin Schmidt. Mainz: Schott's Söhne and Universal Edition, 1975, 1–60; and *Sämtliche Werke.* Section V: Chorwerke, Series B, Vol. 19. Ed. Christian Martin Schmidt. Mainz: Schott's Söhne and Universal Edition, 1977. 1–39.

———. *Letters.* Ed. Erwin Stein, trans. Eithne Wilkins and Ernst Kaiser. Berkeley: University of California Press, 1987.

———. "Ode to Napoleon Buonaparte (Lord Byron) for String Quartet, Piano and Reciter." *Sämtliche Werke,* Section VI: Kammermusik, Series A, Vol. 24: Melodramen und Lieder mit Instrumenten. Ed. Reinhold Brinkmann. Mainz: Schott Musik International, Universal Edition, 1996, 97–166; and *Sämtliche Werke,* Abt. VI: Kammermusik, Series B, vol. 24.2. Ed. Reinhold Brinkmann. Mainz: Schott Musik International, Universal Edition, 1997. 19–141.

———. *Style and Idea: Selected Writings of Arnold Schoenberg.* Ed. Leonard Stein, trans. Leo Black. Berkeley: University of California Press, 1975.

———. "A Survivor from Warsaw." *Sämtliche Werke,* Section V, Series A, Vol. 19, 91–120; and Section V, Series B, Vol. 19. 60–81.

Schoenberg, Randol E. "Arnold Schoenberg and Albert Einstein: Their Relationship and Views on Zionism." *Journal of the Arnold Schoenberg Institute* 10 (1987): 134– w87.

Schoenberg and His World. Ed. Walter Frisch. Princeton, NJ: Princeton University Press, 1999.

A Schoenberg Reader: Documents of a Life. Ed. Joseph Auner. New Haven: Yale University Press, 2003.

Smith, Joan Allen. *Schoenberg and His Circle: A Viennese Portrait.* New York: Schirmer, 1986.

Stein, Leonard. "A Note on the Genesis of the 'Ode to Napoleon.'" *Journal of the Arnold Schoenberg Institute* 2 (1977): 52–54.

Stuckenschmidt, Hans Heinz. *Schoenberg: His Life, World and Work*. Trans. Humphrey Searle. New York: Schirmer, 1978.

Werfel, Franz. *Verdi: A Novel of the Opera*. Trans. Helen Jessiman. New York: Allen, Towne & Heath, 1947.

Zenck, Claudia Maurer. "Challenges and Opportunities of Acculturation: Schoenberg, Krenek, and Stravinsky in Exile." In *Driven into Paradise*, 172–93.

CONCLUSION

Adorno, Theodor W. "What National Socialism Has Done to the Arts." *Gesammelte Werke*, vol. 20.2: 413–29. Frankfurt/Main: Suhrkamp, 1986.

Banham, Reyner. *Los Angeles: The Architecture of Four Ecologies*. Baltimore, MD: Penguin Books, 1971.

Bilski, Emily D., and Emily Braun. "The Salon in Exile." In *Jewish Women and Their Salons: The Power of Conversation*, 138–47, 209–11, 240–41. New York: Jewish Museum; New Haven, CT: Yale University Press, 2005.

Brecht Yearbook 30 (2005): *Who was Ruth Berlau? / Wer war Ruth Berlau?* Ed. Stephen Brockmann. Madison, WI: International Brecht Society, 2005.

Crawford, Dorothy Lamb. *Evenings On and Off the Roof: Pioneering Concerts in Los Angeles, 1939–1971*. Berkeley: University of California Press, 1995.

Deleuze, Gilles, and Félix Guattari. *Kafka: Toward a Minor Literature*. Trans. Dana Polan, foreword by Réda Bensmaïa. Minneapolis: University of Minnesota Press, 1986.

Eichler, Jeremy. "Women Who Conquered Europe with Their Wit." *New York Times*, 4 March 2005, B31, B36.

Giovacchini, Saverio. *Hollywood Modernism: Film and Politics in the Age of the New Deal*. Philadelphia: Temple University Press, 2001.

Gozani, Tal, ed. *Driven into Paradise: L.A.'s European Jewish Émigrés of the 1930s and 1940s: February 3–May 8, 2005*. Los Angeles: Skirball Cultural Center, 2005.

Hampton, Christopher. *Tales from Hollywood*. London: Faber and Faber, 1983.

Hecht, Werner. *Helene Weigel: Eine große Frau des 20. Jahrhunderts*. Introduction by Siegfried Unseld. Frankfurt/Main: Suhrkamp, 2000.

Heinrichsdorff, Amelie. "'Nur eine Frau?' Kritische Untersuchungen zur literaturwissenschaftlichen Vernachlässigung der Exilschriftstellerinnen in Los Angeles: Ruth Berlau, Marta Feuchtwanger, Gina Kaus und Victoria Wolff." Ph.D. diss., University of California, Los Angeles, 1998.

Hohendahl, Peter Uwe. "Reappraisals of : The Legacy of the Frankfurt School in America." In *Reappraisals: Shifting Alignments in Postwar Critical Theory*, 198–228. Ithaca, NY: Cornell University Press, 1991.

Jameson, Fredric. *A Singular Modernity: Essays on the Ontology of the Present*. London: Verso, 2002.

Knight, Christopher. "Portrait of a Cultural Battle: The Display of Looted Klimt

Paintings at LACMA Raises Questions about National Ownership and the Fate of Great Works of Art." *Los Angeles Times,* 4 April 2006, E1, E5.

Lee, Charles. *The Hidden Public: The Story of the Book-of-the-Month Club.* Garden City, NY: Doubleday, 1958.

Matthias, Bettina. "A Home Away from Home? The Hotel as Space of Emancipation in Early Twentieth-Century Austrian Bourgeois Literature." *German Studies Review* 27 (2004): 325–40.

Meyer, Grischa, and Erdmut Wizisla, eds. *Ruth Berlau: Fotografin an Brechts Seite.* Munich: Propyläen, 2003.

Sontag, Susan. "Pilgrimage." In *A Companion to Thomas Mann's* The Magic Mountain, ed. Stephen D. Dowden, 221–39. Columbia, SC: Camden House, 1999.

Viertel, Salka. *The Kindness of Strangers.* New York: Holt, Rinehart & Winston, 1969.

ADDENDA

Gay, Peter. *Modernism: The Lure of Heresy: From Baudelaire to Beckett and beyond.* New York: Norton, 2008.

Horowitz, Joseph. *Artists in Exile: How Refugees from Twentieth-Century War and Revolution Transformed the American Performing Arts.* New York: Harper, 2008.

Jaeger, Roland. *New Weimar on the Pacific: The Pazifische Presse and German Exile Publishing in Los Angeles 1942–1948.* Trans. Marion Philadelphia, ed. Victoria Dailey. Los Angeles: Victoria Dailey, 2000.

Jenemann, David. *Adorno in America.* Minneapolis: University of Minnesota Press, 2007.

Palmier, Jean-Michel. *Weimar in Exile: Exile in Europe and Exile in America.* Transl. David Fernbach. London: Verso, 2006.

Vaget, Hans Rudolf. *Seelenzauber: Thomas Mann und die Musik.* Frankfurt/ Main: S. Fischer, 2006.

Weitz, Eric D. *Weimar Germany: Promise and Tragedy.* Princeton: Princeton University Press, 2007.

Index

347

WEIMAR AND NOW: GERMAN CULTURAL CRITICISM

Edward Dimendberg, Martin Jay, and Anton Kaes, General Editors

Text: 10/13 Sabon
Display: Sabon
Compositor: Binghamton Valley Composition, LLC
Printer and binder: Sheridan Books, Inc.